DATE DUE

F. A. Hayek

STUDIES IN PHILOSOPHY, POLITICS AND ECONOMICS

A CLARION BOOK
PUBLISHED BY SIMON AND SCHUSTER

A Clarion Book
Published by Simon and Schuster
Rockefeller Center, 630 Fifth Avenue
New York, New York 10020
All rights reserved
including the right of reproduction
in whole or in part in any form
Copyright © 1967 by F. A. Hayek
Reprinted by arrangement with University of Chicago Press

First paperback printing 1969

SBN 671-20246-4

Manufactured in the United States of America
Printed by The Murray Printing Co., Forge Village, Mass.
Bound by Electronic Perfect Binders, Inc., Brooklyn, N.Y.

To
Karl Popper

Preface

This volume contains a selection from the work of the last twenty years or so of an economist who discovered that if he was to draw from his technical knowledge conclusions relevant to the public issues of our time, he had to make up his mind on many questions to which economics did not supply an answer. I believe I have spent no less effort to qualify myself for the discussion of those problems of the philosophy of science and of politics that arose out of my work in economics than I had done before I started to write on economics. One effect of this is that I am now at least more aware that in consequence I cannot yet regard myself as a fully trained philosopher or political scientist than I was then aware that I was not yet a fully qualified economist.

The arrangement of the several studies into three parts corresponding to the fields indicated by the title of the volume is somewhat arbitrary. The problems of the philosophy of science and of moral philosophy that are discussed all arose out of the pre-occupation with problems of economic theory, psychology, and social policy, and the studies of problems of politics and economics are also concerned more with issues where the different branches of knowledge intersect than with those that belong only to any one discipline. Yet they seemed to fall naturally into the three groups that justify the title of the volume, which appears better than any other I could think of to indicate the range of interests it covers.

Though I have made no major changes in those of the studies which have appeared earlier, I have revised them carefully, not with an idea of bringing them up to date, but with the aim of expressing better what I meant to say when I first wrote them.

I am still not certain whether I am well advised to include the two speeches (Nos. 9 and 10) which have not been published before. But as they represent the beginning and end of a series of similar efforts in which I devoted my time to bringing together an international group of scholars who were concerned about the same problems which then and ever since have chiefly occupied me, I finally decided that they might be allowed to stand here as an indication of endeavours which have left their mark on much of my other work. The following report recently submitted to a meeting of the Mont Pélèrin Society may serve to indicate the conclusions to which the discussions in that group have led me and at the same time the aim of the more systematic work on which I am now engaged.

Readers of some of my earlier writings may notice a slight change in the tone of my discussion of the attitude which I then called 'scientism'. The reason for this is that Sir Karl Popper has taught me that natural scientists did not really do what most of them not only told us that they did but also urged the representatives of other disciplines to imitate. The difference between the two groups of disciplines has thereby been greatly narrowed and I keep up the argument only because so many social scientists are still trying to imitate what they wrongly believe to be the methods of the natural sciences. The intellectual debt which I owe to this old friend for having taught me this is but one of many, and it is therefore only appropriate that this volume should be in gratitude inscribed to him.

It remains for me to express my thanks to the editors and publishers of the journals and other publications in which some of the following studies have appeared for permission to reprint them, to Dr. Monika Streissler for help in reading the proofs and to Frau Eva von Malchus for preparing the Index.

F. A. HAYEK

Freiburg i. B.
July 1966

Contents

[ix]

Contents

[x]

PART ONE

Philosophy

Das Höchste wäre zu erkennen, dass
alles Faktische schon Theorie ist.
J. W. v. Goethe

CHAPTER ONE

*Degrees of Explanation**

I

The discussion of scientific method has been guided almost entirely by
the example of classical physics. The reason for this is mainly that
certain features of scientific method can be most easily illustrated by
instances from this field, and partly a belief that, because physics is the
most highly developed of all the empirical sciences, it ought to be held
up to all the others for imitation. Whatever truth there may be in this
second consideration ought not, however, to make us overlook the
possibility that some of the characteristic procedures of physics may not
be of universal applicability, and that the procedure of some of the other
sciences, 'natural' or 'social', may differ from that of physics, not because
the former are less advanced, but because the situation in their fields
differs in significant respects from that of physics. More particularly,
what we regard as the field of physics may well be the totality of phenomena where the number of significantly connected variables of different
kinds[1] is sufficiently small to enable us to study them as if they formed a

*Reprinted from the *British Journal for the Philosophy of Science*, VI, 1955 with the last four
paragraphs of the original manuscript restored which had been omitted on the occasion of
the first publication for reasons of space.

The subject of this and the following essay are closely connected, so closely indeed that
they might be regarded as treatments of the same subject at an interval of about eight years.
I have nevertheless decided not only to reprint them both but even to give the earlier one
first place, because they approach the subject from somewhat different angles and cover
different aspects of the problem.

[1] Modern physics has of course resorted to statistics to deal with systems of very large
numbers of variables, but this does not appear to me to be in conflict with the observation
in the text. The statistical technique is in effect a manner of reducing the number of separate
entities, connected by laws which have to be stated, to comparatively few (namely the
statistical collectives) and not a technique for dealing with the interplay of a large number of
such significantly independent variables as the individuals in a social order. The problems of

closed system for which we can observe and control all the determining factors; and we may have been led to treat certain phenomena as lying outside physics precisely because this is not the case. If this were true it would certainly be paradoxical to try to force methods made possible by these special conditions on disciplines regarded as distinct because in their field these conditions do not prevail.

For our attempt to bring out certain aspects of scientific method that are not generally appreciated we will start from the now widely accepted interpretation of theoretical science as a 'hypothetico-deductive' system. One may accept most of the basic ideas underlying this approach and yet feel that it can be interpreted in a manner which makes it inappropriate to some subjects. Its basic conception lends itself to a somewhat narrow interpretation according to which the essence of *all* scientific procedure consists in the discovery of *new* statements ('natural laws' or 'hypotheses') from which testable predictions can be derived. This interpretation may become a serious bar to the penetration of our understanding into fields where certainly at present, and perhaps forever, a different procedure may be our only effective means of obtaining guidance in the complex world in which we live.

The conception of science as a hypothetico-deductive system has been expounded by Karl Popper in a manner which brings out clearly some very important points.[2] He has made it clear that the theoretical sciences are all essentially deductive, that there can be no such logical procedure as 'induction' which leads with necessity from the observation of facts to the formulation of general rules, and that the latter are products of creative acts of the mind which cannot be formalized. He has also emphasized the important point that the conclusions to which theories lead are essentially of the nature of prohibitions: they 'forbid' the occurrence of certain kinds of events and can never be definitely 'verified'

complexity to which the further discussion refers are of the kind which Warren Weaver has described as 'problems of organized complexity' as distinguished from those 'problems of disorganized complexity' with which we can deal by statistical techniques. Cf. Warren Weaver, 'Science and Complexity', *American Scientist*, 1948, and now the fuller version of his views in 'A Quarter Century in the Natural Sciences'. *The Rockefeller Foundation Annual Report*, 1958, pp. 1–15.

[2] Although on some particular points Professor Popper has in recent publications (*The Poverty of Historicism*, London 1957, esp. sections 11 and 12; and *The Open Society*, 1950) improved on his formulations, it is still necessary to go for a full account to his *The Logic of Scientific Discovery* (London, 1959, translated from the German version, Vienna, 1935). In many respects what follows is little more than an elaboration of some of Popper's ideas, particularly of his conception of degrees of testability and of his 'relativization' of his falsifiability criterion. My critical observations are therefore directed solely against certain positivist and operationalist interpretations of the 'hypothetico-deductive' thesis but not against Popper's or similar variants.

but only increasingly confirmed by persistently unsuccessful attempts to prove them false. For what follows, this part of the argument will be accepted.

There is, however, a further and no less illuminating idea contained in this approach which, if accepted too literally, is apt to become misleading. It is what Popper has occasionally expressed in conversation[3] by saying that science does not explain the unknown by the known, as is commonly believed, but, on the contrary, the known by the unknown. What is meant by this apparent paradox is that the advance of knowledge consists in the formulation of new statements which often refer to events which cannot be directly observed and from which, in combination with other statements about particulars, we can derive statements capable of disproof by observation. I do not doubt that it is important to emphasize that additions to knowledge in such instances will be contained in new statements (hypotheses or natural laws) which form part of the basis of our deductive argument; but this seems to me to represent not a general characteristic of all scientific procedure, but one which may be the rule in physics and occasionally also be successful in the biological sciences, but which presupposes conditions which are not present in many other fields.

II

Even in so far as the physical sciences are concerned, the emphasis on the procedure from the hypothesis to be tested to the conclusions which can be proved false may go too far. A large part of the value of these disciplines undoubtedly derives from the fact that once their hypotheses are well accredited we can confidently derive from them conclusions applicable to new circumstances and treat these as true without testing them. The work of the theorist is not concluded when his hypotheses seem sufficiently confirmed. The activity of thinking through all their implications is evidently an activity important and valuable in its own right; and it may sometimes be an activity of great complexity and difficulty, requiring the highest forms of intelligence. Nobody will deny that constant efforts in this direction are part of the regular task of science; in fact, whole theoretical disciplines are concerned almost exclusively with this kind of activity. The question of what is the range of application or the capacity of a theory, whether it can or cannot

---

[3] See now, however, Sir Karl Popper's *Conjectures and Refutations*, London 1963, esp. p. 63: 'scientific explanation is . . . the reduction of the known to the unknown', as well as *ibid.*, pp. 102 and 174.

account for a certain group of observed phenomena, or whether the observed events are within the range of what might have been predicted from it if all the relevant factual data had been known and if we were capable of manipulating them adequately, is often as interesting a problem as that whether the particular conclusion derived from the theory can be confirmed; and it is clearly independent of that question.

These aspects of the work of the theorist become increasingly prominent as we turn from the 'pure' theory of physics to disciplines like astrophysics or the various branches of geophysics (seismology, meteorology, geology, oceanography, etc.) which are sometimes described as 'applied' sciences. This name hardly describes the distinct kind of effort which those disciplines involve. It is used in this context neither to express that, like technology, they serve particular human needs, nor in order to indicate that their applicability is confined to particular regions of time and space. They all aim at developing generic explanations which, at least in principle, are significant apart from the particular events for which they have been worked out: much of the theory of tides as developed in terrestrial oceanography would be applicable to oceans on Mars, etc. What is characteristic of these theories is that they are, in a sense, derivative: they consist of deductions derived from combinations of known laws of physics, and do not, strictly speaking, state distinct laws of their own but elaborate the laws of physics into explanatory patterns appropriate to the peculiar kind of phenomena to which they refer. It is, of course, conceivable that the study of the tides might lead to the discovery of a new natural law; but if it did it would presumably be a new law of physics and not one of oceanography. Yet oceanography will still contain general statements which are not just plain physics but which have been elaborated from the laws of physics in order to account for the joint effects of certain typical constellations of physical events—specific patterns of argument developed to deal with recurring types of situations.

It is, no doubt, desirable that in working out such deductive systems the conclusions should be tested against the facts at every step. We can never exclude the possibility that even the best accredited law may cease to hold under conditions for which it has not yet been tested. But while this possibility always exists, its likelihood in the case of a well-confirmed hypothesis is so small that we often disregard it in practice. The conclusions which we can draw from a combination of well-established hypotheses will therefore be valuable though we may not be in a position to test them.

In a certain sense such a deductive argument, developed to account for an observed phenomenon, does not contain *new* knowledge. To those who are not regularly concerned with the elaboration of such patterns of explanation for typical complex situations the tasks of merely deducing the combined effects of known laws may seem trivial. But this is true only in the sense in which it is also true of mathematics. That certain conclusions are implied by what we know already does not necessarily mean that we are aware of these conclusions, or are able to apply them whenever they would help us to explain what we observe. Nobody could, in fact, work out all the consequences implied by our existing knowledge, or even those of some of the most trivial and undoubted propositions which we employ in daily life; it will often be an exceedingly difficult task to decide how much of what we observe can be explained by laws already known, or could be so explained if we possessed all the relevant data. To squeeze out of what we already know as many significant conclusions as possible is, of course, not a purely deductive task: it must be guided by observation in its choice of problems. But, though observation will raise the problems, the answer will rest on deduction alone.

In the disciplines mentioned, thus, the important question usually is not whether the hypotheses or laws used for the explanation of the phenomena are true, but whether we have selected the appropriate hypotheses from our store of accepted statements and have combined them in the right manner. What will be new about such a 'new' explanation of some phenomena will be the particular combination of theoretical statements with statements about facts regarded as significant for the particular situation (the 'initial' and 'marginal conditions'), not any one of the theoretical statements from which it starts. And the problem will not be whether the model as such is true, but whether it is applicable to (or true *of*) the phenomena it is meant to explain.

We have up to this point spoken mainly of what are called applied branches of physics in order to show that even there much of the undoubtedly theoretical work does not aim at the discovery of new laws and at their confirmation, but at the elaboration from accepted premises of deductive patterns of argument which will account for complex observed facts. If in these instances we can speak of hypotheses which require to be tested, they must be sought in the assertion that this or that pattern fits an observable situation, and not in the conditional statements of which the explanatory pattern itself consists and which is assumed to be true. We shall later discuss the peculiarities of this procedure more fully. At present our aim was merely to stress how comparatively rare an event in the progress even of the physical sciences the discovery of a true new law of nature is, and to suggest how special may be the conditions under which we can hope to discover such new laws of nature.

III

By a scientific prediction we mean the use of a rule or law in order to derive from certain statements about existing conditions statements about what will happen (including statements about what we will find if we search at a particular point). Its simplest form is that of a conditional or 'if then' statement combined with the assertion that the conditions stated in the antecedent are satisfied at a particular time and place. What in this connection is usually not explicitly considered is how specific need be the description of the events mentioned in the law, in the statement of the initial and marginal conditions, and in the prognosis, in order to merit the name of prediction. From the simple examples commonly adduced from physics it is readily concluded that it will generally be possible to specify all those aspects of the phenomenon in which we are interested with any degree of precision which we may need for our purposes. If we represent this form of statement by 'if u and v and w then z', it is often tacitly assumed that at least the description of z will contain all the characteristics of z which are deemed significant for the problem in hand. Where the relations we are studying are between a comparatively small number of measurements, this appears to present no serious difficulties.

The situation is different, however, where the number of significantly interdependent variables is very large and only some of them can in practice be individually observed. The position will here frequently be that if *we already knew* the relevant laws, we could predict that if several hundred specified factors had the values $x_1, x_2, x_3, \ldots x_n$, then there would always occur $y_1, y_2, y_3, \ldots y_n$. But in fact all that our observation suggests may be that if $x_1, x_2, x_3,$ and x_4, then there will occur either (y_1 and y_2) or (y_1 and y_3) or (y_2 and y_3), or some similar situation—perhaps that if $x_1, x_2, x_3,$ and x_4, then there will occur some y_1 and y_2 between which either the relation P or the relation Q will exist. There may be no possibility of getting beyond this by means of observation, because it may in practice be impossible to test all the possible combinations of the factors $x_1, x_2, x_3, x_4, \ldots x_n$. If in the face of the variety and complexity of such a situation our imagination cannot suggest more precise rules than those indicated, no systematic testing will help us over the difficulty.

In situations like these the observation of the complex facts will therefore not enable us to invent new hypotheses from which we can deduce predictions for situations we have not yet observed. We shall not be in a position to discover new natural laws for the kind of complex in question which would enable us to arrive at new predictions. The current view often seems to regard such a situation as beyond the limits of the application of scientific method (at least for the existing state of observational technique) and to accept that for the time being science must stop there. If this were correct, it would be very serious. There is no guarantee that we shall ever be able, physically or conceptually, to handle phenomena of any degree of complexity, nor that phenomena of a degree of complexity exceeding this limit may not be very important.

But if there is no reason to assume that the conditions presupposed by the standard method of physics will be satisfied by all events in which we are interested, there is still no need to despair about our prospects of learning at least something of importance about phenomena where they are not satisfied. But this will require a kind of reversal of what has been described as the standard procedure of physics; we shall here have to proceed in our deductions, not from the hypothetical or unknown to the known and observable, but—as used to be thought to be the normal procedure—from the familiar to the unknown. This is not an entirely satisfactory description of the procedure we shall now have to examine; but it is still true that the older conception of explaining the new by the familiar fits this procedure better than the conception that we proceed from the unknown to the known.

IV

'Explanation'[4] and 'prediction' of course do not refer to an individual event but always to phenomena of a certain kind or class; they will always state only some and never all the properties of any particular phenomenon to which they refer. In addition, each property stated will be expressed not as a unique value or magnitude but as a range, however narrow, within which the property will fall. Because of the limitations of the possible precision of measurement this is true even of the most exact predictions of physics which, strictly speaking, never say more than that

---

[4] I assume that the prejudice of certain earlier positivists against the word 'explanation' is now a thing of the past and that it may be taken for granted that prediction and explanation are merely two aspects of the same process where, in the first instance, known rules are used to derive from the known facts what will follow upon them, while in the second instance these rules are used to derive from the known facts what preceded them. For the purposes of this article it would indeed make no important difference if instead of 'degrees of explanation' we spoke throughout of 'degrees of prediction'. Cf. K. R. Popper, *The Open Society*, 1950, p. 446.

the magnitude in question will fall within a certain interval; and it is still more obviously the case where the prediction is not quantitative.

In ordinary usage we are inclined to admit as predictions only statements which narrow down the admitted phenomena fairly closely, and to draw a distinction between 'positive' predictions such as 'the moon will be full at 5h 22' 16" tomorrow', and merely negative predictions such as 'the moon will not be full tomorrow'. But this is no more than a distinction of degree. Any statement about what we will find or not find within a stated temporal and spatial interval is a prediction and may be exceedingly useful: the information that I will find no water on a certain journey may indeed be more important than most positive statements about what I will find. Even statements which specify no single specific property of what we will find but which merely tell us disjunctively that we will find either x or y or z must be admitted as predictions, and may be important predictions. A statement which excludes only one of all conceivable events from the range of those which may occur is no less a prediction and as such may prove to be false.

V

Where we have to deal with a complex situation in which observation discloses only very limited regularities, be it in the 'applied' branches of physics or in biology or in the social sciences, we usually ask to what extent our existing knowledge of the forces at work, or of the properties of some of the elements of the complex, may account for what we observe. We endeavour to find out whether this may be derived by deduction from what we know about the behaviour under simpler conditions of some of the factors involved. Of course we can never be certain that what we know about the action of those forces under simpler conditions will apply to more complex situations, and we will have no direct way of testing this assumption, since our difficulty is precisely that we are unable to ascertain by observation the presence and specific arrangement of the multiplicity of factors which form the starting point of our deductive reasoning. Neither the assumption that factors of the kind assumed are present, nor of course the validity of the deductive reasoning, need, therefore, be regarded as disproved if the conclusions at which we arrived are not borne out by observation. But though observation of such complex situations cannot decide whether our conditional ('if then') statement is true, it will help us to decide whether to accept it as an explanation of the facts which we observe.

It will be of interest, of course, if we succeed in deducing from our premisses precisely those partial regularities of the complex from which we started. But this, though it may give us satisfaction, does not add to our knowledge. Yet the assertion that what we observe is due to a certain constellation of familiar factors, though we may not be able to test it directly, will usually imply consequences which we can test. The mechanism which we believe to have produced the observed phenomena will be capable of producing some further results but not others. This means that if what we have observed of a given complex of events is due to the assumed mechanism, that complex will also possess certain other characteristics and not be capable of definite other kinds of behaviour. Our tentative explanation will thus tell us what *kinds* of events to expect and which not, and it can be proved false if the phenomena observed show characteristics which the postulated mechanism could not produce. It will thus give us new information by indicating the *range* of phenomena to expect. By providing a schema or framework for the possible results, it not only helps us to order the observational knowledge which we already possess, but it will also provide *niches* for new observations likely to occur, and indicate the directions in which we must expect the phenomena to vary. Not only will the observed facts thus come to 'make sense' and to 'fall into their places', but we shall be able to make predictions about the combinations of events which will not occur if our explanation is correct.

This procedure differs from the supposedly normal procedure of physics in that we do here not *invent* new hypotheses or constructs but merely *select* them from what we know already about some of the elements of the phenomena; in consequence we do not ask whether the hypotheses we used are true or whether the constructs are appropriate, but whether the factors we have singled out are in fact present in the particular phenomena we want to explain, and whether they are relevant and sufficient to explain what we observe. The answer will depend on whether what we observe is of the kind which according to our deductions would occur *if* the postulated factors were present.

VI

The most familiar instance in the natural sciences of this sort of mere 'explanation of the principle'[5] is probably provided by the theory of

---

[5] Though this term is rarely defined, theoretical discussion in biology abounds with statements qualified by the addition of 'in principle', such as 'is in principle specifiable', 'can in principle be ascertained', 'such a reduction is in principle possible', etc. Cf. A. S. Sommerhoff, *Analytical Biology*, London, 1950, pp. iv, v, 27, 30, 180.

evolution by natural selection of the different organisms. It is a theory which neither aims at specific predictions of particular events, nor is based on hypotheses in the sense that the several statements from which it starts are expected to be confirmed or refuted by observation. Although, as is true of any scientific theory, it does delimit a range of facts which are permitted by it against others which it 'forbids', our purpose in examining the facts is not to ascertain whether the different individual premisses from which the theory starts are true, but to test whether the particular combination of undoubted premisses is adequate to arrange the known facts in a meaningful order, and (what in a sense is the same thing) to show why only certain kinds of events are to be expected while others are precluded.

However we prefer to phrase the individual premisses from which we deduce the theory of evolution, they will all be of such a kind that we do not doubt their truth and should not regard them as refuted if the conclusions drawn from them jointly should be contradicted by observation. We can get a considerable distance by starting from the following three assumptions: (i) Organisms which survive to the reproductive stage produce on the average a number of offspring much greater than their own; (ii) While organisms of any one kind produce as a rule only similar organisms, the new individuals are not all completely similar to their parents, and any new properties will in turn be inherited by their offspring; and (iii) Some of these mutations will alter the probability that the individuals affected will in turn produce offspring.[6]

Few people will doubt that these statements are true, or believe that the problem of the theory of evolution is whether they are true or not. The problem is rather whether they are adequate and sufficient to account for the phenomena which we do observe and for the absence of others which do not occur. We want to know what this mechanism of reduplication with transmittable variations and competitive selection can achieve, and this question we can answer only by deductively working out all the implications of these assumptions. We shall accept the conclusions drawn from the premisses and regard them as a satisfactory explanation if they not only allow us to derive from them a process by which the observed phenomena might have been brought about, but if the explanation also points to new (not yet observed) distinctions between what is and what is not possible which are later confirmed by observation.[7]

[6] For a similar listing of these basic assumptions see J. S. Huxley, *Evolution*, London, 1942, p. 14.

[7] A very neat statement of the relation between theory and observation in this field, which is of wider application, occurs in G. S. Carter, *Animal Evolution*, London, 1951,

In some instances such a theory may in fact produce practically no new conclusions but will merely provide a rational foundation for the biologist's knowledge that 'nature does not work that way'. It has even been suggested of the theory of evolution by natural selection that the main objection to it is that it cannot be disproved because 'it appears impossible to indicate any biological phenomena that would plainly disprove it'.[8] This is true only in a limited sense. The individual statements from which it is derived are indeed unlikely to be disproved. But the assertion that the observed differentiation of species is always due to the operation of these factors could be refuted, e.g., if it were observed that after a sudden change in the environment the individuals then living would at once begin to produce offspring possessing a new adaptation to the changed environment. And, in the form in which the premisses have been stated before, their adequacy as an explanation has in fact been shown insufficient by the inheritance of specific attributes of the non-sexual members of certain types of social insects. To account for these, the premisses have to be enlarged to include situations wherein not only the properties of the individual but also properties of other members of the group will affect the chances of successful procreation.

It is worthwhile to pursue a little further the question how much the theory of evolution explains or predicts, and what the causes are of the limitations to what it can do. It can explain or predict only *kinds* of phenomena, defined by very general characteristics: the occurrence, not at a narrowly defined time and place but within a wide range, of changes of certain *types*; or rather the absence of other types of changes in the structure of the succeeding organisms. Disputes which have arisen in the course of the growth of the theory of evolution have thus significantly turned not so much on facts but on such questions as whether the postulated mechanism can account for the evolution having taken place in the time which has been available. And the answer has frequently come, not from the discovery of new facts, but from purely deductive arguments such as the mathematical theory of genetics, while 'experiment and observation did not quite keep up with the mathematical theory of selection'.[9] If we can test the deductions by observation, so much the

---

[8] L. von Bertalanffy, *Problems of Life*, New York, 1952, p. 89
[9] L. von Bertalanffy, *ibid.* p. 83

---

p. 9: 'The palaeontologist may be able to exclude some theories of evolution on the ground that they demand change not in accord with the facts; he claimed to be able to do so for Mendelian theories in their earliest forms' at the start of this century. . . . The part of palaeontology in the study of evolution resembles that of natural selection in the process of evolution; it serves to remove the inefficient, but cannot itself initiate.' See also Popper, *The Poverty of Historicism*, as cited.

better: if we conclude, e.g., that mice of a colour little different from that of the ground are less likely to be caught by owls and will therefore multiply more rapidly than those with a contrasting colour and ultimately dominate the species, it is no doubt desirable that we should be able to confirm this by experiment (as has been done); because it is at least conceivable that such a tendency may be counteracted by another, e.g., by the frequent losses to owls stimulating the fecundity of the species affected (as the proportion of male births among humans was once believed to increase in wartime). But even if such direct confirmation by experiment is not possible, it will be reasonable to accept the deductive conclusions until they are disproved.

VII

The kind of explanation with which we are concerned is in current discussion often referred to as 'model-building'. This expression does not emphasize quite the distinction with which we are concerned since even the most precise predictions of physics are based on the use of 'models' of a formal or material kind.[10] But if the term model is meant to stress that a model always represents only some but not all the features of the original (so that an exact replica of a machine could not appropriately be called a model), it indeed brings out an important feature which all explanations possess but to very different degrees.

This difference of degree is well illustrated by the suspicion with which the physicist frequently regards the formal models employed in the biological and social sciences. To the physicist the value of a model (especially of a mathematical model represented by a set of equations) normally consists in the fact that he can ascertain and insert the relevant variables and thus derive the quantitative values of the events to be predicted or explained. Yet in the disciplines mentioned above similar models are regularly used although the values of the variables cannot in fact be ascertained, and often though there is no prospect of ever ascertaining them. Yet explanatory value is claimed for these models irrespective of this possibility, i.e., although they do not enable us to

---

[10] Cf. A. Rosenblueth and N. Wiener, 'The Rôle of Models in Science,' *Philosophy of Science*, 1945, 12, 317: 'A material model is the representation of a complex system by a system which is assumed simpler and which is also assumed to have some properties similar to those selected for study in the original complex system. A formal model is a symbolic assertion in logical terms of an idealized relatively simple situation showing the structural properties of the original factual system.' In connection with what follows see also K. W. Deutsch, 'Mechanism, Organism, and Society', *Philosophy of Science*, 1951, 18, 3; 'Mechanism, Teleology, and Mind', *Philosophy and Phenomenological Research*, 1952, 12, 185.

predict that such and such a specific event will occur at a particular time and place. Wherein does their explanatory value, then, consist?

The answer should now be obvious. Any model defines a certain range of phenomena which can be produced by the type of situation which it represents. We may not be able directly to confirm that the causal mechanism determining the phenomenon in question is the same as that of the model. But we know that, *if* the mechanism is the same, the observed structures must be capable of showing some kinds of action and unable to show others; and if, and so long as, the observed phenomena keep within the range of possibilities indicated as possible, that is so long as our expectations derived from the model are not contradicted, there is good reason to regard the model as exhibiting the principle at work in the more complex phenomenon.

The peculiar thing about these kinds of models is that, because we have to draw deductions from what we know about some factors contributing to the phenomenon and know nothing about others, our conclusions and predictions will also refer only to some properties of the resulting phenomenon, in other words, to a *kind* of phenomenon rather than to a particular event. Strictly speaking, as we have seen, this is true of all explanations, predictions, or models. Yet there is of course a great difference between the prediction that upon turning a switch the pointer of a measuring instrument will be at a particular figure and the prediction that horses will not give birth to hippogriffs or that, if all commodity prices are fixed by law and demand afterwards increases, people will not be able to buy as much of every commodity as they would wish to buy at these prices.

If we consider a formal model consisting of a system of algebraic equations or 'propositional equations',[11] it will contain assertions about a structure of relations even if we do not know the value of any of the variables, and even if we have only the most general information about the character of the functions occurring in it: it will still exclude the possibility of the occurrence of certain combinations of values in any phenomenon which the model is asserted to represent;[12] it will tell us both what combinations of variables can occur at any time and what range of values the other variables can assume when the value of one or more of the variables is known. Of course, as we become able to insert

[11] i.e., propositional functions for whose variables we will admit only values which make the propositions true. See K. R. Popper, *Logic of Scientific Discovery*, p. 13.

[12] K. R. Popper, *ibid.* 'Even if the system of equations does not suffice for a unique solution, it does not allow every conceivable combination of values to be substituted for the "unknowns" (variables). Rather, the system of equations characterizes certain combinations of values or value systems as admissible.'

more and more definite values for the variables, this range will be narrowed until we reach the point when the system is completely determined and only one value of the remaining variable possible.

It is often not recognized that even the most formal system of equations can thus be used to make predictions and therefore will possess empirical content (though this content would be small), and that it will thus provide an explanation of the common features of a wide range of phenomena—or an explanation of the principle of this kind of phenomenon. This needs to be stressed because of the widespread misconception that the value of such models rests entirely on our ability to specify the values of the variables occurring in them and that they are useless so long as we cannot do this. This is not so: such models are valuable on their own, irrespective of their use for determining particular situations, and even where we know that we shall never have the information which would make this possible. They still do tell us something about the facts and allow us to make prognoses.

But is it not still true that our aim everywhere, as has been said of the theoretical description of nature,[13] should be to formulate theories that can be 'falsified' as easily as possible, i.e., which have as great an empirical content as possible? It is undoubtedly a drawback to have to work with theories which can be refuted only by statements of a high degree of complexity, because anything below that degree of complexity is on that ground alone permitted by our theory.[14] Yet it is still possible that in some fields the more generic theories are the more useful ones and further specification may be of little practical value. Where only the most general patterns can be observed in a considerable number of instances, the endeavour to become more 'scientific' by further narrowing down our formulae may well be a waste of effort; to strive for this in some subjects such as economics has often led to the illegitimate assumption of constants where in fact we have no right to assume the factors in question to be constant.

VIII

Though our conclusions are most readily seen to apply to those disciplines which, like mathematical biology or mathematical economics, employ formalized symbolic models, they are no less true of those biological and social theories which are expressed in ordinary language. While it would be equally incorrect, however, to say that these theories

[13] Popper, *op. cit.*, p. 68.
[14] Popper, *op. cit.*, p. 127.

do not lead to predictions, and while their value does indeed rest on what they predict, it must be recognized that those predictions are so different in character from what is usually understood by this word that not only the physicist but also the ordinary man may well hesitate to accept them as such. They will be mostly negative predictions that such and such things will not occur, and more especially predictions that such and such phenomena will not occur together. These theories equip us with ready-made schemes which tell us that when we observe given patterns of phenomena, certain other patterns are to be expected but not some others. They will show their value through the manner in which the isolated facts which have been known will begin to make sense, will fill the *niches* which the theory provides, and only those. In some respects such theories may seem little more than schemes of classification, yet schemes which provide in advance only for such phenomena or combinations of phenomena as the theories allow to occur. They indicate the range of phenomena to be expected: if the taxonomic scheme of zoology does not provide for winged vertebrates with more than two legs this is the result of a theory which makes it unlikely that such organisms have arisen. If economics tells us that we cannot at the same time maintain fixed rates of foreign exchange and at will control the internal price level of a country by changing the quantity of money, the character of such a 'prediction' is essentially the same as in the previous case. It is because its predictions possess this character that economics, in particular, appears so often to consist merely of variations upon the theme that 'you cannot have your cake and eat it'. The practical value of such knowledge consists indeed largely in that it protects us from striving for incompatible aims. The situation in the other theoretical sciences of society, such as theoretical anthropology, seems to be very much the same: what they tell us is in effect that certain types of institutions will not be found together, that because such and such institutions presuppose certain attitudes on the part of the people (the presence of which can often not be confirmed satisfactorily), only such and such other institutions will be found among people possessing the former (which can be confirmed or refuted by observation).

The limited character of the predictions which these theories enable us to make should not be confused with the question whether they are more or less uncertain than the theories which lead to more specific predictions. They are more uncertain only in the sense that they *leave* more uncertain because they say less about the phenomena, not in the sense that *what* they say is less certain. In so far as the latter sometimes may also be the case, it will be due to a different factor with which we are not here concerned: where we deal with very complex phenomena the *recognition* of the presence of the conditions to which the theory applies may often require the ready perception of patterns or configurations which will demand a special skill which few acquire. The selection and application of the appropriate theoretical scheme thus becomes something of an art where success or failure cannot be ascertained by any mechanical test.[15] The possession of such a ready-made pattern of significant relationships gives us a sort of sense for the physiognomy of events which will guide us in our observation of the environment. But even this constitutes no more than a distinction of degree from the physical sciences: the reading of many instruments also requires very special skills and there will be no other test for its correctness than that the great majority of properly trained observers agree.

IX

The service of a theory which does not tell us what particular events to expect at a definite moment, but only what kinds of events we are to expect within a certain range, or on complexes of a certain type, would perhaps be better described by the term *orientation* than by speaking of prediction. Although such a theory does not tell us precisely what to expect, it will still make the world around us a more familiar world in which we can move with greater confidence that we shall not be disappointed because we can at least exclude certain eventualities. It makes it a more orderly world in which the events make sense because we can at least say in general terms how they hang together and are able to form a coherent picture of them. Though we are not in a position to specify precisely what to expect, or even to list all the possibilities, each observed pattern has meaning in the sense that it limits the possibilities of what else may occur.

Where our predictions are thus limited to some general and perhaps only negative attributes of what is likely to happen, we evidently also shall have little power to control developments.[16] Yet the knowledge of

[15] This is perhaps the place to mention that what we are discussing here is of course not the only difference between the physical and the social sciences, but rather a peculiarity which the latter share with those natural sciences which deal with comparatively complex phenomena. Another and perhaps more important peculiarity of the social sciences is due to the fact that here the *recognition* of the different kinds of facts rests largely on a similarity between the observer and the observed persons. On this see now my essay on 'Rules, Perception and Intelligibility', reprinted as the third essay in the present volume.

[16] While it is evidently possible to predict precisely without being able to control, we shall clearly not be able to control developments further than we can predict the results of our action. A limitation of prediction thus implies a limitation of control, but not *vice versa*.

what kinds of events are to be expected and what not, will nevertheless help us to make our action more effective. Even if we cannot control the external circumstances at all, we may adapt our actions to them. And sometimes, though we may not be able to bring about the particular results we would like, knowledge of the principle of the thing will enable us to make circumstances more favourable to the kinds of events we desire. Of the different classes of events which are to be expected under various combinations of circumstances which we can bring about, some may with greater probability include desirable results than others. An explanation of the principle will thus often enable us to create such favourable circumstances even if it does not allow us to control the outcome. Such activities in which we are guided by a knowledge merely of the principle of the thing should perhaps better be described by the term *cultivation* than by the familiar term 'control'—cultivation in the sense in which the farmer or gardener cultivates his plants, where he knows and can control only some of the determining circumstances, and in which the wise legislator or statesman will probably attempt to cultivate rather than to control the forces of the social process.[17]

But if it is true that in subjects of great complexity we must rely to a large extent on such mere explanations of the principle, we must not overlook some disadvantages connected with this technique. Because such theories are difficult to disprove, the elimination of inferior rival theories will be a slow affair, bound up closely with the argumentative skill and persuasiveness of those who employ them. There can be no crucial experiments which decide between them. There will be opportunities for grave abuses: possibilities for pretentious, over-elaborate theories which no simple test but only the good sense of those equally competent in the field can refute. There will be no safeguards even against sheer quackery. Constant awareness of these dangers is probably the only effective precaution. But it does not help to hold up against this the example of other sciences where the situation is different. It is not because of a failure to follow better counsel, but because of the refractory nature of certain subjects that these difficulties arise. There is no basis for the contention that they are due to the immaturity of the sciences concerned. It would be a complete misunderstanding of the argument of this essay to think that it deals with a provisional and transitory state of the progress of those sciences which they are bound to overcome sooner or later. This may in some instances be possible—but

---

[17] The following paragraphs were for reasons of space omitted on the occasion of the first publication of this essay.

in some of the fields there is good reason to believe that these limitations will be permanent, that explanations of the principles will remain the best we can achieve in them, and that the nature of the subject puts forever beyond our reach the sort of explanation of detail which would enable us to make specific predictions. It is certainly not helpful to discredit what may be the only sort of knowledge we can achieve in these fields.

It seems indeed not improbable that, as the advance of the sciences penetrates further and further into more complex phenomena, theories which merely provide explanations of the principle, or which merely describe a range of phenomena which certain types of structures are able to produce, may become more the rule than the exception. Certain developments of recent years, such as cybernetics, the theory of automata or machines, general system theory, and perhaps also communication theory, seem to belong to this kind. And the more we move into the realm of the very complex, the more our knowledge is likely to be of the principle only, of the significant outline rather than of the detail. Especially where we have to deal with the extreme complexity of human affairs, the hope of ever achieving specific predictions of particulars seems vain. It would appear to be an evident impossibility for a human brain to specify in detail that 'way of acting, feeling, and thinking channelled by a society out of an infinite number and variety of potential ways of thinking', which, in the words of an eminent anthropologist, is the essence of culture.[18]

It cannot be our task here to inquire whether what we have considered with regard to the disciplines which had, from their very beginning, to deal with relatively complex phenomena, may not also become increasingly true of the discipline which was at least able to start with the relatively simple: that is, whether not even physics, as it ceases to treat of a few connected events as if they were closed systems, and at the same time develops in a manner which makes it necessary to define its terms in relation to each other, and in consequence only the theoretical system as a whole but no longer in part can be really falsified,[19] will increasingly have to face the same difficulties with which we are familiar from the biological and social sciences. This would mean that because of the nature of its subject physics comes only at a later stage up against the same sort of obstacles which other disciplines have met earlier, and that the latter, far from being able to learn from physics on this point, indeed had already

[18] A. L. Kroeber, *The Nature of Culture*, Chicago University Press, 1952.
[19] Cf. F. A. Hayek, *The Sensory Order*, London, 1952, pp. 170 *et seq.*

to grapple for a long time with problems of a kind which physicists meet only at a later stage of the development of their science.

In conclusion it should perhaps be stressed that there can never be competition between the two procedures, because what we have called an explanation of the principle will always give us only part of the information which a full explanation would yield where it can be achieved, and because in this sense the former is a less powerful instrument. But it is more powerful in the sense that it can be applied to fields to which the other procedure, for the time being or permanently, cannot be applied at all. Though scientists sometimes talk as if there could be no such fields not accessible to what they regard as the normal scientific method, i.e., fields where we cannot hope to establish by observation the laws of complex phenomena, few would seriously maintain this after reflecting that this belief implies that the human mind must be equipped to deal with the full details of phenomena of any conceivable degree of complexity. This may have some plausibility so long as we think exclusively of the physical world in the narrow sense of the term: it becomes highly doubtful when we think of biological phenomena; and it certainly ceases to be true when we have to deal with some of the activities of man himself. Especially in those fields where the object of our investigation, and our means of investigating and communicating the results, that is our thoughts, our language, and the whole mechanism of communication between men, are partly identical and where in consequence in discussing a system of events we must at the same time move within that system, there are probably definite limits to what we can know. These limits can be ascertained only by studying the *kind* of relations which exist between what can be said within a given system and what can be said about that system. To gain an understanding of such problems it may prove necessary deliberately to cultivate the techniques of explanation of the principle, i.e., the reproduction of a principle on greatly simplified models; and with regard to them the systematic use of this technique may prove the only path to definite knowledge—especially of the limits of what our thought can achieve.

CHAPTER TWO

*The Theory of Complex Phenomena**

1. *Pattern Recognition and Pattern Prediction*

Man has been impelled to scientific inquiry by wonder and by need. Of these wonder has been incomparably more fertile. There are good reasons for this. Where we wonder we have already a question to ask. But however urgently we may want to find our way in what appears just chaotic, so long as we do not know what to look for, even the most attentive and persistent observation of the bare facts is not likely to make them more intelligible. Intimate acquaintance with the facts is certainly important; but systematic observation can start only after problems have arisen. Until we have definite questions to ask we cannot employ our intellect; and questions presuppose that we have formed some provisional hypothesis or theory about the events.[1]

* Reprinted from *The Critical Approach to Science and Philosophy. Essays in Honor of K. R. Popper*, ed. M. Bunge, New York (The Free Press), 1964. The article was there printed (apart from a few stylistic emendations by the editor) in the form in which I had completed the manuscript in December 1961 and without my ever having seen proofs. I have now availed myself of this opportunity to insert some references I had intended to add in the proofs.

[1] See already Aristotle, *Metaphysics*, I, 11, 9, 9826b (Loeb ed. p. 13): 'It is through wonder that men now begin and originally began to philosophize . . . it is obvious that they pursued science for the sake of knowledge, and not for any practical utility'; also Adam Smith, 'The Principles which Lead and Direct Philosophical Inquiries, as Illustrated by the History of Astronomy', in *Essays*, London, 1869, p. 340: 'Wonder, therefore, and not any expectation of advantage from its discoveries, is the first principle which prompts mankind to the study of philosophy, that science which pretends to lay open the concealed connections that unite the various appearances of nature; and they pursue this study for its own sake, as an original pleasure or good in itself, without regarding its tendency to procure them the means of many other pleasures.' Is there really any evidence for the now popular contrary view that, e.g., 'hunger in the Nile Valley led to the development of geometry' (as Gardner Murphy in the *Handbook of Social Psychology*, ed. by Gardner Lindzey, 1954, Vol. II, p. 616, tells us)? Surely the fact that the discovery of geometry turned out to be useful does not prove that it was discovered because of its usefulness. On the fact that economics

Questions will arise at first only after our senses have discerned some recurring pattern or order in the events. It is a re-cognition of some regularity (or recurring pattern, or order), of some similar feature in otherwise different circumstances, which makes us wonder and ask 'why?'[2] Our minds are so made that when we notice such regularity in diversity we suspect the presence of the same agent and become curious to detect it. It is to this trait of our minds that we owe whatever understanding and mastery of our environment we have achieved.

Many such regularities of nature are recognized 'intuitively' by our senses. We see and hear patterns as much as individual events without having to resort to intellectual operations. In many instances these patterns are of course so much part of the environment which we take for granted that they do not cause questions. But where our senses show us new patterns, this causes surprise and questioning. To such curiosity we owe the beginning of science.

Marvellous, however, as the intuitive capacity of our senses for pattern recognition is, it is still limited.[3] Only certain kinds of regular arrangements (not necessarily the simplest) obtrude themselves on our senses. Many of the patterns of nature we can discover only *after* they have been constructed by our mind. The systematic construction of such new patterns is the business of mathematics.[4] The role which geometry plays in this respect with regard to some visual patterns is merely the most familiar instance of this. The great strength of mathe-

---

[2] See K. R. Popper, *The Poverty of Historicism*, London, 1957, p. 121: 'Science . . . cannot start with observations, or with the "collection of data", as some students of method believe. Before we can collect data, our interest in *data of a certain kind* must be aroused: the *problem* always comes first.' Also in his *The Logic of Scientific Discovery*, London, 1959, p. 59: 'observation is always *observation in the light of theories.*'

[3] Although in some respects the capacity of our senses for pattern recognition clearly also exceeds the capacity of our mind for specifying these patterns. The question of the extent to which this capacity of our senses is the result of another kind of (pre-sensory) experience is another matter. See, on this and on the general point that all perception involves a theory or hypothesis, my book *The Sensory Order*, London and Chicago, 1952, esp. para. 7.37. Cf. also the remarkable thought expressed by Adam Ferguson (and probably derived from George Berkeley) in *The History of Civil Society*, London, 1767, p. 39, that 'the inferences of thought are sometimes not to be distinguished from the perception of sense'; as well as H. von Helmholtz's theory of the 'unconscious inferences' involved in most perceptions. For a recent revival of these ideas see N. R. Hanson, *Patterns of Discovery*, Cambridge University Press, 1958, esp. p. 19, and the views on the role of 'hypotheses' in perception as developed in recent 'cognition theory' by J. S. Bruner, L. Postman and others.

[4] Cf. G. H. Hardy, *Mathematician's Apology*, Cambridge University Press, 1941, p. 24: 'A mathematician, like a painter or poet, is a maker of patterns.'

---

has in some degree been an exception to the general rule and has suffered by being guided more by need than by detached curiosity, see my lecture on 'The Trend of Economic Thinking' in *Economica*, 1933.

matics is that it enables us to describe abstract patterns which cannot be perceived by our senses, and to state the common properties of hierarchies or classes of patterns of a highly abstract character. Every algebraic equation or set of such equations defines in this sense a class of patterns, with the individual manifestation of this kind of pattern being particularized as we substitute definite values for the variables.

It is probably the capacity of our senses spontaneously to recognize certain kinds of patterns that has led to the erroneous belief that if we look only long enough, or at a sufficient number of instances of natural events, a pattern will always reveal itself. That this often is so means merely that in those cases the theorizing has been done already by our senses. Where, however, we have to deal with patterns for the development of which there has been no biological reason, we shall first have to invent the pattern before we can discover its presence in the phenomena —or before we shall be able to test its applicability to what we observe. A theory will always define only a kind (or class) of patterns, and the particular manifestation of the pattern to be expected will depend on the particular circumstances (the 'initial and marginal conditions' to which, for the purposes of this article, we shall refer as 'data'). How much in fact we shall be able to predict will depend on how many of those data we can ascertain.

The description of the pattern which the theory provides is commonly regarded merely as a tool which will enable us to predict the particular manifestations of the pattern that will appear in specific circumstances. But the prediction that in certain general conditions a pattern of a certain kind will appear is also a significant (and falsifiable) prediction. If I tell somebody that if he goes to my study he will find there a rug with a pattern made up of diamonds and meanders, he will have no difficulty in deciding 'whether that prediction was verified or falsified by the result',[5] even though I have said nothing about the arrangement, size, colour, etc., of the elements from which the pattern of the rug is formed.

The distinction between a prediction of the appearance of a pattern of a certain class and a prediction of the appearance of a particular instance of this class is sometimes important even in the physical sciences. The mineralogist who states that the crystals of a certain mineral are hexagonal, or the astronomer who assumes that the course of a celestial body in the field of gravity of another will correspond to one of the conic sections, make significant predictions which can be refuted. But in general the physical sciences tend to assume that it will in principle

---

[5] Charles Dickens, *David Copperfield*, p. 1.

always be possible to specify their predictions to any degree desired.[6] The distinction assumes, however, much greater importance when we turn from the relatively simple phenomena with which the natural sciences deal, to the more complex phenomena of life, of mind, and of society, where such specifications may not always be possible.[7]

2. *Degrees of Complexity*

The distinction between simplicity and complexity raises considerable philosophical difficulties when applied to statements. But there seems to exist a fairly easy and adequate way to measure the degree of complexity of different kinds of abstract patterns. The minimum number of elements of which an instance of the pattern must consist in order to exhibit all the characteristic attributes of the class of patterns in question appears to provide an unambiguous criterion.

It has occasionally been questioned whether the phenomena of life, of mind, and of society are really more complex than those of the physical world.[8] This seems to be largely due to a confusion between the degree

---

[6] Though it may be permissible to doubt whether it is in fact possible to predict, e.g., the precise pattern which the vibrations of an airplane will at a particular moment produce in the standing wave on the surface of the coffee in my cup.

[7] Cf. Michael Scriven, 'A Possible Distinction between Traditional Scientific Disciplines and the Study of Human Behavior', *Minnesota Studies in the Philosophy of Science*, I, 1956, p. 332: 'The difference between the scientific study of behavior and that of physical phenomena is thus partly due to the relatively greater complexity of the simplest phenomena we are concerned to account for in a behavioral theory.'

[8] Ernest Nagel, *The Structure of Science*, New York, 1961, p. 505: 'though social phenomena may indeed be complex, it is by no means certain that they are in general more complex than physical and biological phenomena.' See, however, Johann von Neumann, 'The General and Logical Theory of Automata', *Cerebral Mechanism in Behavior*. The Hixon Symposium, New York, 1951, p. 24: 'we are dealing here with parts of logic with which we have practically no experience. The order of complexity is out of all proportion to anything we have ever known.' It may be useful to give here a few illustrations of the orders of magnitude with which biology and neurology have to deal. While the total number of electrons in the Universe has been estimated at 10^{79} and the number of electrons and protons at 10^{100}, there are in chromosomes with 1,000 locations [genes] with 10 allelomorphs 10^{1000} possible combinations; and the number of possible proteins is estimated at 10^{2700} (L. von Bertalanffy, *Problems of Life*, New York, 1952, p. 103). C. Judson Herrick (*Brains of Rats and Men*, New York), suggests that 'during a few minutes of intense cortical activity the number of interneuronic connections actually made (counting also those that are actuated more than once in different associational patterns) may well be as great as the total number of atoms in the solar system' (i.e. 10^{56}); and Ralph W. Gerard (*Scientific American*, September 1953, p. 118) has estimated that in the course of seventy years a man may accumulate 15×10^{12} units of information ('bits'), which is more than 1,000 times larger than the number of nerve cells. The further complications which social relations superimpose upon this are, of course, relatively insignificant. But the point is that if we wanted to 'reduce' social phenomena to physical events, they would constitute an additional complication, superimposed upon that of the physiological processes determining mental events.

of complexity characteristic of a peculiar *kind* of phenomenon and the degree of complexity to which, by a combination of elements, any kind of phenomenon can be built up. Of course, in this manner physical phenomena may achieve any degree of complexity. Yet when we consider the question from the angle of the minimum number of distinct variables a formula or model must possess in order to reproduce the characteristic patterns of structures of different fields (or to exhibit the general laws which these structures obey), the increasing complexity as we proceed from the inanimate to the ('more highly organized') animate and social phenomena becomes fairly obvious.

It is, indeed, surprising how simple in these terms, i.e., in terms of the number of distinct variables, appear all the laws of physics, and particularly of mechanics, when we look through a collection of formulae expressing them.[9] On the other hand, even such relatively simple constituents of biological phenomena as feedback (or cybernetic) systems, in which a certain combination of physical structures produces an overall structure possessing distinct characteristic properties, require for their description something much more elaborate than anything describing the general laws of mechanics. In fact, when we ask ourselves by what criteria we single out certain phenomena as 'mechanical' or 'physical', we shall probably find that these laws are simple in the sense defined. Non-physical phenomena are more complex because we call physical what can be described by relatively simple formulae.

The 'emergence' of 'new' patterns as a result of the increase in the number of elements between which simple relations exist, means that this larger structure as a whole will possess certain general or abstract features which will recur independently of the particular values of the individual data, so long as the general structure (as described, e.g., by an algebraic equation) is preserved.[10] Such 'wholes', defined in terms of certain general properties of their structure, will constitute distinctive objects of explanation for a theory, even though such a theory may be merely a particular way of fitting together statements about the relations between the individual elements.

[9] Cf. Warren Weaver, 'A Quarter Century in the Natural Sciences', *The Rockefeller Foundation Annual Report*, 1958, Chapter I, 'Science and Complexity', which, when writing this, I knew only in the abbreviated version which appeared in the *American Scientist*, XXXVI, 1948.

[10] Lloyd Morgan's conception of 'emergence' derives, *via* G. H. Lewes (*Problems of Life and Mind*, 1st series, Vol. II, problem V, Ch. III, section headed 'Resultants and Emergents', American ed., Boston, 1891, p. 368), from John Stuart Mill's distinction of the 'heteropathic' laws of chemistry and other complex phenomena from the ordinary 'composition of causes' in mechanics, etc. See his *System of Logic*, London, 1843, Bk. III, Ch. 6, in Vol. I, p. 431 of the first edition, and C. Lloyd Morgan, *The Emergence of Novelty*, London, 1933, p. 12.

It is somewhat misleading to approach this task mainly from the angle of whether such structures are 'open' or 'closed' systems. There are, strictly speaking, no closed systems within the universe. All we can ask is whether in the particular instance the points of contact through which the rest of the universe acts upon the system we try to single out (and which for the theory become the data) are few or many. These data, or variables, which determine the particular form which the pattern described by the theory will assume in the given circumstances, will be more numerous in the case of complex wholes and much more difficult to ascertain and control than in the case of simple phenomena.

What we single out as wholes, or where we draw the 'partition boundary',[11] will be determined by the consideration whether we can thus isolate recurrent patterns of coherent structures of a distinct kind which we do in fact encounter in the world in which we live. Many complex patterns which are conceivable and might recur we shall not find it worthwhile to construct. Whether it will be useful to elaborate and study a pattern of a particular kind will depend on whether the structure it describes is persistent or merely accidental. The coherent structures in which we are mainly interested are those in which a complex pattern has produced properties which make self-maintaining the structure showing it.

3. *Pattern Prediction with Incomplete Data*

The multiplicity of even the minimum of distinct elements required to produce (and therefore also of the minimum number of data required to explain) a complex phenomenon of a certain kind creates problems which dominate the disciplines concerned with such phenomena and gives them an appearance very different from that of those concerned with simpler phenomena. The chief difficulty in the former becomes one of in fact ascertaining all the data determining a particular manifestation of the phenomenon in question, a difficulty which is often insurmountable in practice and sometimes even an absolute one.[12] Those mainly concerned with simple phenomena are often inclined to think that where this is the case a theory is useless and that scientific procedure demands that we should find a theory of sufficient simplicity to enable us to derive from it predictions of particular events. To them the theory, the knowledge of the pattern, is merely a tool whose usefulness depends

---

[11] Lewis White Beck, 'The "Natural Science Ideal" in the Social Sciences', *The Scientific Monthly*, LXVIII, June 1949, p. 388.

[12] Cf. F. A. Hayek, *The Sensory Order*, paras. 8.66–8.86.

entirely on our capacity to translate it into a representation of the circumstances producing a particular event. Of the theories of simple phenomena this is largely true.[13]

There is, however, no justification for the belief that it must always be possible to discover such simple regularities and that physics is more advanced because it has succeeded in doing this while other sciences have not yet done so. It is rather the other way round: physics has succeeded because it deals with phenomena which, in our sense, are simple. But a simple theory of phenomena which are in their nature complex (or one which, if that expression be preferred, has to deal with more highly organized phenomena) is probably merely of necessity false—at least without a specified *ceteris paribus* assumption, after the full statement of which the theory would no longer be simple.

We are, however, interested not only in individual events, and it is also not only predictions of individual events which can be empirically tested. We are equally interested in the recurrence of abstract patterns as such; and the prediction that a pattern of a certain kind will appear in defined circumstances is a falsifiable (and therefore empirical) statement. Knowledge of the conditions in which a pattern of a certain kind will appear, and of what depends on its preservation, may be of great practical importance. The circumstances or conditions in which the pattern described by the theory will appear are defined by the range of values which may be inserted for the variables of the formula. All we need to know in order to make such a theory applicable to a situation is, therefore, that the data possess certain general properties (or belong to the class defined by the scope of the variables). Beyond this we need to know nothing about their individual attributes so long as we are content to derive merely the sort of pattern that will appear and not its particular manifestation.

Such a theory destined to remain 'algebraic',[14] because we are in fact unable to substitute particular values for the variables, ceases then to be a mere tool and becomes the final result of our theoretical efforts. Such a theory will, of course, in Popper's terms,[15] be one of small empirical content, because it enables us to predict or explain only certain general

---

[13] Cf. Ernest Nagel, 'Problems of Concept and Theory Formation in the Social Sciences', in *Science, Language and Human Rights* (American Philosophical Association, Eastern Division, Vol. 1), University of Pennsylvania Press, 1952, p. 620: 'In many cases we are ignorant of the appropriate initial and boundary conditions, and cannot make precise forecasts even though available theory is adequate for that purpose.'

[14] The useful term 'algebraic theories' was suggested to me by J. W. N. Watkins.

[15] K. R. Popper, *The Logic of Scientific Discovery*, London, 1959, p. 113.

features of a situation which may be compatible with a great many particular circumstances. It will perhaps enable us to make only what M. Scriven has called 'hypothetical predictions',[16] i.e., predictions dependent on yet unknown future events; in any case the range of phenomena compatible with it will be wide and the possibility of falsifying it correspondingly small. But as in many fields this will be for the present, or perhaps forever, all the theoretical knowledge we can achieve, it will nevertheless extend the range of the possible advance of scientific knowledge.

The advance of science will thus have to proceed in two different directions: while it is certainly desirable to make our theories as falsifiable as possible, we must also push forward into fields where, as we advance, the degree of falsifiability necessarily decreases. This is the price we have to pay for an advance into the field of complex phenomena.

4. *Statistics Impotent to Deal with Pattern Complexity*

Before we further illustrate the use of those mere 'explanations of the principle'[17] provided by 'algebraic' theories which describe only the general character of higher-level generalities, and before we consider the important conclusions which follow from the insight into the boundaries of possible knowledge which our distinction provides, it is necessary to turn aside and consider the method which is often, but erroneously, believed to give us access to the understanding of complex phenomena: statistics. Because statistics is designed to deal with large numbers it is often thought that the difficulty arising from the large number of elements of which complex structures consist can be overcome by recourse to statistical techniques.

Statistics, however, deals with the problem of large numbers essentially by eliminating complexity and deliberately treating the individual elements which it counts as if they were not systematically connected. It avoids the problem of complexity by substituting for the information on the individual elements information on the frequency with which their different properties occur in classes of such elements, and it deliberately disregards the fact that the relative position of the different elements in a structure may matter. In other words, it proceeds

---

[16] M. Scriven, 'Explanation and Prediction in Evolutionary Theory', *Science*, August 28, 1959, p. 478 and cf. K. R. Popper, 'Prediction and Prophecy in the Social Sciences' (1949), reprinted in his *Conjectures and Refutations*, London, 1963, especially pp. 339 *et seqq.*

[17] Cf. F. A. Hayek, 'Degrees of Explanation', *The British Journal for the Philosophy of Science*, VI, No. 23, 1955, now reprinted as the first essay of the present collection.

on the assumption that information on the numerical frequencies of the different elements of a collective is enough to explain the phenomena and that no information is required on the manner in which the elements are related. The statistical method is therefore of use only where we either deliberately ignore, or are ignorant of, the relations between the individual elements with different attributes, i.e., where we ignore or are ignorant of any structure into which they are organized. Statistics in such situations enables us to regain simplicity and to make the task manageable by substituting a single attribute for the unascertainable individual attributes in the collective. It is, however, for this reason irrelevant to the solution of problems in which it is the relations between individual elements with different attributes which matters.

Statistics might assist us where we had information about many complex structures of the same kind, that is, where the complex phenomena and not the elements of which they consist could be made the elements of the statistical collective. It may provide us, e.g., with information on the relative frequency with which particular properties of the complex structures, say of the members of a species of organisms, occur together; but it presupposes that we have an independent criterion for identifying structures of the kind in question. Where we have such statistics about the properties of many individuals belonging to a class of animals, or languages, or economic systems, this may indeed be scientifically significant information.[18]

How little statistics can contribute, however, even in such cases, to the explanation of complex phenomena is clearly seen if we imagine that computers were natural objects which we found in sufficiently large numbers and whose behaviour we wanted to predict. It is clear that we should never succeed in this unless we possessed the mathematical knowledge built into the computers, that is, unless we knew the theory determining their structure. No amount of statistical information on the correlation between input and output would get us any nearer our aim. Yet the efforts which are currently made on a large scale with regard to the much more complex structures which we call organisms are of the same kind. The belief that it must be possible in this manner to discover by observation regularities in the relations between input and output without the possession of an appropriate theory in this case appears even more futile and naïve than it would be in the case of the computers.[19]

While statistics can successfully deal with complex phenomena where

---

[18] See F. A. Hayek, *The Counter-Revolution of Science*, Glencoe, Ill., 1952, pp. 60–63.
[19] Cf. J. G. Taylor, 'Experimental Design: A Cloak for Intellectual Sterility', *The British Journal of Psychology*, 49, 1958, esp. pp. 107–8.

these are the elements of the population on which we have information, it can tell us nothing about the structure of these elements. It treats them, in the fashionable phrase, as 'black boxes' which are presumed to be of the same kind but about whose identifying characteristics it has nothing to say. Nobody would probably seriously contend that statistics can elucidate even the comparatively not very complex structures of organic molecules, and few would argue that it can help us to explain the functioning of organisms. Yet when it comes to accounting for the functioning of social structures, that belief is widely held. It is here of course largely the product of a misconception about what the aim of a theory of social phenomena is, which is another story.

5. *The Theory of Evolution as an Instance of Pattern Prediction*

Probably the best illustration of a theory of complex phenomena which is of great value, although it describes merely a general pattern whose detail we can never fill in, is the Darwinian theory of evolution by natural selection. It is significant that this theory has always been something of a stumbling block for the dominant conception of scientific method. It certainly does not fit the orthodox criteria of 'prediction and control' as the hallmarks of scientific method.[20] Yet it cannot be denied that it has become the successful foundation of a great part of modern biology.

Before we examine its character we must clear out of the way a widely held misconception as to its content. It is often represented as if it consisted of an assertion about the succession of particular species of organisms which gradually changed into each other. This, however, is not the theory of evolution but an application of the theory to the particular events which took place on Earth during the last two billion years or so.[21] Most of the misapplications of evolutionary theory (parti-

---

[20] Cf., e.g., Stephen Toulmin, *Foresight and Prediction*, London, 1961, p. 24: 'No scientist has ever used this theory to foretell the coming into existence of creatures of a novel species, still less verified his forecast.'

[21] Even Professor Popper seems to imply this interpretation when he writes (*Poverty of Historicism*, p. 107) that 'the evolutionary hypothesis is not a universal law of nature but a particular (or, more precisely, singular) historical statement about the ancestry of a number of terrestrial plants and animals'. If this means that the essence of the theory of evolution is the assertion that particular species had common ancestors, or that the similarity of structure always means a common ancestry (which was the hypothesis from which the theory of evolution was derived), this is emphatically not the main content of the present theory of evolution. There is, incidentally, some contradiction between Popper's treatment of the concept of 'mammals' as a universal (*Logic*, p. 65) and the denial that the evolutionary hypothesis describes a universal law of nature. The same process might have produced mammals on other planets.

cularly in anthropology and the other social sciences) and its various abuses (e.g., in ethics) are due to this erroneous interpretation of its content.

The theory of evolution by natural selection describes a kind of process (or mechanism) which is independent of the particular circumstances in which it has taken place on Earth, which is equally applicable to a course of events in very different circumstances, and which might result in the production of an entirely different set of organisms. The basic conception of the theory is exceedingly simple and it is only in its application to the concrete circumstances that its extraordinary fertility and the range of phenomena for which it can account manifests itself.[22] The basic proposition which has this far-reaching implication is that a mechanism of reduplication with transmittable variations and competitive selection of those which prove to have a better chance of survival will in the course of time produce a great variety of structures adapted to continuous adjustment to the environment and to each other. The validity of this general proposition is not dependent on the truth of the particular applications which were first made of it: if, for example, it should have turned out that, in spite of their structural similarity, man and ape were not joint descendants from a comparatively near common ancestor but were the product of two convergent strands starting from ancestors which differed much more from each other (such as is true of the externally very similar types of marsupial and placental carnivores), this would not have refuted Darwin's general theory of evolution but only the manner of its application to the particular case.

The theory as such, as is true of all theories, describes merely a range of possibilities. In doing this it excludes other conceivable courses of events and thus can be falsified. Its empirical content consists in what it forbids.[23] If a sequence of events should be observed which cannot be fitted into its pattern, such as, e.g., that horses suddenly should begin to give birth to young with wings, or that the cutting off of a hind-paw in successive generations of dogs should result in dogs being born without that hind-paw, we should regard the theory as refuted.[24]

The range of what is permitted by the theory is undeniably wide. Yet one could also argue that it is only the limitation of our imagination which prevents us from being more aware of how much greater is the

---

[22] Charles Darwin himself well knew, as he once wrote to Lyell, that 'all the labour consists in the application of the theory' (quoted by C. C. Gillispie, *The Edge of Objectivity*, Princeton, 1960, p. 314).

[23] K. R. Popper, *Logic*, p. 41.

[24] Cf. Morton Beckner, *The Biological Way of Thought*, Columbia University Press, 1954, p. 241.

range of the prohibited—how infinite is the variety of conceivable forms of organisms which, thanks to the theory of evolution, we know will not in the foreseeable future appear on Earth. Commonsense may have told us before not to expect anything widely different from what we already knew. But exactly what kinds of variations are within the range of possibility and what kinds are not, only the theory of evolution can tell us. Though we may not be able to write down an exhaustive list of the possibilities, any specific question we shall, in principle, be able to answer.

For our present purposes we may disregard the fact that in one respect the theory of evolution is still incomplete because we still know only little about the mechanism of mutation. But let us assume that we knew precisely the circumstances in which (or at least the probability that in given conditions) a particular mutation will appear, and that we similarly knew also the precise advantages which any such mutation would in any particular kind of environment confer upon an individual of a specific constitution. This would not enable us to explain why the existing species or organisms have the particular structures which they possess, nor to predict what new forms will spring from them.

The reason for this is the actual impossibility of ascertaining the particular circumstances which, in the course of two billion years, have decided the emergence of the existing forms, or even those which, during the next few hundred years, will determine the selection of the types which will survive. Even if we tried to apply our explanatory scheme to a single species consisting of a known number of individuals each of which we were able to observe, and assuming that we were able to ascertain and record every single relevant fact, their sheer number would be such that we should never be able to manipulate them, i.e., to insert these data into the appropriate blanks of our theoretical formula and then to solve the 'statement equations' thus determined.[25]

What we have said about the theory of evolution applies to most of the rest of biology. The theoretical understanding of the growth and functioning of organisms can only in the rarest of instances be turned into specific predictions of what will happen in a particular case, because we can hardly ever ascertain all the facts which will contribute to determine the outcome. Hence, 'prediction and control, usually regarded as essential criteria of science, are less reliable in biology'.[26] It deals with pattern-building forces, the knowledge of which is useful for creating

[25] K. R. Popper, *Logic*, p. 73.
[26] Ralph S. Lillie, 'Some Aspects of Theoretical Biology', *Philosophy of Science*, XV, 2, 1948, p. 119.

conditions favourable to the production of certain kinds of results, while it will only in comparatively few cases be possible to control all the relevant circumstances.

6. *Theories of Social Structures*

It should not be difficult now to recognize the similar limitations applying to theoretical explanations of the phenomena of mind and society. One of the chief results so far achieved by theoretical work in these fields seems to me to be the demonstration that here individual events regularly depend on so many concrete circumstances that we shall never in fact be in a position to ascertain them all; and that in consequence not only the ideal of prediction and control must largely remain beyond our reach, but also the hope remain illusory that we can discover by observation regular connections between the individual events. The very insight which theory provides, for example, that almost any event in the course of a man's life may have some effect on almost any of his future actions, makes it impossible that we translate our theoretical knowledge into predictions of specific events. There is no justification for the dogmatic belief that such translation must be possible if a science of these subjects is to be achieved, and that workers in these sciences have merely not yet succeeded in what physics has done, namely to discover simple relations between a few observables. If the theories which we have yet achieved tell us anything, it is that no such simple regularities are to be expected.

I will not consider here the fact that in the case of mind attempting to explain the detail of the working of another mind of the same order of complexity, there seems to exist, in addition to the merely 'practical' yet nevertheless unsurmountable obstacles, also an absolute impossibility: because the conception of a mind fully explaining itself involves a logical contradiction. This I have discussed elsewhere.[27] It is not relevant here because the practical limits determined by the impossibility of ascertaining all the relevant data lie so far inside the logical limits that the latter have little relevance to what in fact we can do.

In the field of social phenomena only economics and linguistics[28]

---

[27] See *The Sensory Order*, 8.66–8.86, also *The Counter-Revolution of Science*, Glencoe, I, 22 1952, p. 48, and the following essay in the present volume.

[28] See particularly Noam Chomsky, *Syntactic Structures*, 'sGravenhage, 1957, who characteristically seems to succeed in building up such a theory after frankly abandoning the striving after an inductivist 'discovery procedure' and substituting for it the search after an 'evaluation procedure' which enables him to eliminate false theories of grammars and where these grammars may be arrived at 'by intuition, guess-work, all sorts of partial methodological hints, reliance on past experience, etc.' (p. 56).

seem to have succeeded in building up a coherent body of theory. I shall confine myself here to illustrating the general thesis with reference to economic theory, though most of what I have to say would appear to apply equally to linguistic theory.

Schumpeter well described the task of economic theory when he wrote that 'the economic life of a non-socialist society consists of millions of relations or flows between individual firms and households. We can establish certain theorems about them, but we can never observe them all.'[29] To this must be added that most of the phenomena in which we are interested, such as competition, could not occur at all unless the number of distinct elements involved were fairly large, and that the overall pattern that will form itself is determined by the significantly different behaviour of the different individuals so that the obstacle of obtaining the relevant data cannot be overcome by treating them as members of a statistical collective.

For this reason economic theory is confined to describing kinds of patterns which will appear if certain general conditions are satisfied, but can rarely if ever derive from this knowledge any predictions of specific phenomena. This is seen most clearly if we consider those systems of simultaneous equations which since Léon Walras have been widely used to represent the general relations between the prices and the quantities of all commodities bought and sold. They are so framed that *if* we were able to fill in all the blanks, i.e., *if* we knew all the parameters of these equations, we could calculate the prices and quantities of all the commodities. But, as at least the founders of this theory clearly understood, its purpose is not 'to arrive at a numerical calculation of prices', because it would be 'absurd' to assume that we can ascertain all the data.[30]

The prediction of the formation of this general kind of pattern rests on certain very general factual assumptions (such as that most people engage in trade in order to earn an income, that they prefer a larger income to a smaller one, that they are not prevented from entering whatever trade they wish, etc.,—assumptions which determine the scope of the variables but not their particular values); it is, however, not dependent on the knowledge of the more particular circumstances which we would have to know in order to be able to predict prices or quantities of particular commodities. No economist has yet succeeded in making a fortune by buying or selling commodities on the basis of his scientific prediction of future prices (even though some may have done so by selling such predictions).

---

[29] J. A. Schumpeter, *History of Economic Analysis*, Oxford University Press, 1954, p. 241.
[30] V. Pareto, *Manuel d'économie politique*, 2nd ed., Paris, 1927, pp. 223-4.

To the physicist it often seems puzzling why the economist should bother to formulate those equations although admittedly he sees no chance of determining the numerical values of the parameters which would enable him to derive from them the values of the individual magnitudes. Even many economists seem loath to admit that those systems of equations are not a step towards specific predictions of individual events but the final results of their theoretical efforts, a description merely of the general character of the order we shall find under specifiable conditions which, however, can never be translated into a prediction of its particular manifestations.

Predictions of a pattern are nevertheless both testable and valuable. Since the theory tells us under which general conditions a pattern of this sort will form itself, it will enable us to create such conditions and to observe whether a pattern of the kind predicted will appear. And since the theory tells us that this pattern assures a maximization of output in a certain sense, it also enables us to create the general conditions which will assure such a maximization, though we are ignorant of many of the particular circumstances which will determine the pattern that will appear.

It is not really surprising that the explanation of merely a sort of pattern may be highly significant in the field of complex phenomena but of little interest in the field of simple phenomena, such as those of mechanics. The fact is that in studies of complex phenomena the general patterns are all that is characteristic of those persistent wholes which are the main object of our interest, because a number of enduring structures have this general pattern in common and nothing else.[31]

7. *The Ambiguity of the Claims of Determinism*

The insight that we will sometimes be able to say that data of a certain class (or of certain classes) will bring about a pattern of a certain kind, but will not be able to ascertain the attributes of the individual elements which decide which particular form the pattern will assume, has consequences of considerable importance. It means, in the first instance, that when we assert that we know how something is determined, this state-

[31] A characteristic instance of the misunderstanding of this point (quoted by E. Nagel, l.c., p. 61) occurs in Charles A. Beard, *The Nature of the Social Sciences*, New York, 1934, p. 29, where it is contended that if a science of society 'were a true science, like that of astronomy, it would enable us to predict the essential movements of human affairs for the immediate and the indefinite future, to give pictures of society in the year 2000 or the year 2500 just as astronomers can map the appearances of the heavens at fixed points of time in the future.'

ment is ambiguous. It may mean that we merely know what class of circumstances determines a certain kind of phenomena, without being able to specify the particular circumstances which decide which member of the predicted class of patterns will appear; or it may mean that we can also explain the latter. Thus we can reasonably claim that a certain phenomenon is determined by known natural forces and at the same time admit that we do not know precisely how it has been produced. Nor is the claim invalidated that we can explain the principle on which a certain mechanism operates if it is pointed out that we cannot say precisely what it will do at a particular place and time. From the fact that we do know that a phenomenon is determined by certain kinds of circumstances it does not follow that we must be able to know even in one particular instance all the circumstances which have determined all its attributes.

There may well be valid and more grave philosophical objections to the claim that science can demonstrate a universal determinism; but for all practical purposes the limits created by the impossibility of ascertaining all the particular data required to derive detailed conclusions from our theories are probably much narrower. Even if the assertion of a universal determinism were meaningful, scarcely any of the conclusions usually derived from it would therefore follow. In the first of the two senses we have distinguished we may, for instance, well be able to establish that every single action of a human being is the necessary result of the inherited structure of his body (particularly of its nervous system) and of all the external influences which have acted upon it since birth. We might even be able to go further and assert that if the most important of these factors were in a particular case very much the same as with most other individuals, a particular class of influences will have a certain kind of effect. But this would be an empirical generalization based on a *ceteris paribus* assumption which we could not verify in the particular instance. The chief fact would continue to be, in spite of our knowledge of the principle on which the human mind works, that we should not be able to state the full set of particular facts which brought it about that the individual did a particular thing at a particular time. The individual personality would remain for us as much a unique and unaccountable phenomenon which we might hope to influence in a desirable direction by such empirically developed practices as praise and blame, but whose specific actions we could generally not predict or control, because we could not obtain the information on all the particular facts which determined it.

8. *The Ambiguity of Relativism*

The same sort of misconception underlies the conclusions derived from the various kinds of 'relativism'. In most instances these relativistic positions on questions of history, culture, or ethics are derived from the erroneous interpretations of the theory of evolution which we have already considered. But the basic conclusion that the whole of our civilization and all human values are the result of a long process of evolution in the course of which values, as the aims of human activity appeared, continue to change, seems inescapable in the light of our present knowledge. We are probably also entitled to conclude that our present values exist only as the elements of a particular cultural tradition and are significant only for some more or less long phase of evolution— whether this phase includes some of our pre-human ancestors or is confined to certain periods of human civilization. We have no more ground to ascribe to them eternal existence than to the human race itself. There is thus one possible sense in which we may legitimately regard human values as relative and speak of the probability of their further evolution.

But it is a far cry from this general insight to the claims of the ethical, cultural, or historical relativists or of evolutionary ethics. To put it crudely: while we know that all those values are relative to something, we do not know to what they are relative. We may be able to indicate the general class of circumstances which have made them what they are, but we do not know the particular conditions to which the values we hold are due, or what our values would be if those circumstances had been different. Most of the illegitimate conclusions are the result of the erroneous interpretation of the theory of evolution as the empirical establishment of a trend. Once we recognize that it gives us no more than a scheme of explanation which might be sufficient to explain particular phenomena *if* we knew all the facts which have operated in the course of history, it becomes evident that the claims of the various kinds of relativism (and of evolutionary ethics) are unfounded. Though we may meaningfully say that our values are determined by a class of circumstances definable in general terms, so long as we cannot state which particular circumstances have produced the existing values, or what our values would be under any specific set of other circumstances, no significant conclusions follow from the assertion.

It deserves brief notice in passing how radically opposed are the practical conclusions which are derived from the same evolutionary approach according as it is assumed that we can or cannot in fact know enough about the circumstances to derive specific conclusions from our theory. While the assumption of a sufficient knowledge of the concrete facts generally produces a sort of intellectual hubris which deludes itself that reason can judge all values, the insight into the impossibility of such full knowledge induces an attitude of humility and reverence towards that experience of mankind as a whole that has been precipitated in the values and institutions of existing society.

A few observations ought to be added here about the obvious significance of our conclusions for assessing the various kinds of 'reductionism'. In the sense of the first of the distinctions which we have repeatedly made—in the sense of general description—the assertion that biological or mental phenomena are 'nothing but' certain complexes of physical events, or that they are certain classes of structures of such events, these claims are probably defensible. But in the second sense—specific prediction—which alone would justify the more ambitious claims made for reductionism, they are completely unjustified. A full reduction would be achieved only if we were able to substitute for a description of events in biological or mental terms a description in physical terms which included an exhaustive enumeration of all the physical circumstances which constitute a necessary and sufficient condition of the biological or mental phenomena in question. In fact such attempts always consist—and can consist only—in the illustrative enumeration of classes of events, usually with an added 'etc.', which might produce the phenomenon in question. Such 'etc.-reductions' are not reductions which enable us to dispense with the biological or mental entities, or to substitute for them a statement of physical events, but are mere explanations of the general character of the kind of order or pattern whose specific manifestations we know only through our concrete experience of them.[32]

9. *The Importance of Our Ignorance*

Perhaps it is only natural that in the exuberance generated by the successful advances of science the circumstances which limit our factual knowledge, and the consequent boundaries imposed upon the applicability of theoretical knowledge, have been rather disregarded. It is high time, however, that we take our ignorance more seriously. As Popper and others have pointed out, 'the more we learn about the world, and the deeper our learning, the more conscious, specific, and articulate will be

[32] Cf. My *Counter-Revolution of Science*, pp. 48 *et seqq.*, and William Craig, 'Replacement of Auxiliary Expressions', *The Philosophical Review*, 65, 1956.

our knowledge of what we do not know, our knowledge of our ignorance'.[33] We have indeed in many fields learnt enough to know that we cannot know all that we would have to know for a full explanation of the phenomena.

These boundaries may not be absolute. Though we may never know as much about certain complex phenomena as we can know about simple phenomena, we may partly pierce the boundary by deliberately cultivating a technique which aims at more limited objectives—the explanation not of individual events but merely of the appearance of certain patterns or orders. Whether we call these mere explanations of the principle or mere pattern predictions or higher-level theories does not matter. Once we explicitly recognize that the understanding of the general mechanism which produces patterns of a certain kind is not merely a tool for specific predictions but important in its own right, and that it may provide important guides to action (or sometimes indications of the desirability of no action), we may indeed find that this limited knowledge is most valuable.

What we must get rid of is the naïve superstition that the world must be so organized that it is possible by direct observation to discover simple regularities between all phenomena and that this is a necessary presupposition for the application of the scientific method. What we have by now discovered about the organization of many complex structures should be sufficient to teach us that there is no reason to expect this, and that if we want to get ahead in these fields our aims will have to be somewhat different from what they are in the fields of simple phenomena.

10. *A Postscript on the Role of 'Laws' in the Theory of Complex Phenomena*[34]

Perhaps it deserves to be added that the preceding considerations throw some doubt on the widely held view that the aim of theoretical science is to establish 'laws'—at least if the word 'law' is used as com-

[33] K. R. Popper, 'On the Sources of Knowledge and Ignorance', *Proceedings of the British Academy*, 46, 1960, p. 69. See also Warren Weaver, 'A Scientist Ponders Faith', *Saturday Review*, January 3, 1959: 'Is science really gaining in its assault on the totality of the unsolved? As science learns one answer, it is characteristically true that it also learns several new questions. It is as though science were working in a great forest of ignorance, making an ever larger circular clearing within which, not to insist on the pun, things are clear. . . . But, as that circle becomes larger and larger, the circumference of contact with ignorance also gets longer and longer. Science learns more and more. But there is an ultimate sense in which it does not gain; for the volume of the appreciated but not understood keeps getting larger. We keep, in science, getting a more and more sophisticated view of our ignorance.'

[34] This last section of this essay was not contained in the version originally published and has been added to this reprint.

monly understood. Most people would probably accept some such definition of 'law' as that 'a scientific law is the rule by which two phenomena are connected with each other according to the principle of causality, that is to say, as cause and effect.'[35] And no less an authority than Max Planck is reported to have insisted that a true scientific law must be expressible in a single equation.[36]

Now the statement that a certain structure can assume only one of the (still infinite) number of states defined by a system of many simultaneous equations is still a perfectly good scientific (theoretical and falsifiable) statement.[37] We might still call, of course, such a statement a 'law', if we so wish (though some people might rightly feel that this would do violence to language); but the adoption of such a terminology would be likely to make us neglectful of an important distinction: for to say that such a statement describes, like an ordinary law, a relation between cause and effect would be highly misleading. It would seem, therefore, that the conception of law in the usual sense has little application to the theory of complex phenomena, and that therefore also the description of scientific theories as 'nomologic' or 'nomothetic' (or by the German term *Gesetzeswissenschaften*) is appropriate only to those two-variable or perhaps three-variable problems to which the theory of simple phenomena can be reduced, but not to the theory of phenomena which appear only above a certain level of complexity. If we assume that all the other parameters of such a system of equations describing a complex structure are constant, we can of course still call the dependence of one of the latter on the other a 'law' and describe a change in the one as 'the cause' and the change in the other as 'the effect'. But such a 'law' would be valid only for one particular set of values of all the other parameters and would change with every change in any one of them. This would evidently not be a very useful conception

[35] The particular wording which I happened to come across while drafting this is taken from H. Kelsen, 'The Natural Law Doctrine Before the Tribunal of Science' (1949), reprinted in *What is Justice?*, University of California Press, 1960, p. 139. It seems to express well a widely held view.

[36] Sir Karl Popper comments on this that it seems extremely doubtful whether any *single* one of Maxwell's equations could be said to express anything of real significance if we knew none of the others; in fact, it seems that the repeated occurrence of the symbols in the various equations is needed to secure that these symbols have the intended meanings.

[37] Cf. K. R. Popper, *Logic of Scientific Discovery*, § 17, p. 73: 'Even if the system of equations does not suffice for a unique solution, it does not allow every conceivable combination of values to be substituted for the "unknowns" (variables). Rather, the system of equations characterizes certain combinations of values or value systems as admissible, and others as inadmissible; it distinguishes the class of admissible value systems from the class of inadmissible value systems.' Note also the application of this in the following passages to 'statement equations'.

of a 'law', and the only generally valid statement about the regularities of the structure in question is the whole set of simultaneous equations from which, if the values of the parameters are continuously variable, an infinite number of particular laws, showing the dependence of one variable upon another, could be derived.

In this sense we may well have achieved a very elaborate and quite useful theory about some kind of complex phenomenon and yet have to admit that we do not know of a single law, in the ordinary sense of the word, which this kind of phenomenon obeys. I believe this to be in a great measure true of social phenomena: though we possess theories of social structures, I rather doubt whether we know of any 'laws' which social phenomena obey. It would then appear that the search for the discovery of laws is not an appropriate hall-mark of scientific procedure but merely a characteristic of the theories of simple phenomena as we have defined these earlier; and that in the field of complex phenomena the term 'law' as well as the concepts of cause and effect are not applicable without such modification as to deprive them of their ordinary meaning·

In some respect the prevalent stress on 'laws', i.e., on the discovery of regularities in two-variable relations, is probably a result of inductivism, because only such simple co-variation of two magnitudes is likely to strike the senses before an explicit theory or hypothesis has been formed. In the case of more complex phenomena it is more obvious that we must have our theory first before we can ascertain whether the things do in fact behave according to this theory. It would probably have saved much confusion if theoretical science had not in this manner come to be identified with the search for laws in the sense of a simple dependence of one magnitude upon another. It would have prevented such misconception as that, e.g., the biological theory of evolution proposed some definite 'law of evolution' such as a law of the necessary sequence of certain stages or forms. It has of course done nothing of the kind and all attempts to do this rest on a misunderstanding of Darwin's great achievement. And the prejudice that in order to be scientific one must produce laws may yet prove to be one of the most harmful of methodological conceptions. It may have been useful to some extent for the reason given by Popper, that 'simple statements . . . are to be prized more highly'[38] in all fields where simple statements are significant. But it seems to me that there will always be fields where it can be shown that all such simple statements must be false and where in consequence also the prejudice in favour of 'laws' must be harmful.

[38] *Ibid.*, p. 142.

CHAPTER THREE

Rules, Perception and Intelligibility[*][1]

1. Rule-guided Action

The most striking instance of the phenomenon from which we shall start is the ability of small children to use language in accordance with the rules of grammar and idiom of which they are wholly unaware. 'Perhaps there is', Edward Sapir wrote thirty-five years ago, 'a far-reaching moral in the fact that even a child may speak the most difficult language with idiomatic ease but that it takes an unusually analytical type of mind to define the mere elements of that incredibly subtle linguistic mechanism which is but a plaything in the child's unconscious.'[2]

The phenomenon is a very comprehensive one and includes all that we call skills. The skill of a craftsman or athlete which in English is described as 'knowledge how' (to carve, to ride a bicycle, to ski, or to tie a knot) belongs to this category. It is characteristic of these skills that we are usually not able to state explicitly (discursively) the manner of acting which is involved. A good example is given in another connection by M. Friedman and L. J. Savage:

> Consider the problem of predicting, before each shot, the direction of travel of a billiard-ball hit by an expert billiards player. It would be possible to construct one or more mathematical formulas that would give the

---

* Reprinted from the *Proceedings of the British Academy*, XLVIII, 1962, London, 1963.

[1] Numbers in footnotes refer to the Bibliography at the end of this chapter.

[2] E. Sapir (52, p. 549). Further insight into the nature of grammatical order makes this achievement of children appear even more remarkable, and R. B. Lees was recently moved to observe (32, p. 408) that 'in the case of this typically human and culturally universal phenomenon of speech, the simplest model that we can construct to account for it reveals that a grammar is of the same order as a predictive theory. If we are to account adequately for the indubitable fact that a child by the age of five or six has somehow reconstructed for himself the theory of this language, it would seem that our notions of human learning are due for some considerable sophistication'.

directions of travel that would score points and, among these, would indicate the one (or more) that would leave the balls in the best positions. The formulas might, of course, be extremely complicated, since they would necessarily take account of the location of the balls in relation to one another and of the cushions and of the complicated phenomena induced by 'english'. Nonetheless, it seems not at all unreasonable that excellent predictions would be yielded by the hypothesis that the billiards player made his shots *as if* he knew the formulas, could estimate accurately by eye the angles, etc., describing the location of the balls, could make lightning calculations from the formulas, and could then make the ball travel in the direction indicated by the formulas.[3]

(A being endowed with intellectual powers of a higher order would probably describe this by saying that the billiards player acted as if he could think.)

So far as we are able to describe the character of such skills we must do so by stating the rules governing the actions of which the actors will usually be unaware. Unfortunately, modern English usage does not permit generally to employ the verb 'can' (in the sense of the German *können*) to describe all those instances in which an individual merely 'knows how' to do a thing. In the instances so far quoted it will probably be readily granted that the 'know how' consists in the capacity to act according to rules which we may be able to discover but which we need not be able to state in order to obey them.[4] The problem is, however, of

---

[3] M. Friedman and L. J. Savage (8, p. 87).

[4] Cf. Gilbert Ryle (48) and (49, Chapter 2). The almost complete loss of the original connotation of 'can' in English, where it can scarcely any longer be used in the infinitive form, is not only an obstacle to the easy discussion of these problems but also a source of confusion in the international communication of ideas. If a German says 'Ich weiß, wie man Tennis spielt' this does not necessarily imply that he knows how to play tennis, which a German would express by saying 'Ich kann Tennis spielen'. In German the former phrase states the explicit knowledge of the rules of the game and may—if the speaker had made special motion studies—refer to the rules by which the skill of a player can be described, a skill which the speaker who claims to know these rules need not possess. German, in fact, has three terms for the English 'to know': *wissen*, corresponding to 'know that', *kennen*, corresponding to 'be acquainted with', and *können*, corresponding to 'know how'. See the interesting discussion in H. von Helmholtz (21, pp. 92 *et seqq.*). The passage is inevitably rendered only imperfectly in the English translation of this work.

Compare also on the whole issue Michael Polanyi (45), especially the chapters on 'Skills' and 'Articulation' and the penetrating observations in Adam Ferguson (7, p. 50): 'It is fortunate in this, as in other articles to which speculation and theory are applied, that nature proceeds in her course, whilst the curious are busied in the search for her principles. The peasant, or the child, can reason and judge, and speak his language with discernment, a consistency, and a regard for analogy, which perplex the logician, the moralist, and the grammarian, when they would find the principles upon which the proceeding is founded, or when they would bring to general rules what is so familiar, and so well sustained in particular cases.'

much wider significance than will perhaps be readily conceded. If what is called the *Sprachgefühl* consists in our capacity to follow yet unformulated rules,[5] there is no reason why, for example, the sense of justice (the *Rechtsgefühl*) should not also consist in such a capacity to follow rules which we do not know in the sense that we can state them.[6]

From these instances where action is guided by rules (movement patterns, ordering principles, etc.) which the acting person need not explicitly know (be able to specify, discursively to describe, or 'verbalize'),[7] and where the nervous system appears to act as what may be called a 'movement pattern effector', we must now turn to the corresponding and no less interesting instances where the organism is able to recognize actions conforming to such rules or patterns without being consciously aware of the elements of these patterns, and therefore must be presumed to possess also a kind of 'movement pattern detector'.

2. *Rule-guided Perception*

Again the capacity of the child to understand various meanings of sentences expressed by the appropriate grammatical structure provides the most conspicuous example of the capacity of rule-perception. Rules which we cannot state thus do not govern only our actions. They also govern our perceptions, and particularly our perceptions of other people's actions. The child who speaks grammatically without knowing the rules of grammar not only understands all the shades of meaning expressed by others through following the rules of grammar, but may also be able to correct a grammatical mistake in the speech of others.

This capacity of perceiving rules (or regularity, or patterns) in the action of others is a very general and important phenomenon. It is an instance of *Gestalt* perception, but of a perception of configurations of a peculiar kind. While in the more familiar instances we are able to specify (explicitly or discursively to describe, or explicate) the configurations which are recognized as the same, and therefore also are able deliberately to reproduce the stimulus situation which will produce the same perception in different people, all we often know in the instances which belong here and which will be the main subject of this paper is that a

---

[5] Cf. F. Kainz (23, p. 343): 'Die Normen, die das Sprachverwenden steuern, das Richtige vom Falschen sondern, bilden in ihrer Gesamtheit das Sprachgefühl.'

[6] Cf. L. Wittgenstein (66, p. 185e): ' "Knowing" it only means: being able to describe it.'

[7] Since the meaning of many of the terms we shall have to use is somewhat fluid, we shall occasionally resort to the device of cumulating near-synonyms which, although not identical in their meaning, by the range of overlap of meaning define more precisely the sense in which we use these terms.

particular situation is recognized by different persons as one of a certain kind.

To these classes of structures of events which are 'known by none, and understood by all'[8] belong in the first instance gestures and facial expressions. It is significant that the capacity to respond to signs of which we are not conscious decreases as we move from members of our own culture to those of different cultures, but that in some measure it also exists in our mutual relations to (and also between) higher animals.[9] The phenomenon has in recent years received a good deal of attention under the heading of 'physiognomy perception'[10]; it seems, however, to be of much wider occurrence than this term at first suggests. It guides not only our perception of expression but also our recognition of action as directed or purposive;[11] and it colours also our perception of non-human and inanimate phenomena. It would lead too far to consider here the important contributions made to the knowledge of these phenomena by ethology, particularly by the studies of birds by O. Heinroth, K. Z. Lorenz, and N. Tinbergen,[12] though their descriptions of the 'infective' character of certain types of movement and of the 'innate releasing mechanism' as a 'perceptual function' are highly relevant. We shall on the whole have to confine ourselves to the problems in man with an occasional look at other higher animals.

3. *Imitation and Identification*

The main difficulty which has to be overcome in accounting for these phenomena is most clearly seen in connection with the phenomenon of

[8] E. Sapir (52, p. 556): 'In spite of these difficulties of conscious analysis, we respond to gestures with an extreme alertness and, one might almost say, in accordance with an elaborate and secret code that is written nowhere, known by none, and understood by all.' Compare also Goethe's expression 'Ein jeder lebt's, nicht allen ist's bekannt'.

[9] Wolfgang Köhler (27, p. 307) reports that the chimpanzee 'at once correctly interprets the slightest changes of human expression, whether menacing or friendly'; and H. Hediger (18, p. 282) writes: 'Im Tierreich, namentlich bei den Säugetieren, besteht eine weitver-breitete und überraschend hohe Fähigkeit, menschliche Ausdruckserscheinungen ganz allgemein aufs feinste zu interpretieren.' R. E. Miller and his collaborators (37, p. 158) have shown 'that the effect of fear and/or anxiety can be perceived or discriminated by rhesus monkeys in the facial expression and posture of other monkeys'. For an illustration of the reverse relation, man recognizing the actions of apes as meaningful, see the description of observations of chimpanzees in the wild in A. Kortlandt (30).

[10] See H. Werner (63 and 64), F. Heider (19), and now J. Church (6) where, after completing this paper, I found much support for its argument.

[11] See, particularly, F. G. From (9) and E. Rubin (50), as well as G. W. Allport (2, p. 520), who sums up by saying that 'the key to person perception lies in our attention to what the other is *trying to do*'.

[12] See (20), (33 and 34), and (58) respectively.

imitation. The attention paid to this by psychologists has fluctuated greatly and after a period of neglect it seems again to have become respectable.[13] The aspect which concerns us here probably has not again been stated more clearly since it was first pointed out at the end of the eighteenth century by Dugald Stewart.[14] It concerns a difficulty which is commonly overlooked because imitation is most frequently discussed in connection with speech where it is at least plausible to assume that the sounds emitted by an individual are perceived by him as similar to those produced by another.

The position is very different, however, in the case of gestures, postures, gait, and other movements and particularly in that of facial expressions, where the movements of one's own body are perceived in a manner altogether different from that in which the corresponding movements of another person are perceived. Whatever in this respect may be the capacities of the newborn infant,[15] there can be no doubt that not only do human beings soon learn to recognize and to imitate complex movement patterns, but also that the various forms of 'infection' which occur in all forms of group life presuppose some such identification of the observed movements of another with one's own movements.[16] Whether it is the bird which is induced to fly (or preen, scratch, shake itself, etc.) by the sight of other birds doing so, or man induced to yawn or stretch by seeing others doing the same, or the more deliberate imitation practised in mimicry or learning a skill, what happens in all these instances is that an observed movement is directly translated into the corresponding action, often without the observing and imitating individual being aware of the elements of which the action consists or (in the case of man) being able to state what he observes and does.[17]

[13] For a survey see N. E. Miller and J. Dollard (36, especially appendix 2), and cf. also H. F. Harlow (14, p. 443), K. Koffka (28, pp. 307–19), and G. W. Allport (2, Chapter I).

[14] Dugald Stewart (56, chapter on 'Sympathetic Imitation').

[15] For the latest experimental results and the earlier literature on the smiling response of infants, see R. Ahrens (1), K. Goldstein (11), H. Plessner (44), and F. J. J. Buytendijk (5a).

[16] Cf. Dugald Stewart (56, p. 139): 'To bestow upon [this theory of imitation] even the shadow of plausibility, it must be supposed further, that the infant has the aid of a mirror, to enable it to know the existence of its own smile, and what sort of appearance these smiles exhibit to the eye . . . this throws no light whatever on the present difficulty till it is further explained by what process the child learns to *identify* what it feels, or is conscious of, in its own countenance, with what it sees on the countenance of others.' (Italics added and original italics omitted.)

[17] Cf. P. Schilder (53, p. 244): 'real imitation actions . . . are due to the fact that the visual presentation of the movement of another is apt to evoke the representation of a similar movement of one's own body, which, like all motor representations, tends to realize itself immediately in movements. Many of the imitation movements of children are of this class.' The extensive experimental work done on this phenomenon in recent times with the help of elaborate apparatus, photography, etc., has not taught us much more

Our capacity to imitate someone's gait, postures, or grimaces certainly does not depend on our capacity to describe these in words. We are frequently unable to do the latter, not merely because we lack the appropriate words but because we are unaware both of the elements of which these patterns are made up and of the manner in which they are related. We may well have a name for the whole,[18] or sometimes use comparisons with movements of animals ('creeping', 'ferocious') and the like, or describe conduct as expressive of an attribute of character such as 'furtive', 'timid', 'determined', or 'proud'. In one sense we thus know what we observe, but in another sense we do not know what it is that we thus observe.

Imitation is of course only one particularly obvious instance of the many in which we recognize the actions of others as being of a known kind, of a kind, however, which we are able to describe only by stating the 'meaning' which these actions have to us and not by pointing out the elements from which we recognize this meaning. Whenever we conclude that an individual is in a certain mood, or acts deliberately or purposively or effortlessly, seems to expect[19] something or to threaten or comfort another, etc., we generally do not know, and would not be able to explain, how we know this. Yet we generally act successfully on the basis of such 'understanding' of the conduct of others.

All these instances raise a problem of 'identification', not in the special psycho-analytical but in the ordinary sense of the term, the sense in which some movement (or posture, etc.) of our own which is perceived through one sense is recognized as being of the same kind as the movements of other people which we perceive through another sense. Before imitation is possible, identification must be achieved, i.e., the correspondence established between movement patterns which are perceived through different sense modalities.

4. *The Transfer of Learnt Rules*

The recognition of a correspondence between patterns made up of different sensory elements (whether belonging to the same or to different

than Adam Smith knew when he wrote ('Theory of Moral Sentiments', in *Essays*, London, 1869, p. 10) that 'the mob, when they are gazing at a dancer at the slack rope, naturally writhe and twist and balance their own bodies, as they see him do, and as they feel that they themselves must do if in his situation'.

[18] G. Kietz (24, p. 1) lists 59 verbs and 67 adjectives which are used in the region of Leipzig to describe distinguishable kinds of gait.

[19] Even the author of *A Glossary of Some Terms used in the Objective Science of Behaviour* (61, s.v. 'expect') finds himself forced to say that 'If one does not "intuitively know" what *expect* means, one is lost'.

sense modalities) presupposes a mechanism of sensory pattern transfer, that is, a mechanism for the transfer of the capacity to discern an abstract order or arrangement from one field to another. That such a capacity should exist seems not implausible as a similar transfer of learning in the motor sphere is a well-established fact: skills learnt with one hand are readily transferred to the other, etc.[20] It has recently also been demonstrated that, for example, monkeys trained to respond to differences in simple rhythms of light signals (opening a door on two signals of equal duration and not opening it on two signals of unequal duration) at once transferred this response to the corresponding rhythms of sound signals.[21] In the field of perception many of the *Gestalt* phenomena, such as the transposition of a melody, also imply the operation of the same principle. The prevalent views on the nature of perception, however, do not supply us with an adequate account of how such a transfer is brought about.[22]

Such a mechanism is not difficult to conceive. The main point to keep in mind is that in order that any two different sensory elements ('elementary sense qualities' or more complex percepts) should be capable of taking the same place in a pattern of a certain kind, they must have certain attributes in common. Unless both can vary along some such scale as large: small, strong : weak, of long duration : of short duration, etc., they cannot serve in the same place as constituents of similar patterns. The most important of these common properties of different kinds of sensations which enables them to take the same place in a pattern of a certain kind is their common space-time framework: while visual, tactile, kinesthetic, and auditory sensations may have the same rhythm, and the first three of them also form the same spatial patterns, this is not possible for sensations of smell and taste.[23]

---

[20] A convenient survey of the facts is given by R. S. Woodworth and H. Schlossberg (67, Chapter 24), where also instances of the transfer of 'perceptual skills' are given. See also K. S. Lashley (31), a paper full of significant suggestions on our problem.

[21] L. C. Stepien and others (55, pp. 472–3).

[22] In modern discussions of these problems resort is generally had to the somewhat vague conception of the 'schema'. For recent discussions of this, see R. C. Oldfield and O. L. Zangwill (42), R. C. Oldfield (41), and M. D. Vernon (60). We shall not use it here as a technical term because by its various uses it has acquired a penumbra of undesirable connotations.

[23] It is becoming increasingly clear that even the perception of spatial patterns, which we are inclined to ascribe to the simultaneous occurrence of the sensory elements from which the patterns are made up, rests largely on a process of visual or tactual scanning and on the perception of 'gradients', i.e., on the particular sequence of stimuli being recognized as following a rule. Hence, as K. S. Lashley has pointed out (31, p. 128), 'spatial and temporal order thus appear to be almost completely interchangeable in cerebral action'. It would seem as if the task of the theory of perception were increasingly becoming the discovery of

These common attributes that the separate sensations must possess in order to be capable of forming the same abstract patterns must evidently have some distinct neural correlates (impulses in particular groups of neurons which represent them), because only thus can they in some respect have the same effect on our mental processes and actions: if different sensations lead us to describe them as 'large' or 'intense' or 'long', the impulses corresponding to them must at some stage of the hierarchical order of evaluation (classification)[24] reach the same pathways. Once, however, we recognize that in order to possess similar attributes the sensations caused by different nerve impulses must have some identical elements among the 'following'[25] which determines their quality, the problem of the transfer of a pattern that has been learnt in one sensory field to another presents no serious difficulty.

If a certain order or sequence of sensory elements possessing given attributes has acquired a distinctive significance, this significance will be determined by the classification as equivalent of the neural events standing for those attributes and it will thus automatically apply to them also when they are evoked by other sensations than those in connection with which the pattern has been learnt in the first instance. Or, to put this differently, sensations which have common attributes will be capable of forming elements of the same pattern and this pattern will be recognized as one of the same kind even if it has never been experienced before in connection with the particular elements, because the otherwise qualitatively different sensations will have among the impulses determining their quality some which uniquely determine the abstract attribute in question; and whenever the capacity of recognizing an abstract rule which the arrangement of these attributes follows has been acquired in one field, the same master mould will apply when the signs for those abstract attributes are evoked by altogether different elements. It is the classification of the structure of relationships between these abstract attributes which constitutes the recognition of the patterns as the same or different.

[24] For a systematic exposition of the theory underlying this statement see F. A. Hayek (16).

[25] See (16, para. 3.34).

the rules according to which various constellations of physical data are translated into perceptual categories so that a great variety of sets of physical facts are interpreted as the same phenomenal situation. This development traces back to H. von Helmholtz's conception of the 'unconscious inference' (21), has been developed particularly by J. C. Gibson (10), and has recently produced the most remarkable results in Ivo Kohler's demonstration (29) of the 'general rules' by which the visual system learns to correct exceedingly complex and variable distortions produced by prismatic spectacles when the eye or the head moves.

5. *Behaviour Patterns and Perception Patterns*

In the course of its development[26] any organism will acquire a large repertoire of such perceptual patterns to which it can specifically respond, and among this repertoire of patterns some of the earliest and most firmly embedded will be those due to the proprioceptive (kinesthetic) recording of movement patterns of its own body, movement patterns which in many instances will be guided by innate organization and probably be directed sub-cortically, yet reported to and recorded at higher levels. The term 'movement pattern' in this connection hardly suggests the complexity or variety of the attributes of the movements involved. Not only does it include relative movements of rigid bodies and various bending or elastic movements of flexible bodies, but also continuous and discontinuous, rhythmic and a-rhythmic changes of speed, etc. The opening and closing of jaws or beaks or the characteristic movements of limbs are relatively simple instances of such patterns. They can generally be analysed into several separate movements which together produce the pattern in question.

The young animal for which every day begins with the sight of his elders and siblings yawning and stretching, grooming and defecating, scanning the environment, and so on, and who soon learns to recognize these basic schemata as the same as its own innate movement patterns connected with certain moods (or dispositions, or sets), will tend to place into these perceptual categories everything which approximately fits them. These patterns will provide the master moulds (templates, schemata, or *Schablonen*) in terms of which will be perceived many other complex phenomena in addition to those from which the patterns are derived. What at first may have originated with an innate and fairly specific movement pattern may thus become a learnt and abstract mould for classifying perceived events. ('Classifying' stands here, of course, for a process of channelling, or switching, or 'gating', of the nervous impulses so as to produce a particular disposition or set.)[27] The effect of perceiving that events occur according to a rule will thus be that another rule is imposed upon the further course of the processes in the nervous system.

The phenomenal (sensory, subjective, or behavioural)[28] world in which such an organism lives will therefore be built up largely of move-

---

[26] The expression 'development' is used to include not only ontogenetic but also phylogenetic processes.

[27] See (15, Chapter iii).

[28] In contrast to objective, physical, scientific, etc. See (16, para. 1.10).

ment patterns characteristic of its own kind (species or wider group). These will be among the most important categories in terms of which it perceives the world and particularly most forms of life. Our tendency to personify (to interpret in anthropomorphic or animistic terms) the events we observe is probably the result of such an application of schemata which our own bodily movements provide. It is they which make, though not yet intelligible, at least perceivable (comprehensible or meaningful) complexes of events which without such perceptual schemata would have no coherence or character as wholes.

It is not surprising that the explicit evoking of these anthropomorphic interpretations should have become one of the main tools of artistic expression by which the poet or painter can conjure up the character of our experiences in an especially vivid manner. Expressions such as that a thundercloud leans threateningly over us, or that a landscape is peaceful or smiling or sombre or wild, are more than merely metaphors. They describe true attributes of our experiences in the terms in which they occur. This does not mean that these attributes belong to the objective events in any other sense than that we intuitively ascribe them to those events. But they are nevertheless part of the environment as we know it and as it determines our conduct. And, as we shall see, if our perceptions in those instances do not in fact help us to understand nature, the fact that sometimes those patterns we read (or project) into nature are all that we know and all that determines our action makes it an essential datum in our efforts to explain the results of human interaction.

The conception that we often perceive patterns without being aware of (or even without perceiving at all) the elements of which they are made up conflicts with the deeply ingrained belief that all recognition of 'abstract' forms is 'derived' from our prior perception of the 'concrete': the assumption that we must first perceive particulars in all their richness and detail before we learn to abstract from them those features which they have in common with other experiences. But, although there exists some clinical evidence that the abstract is often dependent on the functioning of higher nervous centres and that the capacity to form abstract conceptions may be lost while more concrete images are still retained, this is clearly not always so[29]. Nor would it prove that the concrete is chronologically prior. It is at least highly probable that we often perceive only highly abstract features, that is, an order of stimuli which individually are not perceived at all or at least are not identified.[30]

[29] Cf. Roger W. Brown (3, pp. 264–98), and (16, paras. 6.33–6.43).

[30] Cf. J. Church (6, p. 111): 'It is perfectly possible to see something well enough to sense that it is something dangerous or something attractive but not well enough to know what it is.'

6. Specifiable and Non-specifiable Patterns

The fact that we sometimes perceive patterns which we are unable to specify has often been noticed, but it has scarcely yet been given its proper place in our general conception of our relations to the outside world. It will therefore be useful to contrast it explicitly with the two more familiar ways in which patterns play a role in the interpretation of our surroundings. The instance which is familiar to everybody is that of the sensory perception of patterns, such as geometrical figures, which we can also explicitly describe. That the ability intuitively to perceive and the ability discursively to describe a pattern are not the same thing, however, has become evident in the course of the advance of science, which has increasingly led to the interpretation of nature in terms of patterns which can be constructed by our intellect but not intuitively pictured (such as patterns in multidimensional space). Mathematics and logic are largely occupied with the making of new patterns which our perception does not show us but which later may or may not be found to describe relations between observable elements.[31]

In the third case, the one which interests us here, the relation is the reverse: our senses recognize (or better: 'project', or 'read into' the world) patterns which we are in fact not able discursively to describe[32] and perhaps may never be able to specify. That there exist instances where we do recognize such patterns intuitively long before we can describe them the instance of language alone sufficiently demonstrates. But once the existence of some such cases is demonstrated, we must be prepared to discover that they are more numerous and significant than we are immediately aware of. Whether in all such instances we shall, even in principle, be able explicitly to describe the structures which our senses spontaneously treat as instances of the same pattern we shall have to consider at the end of this paper.

The fact that we recognize patterns which we cannot specify does not, of course, mean that such perceptions can legitimately serve as elements of scientific explanation (though they may provide the 'intuitions' which usually precede the conceptual formulation).[33] But, though such per-

---

[31] Cf. F. A. Hayek (17), now reprinted as the second essay in the present volume.

[32] Compare Goethe's remark that 'Das Wort bemüht sich nur umsonst, Gestalten schöpferisch aufzubauen'. See also E. H. Gombrich (12, pp. 103–5 and 307–13) and particularly his observation (p. 307) that 'it almost looks as if the eye knew of meanings of which the mind knows nothing'.

[33] It is a different matter that in medical and other diagnoses 'physiognomy perception' plays a very important role as a guide to practice. Even here, however, it cannot directly enter theory. On its role cf. M. Polanyi (45a). See on these problems also H. Klüver (25,

ceptions do not provide a scientific explanation, they not only raise a problem for explanation; we must also take into account in explaining the effects of men's actions that they are guided by such perceptions. We shall have to return to this problem later. At this stage it should merely be pointed out that it is entirely consistent, on the one hand, to deny that 'wholes' which are intuitively perceived by the scientist may legitimately figure in his explanations and, on the other, to insist that the perception of such wholes by the persons whose interactions are the object of investigation must form a datum for scientific analysis. We shall find that perceptions of this sort, which the radical behaviourists wish to disregard because the corresponding stimuli cannot be defined in 'physical terms', are among the chief data on which our explanations of the relations between men must be built.[34]

In a certain sense it is generally true that the requirement that the terms in which an explanation runs must be fully specifiable applies only to the theory (the general formula or the abstract pattern) and not to the particular data which must be inserted in place of the blanks to make it applicable to particular instances. So far as the recognition of the particular conditions is concerned to which a theoretical statement is applicable, we always have to rely on interpersonal agreement, whether the conditions are defined in terms of sensory qualities such as 'green' or 'bitter', or in terms of point coincidences, as is the case where we measure. In these familiar instances this raises in general no difficulty, not only because agreement between different observers is very high, but also because we know how to create the conditions in which different persons will experience the same perceptions. The physical circumstances which produce these sensations can be deliberately manipulated and generally assigned to defined space-time regions which are for the observer 'filled' with the sensory quality in question. We will also find in general that what appears as alike to different people will also have the

[34] It is difficult to say how far such perceptions of non-specifiable patterns fit the usual conception of 'sense data', 'data of observation', 'perceptual data', 'empirical ultimates', or 'objective facts', and perhaps even whether we can still speak of perception by the senses or should rather speak of perception by the mind. It would seem as if the whole phenomenon we are considering could not be fitted into the sensualist philosophy from which those conceptions derive. It is clearly not true, as is implied in those terms, that all we experience we must also be in a position to describe. Though we may have a name for such unspecifiable perceptions which our fellows understand, we should have no way of explaining what they are to a person who does not already in some sense perceive the same complexes of events of which we cannot further explain what they have in common.

pp. 7-9) and K. Z. Lorenz (34, p. 176) who suggests that 'no important scientific fact has ever been "proved" that has not previously been simply and immediately seen by intuitive *Gestalt* perception'.

same effects on other objects; and we regard it as a rather surprising exception if what appears as alike to us acts differently on other objects, or if what appears different to us acts alike on other objects.[35] Yet we can experiment with the stimuli to which such perceptions are due, and though in the last resort the applicability of our theoretical model also rests on agreement on sense perceptions, we can push these, as it were, as far back as we wish.

The situation is different where we cannot specify the structures of elements which people in fact treat as the same pattern and call by the same name. Though in one sense people know in those instances what they perceive, in another they do not know what it is that they thus perceive. While all observers may in fact agree that a person is happy, or acts deliberately or clumsily, or expects something, etc., they cannot for persons who do not know what these terms mean provide what is sometimes misleadingly called an 'ostensive' definition because they cannot point to those parts of the observed environment from which they recognize those attributes.

The intelligibility of communications intended to be understood (or the comprehension of their meaning) on the basis of the perception of the rules which they follow is merely the most conspicuous instance of a phenomenon of much wider occurrence. What we perceive in watching other people (and in some measure also in watching other living things)[36] is not so much particular movements but a purpose or mood or attitude (disposition or set) which we recognize from we do not know what. It is from such perceptions that we derive most of the information which makes the conduct of others intelligible to us. What we recognize as purposive conduct is conduct following a rule with which we are acquainted but which we need not explicitly know. Similarly, that an approach of another person is friendly or hostile, that he is playing a game or willing to sell us some commodity or intends to make love, we recognize without knowing what we recognize it from. In general, we do not know in those instances what psychologists call the 'clues' (or 'cues') from which men recognize what to them is the significant aspect of the situation; and in most instances there will in fact be no specific clues in the sense of single events but merely a pattern of a certain kind which has a meaning to them.

---

[35] See (16, paras. 1.6–1.21) and (15, pp. 18–24)

[36] If the vitalists find causal explanations of the phenomena of life so unsatisfactory, it is probably because such explanations do not fully account for those features by which we unitively recognize something as living.

7. *The Multiple Chain of Rules*

We have called the phenomena we are discussing 'rule perception' (though 'regularity perception' would perhaps be more appropriate).[37] That expression has the advantage over such terms as 'pattern perception' and the like in that it more strongly suggests that such perceptions may be of any degree of generality or abstractness, that it clearly includes temporal as well as spatial orders, and that it is compatible with the fact that the rules to which it refers interact in a complex structure. It is also helpful in bringing out the connection between the rules governing perception and the rules governing action.[38]

No attempt will be made here to define 'rule'. It should be noted, however, that in describing the rules on which a system acts, at least some of these rules will have to be given the form of imperatives or norms, i.e., the form 'if A, then do B', though once a framework of such imperatives has been established, within it indicative rules such as 'if A, then B' may be used to determine the premisses of the imperative rules. But while all the indicative rules could be restated as imperative rules (namely in the form 'if A, then do as if B'), the reverse is not true.

The unconscious rules which govern our action are often represented as 'customs' or 'habits'. These terms are somewhat misleading, however, because they are usually understood to refer to very specific or particular actions. But the rules of which we are speaking generally control or circumscribe only certain aspects of concrete actions by providing a general schema which is then adapted to the particular circumstances. They will often merely determine or limit the range of possibilities within which the choice is made consciously.[39] By eliminating certain kinds of action altogether and providing certain routine ways of achieving the object, they merely restrict the alternatives on which a conscious choice is required. The moral rules, for example, which have become part of a man's nature will mean that certain conceivable choices will not appear at all among the possibilities between which he chooses. Thus even decisions which have been carefully considered will in part be determined by rules of which the acting person is not aware. Like scientific

---

[37] Cf. O. G. Selfridge (54, p. 345): 'A pattern is equivalent to a set of rules for recognizing it,' and (p. 346): 'By pattern recognition is meant classifying patterns into learnt categories.'

[38] The crucial significance of the concept of rule in this connection was brought home to me by reading T. S. Szasz (57) and R. S. Peters (43), which helped me to bring together various strands of thought starting from different origins.

[39] Cf. G. Humphrey (22, esp. p. 255) who distinguishes with respect to habits between the fixed strategy and the variable tactics.

laws,[40] the rules which guide an individual's action are better seen as determining what he will not do rather than what he will do.

The relations between rules of perception and rules of action are complex. So far as the perception of actions of other individuals is concerned, we have seen that in the first instance the perceiving individual's own action patterns provide the master moulds by which the action patterns of other individuals are recognized. But recognizing an action pattern as one of a class determines merely that it has the same meaning as others of the same class, but not yet what that meaning is. The latter rests on the further pattern of action, or set of rules, which in response to the recognition of a pattern as one of a certain kind the organism imposes upon its own further activities.[41] Every perception of a rule in the external events as well as every single perceived event, or any need arising out of the internal processes of the organism, thus adds to or modifies the set of rules governing the further responses to new stimuli. It is the total of such activated rules (or conditions imposed upon further action) which constitutes what is called the 'set' (disposition) of the organism at any particular moment, and the significance of newly received signals consists in the manner in which they modify this complex of rules.[42]

The complexity of the arrangement in which these rules may be super-imposed and interrelated is difficult briefly to indicate. We must assume that there exists not only on the perceptual side a hierarchy of super-imposed classes of classes, etc., but that similarly also on the motor side not merely dispositions to act according to a rule but dispositions to change dispositions and so on will operate chains which may be of considerable length. Indeed, in view of the inter-connections between the sensory and the motor elements on all levels, it becomes impossible clearly to distinguish between an ascending (sensory) and descending (motor) branch of the process; we should conceive of the whole rather

---

[40] Cf. K. R. Popper (46).

[41] I presume that it is this circular connection between action patterns and perception patterns which V. von Weizsäcker had in mind in speaking of the *Gestaltkreis* (65). In this connection it should be mentioned that, apart from the *Gestalt* theorists, those who have given most attention to the phenomena discussed here were mainly students influenced by phenomenologist or existentialist conceptions, though I find myself unable to accept their philosophical interpretations. See particularly F. J. J. Buytendijk (5), M. Merleau-Ponty (35), and H. Plessner (44). Cf. also (15, paras. 4.45–4.63 and 5.63–5.75).

[42] That the arrival of additional modifiers of an action that may already be sufficiently determined by other circumstances does not lead to over-determination presupposes an organization more complex than that represented, for example, by a system of simultaneous equations, something in which a 'normal' (general purpose or routine) instruction can be superseded by another containing more specific information.

as one continuous stream in which the connection between any group of stimuli and any group of responses is effected by many arcs of different length, with the longer ones not only controlling the results of the shorter ones but in turn being controlled by the ongoing processes in the higher centres through which they pass. The first step in the successive classification of the stimuli must thus be seen as at the same time the first step in a successive imposition of rules on action, and the final specification of a particular action as the last step of many chains of successive classifications of stimuli according to the rules to which their arrangement corresponds.[43]

It would seem to follow from this that the meaning (connotation, intension) of a symbol or concept will normally be a rule imposed on further mental processes which itself need not be conscious or specifiable. This would imply that such a concept need not be accompanied by an image or have an external 'referent': it merely puts into operation a rule which the organism possesses. This rule imposed upon the further processes should, of course, not be confused with the rule by which the symbol or action having the meaning is recognized. Nor must we expect to find any simple correspondence between the structure of any system of symbols and the structure of meaning: what we have to deal with is a set of relations between two systems of rules. A great part of the current philosophies of 'symbolism' seem in this respect to be barking up the wrong tree—not to speak of the paradox of a 'theory of communication' which believes that it can account for communication while disregarding meaning or the process of understanding.

8. Γνῶσις τοῦ ὁμοίου τῷ ὁμοίῳ

We have yet to consider more closely the role which the perception of the meaning of other people's action must play in the scientific explanation of the interaction of men. The problem which arises here is known in the discussion of the methodology of the social sciences as that of *Verstehen* (understanding). We have seen that this understanding of the meaning of actions is of the same kind as the understanding of communications (i.e., of action intended to be understood). It includes what the eighteenth-century authors described as sympathy and what has more recently been discussed under the heading of 'empathy' (*Einfühlung*). Since we shall be concerned chiefly with the use of these perceptions as data for the theoretical social sciences, we shall concentrate on what is sometimes called rational understanding (or rational

43 Cf. (16, paras. 4.45–4.63 and 5.63–5.75).

reconstruction), that is, on the instances where we recognize that the persons in whose actions we are interested base their decisions on the meaning of what they perceive. The theoretical social sciences do not treat all of a person's actions as an unspecifiable and unexplainable whole but, in their efforts to account for the unintended consequences of individual actions, endeavour to reconstruct the individual's reasoning from the data which to him are provided by the recognition of the actions of others as meaningful wholes. We shall indicate this limitation by speaking of *intelligibility* and of *comprehending the meaning* of human action rather than of understanding.[44]

The chief question we shall have to consider is that of what, and how much, we must have in common with other people in order to find their actions intelligible or meaningful. We have seen that our capacity to recognize action as following rules and having meaning rests on ourselves already being equipped with these rules. This 'knowledge by acquaintance' presupposes therefore that some of the rules in terms of which we perceive and act are the same as those by which the conduct of those whose actions we interpret is guided.

The contention that intelligibility of human action presupposes a certain likeness between actor and the interpreter of his actions has led to the misunderstanding that this means that, for example, 'only a war-like historian can tackle a Genghis Khan or a Hitler'.[45] This, of course, is not implied in the contention. We need not be wholly alike or even have a similar character with those whose communications or other actions we find intelligible, but we must be made up of the same ingredients, however different the mixture may be in the particular instances. The requirement of likeness is of the same kind as in the case of understanding language, although in the latter case the specificity of languages to particular cultures adds an extra requirement which is not needed for the interpretation of the meaning of many other actions. One need clearly not be frequently or even ever violently angry to be familiar with the rage pattern or to recognize and interpret a choleric temper.[46] Nor need

---

[44] See L. von Mises (38 and 39), who distinguishes between *Begreifen* and *Verstehen*, though I prefer to render his *Begreifen* by 'comprehension' rather than by his own English term 'conception'. To the first of his works cited I owe also the quotation from Empedocles used as the heading of this section, which is derived from Aristotle, *Metaphysics*, ii.4,1000^{b}5. A careful analysis of the whole problem of *Verstehen* which deserves to be better known will be found in H. Gomperz (13).

[45] J. W. N. Watkins (62, p. 740).

[46] Cf. R. Redfield (47): 'The anthropologist demonstrates the existence of human nature whenever he finds out what an exotic people are thinking and feeling. He can do this only by supposing that they have in common with him certain acquired propensities of attitude; these are human nature. To be able to find out what it is that a Zuni Indian is ashamed of, one must first know what it is to be ashamed.'

one be at all like Hitler to understand his reasoning in a way one cannot understand the mental processes of an imbecile. Nor does one have to like the same things as another to know what 'liking' means.[47] Intelligibility is certainly a matter of degree and it is a commonplace that people who are more alike also understand each other better. Yet this does not alter the fact that even in the limiting case of the restricted understanding which occurs between men and higher animals, and still more in the understanding between men of different cultural backgrounds or character, intelligibility of communications and other acts rests on a partial similarity of mental structure.

It is true that there is no systematic procedure by which we are able to decide in a particular instance whether our comprehension of the meaning of the action of others is correct, and also that for this reason we can never be certain of this sort of fact. But of this those who guide their action by physiognomic perceptions are generally also aware, and the degree of confidence they attach to their knowledge of the meaning of another man's action is as much a datum by which they orient themselves as the meaning itself, and must therefore in the same manner enter our scientific account of the effects of the interactions of many men.

9. *Supra-conscious Rules and the Explanation of Mind*

So far our argument has rested solely on the uncontestable assumption that we are not in fact able to specify all the rules which govern our perceptions and actions. We still have to consider the question whether it is conceivable that we should ever be in a position discursively to describe all (or at least any one we like) of these rules, or whether mental activity must always be guided by some rules which we are in principle not able to specify.

If it should turn out that it is basically impossible to state or communicate all the rules which govern our actions, including our communications and explicit statements, this would imply an inherent limitation of our possible explicit knowledge and, in particular, the impossibility of ever fully explaining a mind of the complexity of our own. Yet, though I am not able to supply a strict proof, this seems to me indeed to follow from the preceding considerations.

If everything we can express (state, communicate) is intelligible to others only because their mental structure is governed by the same rules

---

47 Cf. H. Klüver (26, p. 286): 'It should be realized that "emotional" or "affective" qualities may become visible as "physiognomic" properties without emotional states or events occurring in the observer or the observed object. We may see, for instance, "sadness" or "aggressiveness" in a face without being emotionally affected.'

as ours, it would seem that these rules themselves can never be communicated. This seems to imply that in one sense we always know not only more than we can deliberately state but also more than we can be aware of or deliberately test; and that much that we successfully do depends on presuppositions which are outside the range of what we can either state or reflect upon. This application to all conscious thought of what seems obviously true of verbal statements seems to follow from the fact that such thought must, if we are not to be led into an infinite regress, be assumed to be directed by rules which in turn cannot be conscious—by a supra-conscious[48] mechanism which operates upon the contents of consciousness but which cannot itself be conscious.[49]

The main difficulty of admitting the existence of such supra-conscious processes is probably our habit of regarding conscious thought and explicit statements as in some sense the highest level of mental functions. While we are clearly often not aware of mental processes because they have not yet risen to the level of consciousness but proceed on what are (both physiologically and psychologically) lower levels, there is no reason why the conscious level should be the highest level, and there are many grounds which make it probable that, in order to be conscious, processes must be guided by a supra-conscious order which cannot be the object of its own representations. Mental events may thus be unconscious and uncommunicable because they proceed on too high a level as well as because they proceed on too low a level.

To put this differently: if 'to have meaning' is to have a place in an order which we share with other people, this order itself cannot have meaning because it cannot have a place in itself. A point may have a distinct place in a network of lines which differentiates it from all other points in that network; and, similarly, a complex structure of relationships may be distinguished from all other similar structures by a place in a more comprehensive structure which gives each element of the first structure and its relations a distinct 'place'. But the distinguishing

---

[48] Or better, perhaps, 'meta-conscious', since the problem is essentially the same as those which have given rise to meta-mathematics, meta-languages, and meta-legal rules.

[49] Twenty years ago I suggested (15, p. 48) that it would seem that any mechanism of classification would always have to possess a degree of complexity greater than any one of the different objects it classifies, and if this is correct it would follow that it is impossible that our brain should ever be able to produce a complete explanation of the particular ways in which it classifies stimuli (as distinguished from a mere explanation of the principle); and ten years later I attempted to state the argument more fully (16, paras. 8.66–8.68). It now seems to me as if this would follow from what I understand to be Georg Cantor's theorem in the theory of sets according to which in any system of classification there are always more classes than things to be classified, which presumably implies that no system of classes can contain itself. But I do not feel competent to attempt such a proof.

character of such an order could never be defined by its place in itself, and a mechanism possessing such an order, though it may be able to indicate meaning by reference to such a place, can never by its action so reproduce the set of relations which defines this place as to distinguish it from another such set of relations.

It is important not to confuse the contention that any such system must always act on some rules which it cannot communicate with the contention that there are particular rules which no such system could ever state. All the former contention means is that there will always be some rules governing a mind which that mind in its then prevailing state cannot communicate, and that, if it ever were to acquire the capacity of communicating these rules, this would presuppose that it had acquired further higher rules which make the communication of the former possible but which themselves will still be incommunicable.

To those familiar with the celebrated theorem due to Kurt Gödel it will probably be obvious that these conclusions are closely related to those Gödel has shown to prevail in formalized arithmetical systems.[50] It would thus appear that Gödel's theorem is but a special case of a more general principle applying to all conscious and particularly all rational processes, namely the principle that among their determinants there must always be some rules which cannot be stated or even be conscious. At least all we can talk about and probably all we can consciously think about presupposes the existence of a framework which determines its meaning, i.e., a system of rules which operate us but which we can neither state nor form an image of and which we can merely evoke in others in so far as they already possess them.

It would lead too far if we were here to attempt an examination of the processes by which the manipulation of rules of which we are conscious may lead to the building up of further meta-conscious rules, in terms of which we may then be able explicitly to formulate rules of which we were formerly unconscious. It seems probable that much of the mysterious powers of scientific creativity are due to processes of this sort which involve a restructuring of the supra-conscious matrix in which our conscious thought moves.

We must be content here with providing a framework within which the problem of meaning (intelligibility, significance, understanding) can be meaningfully discussed. To pursue it further would demand the construction of a formal model of a causal system capable not only of recognizing rules in the observed events and responding to them according to another set of rules, different from, yet related to the former,

[50] See E. Nagel and J. R. Newman (40) for a semi-popular exposition.

but also able to communicate its perceptions and actions to another system of the same sort, and the demonstration that two such communicating systems must be governed by a common set of rules which cannot be communicated between them. This, however, is a task which would exceed not only the scope of this paper but also the powers of its author.

BIBLIOGRAPHY

1. R. Ahrens, 'Beitrag zur Entwicklung der Physiognomie- und Mimiker-kenntnis', *Z. f. exp. u. ang. Psychologie*, 1954.
2. Gordon W. Allport, *Pattern and Growth of Personality*, New York, 1961.
3. Roger W. Brown, *Words and Things*, Glencoe, Ill., 1958.
4. J. S. Bruner, J. J. Goodnow, and G. A. Austin, *A Study of Thinking*, New York, 1956.
5. F. J. J. Buytendijk, *Allgemeine Theorie der menschlichen Haltung und Bewegung*, Berlin-Heidelberg, 1956.
5a. ——, 'Das erste Lächeln des Kindes', *Psyche*, 2, 1957.
6. Joseph Church, *Language and the Discovery of Reality*, New York, 1961.
7. Adam Ferguson, *An Essay on the History of Civil Society*, London, 1767.
8. Milton Friedman and L. J. Savage, 'The Utility Analysis of Choice involving Risk' (*J. of Pol. Econ.*, 56, 1948), reprinted in G. J. Stigler and K. E. Boulding (eds.), *Readings in Price Theory*, Chicago, 1952.
9. Franz G. From, 'Perception and Human Action', in H. P. David and J. C. Breugelmann (eds.), *Perspectives in Personality Research*, New York, 1960.
10. James C. Gibson, *The Perception of the Visual World*, Boston, 1950.
11. Kurt Goldstein, 'The Smiling of the Infant and the Problem of Understanding the "Other" ', *J. Psychology*, 44, 1957.
12. E. H. Gombrich, *Art and Illusion*, New York, 1960.
13. Heinrich Gomperz, *Über Sinn und Sinngebilde, Verstehen und Erklären*, Tübingen, 1929.
14. Harry F. Harlow, 'Social Behavior in Primates', in C. P. Stone (ed.), *Comparative Psychology*, 3rd ed., New York, 1951.
15. F. A. Hayek, 'Scientism and the Study of Society', Part II, *Economica*, N.S., 10, 1942, reprinted in *The Counter-Revolution of Science*, Glencoe, Ill., 1952.
16. ——, *The Sensory Order*, London and Chicago, 1952.
17. ——, 'The Theory of Complex Phenomena', in M. Bunge (ed.), *The Critical Approach to Science and Philosophy*. Essays in Honor of Karl Popper, New York, 1964, now reprinted as the second essay in the present volume.
18. H. Hediger, *Skizzen zu einer Tierpsychologie im Zoo und im Zirkus*, Stuttgart, 1954.

19. Fritz Heider, *The Psychology of Interpersonal Relations*, New York, 1958.

20. O. Heinroth, 'Über bestimmte Bewegungsweisen von Wirbeltieren', *Sitzungsberichte der Gesellschaft naturforschender Freunde*, Berlin, 1931.

21. H. von Helmholtz, *Populäre wissenschaftliche Vorträge*, 2. Heft, Braunschweig, 1871.

22. G. Humphrey, *The Nature of Learning*, London, 1933.

23. F. Kainz, *Psychologie der Sprache*, 4. Band, Stuttgart, 1956.

24. G. Kietz, *Der Ausdrucksgehalt des menschlichen Ganges* (Beiheft 93 to *Zeitschr. f. ang. Psychologie u. Charakterkunde*), Leipzig, 1948.

25. Heinrich Klüver, *Behavior Mechanisms in Monkeys*, Chicago, 1933.

26. ——, 'Functional Significance of the Geniculo-Striate System', *Biological Symposia*, 7, 1942.

27. Wolfgang Köhler, *The Mentality of Apes*, New York, 1925.

28. Kurt Koffka, *Growth of the Mind*, New York, 1925.

29. Ivo Kohler, 'Experiments with Goggles', *Scientific American*, May 1962.

30. Adriaan Kortlandt, 'Chimpanzees in the Wild', *Scientific American*, May 1962.

31. K. S. Lashley, 'The Problem of Serial Order in Behavior', in L. Jeffress (ed.), *Hixon Symposium on Cerebral Mechanism in Behavior*, New York, 1951.

32. Robert B. Lees, Review of N. Chomsky, *Syntactic Structures, Language*, 33, 1957.

33. K. Z. Lorenz, 'The Comparative Method in Studying Innate Behaviour', in *Physiological Mechanisms in Animal Behaviour* (Symposia of the Society for Experimental Biology, No. 4), Cambridge, 1950.

34. ——, 'The Role of Gestalt Perception in Animal and Human Behaviour', in L. L. Whyte (ed.), *Aspects of Form*, London, 1951.

35. M. Merleau-Ponty, *La Structure du Comportement*, Paris, 1942.

36. N. E. Miller and J. Dollard, *Social Learning and Imitation*, Yale University Press, 1941.

37. R. E. Miller, J. V. Murphy, and I. A. Mirsky, 'Non-verbal Communication of Affect', *J. Clin. Psych.*, 15, 1959.

38. Ludwig von Mises, 'Begreifen und Verstehen' (1930), trsl. by G. Reisman as 'Conception and Understanding', in L. von Mises, *Epistemological Problems of Economics*, New York, 1960.

39. ——, *Human Action*, Yale University Press, 1949.

40. Ernest Nagel and James R. Newman, *Gödel's Proof*, New York University Press, 1958.

41. R. C. Oldfield, 'Memory Mechanism and the Theory of Schemata', *Brit. J. of Psych.* (Gen. Sect.), 45, 1954.

42. —— and O. L. Zangwill, 'Head's Concept of the Schema and its Application to Contemporary British Psychology', *Brit. J. of Psych.*, 1942–3.

43. R. S. Peters, *The Concept of Motivation*, London, 1958.

44. H. Plessner, 'Die Deutung des mimischen Ausdrucks' (1925-6), reprinted in H. Plessner, *Zwischen Philosophie und Gesellschaft*, Bern, 1953.
45. Michael Polanyi, *Personal Knowledge, Towards a Post-Critical Philosophy*, London, 1959.
45a. ――, 'Knowing and Being', *Mind*, 70, 1961.
46. Karl R. Popper, *The Logic of Scientific Discovery*, London, 1959.
47. Robert Redfield, 'Social Science among the Humanities', *Measure*, 1, 1950.
48. Gilbert Ryle, 'Knowing How and Knowing That', *Proc. Arist. Soc.*, 1945-6.
49. ――, *The Concept of Mind*, London, 1949.
50. E. Rubin, 'Bemerkungen über unser Wissen von anderen Menschen', in E. Rubin, *Experimenta Psychologica*, Copenhagen, 1949.
51. J. Ruesch and W. Kees, *Non-verbal Communication*, University of Colorado Press, 1956.
52. Edward Sapir, 'The Unconscious Patterning of Behaviour in Society' (1927), in *Selected Writings of Edward Sapir*, ed. by D. G. Mandelbaum, University of California Press, 1949.
53. Paul Schilder, *The Image and Appearance of the Human Body*, London, 1936.
54. O. G. Selfridge, 'Pattern Recognition and Learning', in Colin Cherry (ed.), *Information Theory*, Third London Symposium, London, 1956.
55. L. C. Stepien, J. P. Cordeau, and T. Rasmussen, 'The Effect of Temporal Lobe and Hippocampal Lesions on Auditory and Visual Recent Memory in Monkeys', *Brain*, 83, 1960.
56. Dugald Stewart, *Elements of the Philosophy of the Human Mind*, in *Collected Works*, Vol. 4, Edinburgh, 1854.
57. Thomas S. Szasz, *The Myth of Mental Illness: Foundations of a Theory of Personal Conduct*, New York, 1961.
58. N. Tinbergen, *The Study of Instinct*, Oxford, 1951.
59. M. D. Vernon, 'The Function of Schemata in Perceiving', *Psych. Rev.*, 62, 1955.
60. ――, *The Psychology of Perception*, London, 1962.
61. W. S. Verplanck, *A Glossary of some Terms used in the Objective Science of Behaviour*, Supplement to *Psych. Rev.*, 64, 1947.
62. J. W. N. Watkins, 'Ideal Types and Historical Explanation', in H. Feigl and M. Brodbeck (eds.), *Readings in the Philosophy of Science*, New York, 1953.
63. Heinz Werner, *Comparative Psychology of Mental Development*, rev. ed., Chicago, 1948.
64. ―― and others, 'Studies in Physiognomic Perception', *J. of Psych.*, 38-46, 1954-8.
65. Viktor von Weizsäcker, *Der Gestaltkreis*, 3rd ed., Stuttgart, 1947.
66. Ludwig Wittgenstein, *Philosophical Investigations*, Oxford, 1953.
67. R. S. Woodworth and H. Schlossberg, *Experimental Psychology*, rev. ed., New York, 1955.

CHAPTER FOUR

Notes on the Evolution of Systems of Rules of Conduct

(The Interplay between Rules of Individual Conduct and the Social Order of Actions)

I

The purpose of these notes is to clarify the conceptual tools with which we describe facts, not to present new facts. More particularly, their aim is to make clear the important distinction between the systems of rules of conduct which govern the behaviour of the individual members of a group (or of the elements of any order) on the one hand and, on the other hand, the order or pattern of actions which results from this for the group as a whole.[1] It does not matter for this purpose whether the individual members which make up the group are animals or men,[2] nor whether the rules of conduct are innate (transmitted genetically) or learnt (transmitted culturally). We know that cultural transmission by learning occurs at least among some of the higher animals, and there can be no doubt that men also obey some rules of conduct which are innate. The two sorts of rules will therefore often interact. Throughout it

---

[1] We shall use '(social) order' and '(social) pattern' interchangeably to describe the structure of the actions of all the members of a group, but shall avoid the more common term 'social organization', because 'organization' has an intentionalist (anthropomorphic) connotation and is therefore better reserved for orders which are the product of design. Similarly we shall occasionally use the pairs of concepts 'order and its elements' and 'groups and individuals' interchangeably, although the former is of course the more general term of which the relation between group and individual is a particular instance.

[2] Or even whether they are living organisms or perhaps some sort of reduplicating mechanical structures. Cf. L. S. Penrose, 'Self-Reproducing Machines', *Scientific American*, June 1959.

should be clearly understood that the term 'rule' is used for a statement by which a regularity of the conduct of individuals can be described, irrespective of whether such a rule is 'known' to the individuals in any other sense than that they normally act in accordance with it. We shall not consider here the interesting question of how such rules can be transmitted culturally long before the individuals are capable of stating them in words and therefore of explicitly teaching them, or how they learn abstract rules 'by analogy' from concrete instances.

That the systems of rules of individual conduct and the order of actions which results from the individuals acting in accordance with them are not the same thing should be obvious as soon as it is stated, although the two are in fact frequently confused. (Lawyers are particularly prone to do so by using the term 'order of law' for both.) Not every system of rules of individual conduct will produce an overall order of the actions of a group of individuals; and whether a given system of rules of individual conduct will produce an order of actions, and what kind of order, will depend on the circumstances in which the individuals act. The classical instance in which the very regularity of the behaviour of the elements produces 'perfect disorder' is the second law of thermo-dynamics, the entropy principle. It is evident that in a group of living beings many possible rules of individual conduct would also produce only disorder or make the existence of the group as such impossible. A society of animals or men is always a number of individuals observing such common rules of conduct as, in the circumstances in which they live, will produce an order of actions.

For the understanding of animal and human societies the distinction is particularly important because the genetic (and in a great measure also the cultural) *transmission* of rules of conduct takes place *from individual to individual*, while what may be called the natural *selection* of rules will operate on the basis of the greater or lesser efficiency of the resulting *order of the group*.[3] For the purposes of this discussion we shall define the different kinds of elements of which groups consist by the rules of conduct which they obey, and regard the appearance of a transmittable 'mutation' of these rules of individual conduct as the equivalent of the appearance of new elements, or as a progressive change in the character of all the elements of the group.

---

[3] Cf. Alexander Carr-Saunders, *The Population Problem*, London, 1922, p. 223: 'Those groups practising the most advantageous customs will have an advantage in the constant struggle with adjacent groups.'

II

The necessity of distinguishing between the order of actions of the group and the rules of conduct of the individuals may be further supported by the following considerations:

1. A particular order of actions can be observed and described without knowledge of the rules of conduct of the individuals which bring it about: and it is at least conceivable that the same overall order of actions may be produced by different sets of rules of individual conduct.

2. The same set of rules of individual conduct may in some circumstances bring about a certain order of actions, but not do so in different external circumstances.

3. It is the resulting overall order of actions but not the regularity of the actions of the separate individuals as such which is important for the preservation of the group; and a certain kind of overall order may in the same manner contribute to the survival of the members of the group whatever the particular rules of individual conduct which bring it about.

4. The evolutionary selection of different rules of individual conduct operates through the viability of the order it will produce, and any given rules of individual conduct may prove beneficial as part of one set of such rules, or in one set of external circumstances, and harmful as part of another set of rules or in another set of external circumstances.

5. Although the overall order of actions arises in appropriate circumstances as the joint product of the actions of many individuals who are governed by certain rules, the production of the overall order is of course not the conscious aim of individual action since the individual will not have any knowledge of the overall order, so that it will not be an awareness of what is needed to preserve or restore the overall order at a particular moment but an abstract rule which will guide the actions of the individual.

6. The concrete individual action will always be the joint effect of internal impulses, such as hunger, the particular external events acting upon the individual (including the actions of other members of the group), and the rules applicable to the situation thus determined. The rules upon which different individual members of a group will at any moment act may therefore be different either because the drives or external circumstances acting upon them make different rules applicable, or because different rules apply to different individuals according to age, sex, status, or some particular state in which each individual finds itself at the moment.

7. It is important always to remember that a rule of conduct will never

by itself be a sufficient cause of action but that the impulse for actions of a certain kind will always come either from a particular external stimulus or from an internal drive (and usually from a combination of both), and that the rules of conduct will always act only as a restraint on actions induced by other causes.

8. The orderliness of the system of actions will in general show itself in the fact that actions of the different individuals will be so co-ordinated, or mutually adjusted to each other, that the result of their actions will remove the initial stimulus or make inoperative the drive which has been the cause of activity.

9. The difference between the orderliness of the whole and the regularity of the actions of any of its individual parts is also shown by the fact that a whole may be orderly without the action of any particular individual element showing any regularity. This might be the case, for instance, if the order of the whole were brought about by an authority commanding all particular actions and choosing the individuals who have to perform any one action at a given moment at random, say by drawing lots. There might in such a group well exist a recognizable order in the sense that certain roles were always filled by somebody; but no rules guiding the actions of any one individual (other than perhaps the commanding authority) could be formulated. The actions taken there by any one individual would not be derived by means of a rule from any of its properties or any of the circumstances acting on it (other than the commands of the organizer).

III

The most easily observed instances in which the rules of individual conduct produce an overall order are those where this order consists in a spatial pattern such as will occur in the marching, defence, or hunting of a group of animals or men. The arrow formation of migrating wild geese, the defensive ring of the buffaloes, or the manner in which lionesses drive the prey towards the male for the kill, are simple instances in which presumably it is not an awareness of the overall pattern by the individual but some rules of how to respond to the immediate environment which co-ordinate the actions of the several individuals.

More instructive are the abstract and more complex orders based on a division of labour which we find in such insect societies as those of bees, ants, and termites. There is perhaps less temptation in these instances to ascribe the changes in the activities of the individual either to a central command or to an 'insight' on the part of the individual into what at the particular moment is needed by the whole. There can be little doubt that the successive activities which a worker bee performs at the different stages of its career, at intervals varying in length according to the requirements of the situation[4] (and apparently even reverting to stages already passed when the 'needs' of the hive require it), could be explained by comparatively simple rules of individual conduct, if we only knew them. Similarly the elaborate structures which termites build, the genetics of which A. E. Emerson has so revealingly described,[5] must ultimately be accounted for by innate rules of conduct of the individuals of which we are largely ignorant.

When we are concerned with primitive human societies, on the other hand, it is often easier to ascertain the rules of individual conduct than to trace from them the resulting overall and often highly abstract order. The individuals will often themselves be able to tell us what they regard as appropriate action in different circumstances, though they may be able to do this only for particular instances but not to articulate the rules in accordance with which they act;[6] but the 'functions' which these rules serve we shall be able to discover only after we have reconstructed the overall order which is produced by actions in accordance with them. The individual may have no idea what this overall order is that results from his observing such rules as those concerning kinship and inter-marriage, or the succession to property, or which function this overall order serves. Yet all the individuals of the species which exist will behave in that manner because groups of individuals which have thus behaved have displaced those which did not do so.[7]

IV

The overall order of actions in a group is in two respects more than the totality of regularities observable in the actions of the individuals and cannot be wholly reduced to them. It is so not only in the trivial sense in which a whole is more than the mere *sum* of its parts but presupposes also that these elements are related to each other in a particular manner.[8] It is

---

[4] See K. von Frisch, *The Dancing Bees*, New York, 1955.

[5] A. E. Emerson, 'Termite Nests—A Study of Phylogeny of Behavior', *Ecological Monographs*, VIII, 1938.

[6] Cf. Edward Sapir, *The Selected Writings*, ed. D. G. Mandelbaum, University of California Press, 1949, p. 548 *et seq.*

[7] Ample further illustrations of the kind of orders briefly sketched in this section will be found in V. C. Wynne-Edwards, *Animal Dispersion in Relation to Social Behaviour*, Edinburgh, 1962; Anne Roe and G. G. Simpson, *Behavior and Evolution*, Yale University Press, 1958; and Robert Ardrey, *The Territorial Imperative*, New York, 1966.

[8] Cf. K. R. Popper, *The Poverty of Historicism*, London, 1957, section 7, and Ernest Nagel, *The Structure of Science*, New York, 1961, pp. 380–97.

more also because the existence of those relations which are essential for the existence of the whole cannot be accounted for wholly by the inter-action of the parts but only by their interaction with an outside world both of the individual parts and the whole. If there exist recurrent and persistent structures of a certain type (i.e., showing a certain order), this is due to the elements responding to external influences which they are likely to encounter in a manner which brings about the preservation or restoration of this order; and on this, in turn, may be dependent the chances of the individuals to preserve themselves.

From any given set of rules of conduct of the elements will arise a steady structure (showing 'homeostatic' control) only in an environment in which there prevails a certain probability of encountering the sort of circumstances to which the rules of conduct are adapted. A change of environment may require, if the whole is to persist, a change in the order of the group and therefore in the rules of conduct of the individuals; and a spontaneous change of the rules of individual conduct and of the resulting order may enable the group to persist in circumstances which, without such change, would have led to its destruction.

These considerations are mainly intended to bring out that systems of rules of conduct will develop as wholes, or that the selection process of evolution will operate on the order as a whole; and that, whether a new rule will, in combination with all the other rules of the group, and in the particular environment in which it exists, increase or decrease the efficiency of the group as a whole, will depend on the order to which such individual conduct leads. One consequence of this is that a new rule of individual conduct which in one position may prove detrimental, may in another prove to be beneficial. Another is that changes in one rule may make beneficial other changes, both of a behavioural or somatic character, which before were harmful. It is thus likely that even culturally transmitted patterns of individual behaviour (or the resulting patterns of action of the group) may contribute to determine the selection among genetic changes of a behavioural or somatic kind.[9]

It is evident that this interplay of the rules of conduct of the in-dividuals with the actions of other individuals and the external circum-stances in producing an overall order may be a highly complex affair. The whole task of social theory consists in little else but an effort to reconstruct the overall orders which are thus formed, and the reason why that special apparatus of conceptual construction is needed which social theory represents is the complexity of this task. It will also be clear that such a distinct theory of social structures can provide only an explanation

[9] Cf. Sir Alister Hardy, *The Living Stream*, London 1966, especially lecture II.

of certain general and highly abstract features of the different types of structures (or only of the 'qualitative aspects'), because these abstract features will be all that all the structures of a certain type will have in common, and therefore all that will be predictable or provide useful guidance for action.

Of theories of this type economic theory, the theory of the market order of free human societies, is so far the only one which has been systematically developed over a long period and, together with linguistics, perhaps one of a very few which, because of the peculiar complexity of their subject, require such elaboration. Yet, though the whole of economic theory (and, I believe, of linguistic theory) may be interpreted as nothing else but an endeavour to reconstruct from regularities of the individual actions the character of the resulting order, it can hardly be said that economists are fully aware that this is what they are doing. The nature of the different kinds of rules of individual conduct (some voluntarily and even unconsciously observed and some enforced), which the formation of the overall order presupposes, is frequently left obscure.[10] The important question of which of these rules of individual action can be deliberately and profitably altered, and which are likely to evolve gradually with or without such deliberate collective decisions as legislation involves, is rarely systematically considered.

V

Although the existence and preservation of the order of actions of a group can be accounted for only from the rules of conduct which the individuals obey, these rules of individual conduct have developed because the individuals have been living in groups whose structures have gradually changed. In other words, the properties of the individuals which are significant for the existence and preservation of the group, and through this also for the existence and preservation of the individuals themselves, have been shaped by the selection of those from the individuals living in groups which at each stage of the evolution of the group tended to act according to such rules as made the group more efficient.

Thus for the explanation of the functioning of the social order at any one time the rules of individual conduct must be assumed to be given. Yet these rules have been selected and formed by the effects they have

[10] As is shown by the unprofitable discussions about the degree of 'rationality' which economic theory is alleged to assume. What is said above, incidentally, also implies that social theory is, strictly speaking, not a science of behaviour and that to regard it as part of 'behavioural science' is at least misleading.

on the social order; and in so far as psychology does not wish to content itself with describing the rules which individuals actually obey, but undertakes to explain why they observe these rules, at least a great part of it will have to become evolutionary social psychology. Or, to put this differently, though social theory constructs social orders from the rules of conduct assumed to be given at any one time, these rules of conduct have themselves developed as part of a larger whole, and at each stage of this development the then prevailing overall order determined what effect any one change in the rules of individual conduct had.

Though we cannot here further pursue the question of the relation of psychology to social theory, it will contribute to the main purpose of these notes if we add a few remarks on the difference between an order which is brought about by the direction of a central organ such as the brain, and the formation of an order determined by the regularity of the actions towards each other of the elements of a structure. Michael Polanyi has usefully described this distinction as that between a monocentric and a polycentric order.[11] The first point which it is in this connection important to note is that the brain of an organism which acts as the directing centre for that organism is itself in turn a polycentric order, that is, that its actions are determined by the relation and mutual adjustment to each other of the elements of which it consists.

As we are all tempted to assume that wherever we find an order it must be directed by a central organ, which, if we applied this to the brain, evidently would lead to an infinite regress, it will be useful briefly to consider the advantage derived from the fact that one such polycentric order is set aside in a part of the whole and governs the action of the rest. This advantage consists in the possibility of trying out beforehand on a model the various alternative complexes of actions and selecting from them the most promising before action is taken by the whole organism. There is no reason why any one of these complex patterns of actions should not be determined by the direct interaction of the parts without this pattern being first formed in another centre, and then directed by it. The unique attribute of the brain is that it can produce a representative model on which the alternative actions and their consequences can be tried out beforehand. The structure which the brain directs may have a repertoire of possible patterns of actions quite as big as the one the brain can pre-form; but if it actually had to take that action before it was tried out on a model, it might discover its harmful effects only when it was too late and it might be destroyed as a result. If, on the other hand, such action is

[11] M. Polanyi, *The Logic of Liberty*, London, 1951, especially Chapters 8 and 9.

first tried out on a model in a separate part of the whole set aside for the purpose, not the actual effect but a representation of the effect to be expected will act as a signal that the particular action is not to be taken.

There is, therefore, no reason why a polycentric order in which each element is guided only by rules and receives no orders from a centre should not be capable of bringing about as complex and apparently as 'purposive' an adaptation to circumstances as could be produced in a system where a part is set aside to preform such an order on an analogue or model before it is put into execution by the larger structure. In so far as the self-organizing forces of a structure as a whole lead at once to the right kind of action (or to tentative actions which can be retraced before too much harm is done), such a single-stage order need not be inferior to a hierarchic one in which the whole merely carries out what has first been tried out in a part. Such a non-hierarchic order dispenses with the necessity of first communicating all the information on which its several elements act to a common centre and conceivably may make the use of more information possible than could be transmitted to, and digested by, a centre.

Such spontaneous orders as those of societies, although they will often produce results similar to those which could be produced by a brain, are thus organized on principles different from those which govern the relations between a brain and the organism which it directs. Although the brain may be organized on principles similar to those on which a society is organized, society is not a brain and must not be represented as a sort of super-brain, because in it the acting parts and those between which the relations determining the structure are established are the same, and the ordering task is not deputized to any part in which a model is preformed.

VI

The existence of such ordered structures as galaxies, solar systems, organisms, and social orders in a multiplicity of instances showing certain common features and observing as wholes regularities which cannot be wholly reduced to the regularities of the parts, because they also depend on the interaction of the whole with the environment which placed and keeps the part in the order necessary for the specific behaviour of the whole, creates certain difficulties for a theory of scientific method which regards as its aim the discovery of 'universal laws of nature'. Though it is reasonable to believe that structures of the kind will in a definable environment always behave as they do, the existence of such structures may in fact depend not only on that environment, but also on the existence in the past of many other environments, indeed on a definite sequence of such environments which have succeeded in that order only once in the history of the universe. The theoretical disciplines which are concerned with the structures of such complexes have thus an object the very existence of which is due to circumstances (and a process of evolution determined by them) which, though in principle repeatable, may in fact have been unique and never occur again. In consequence, the laws which govern the behaviour of these complexes, though 'in principle universally valid' (whatever that means), apply in fact only to structures to be found in a particular space-time sector of that universe.

Just as apparently the existence of life on earth is due to events which could have happened only in the peculiar conditions prevailing during an early phase of its history, so the existence of our kind of society, and even of human beings thinking as we do, may be due to phases in the evolution of our species without which neither the present order nor the existing kinds of individual minds could have arisen, and from the legacy of which we can never wholly free ourselves. We can judge and modify all our views and beliefs only within a framework of opinions and values which, though they will gradually change, are for us a given result of that evolution.

Yet the problem of the formation of such structures is still a theoretical and not a historical problem, because it is concerned with those factors in a sequence of events which are in principle repeatable, though in fact they may have occurred only once. We may call the answer 'conjectural history' (and much of modern social theory derives indeed from what the eighteenth-century thinkers called conjectural history), if we remain aware that the aim of such 'conjectural history' is not to account for all particular attributes which a unique event possesses, but only for those which under conditions which may be repeated can be produced again in the same combination. Conjectural history in this sense is the reconstruction of a hypothetical kind of process which may never have been observed but which, if it had taken place, would have produced phenomena of the kind we observe. The assumption that such a process has taken place may be tested by seeking for yet unobserved consequences which follow from it, and by asking whether all regular structures of the kind in question which we find can be accounted for by that assumption.

As was clearly recognized by Carl Menger, in the sphere of complex phenomena *'this genetic element is inseparable from the idea of theoretical sciences*'.[12] Or, to put it differently, the existence of the structures with which the theory of complex phenomena is concerned can be made intelligible only by what the physicists would call a cosmology, that is, a theory of their evolution.[13] The problem of how galaxies or solar systems are formed and what is their resulting structure is much more like the problems which the social sciences have to face than the problems of mechanics; and for the understanding of the methodological problems of the social sciences a study of the procedures of geology or biology is therefore much more instructive than that of physics. In all these fields the structures or steady states which they study, the kind of objects with which they are concerned, though they may within a particular space-time region occur in millions or billions of instances, can be fully accounted for only by considering also circumstances which are not properties of the structures themselves but particular facts of the environment in which they have developed and exist.

VII

Societies differ from simpler complex structures by the fact that their elements are themselves complex structures whose chance to persist depends on (or at least is improved by) their being part of the more comprehensive structure. We have to deal here with integration on at least two different levels,[14] with on the one hand the more comprehensive order assisting the preservation of ordered structures on the lower level, and, on the other, the kind of order which on the lower level determines the regularities of individual conduct assisting the prospect of the survival of the individual only through its effect on the overall order of the society. This means that the individual with a particular structure and behaviour owes its existence in this form to a society of a particular structure, because only within such a society has it been advantageous to develop some of its peculiar characteristics, while the order of society

[12] Carl Menger, *Untersuchungen über die Methode der Socialwissenschaften und der Politischen Ökonomie insbesondere*, Leipzig, 1883, p. 88, English translation by F. J. Nock, ed. by Louis Schneider under the title *Problems of Economics and Sociology*, Urbana, Ill., 1963, p. 94. Italics in the original.

[13] I assume it need not be stressed here that a theory of evolution does not imply 'laws of evolution' in the sense of necessary sequences of particular forms or stages, a mistake often made by the same people who interpret the genetical as a historical problem. A theory of genetics describes a mechanism capable of producing an infinite variety of particular results.

[14] Cf. R. Redfield (ed.), *Levels of Integration in Biological and Social Systems* (*Biological Symposia*, ed. J. Catell, Vol. VIII) Lancaster, Penn., 1941. 'Integration', in this context, means of course simply the formation of an order or the incorporation in an already existing order.

in turn is a result of these regularities of conduct which the individuals have developed in society.

This implies a sort of inversion of the relation between cause and effect in the sense that the structures possessing a kind of order will exist because the elements do what is necessary to secure the persistence of that order. The 'final cause' or 'purpose', i.e., the adaptation of the parts to the requirements of the whole, becomes a necessary part of the explanation of why structures of the kind exist: we are bound to explain the fact that the elements behave in a certain way by the circumstance that this sort of conduct is most likely to preserve the whole—on the preservation of which depends the preservation of the individuals, which would therefore not exist if they did not behave in this manner. A 'teleological' explanation is thus entirely in order so long as it does not imply design by a maker but merely the recognition that the kind of structure would not have perpetuated itself if it did not act in a manner likely to produce certain effects,[15] and that it has evolved through those prevailing at each stage who did.

The reason why we are reluctant to describe such actions as purposive is that the order which will form as the result of these actions is of course in no sense 'part of the purpose' or of the motive of the acting individuals. The immediate cause, the impulse which drives them to act, will be something affecting them only; and it is merely because in doing so they are restrained by rules that an overall order results, while this consequence of observing these rules is wholly beyond their knowledge or intentions. In Adam Smith's classical phrase, man 'is led to promote an end which is no part of his intentions',[16] just as the animal defending its territory has no idea that it thereby contributes to regulate the numbers of its species.[17] It was indeed what I have elsewhere called the twin ideas of evolution and spontaneous order,[18] the great contributions of Bernard Mandeville and David Hume, of Adam Ferguson and Adam Smith, which have opened the way for an understanding, both in biological and social theory, of that interaction between the regularity of the conduct of the elements and the regularity of the resulting structure. What they

---

[15] Cf. David Hume, *Dialogues Concerning Natural Religion* (1779), in *A Treatise of Human Nature*, ed. T. H. Green and T. H. Grose, new ed., London, 1890, Vol. II, pp. 428–9: 'I would fain know how an animal could subsist unless its parts were so adjusted? . . . No form . . . can subsist unless it possesses those powers and organs, requisite for its subsistence: some new order of œconomy must be tried, and so on, without intermission, till at last some order which can support and maintain itself, is fallen upon.'

[16] Adam Smith, *Wealth of Nations*, ed. Cannan, I, p. 421.

[17] See V. C. Wynne-Edwards, *op. cit.*

[18] See my lecture, 'Dr. Bernard Mandeville', *Proceedings of the British Academy*, LII, 1966.

did not make clear, and what even in the subsequent development of social theory has not been brought out with sufficient clarity, is that it is always some regularity in the behaviour of the elements which produces, in interaction with the environment, what may be a wholly different regularity of the actions of the whole.

Earlier groping efforts towards such an understanding which have left their traces on modern jurisprudence ran in terms of the adequacy of the rules of individual conduct to the *natura rei*, the nature of the thing. By this was meant just that overall order which would be affected by a change in any one of the rules of individual conduct—with the consequence that the effects of such a change in any one rule can be assessed only out of an understanding of all the factors determining the overall order. The true element in this is that the normative rules often serve to adapt an action to an order which exists as a fact. That there always exists such an order beyond the regularities of the actions of any one individual, an order at which the particular rules 'aim' and into which any one new rule has to be fitted, is the insight which only a theory of the formation of that overall order can adequately give.

VIII

A few observations may be added in conclusion on certain peculiarities of social orders which rest on learnt (culturally transmitted) rules in addition to the innate (genetically transmitted) ones. Such rules will presumably be less strictly observed and it will need some continuous outside pressure to secure that individuals will continue to observe them. This will in part be effected if behaviour according to the rules serves as a sort of mark of recognition of membership of the group. If deviant behaviour results in non-acceptance by the other members of the group, and observance of the rules is a condition of successful co-operation with them, an effective pressure for the preservation of an established set of rules will be maintained. Expulsion from the group is probably the earliest and most effective sanction or 'punishment' which secures conformity, first by mere actual elimination from the group of the individuals who do not conform while later, in higher stages of intellectual development, the fear of expulsion may act as a deterrent.

Such systems of learnt rules will probably nevertheless be more flexible than a system of innate rules and a few more remarks on the process by which they may change will be in place. This process will be closely connected with that by which individuals learn by imitation how to observe abstract rules; a process of which we know very little.

One factor influencing it will be the order of dominance of the individuals within the group. There will be, on the one end of the scale, a greater margin of tolerance for the young who are still in the process of learning and who are accepted as members of the group, not because they have already learnt all the rules peculiar to the group, but because as natural offspring they are attached to particular adult members of the group. On the other end of the scale there will be dominant old individuals who are firmly set in their ways and not likely to change their habits, but whose position is such that if they do acquire new practices they are more likely to be imitated than to be expelled from the group. The order of rank is thus undoubtedly an important factor in determining what alterations will be tolerated or will spread, though not necessarily in the sense that it will always be the high-ranking who initiate change.[19]

A point which deserves more consideration than it usually receives, however, is that the preference for acting according to established rules, and the fear of the consequences if one deviates from them, is probably much older and more basic than the ascription of these rules to the will of a personal, human or super-natural, agent, or to the fear of punishment that may be inflicted by such an agent. The partial awareness of a regularity of the world, of the difference between a known and predictable and an unknown and unpredictable part of the events in the environment, must create a preference for the kinds of actions whose consequences are predictable and a fear of the kinds of actions whose consequences are unpredictable. Though in an animistically interpreted world this fear is likely to become a fear of retribution by the agent whose will is disregarded, such a fear of the unknown or unusual action must operate much earlier to keep the individual to the tried ways. The knowledge of some regularities of the environment will create a preference for those kinds of conduct which produce a confident expectation of certain consequences, and an aversion to doing something unfamiliar and fear when it has been done. This establishes a sort of connection between the knowledge that rules exist in the objective world and a disinclination to deviate from the rules commonly followed in action, and therefore also between the belief that events follow rules and the feeling that one 'ought' to observe rules in one's conduct.

Our knowledge of fact (and especially of that complex order of society

---

[19] It would seem, e.g., that among monkeys new food habits are acquired more readily by the young and may then spread to the older members of the group: see the observations by J. Itani reported by S. Kawamura, 'The Process of Sub-cultural Propagation among Japanese Macaques', in Charles H. Southwick (ed.), *Primate Social Behavior*, Princeton, 1963, p. 85.

within which we move as much as within the order of nature) tells us mainly what will be the consequences of some of our actions in some circumstances. While this will help us to decide what to do if we want to obtain a particular result, or are driven by a particular impulse, it needs to be supplemented in a largely unknown world by some principle which inhibits actions to which our internal drives might lead us but which are inappropriate to the circumstances. The rules of fact which one knows can be relied upon only so long as one plays the game oneself according to the rules, i.e., keeps within the kind of actions the consequences of which are tolerably predictable. Norms are thus an adaptation to a factual regularity on which we depend but which we know only partially and on which we can count only if we observe those norms. If I know that if I do not observe the rules of my group, not only will I not be accepted and in consequence not be able to do most of the things I want to do and must do to preserve my life, but also that, if I do not observe these rules, I may release the most terrifying events and enter a world in which I can no longer orient myself, such rules will be as much a necessary guidance to successful action as rules that tell me how the objects in my environment will behave. The factual belief that such and such is the only way in which a certain result can be brought about, and the normative belief that this is the only way in which it ought to be pursued, are thus closely associated. The individual will feel that it exposes itself to dangers by transgressing the rules even if there is nobody there to punish it, and the fear of this will keep even the animal to the customary way. But once such rules are deliberately taught, and taught in an animistic language, they come almost inevitably to be associated with the will of the teacher or the punishment or the supernatural sanctions threatened by him.

Man does not so much choose between alternative actions according to their known consequences as prefer those the consequences of which are predictable over those the consequences of which are unknown. What he most fears, and what puts him in a state of terror when it has happened, is to lose his bearings and no longer to know what to do. Though we all tend to associate conscience with the fear of blame or punishment by another will, the state of mind which it represents is psychologically little different from the alarm experienced by somebody who, while manipulating a powerful and complicated machinery, has inadvertently pulled the wrong levers and thereby produced wholly unexpected movements. The resulting feeling that something dreadful is going to happen because one has infringed rules of conduct is but one form of the panic produced when one realizes that one has entered an unknown world. A bad conscience is the fear of the dangers to which one has thus exposed oneself by having left the known path and entered such an unknown world. The world is fairly predictable only so long as one adheres to the established procedures, but it becomes frightening when one deviates from them.

In order to live successfully and to achieve one's aims within a world which is only very partially understood, it is therefore quite as important to obey certain inhibiting rules which prevent one from exposing oneself to danger as to understand the rules on which this world operates. Taboos or negative rules acting through the paralysing action of fear will, as a kind of knowledge of what *not* to do, constitute just as significant information about the environment as any positive knowledge of the attributes of the objects of this environment. While the latter enables us to predict the consequences of particular actions, the former just warns us not to take certain kinds of action. At least so long as the normative rules consist of prohibitions, as most of them probably did before they were interpreted as commands of another will, the 'Thou shalt not' kind of rule may after all not be so very different from the rules giving us information about what is.[20]

---

[20] The possibility contemplated here is not that all normative rules can be interpreted as descriptive or explanatory rules, but that the latter may be meaningful only within a framework of a system of normative rules.

CHAPTER FIVE

Kinds of Rationalism*

I

In the course of my critical examination of certain dominant beliefs of
our time I have sometimes had to make a difficult choice. It often happens
that quite specific demands are labelled by a perfectly good word which
in its more general sense describes a thoroughly desirable and generally
approved activity. Indeed the specific demands which I find necessary to
oppose are often the result of the belief that, if a certain attitude is usually
beneficial, it must be beneficial in all applications. The difficulty which
this creates for the critic of current beliefs I have first encountered in
connection with the word 'planning'. That we should think out beforehand what we are going to do, that a sensible ordering of our lives
demands that we should have a clear conception of our aims before we
start acting, seems so obvious that it appears difficult to believe that the
demand for planning should ever be wrong. All economic activity, in
particular, is planning decisions about the use of resources for all the
competing ends. It would, therefore, seem particularly absurd for an
economist to oppose 'planning' in this most general sense of the word.

But in the 1920's and 1930's this good word had come to be widely
used in a narrower and more specific sense. It had become the accepted
slogan for the demand, not that each of us should intelligently plan his
economic activities, but that the economic activities of all should be
centrally directed according to a single plan laid down by a central
authority. 'Planning' thus meant central collectivist planning, and the
discussion whether to plan or not to plan referred exclusively to this
issue. This circumstance, that the good word 'planning' had been

* A lecture delivered on April 27, 1964 at Rikkyo University, Tokyo and published
in *The Economic Studies Quarterly*, Tokyo, Vol. XV, 3, 1965.

appropriated by the central planners for their particular schemes, created for the opponents of these proposals a delicate problem. Were they to try to rescue the good word for its legitimate uses, insisting that a free economy rested on the separate plans of many individuals, and indeed gave the individual more scope for planning his life than a centrally planned system? Or ought they to accept the narrow sense in which the term had come to be used and to direct their criticism simply against 'planning'?

Rightly or wrongly, I decided, somewhat to the discomfort of my friends, that things had already gone too far and that it was too late to vindicate the word for its legitimate uses. Just as my opponents argued simply for planning, meaning thereby central planning of all economic activity, I directed my criticism simply against 'planning'—leaving to my adversaries the advantage of the good word and laying myself open to the charge of opposing the use of our intelligence in the ordering of our affairs. Yet I still believe that as things then were, such a head-on attack on 'planning' was necessary to dethrone what had become a shibboleth.

More recently, I have encountered similar difficulties with the blessed word 'social'. Like 'planning' it is one of the fashionable good words of our time, and in its original meaning of belonging to society it could be a very useful word. But in its modern usage in such connections as 'social justice' (one would have thought that all justice is a social phenomenon!), or when our social duties are contrasted with mere moral duties, it has become one of the most confusing and harmful words of our time, not only itself empty of content and capable of being given any arbitrary content one likes, but depriving all terms with which it is combined (as in the German *soziale Marktwirtschaft* or *sozialer Rechtsstaat*) of any definite content. In consequence I felt obliged to take a position against the word 'social', and to demonstrate that in particular the concept of social justice had no meaning whatever, calling up a misleading mirage which clear-thinking people ought to avoid. But this attack on one of the sacred idols of our time again made many people regard me as an irresponsible extremist, entirely out of sympathy with the spirit of our time.

One more example of such a good word which, if it had not been given a special meaning, I should readily have used to describe my own position, but which I felt forced to turn against, is 'positive' or 'positivist'. Again the special sense which has been given to it has created a situation where I felt forced to leave this perfectly good word to my opponents and find myself an 'anti-positivist', although what I defend is quite as much positive science as the doctrines of the self-appointed positivists.

II

I am now, however, involved in another conflict of opinion where I do not dare to do the same without a good deal of explanation. The general social philosophy which I hold has sometimes been described as anti-rationalist, and at least with regard to my main intellectual forebears in this respect, B. Mandeville, David Hume and Carl Menger, I have, like others, occasionally myself used that term. Yet this has given rise to so many misunderstandings that it seems to me now a dangerous and misleading expression which ought to be avoided.

We have to deal here once again with a situation in which one group of thinkers have effectively claimed for themselves the only proper use of the good word and have in consequence come to be called rationalists. It was almost inevitable that those who did not agree with their views on the proper use of reason should have been labelled 'anti-rationalists'. This gave the impression as if the latter rated reason less highly, while in fact they were anxious to make reason more effective and pleaded that an effective use of reason required a proper insight into the limits of the effective use of individual reason in regulating relations between many reasonable beings.

There seems to me to exist a sort of rationalism which, by not recognizing these limits of the powers of individual reason, in fact tends to make human reason a less effective instrument than it could be. This sort of rationalism is a comparatively new phenomenon, though its roots go back to ancient Greek philosophy. Its modern influence, however, begins only in the sixteenth and seventeenth century and particularly with the formulation of its main tenets by the French philosopher, René Descartes. It was mainly through him that the very term 'reason' changed its meaning. To the medieval thinkers reason had meant mainly a capacity to recognize truth, especially moral truth,[1] when they met it, rather than a capacity of deductive reasoning from explicit premisses. And they were very much aware that many of the institutions of civilization were not the inventions of the reason but what, in explicit contrast to all that was invented, they called 'natural', i.e., spontaneously grown.

It was against this older natural law theory which did recognize that much of the institution of civilization was not the product of deliberate

---

[1] Cf. John Locke, *Essays on the Laws of Nature* (1676), ed. W. von Leyden, Oxford (Clarendon Press), 1954, p. 111: 'By reason, however, I do not think is meant here that faculty of the understanding which forms trains of thought and deduces proofs, but certain definite principles of action from which spring all virtues and whatever is necessary for the proper moulding of morals.'

human design that the new rationalism of Francis Bacon, Thomas Hobbes and particularly René Descartes contended that all the useful human institutions were and ought to be deliberate creation of conscious reason. This reason was conceived as to the Cartesian *esprit géométrique,* a capacity of the mind to arrive at the truth by a deductive process from a few obvious and undoubtable premisses.

It seems to me that the best name for this kind of naïve rationalism is rationalist constructivism. It is a view which in the social sphere has since wrought unmeasurable harm, whatever its great achievements in the sphere of technology may have been. (If it be thought that by labelling this view 'constructivism' I am once again presenting my opponents with a good word, I should plead that this term was used in precisely this sense already by one of the greatest of the nineteenth-century liberals, W. E. Gladstone. He used it as a name for the attitude for which in the past I had no better term than the 'engineering type of mind'. 'Constructivism' now seems to me the best label for the practical attitude which regularly accompanies what in the field of theory I have described as 'scientism'.[2])

The ascendancy of this view in the seventeenth century implied in fact a relapse into an earlier naïve way of thinking, into a view which habitually assumed a personal inventor for all human institutions, be it language or writing, laws or morals. It is no accident that Cartesian rationalism was completely blind to the forces of historical evolution. And what it applied to the past it proclaimed as programme for the future: that man in the full knowledge of what he was doing should deliberately create such a civilization and social order as the process of his reason enabled him to design. Rationalism in this sense is the doctrine which assumes that all institutions which benefit humanity have in the past and ought in the future to be invented in clear awareness of the desirable effects that they produce; that they are to be approved and respected only to the extent that we can show that the particular effects they will produce in any given situation are preferable to the effects another arrangement would produce; that we have it in our power so to shape our institutions that of all possible sets of results that which we prefer to all others will be realized; and that our reason should never resort to automatic or mechanical devices when conscious consideration of all factors would make preferable an outcome different from that of the spontaneous process. It is from this kind of social rationalism or constructivism that all modern socialism, planning and totalitarianism derives.

[2] Cf. my *The Counter-Revolution of Science,* Glencoe, Ill., 1952.

III

Our issue may now be pointed by asking whether, as Cartesian rationalism and all its descendents assume, human civilization is the product of human reason, or whether it is not the other way round and we should regard human reason as the product of a civilization which was not deliberately made by man but which had rather grown by a process of evolution. This is, of course, in a way a 'hen or egg' kind of question—nobody will deny that the two phenomena constantly interact. But the typical view of Cartesian rationalism is to insist throughout on the first interpretation, on a pre-existing human reason designing institutions. From the 'social contract' to the view that law is the creation of the State, and that because we have made our institutions we can also change them at will, the whole thinking of our modern age is permeated by the offsprings of this tradition. It is characteristic of this view also that it has no place for social theory proper: because the problems of social theory arise out of the fact that the individual efforts of man do often produce an order which, although unintended and unforeseen, turns out to be indispensable for the realization of what men strive for.

It deserves mention that in this respect the two-hundred and more years of effort of social and particularly economic theorists are now receiving unexpected support from the new science of social anthropology: its investigations show in more and more fields how what has long been regarded as the invention of reason was in fact the outcome of a process of evolution and selection very similar to that which we find in the biological field. I called it a new science—but in fact the social anthropologists merely continue work which Mandeville, Hume, and his successors among the Scottish philosophers had commenced, but which was largely forgotten when their later followers more and more confined themselves to the narrow field of economics.

In its more general form the main result of this development is thus the insight that even man's capacity to think is not a natural endowment of the individual but a cultural heritage, something transmitted not biologically but through example and teaching—mainly through, and implicit in, the teaching of language. The extent to which the language which we learn in early childhood determines our whole manner of thinking and our view and interpretation of the world is probably much greater than we are yet aware of. It is not merely that the knowledge of earlier generations is communicated to us through the medium of language; the structure of the language itself implies certain views about the nature of the world; and by learning a particular language we acquire a certain picture of the world, a framework of our thinking within which we henceforth move without being aware of it. As we learn as children to use our language according to rules which we do not explicitly know, so we learn with language not only to act according to the rules of language, but according to many other rules of interpreting the world and of acting appropriately, rules which will guide us though we have never explicitly formulated them. This phenomenon of implicit learning is clearly one of the most important parts of cultural transmission, but one which we as yet only imperfectly understand.

IV

The fact to which I have just referred probably means that in all our thinking we are guided (or even operated) by rules of which we are not aware, and that our conscious reason can therefore always take account only of some of the circumstances which determine our actions. That rational thought was only one element among those which guide us has of course long been recognized. It was expressed in the scholastic maxim that *ratio non est judex, sed instrumentum*—that reason is not the judge but an instrument. But clear awareness came only with David Hume's demonstration (directed against the constructivist rationalism of his time) that 'the rules of morality are not the conclusions of our reason'. This applies, of course, to all our values, which are the ends which reason serves but which reason cannot determine. This does not mean that reason has no function in deciding in conflicts of values—and all moral problems are problems created by conflicts of values. But nothing shows better the limited role of reason in this connection than a closer analysis of how we decide such conflicts. Reason can only help us to see what are the alternatives before us, which are the values which are in conflict, or which of them are true ultimate values and which are, as is often the case, only mediate values which derive their importance from serving other values. Once this task is accomplished, however, reason cannot help us further. It must accept as given the values which it is made to serve.

That values nevertheless serve a function or 'purpose' which scientific analysis may be able to discover is a different matter. It will help to distinguish further between the different types of rationalism if we examine somewhat more closely the character of these attempts to explain why we hold the values which we do. The best known of these theories concerning moral rules is utilitarianism. It occurs in two forms which provide the best illustration of the difference between the legitimate use of reason in the discussion of values and that false 'constructivist' rationalism which ignores the limitations that are set to the powers of reason.

Utilitarianism appears in its first and legitimate form in the work of the same David Hume who was so emphatic that 'reason of itself is utterly impotent' to create moral rules, but who at the same time insisted that the obedience to moral and legal rules which nobody had invented or designed for that purpose was essential for the successful pursuit of men's aims in society. He showed that certain abstract rules of conduct came to prevail because those groups who adopted them became as a result more effective in maintaining themselves. What he stressed in this respect was above all the superiority of an order which will result when each member obeys the same abstract rules, even without understanding their significance, compared with a condition in which each individual action was decided on the grounds of expediency, i.e., by explicitly considering all the concrete consequences of a particular action. Hume is not concerned with any recognizable utility of the particular action, but only with the utility of a universal application of certain abstract rules including those particular instances in which the immediate known results of obeying the rules are not desirable. His reason for this is that human intelligence is quite insufficient to comprehend all the details of the complex human society, and it is this inadequacy of our reason to arrange such an order in detail which forces us to be content with abstract rules; and further that no single human intelligence is capable of inventing the most appropriate abstract rules because those rules which have evolved in the process of growth of society embody the experience of many more trials and errors than any individual mind could acquire.

Authors in the Cartesian tradition like Helvetius and Beccaria, or their English followers Bentham and Austin down to G. E. Moore, turned this *generic utilitarianism*, which searched for the utility embodied in the abstract rules evolved by successive generations, into a *particularist utilitarianism* which in its ultimate consequences amounts to a demand that every action should be judged in full awareness of all its foreseeable results—a view which in the last resort tends to dispense with all abstract rules and leads to the claim that man can achieve a desirable order of society by concretely arranging all its parts in full knowledge of all the relevant facts. While the generic utilitarianism of Hume thus rests on a recognition of the limitations of our reason and expects its fullest use from a strict obedience to abstract rules, the constructivist particularist utilitarianism rests on the belief that reason is capable of directly manipulating all the details of a complex society.

V

The attitudes of the different kinds of rationalism to abstraction require somewhat fuller discussion because they are the source of frequent confusion. Perhaps the difference is best explained by saying that those who recognize the limits of the powers of reason want to use abstraction to extend it by achieving at least some degree of order in the complex of human affairs, where they know it is impossible to master the full detail, while the constructivist rationalist values abstraction only as an instrument in determining particulars. To the first, as de Tocqueville expressed it, 'general ideas are not proof of the strength but rather of the insufficiency of the human intellect', to the second they are a tool which is to give us unlimited power over the particular. In the philosophy of science this difference manifests itself in the belief of the adherents of the second view that the value of a theory must be judged by its capacity to predict particular events, i.e., on our ability to fill in the general pattern described by the theory with sufficient concrete facts to specify its particular manifestation, while of course the prediction that a kind of pattern will appear is also a falsifiable statement. In moral philosophy the constructivist rationalism tends to disdain any reliance on abstract mechanical rules and to regard as truly rational only behaviour such as is based on decisions which judge each particular situation 'on its merits', and chooses between alternatives in concrete evaluation of the known consequences of the various possibilities.

It is fairly obvious that this kind of rationalism must lead to the destruction of all moral values and to the belief that the individual should be guided only by his personal evaluation of the particular ends he pursues, and that it tends to justify all means by the ends pursued. The state of mind which it produces has been well described in an autobiographical essay by the late Lord Keynes. Describing the views he and his friends had held in the early years of the century—and he himself admittedly still held thirty years later—he wrote:

> We entirely repudiated a personal liability on us to obey general rules. We claimed the right to judge every individual case on its merits, and the wisdom, experience and self-control to do so successfully. This was a very important part of our faith, violently and aggressively held, and for the outer world it was our most obvious and dangerous characteristic. We repudiated entirely costumary morals, conventions and traditional wisdom. We were, that is to say, in the strict sense of the term, immoralists. The consequences of being found out had, of course, to be considered for what they were worth. But we recognized no moral obligation on us, no inner

sanction, to conform or to obey. Before heaven we claimed to be our own judge in our own case.[3]

It is to be noticed that this statement implies not only a rejection of traditional moral rules but of all commitment to any kind of binding abstract rules of conduct, moral or other. It implies the claim that man's intelligence is adequate to order his life successfully without availing himself of the aid which general rules or principles can give him, in other words, the claim that man is capable of co-ordinating his activities successfully through a full explicit evaluation of the consequences of all possible alternatives of action, and in full knowledge of all the circumstances. This, of course, involves not only a colossal presumption concerning our intellectual powers, but also a complete misconception of the kind of world in which we live. It treats our practical problems as if we knew all the facts and the task of coping with them were a purely intellectual one. I am afraid much of modern social theory also has been deprived of value by this same assumption. The crucial fact of our lives is that we are *not* omniscient, that we have from moment to moment to adjust ourselves to new facts which we have not known before, and that we can therefore not order our lives according to a preconceived detailed plan in which every particular action is beforehand rationally adjusted to every other.

Since our whole life consists in facing ever new and unforeseeable circumstances, we cannot make it orderly by deciding in advance all the particular actions we shall take. The only manner in which we can in fact give our lives some order is to adopt certain abstract rules or principles for guidance, and then strictly adhere to the rules we have adopted in our dealing with the new situations as they arise. Our actions form a coherent and rational pattern, not because they have been decided upon as part of a single plan thought-out beforehand, but because in each successive decision we limit our range of choice by the same abstract rules.

Considering how important is this adherence to rules in making our lives orderly, it is curious how little the connection between such abstract rules and the achievement of an overall order has been studied. We all know of course that in fact we have learned to act according to rules in order to give our successive action some coherence, that we adopt general rules for our lives not only to save us the trouble of reconsidering certain questions every time they arise, but mainly because only thus can we produce something like a rational whole. I cannot

[3] J. M. Keynes, *Two Memoirs: Dr. Melchior; a defeated enemy and My Early Beliefs*, Intro. by D. Garnett, London: Rupert Hart-Davis, 1949, pp. 97–8.

attempt here a more systematic discussion of the relation between the abstract rules followed in all the separate decisions and the abstract overall pattern which will thereby result. But there is one significant point I must mention briefly. If we want in this manner to achieve an overall order of our affairs, it is requisite that we follow the general rule in all instances and not only when there is no special reason to do otherwise. This may imply that we must deliberately disregard some knowledge of particular consequences which obedience to the rule in the given instance may produce. Here I think a true insight into the significance of behaviour according to rules demands a much more rigid adherence to them than would be conceded by the constructivist rationalists who would accept abstract rules at best as a substitute for a decision in full evaluation of all the particular circumstances and would regard it as desirable to depart from the rules whenever there is special reason for doing so.

Lest I be misunderstood I ought here briefly to say that when I speak of rigidly adhering to rules I do of course not mean isolated single rules but always a whole system of rules where often one rule will modify the consequences which we have to draw from another. More precisely, I ought to speak of a hierarchy of rules of different degrees of importance. But I cannot here go further into this important question than is necessary to prevent the misunderstanding that any one rule in isolation will normally be sufficient to solve our problems.

VI

What I have said about the need of abstract rules for the co-ordination of the successive actions of any man's life in ever new and unforeseen circumstances applies even more to the co-ordination of the actions of many different individuals in concrete circumstances which are known only partially to each individual and become known to him only as they arise. This brings me to what in my personal development was the starting point of all these reflections, and which may explain why, though at one time a very pure and narrow economic theorist, I was led from technical economics into all kinds of questions usually regarded as philosophical. When I look back, it seems to have all begun, nearly thirty years ago, with an essay on 'Economics and Knowledge'[4] in which I examined what seemed to me some of the central difficulties of pure economic theory. Its main conclusion was that the task of economic

---

[4] *Economica*, N.S., IV, 1937, reprinted in *Individualism and Economic Order*, London and Chicago, 1949.

theory was to explain how an overall order of economic activity was achieved which utilized a large amount of knowledge which was not concentrated in any one mind but existed only as the separate knowledge of thousands or millions of different individuals. But it was still a long way from this to an adequate insight into the relations between the abstract rules which the individual follows in his actions, and the abstract overall order which is formed as a result of his responding, within the limits imposed upon him by those abstract rules, to the concrete particular circumstances which he encounters. It was only through a re-examination of the age-old concept of freedom under the law, the basic conception of traditional liberalism, and of the problems of the philosophy of law which this raises, that I have reached what now seems to me a tolerably clear picture of the nature of the spontaneous order of which liberal economists have so long been talking.

It turns out to be an instance of a general method of indirectly creating an order in situations where the phenomena are far too complex to allow us the creation of an order by separately putting each element in its appropriate place. It is a sort of order over the particular manifestation of which we have little control, because the rules which determine it determine only its abstract character, while the detail depends on the particular circumstances known only to its individual members. It is therefore an order which we cannot improve upon but only disturb by attempting to change by deliberate arrangement any one part of it. The only way in which we can effectively improve it is by improving the abstract rules which guide the individuals. This, however, is of necessity a slow and difficult task, because most of the rules which do govern existing society are not the result of our deliberate making, and in consequence we often understand only very imperfectly what depends on them. As I have mentioned before, they are the product of a slow process of evolution in the course of which much more experience and knowledge has been precipitated in them than any one person can fully know. This means that, before we can hope successfully to improve them, we must learn to comprehend much better than we do now in what manner the man-made rules and the spontaneous forces of society interact. This will require not only a much closer collaboration between the specialists in economics, law, and social philosophy than we have had in recent times; even after we have achieved this, all we can hope for will be a slow experimental process of gradual improvement rather than any opportunity for drastic change.

It is perhaps understandable that constructivist rationalists, in their pride in the great powers of human reason, should have revolted against the demand for a submission to rules whose significance they do not fully understand, and which produce an order which we cannot predict in detail. That we should not be able fully to shape human affairs according to our wishes went much against the grain of generations which believed that by the full use of his reason man could make himself fully master of his fate. It seems, however, that this desire to make everything subject to rational control, far from achieving the maximal use of reason, is rather an abuse of reason based on a misconception of its powers, and in the end leads to a destruction of that free interplay of many minds on which the growth of reason nourishes itself. True rational insight into the role of conscious reason seems indeed to indicate that one of the most important uses is the recognition of the proper limits of rational control. As the great Montesquieu clearly pointed out at the height of the 'age of reason': *la raison même a besoin de limites.*

VII

In conclusion I would like to say a few words in explanation of why I have chosen this particular topic for what I regard as my chief public address in Japan—the address to the University which has so graciously received me as one of its members. I do not think I am wrong in thinking that the cult of the explicit use of reason, which has been so important an element in the development of European civilization during the last three hundred years, has not played the same role in the indigenous Japanese evolution. Nor can it probably be denied that the deliberate use of reason as a critical instrument in the seventeenth, eighteenth and nineteenth centuries is perhaps the main cause of the more rapid development of the European civilization. It was therefore only natural that, when Japanese thinkers began to study the different strands in the development of European thought, they should have been most attracted by those schools which seemed to represent this rationalist tradition in its most extreme and explicit form. To those who were seeking the secret of Western rationalism, the study of the most extreme form of it, what I have called constructivist rationalism and what I regard as an illegitimate and erroneous exaggeration of a characteristic element of the European tradition, was bound to appear as the most promising path to the discovery of this secret.

Thus it came about that of the various traditions of European philosophy that which goes back to Plato in ancient Greece and then was revived by Descartes and Hobbes in the seventeenth century and which, with Rousseau, Hegel, and Marx and later the philosophical and legal positivists, had carried this cult of reason furthest, was most widely studied by the Japanese. The chief purpose of what I have said was to warn you that the very schools which have carried furthest what may seem most characteristic of the European tradition may have gone as far wrong in one direction as those who have not fully appreciated the value of conscious reason have gone in another. Reason is like a dangerous explosive which, handled cautiously, will be most beneficial, but if handled incautiously may blow up a civilization.

Fortunately, this constructivist rationalism is not the only philosophy which the European tradition has to offer—even if it must be admitted that it has tinged the views of some of its greatest philosophers, including even Immanuel Kant. But at least outside the communist world (where constructivist rationalism has indeed blown up a civilization) you will also find another, more modest and less ambitious tradition, a tradition which is less given to building magnificent philosophical systems but which has probably done more to create the foundation of modern European civilization and particularly the political order of liberalism (while constructivist rationalism has always and everywhere been profoundly anti-liberal). It is a tradition which also goes back to classical antiquity, to Aristotle and Cicero, which was transmitted to our modern age mainly through the work of St. Thomas Aquinas, and during the last few centuries was developed mainly by political philosophers. In the eighteenth century it was mainly opponents of Cartesian rationalism like Montesquieu, David Hume and the Scottish philosophers of his school, in particular Adam Smith, who built up a true theory of society and of the role of reason in the growth of civilization. We owe much also to the great classical German liberals, Kant and Humboldt, who, however, as is true also of Bentham and the English utilitarians, did not wholly escape the fatal attraction of Rousseau and French rationalism. In its purer form we then find the political philosophy of this school once more in Alexis de Tocqueville and Lord Acton; and the foundation of its social theory was clearly restated, for the first time after David Hume, in the work of the founder of the Austrian School of Economics, Carl Menger. Among contemporary philosophers it is particularly Professor Karl R. Popper who has provided important new philosophical foundations for this strand of thought. He has coined for it the name 'critical rationalism', which I think very happily expresses the contrast to the naïve rationalism or constructivism. It seems to me the best term for describing the general position which I regard as the most reasonable one.

It was one of the chief aims of my talk to draw your attention to this tradition. I believe that if you will examine it you will find less that is new and startling in it than earlier generations of Japanese found in the extreme rationalism of the Descartes-Hegel-Marx school. You may find it at first less fascinating and exciting—it does not carry with it the peculiar fascination or even intoxication which the cult of pure reason engenders. But I hope you will find it not only more congenial. It seems to me that, because it is not a one-sided exaggeration which has its roots in a peculiar phase of European intellectual development, but provides a true theory of human nature, it should offer a foundation to the development of which your own experience should enable you to make important contributions. It is a view of mind and society which provides an appropriate place for the role which tradition and custom play in their development. It makes us see much to which those brought up on the crude forms of rationalism are often blind. It shows us that sometimes grown institutions which nobody has invented may provide a better framework for cultural growth than more sophisticated designs.

President Matsushita,[5] on another occasion, asked me a question which goes right to the heart of the matter but which I was not then at once able to answer. He asked, if I understood him rightly, whether a people who relied on convention rather than invention for its institutions may not sometimes provide more freedom for the individual and therefore more scope for evolution than those who attempted deliberately to construct all institutions, or tried to remake them according to the principles of reason. I believe the answer is Yes. Until we have learnt to recognize the proper limits of reason in the arrangement of social affairs, there is great danger that in trying to force on society what we think is a rational pattern we may smother that freedom which is the main condition for gradual improvement.

---

[5] Dr. Masatoshi Matsushita, President of Rikkyo University, who took the chair when this lecture was delivered.

CHAPTER SIX

The Results of Human Action but not of Human Design*[1]

The belief in the superiority of deliberate design and planning over the spontaneous forces of society enters European thought explicitly only through the rationalist constructivism of Descartes. But it has its sources in a much older erroneous dichotomy which derives from the ancient Greeks and still forms the greatest obstacle to a proper understanding of the distinct task of both social theory and social policy. This is the misleading division of all phenomena into those which are 'natural' and those which are 'artificial'.[2] Already the sophists of the fifth century B.C. had struggled with the problem and stated it as the false alternative that institutions and practices must be either due to nature (*physei*) or due to convention (*thesei* or *nomō*); and through Aristotle's adoption of this division it has become an integral part of European thought.

It is misleading, however, because those terms make it possible to include a large and distinct group of phenomena either under the one or the other of the two terms, according as to which of two possible definitions is adopted that were never clearly distinguished and are to the present day constantly confused. Those terms could be used to describe either the contrast between something which was independent

---

* A French translation of this essay was published in: *Les Fondements Philosophiques des Systèmes Economiques*. Textes de Jacques Rueff et essais rédigés en son honneur., Paris 1967.

[1] Adam Ferguson, *An Essay on the History of Civil Society*, London, 1767, p. 187: 'Nations stumble upon establishments, which are indeed the result of human action, but not the execution of any human design.' Ferguson refers in this connection to the *Mémoires du Cardinal de Retz*, presumably the reference (ed. Paris, 1820, Vol. II, p. 497) to President de Bellièvre's statement that Cromwell once told him that 'on ne montait jamais si haut que quand on ne sait où l'on va.'

[2] Cf. F. Heinimann, *Nomos und Physis*, Basel, 1945.

[96]

of human action and something which was the result of human action, or to describe the contrast between something which had come about without, and something which had come about as a result of, human design. This double meaning made it possible to represent all those institutions which in the eighteenth century Adam Ferguson at last clearly singled out as due to human action but not to human design either as natural or as conventional according as one or the other of these distinctions was adopted. Most thinkers, however, appear to have been hardly aware that there were two different distinctions possible.

Neither the Greeks of the fifth century B.C. nor their successors for the next two thousand years developed a systematic social theory which explicitly dealt with those unintended consequences of human action or accounted for the manner in which an order or regularity could form itself among those actions which none of the acting persons had intended. It therefore never became clear that what was really required was a threefold division which inserted between the phenomena which were natural in the sense that they were wholly independent of human action, and those which were artificial or conventional[3] in the sense that they were the product of human design, a distinct middle category comprising all those unintended patterns and regularities which we find to exist in human society and which it is the task of social theory to explain. We still suffer, however, from the lack of a generally accepted term to describe this class of phenomena; and to avoid continuing confusion it seems to be urgently necessary that one should be adopted. Unfortunately the most obvious term which should be available for that purpose, namely 'social', has by a curious development come to mean almost the opposite of what is wanted: as a result of the personification of society, consequent on the very failure to recognize it as a spontaneous order, the word 'social' has come to be generally used to describe the aims of deliberate concerted action. And the new term 'societal' which, conscious of the difficulty, some sociologists have attempted to introduce, appears to have small prospect of establishing itself to fill that urgent need.[4]

It is important to remember, however, that up to the appearance of modern social theory in the eighteenth century, the only generally

---

[3] The ambiguity of the term 'conventional', which may refer either to explicit agreement or to habitual practices and their results, has further contributed to enhance the confusion.

[4] See F. Stuart Chapin, *Cultural Change*, New York, 1928 and M. Mandelbaum, 'Societal Facts' in Patrick Gardiner, ed. *Theories of History*, London, 1959. The term 'cultural' which social anthropologists have adopted as a technical term to describe these phenomena will hardly do for general usage, since most people would hesitate to include, e.g., cannibalism under 'cultural' institutions.

understood term through which it could be expressed that certain observed regularities in human affairs were not the product of design was the term 'natural'. And, indeed, until the rationalist reinterpretation of the law of nature in the seventeenth century, the term 'natural' was used to describe an orderliness or regularity that was not the product of deliberate human will. Together with 'organism' it was one of the two terms generally understood to refer to the spontaneously grown in contrast to the invented or designed. Its use in this sense had been inherited from the stoic philosophy, had been revived in the twelfth century,[5] and it was finally under its flag that the late Spanish Schoolmen developed the foundations of the genesis and functioning of spontaneously formed social institutions.[6]

It was through asking how things would have developed if no deliberate acts of legislation had ever interfered that successively all the problems of social and particularly economic theory emerged. In the seventeenth century, however, this older natural law tradition was submerged by another and very different one, a view which in the spirit of the then rising constructivist rationalism interpreted the 'natural' as the product of designing reason.[7] It was finally in reaction to this Cartesian rationalism that the British moral philosophers of the eighteenth century, starting from the theory of the common law as much as

---

[5] Cf. particularly the account in Sten Gagnér, *Studien zur Ideengeschichte der Gesetzgebung*, Uppsala, 1960, pp. 225–40 of the work of Guillaume des Conches, especially the passage quoted p. 231: 'Et est positiva que est ab hominibus inventa. . . . Naturalis vero que non est homine inventa.'

[6] See particularly Luis Molina, *De iustitia et iure*, Cologne, 1596–1600, esp. tom. II, disp. 347, No. 3, where he says of natural price that 'naturale dicitur, quoniam et ipsis rebus, seclusa quacumque humana lege eo decreto consurgit, dependetur tamen a multis circumstantiis, quibus variatur, atque ab hominum affectu, ac aestimatione, comparatione diversum usum, interdum pro solo hominum beneplacito et arbitrio'. In an interesting but unpublished doctoral thesis of Harvard University, W. S. Joyce, *The Economics of Louis de Molina*, 1948 (p. 2 of the Appendix 'Molina on Natural Law'), the author rightly says that 'Molina explains that unlike positive law, natural law is "de objecto"—an untranslatable but very handy scholastic term which means very much "in the nature of the case"—because from the very nature of the thing (*ex ipsamet natura rei*) it follows that, for the preservation of virtue or the avoiding of vice, that action should be commanded or forbidden, which the natural law commands or forbids. "Hence," Molina continues, "what is commanded or forbidden results from the nature of the case and not from the arbitrary will (*ex voluntate et libito*) of the legislator."

[7] The change in the meaning of the concept of reason which this transition involves is clearly shown by a passage in John Locke's early *Essays on the Law of Nature* (ed. by W. von Leyden, Oxford, 1954, p. 111) in which he explains that 'By reason, however, I do not think is meant here that faculty of the understanding which forms trains of thought and deduces proofs, but certain definite principles of action from which spring all virtues and whatever is necessary for the proper moulding of morals.' Cf. also *ibid.*, p. 149: 'For right reason of this sort is nothing but the law of nature itself already known.'

from that of the law of nature, built up a social theory which made the undesigned results of individual action its central object, and in particular provided a comprehensive theory of the spontaneous order of the market.

There can be little question that the author to whom more than to any other this 'anti-rationalist' reaction is due was Bernard Mandeville.[8] But the full development comes only with Montesquieu[9] and particularly with David Hume,[10] Josiah Tucker, Adam Ferguson, and Adam Smith. The uncomprehending ridicule later poured on the latter's expression of the 'invisible hand' by which 'man is led to promote an end which was no part of his intention',[11] however, once more submerged this profound insight into the object of all social theory, and it was not until a century later that Carl Menger at last resuscitated it in a form which now, yet

---

[8] The basic idea is already contained in many passages of the original poems of 1705, especially

> The worst of all the multitude
> Did something for the common good,

but the fully developed conception occurs only in the second part of the prose commentary added more than twenty years later to *The Fable of the Bees* (see ed. by F. B. Kaye, Oxford, 1924, Vol. II, esp. pp. 142, 287–8, and 349–50 and compare Chiaki Nishiyama, *The Theory of Self-Love. An Essay in the Methodology of the Social Sciences, etc.*, Chicago Ph.D. thesis, June 1960—esp. for the relation of Mandeville's theories to Menger's).

[9] On the influence of Mandeville on Montesquieu see J. Dedieu, *Montesquieu et la Tradition Politique Anglaise*, Paris, 1909.

[10] David Hume, *Works*, ed. by T. H. Green and T. H. Grose, Vol. I and II, *A Treatise on Human Nature*, Vol. III and IV, *Essays, Moral, Political, and Literary*, esp. II, p. 296: 'advantageous to the public though it be not intended for that purpose by the inventors'; also III, p. 99: 'if the particular checks and controls, provided by the constitution . . . made it not the interest, even of bad men, to act for the public good'; as well as II, p. 289: 'I learn to do a service to another without bearing him a real kindness'; and II, p. 195: 'all these institutions arise merely from the necessity of human society.' It is interesting to observe the terminological difficulties into which Hume is led because, as a result of his opposition to contemporary natural law doctrines, he has chosen to describe as 'artifact', 'artifice', and 'artificial' precisely what the older natural law theorists had described as 'natural', cf. esp. II, p. 258: 'where an invention is obvious and absolutely necessary, it may as probably be said to be natural as anything that proceeds immediately from original principles; without the intervention of thought and reflection. Though the rules of justice be *artificial*, they are not *arbitrary*. Nor is the expression improper to call them *Laws of Nature*; if by natural we understand what is common to any species, or even if we confine it to mean what is inseparable from the species.' Cf. my essay on 'The Legal and Political Philosophy of David Hume', reprinted in this volume. Professor Bruno Leoni has drawn my attention to the fact that Hume's use of 'artificial' in this connection derives probably from Edward Coke's conception of law as 'artificial reason' which is of course closer to the meaning the later scholastics had given to 'natural' than to the usual meaning of 'artificial'.

[11] Adam Smith, *An Inquiry into the Nature and Causes of the Wealth of Nations* (1776), Bk. IV, ii, ed. E. Cannan, London, 1904, Vol. I, p. 421.

another eighty years later, seems to have become widely accepted,[12] at least within the field of social theory proper.

There was perhaps some excuse for the revulsion against Smith's formula because he may have seemed to treat it as too obvious that the order which formed itself spontaneously was also the best order possible. His implied assumption, however, that the extensive division of labour of a complex society from which we all profited could only have been brought about by spontaneous ordering forces and not by design was largely justified. At any rate, neither Smith nor any other reputable author I know has ever maintained that there existed some original harmony of interests irrespective of those grown institutions. What they did maintain, and what one of Smith's contemporaries, indeed, expressed much more clearly than Smith himself ever did, was that institutions had developed by a process of the elimination of the less effective which did bring about a reconciliation of the divergent interests. Josiah Tucker's claim was not that 'the universal mover of human nature, self love' always did receive, but that 'it may receive such a direction in this

---

[12] Carl Menger, *Untersuchungen über die Methode der Socialwissenschaften und der Politischen Ökonomie insbesondere*, Leipzig, 1883, p. 182: 'die unbeabsichtigte Resultante individueller, d.i. individuellen Interessen verfolgender Bestrebungen der Volksglieder . . . die unbeabsichtigte sociale Resultante individuell teleologischer Faktoren' (in the English translation of this work by F. J. Nock, ed. by L. Schneider, *Problems of Economics and Sociology*, Urbana, 1963, p. 158). The more recent revival of this conception seems to date from my own article on 'Scientism and the Study of Society', *Economica*, N. S. IX/35, August 1942, p. 276 (in the reprint in *The Counter-Revolution of Science*, Glencoe, Ill. , 1952, p. 25) where I argued that the aim of social studies is 'to explain the unintended or undesigned results of many men'. From this it appears to have been adopted by Karl Popper, 'The Poverty of Historicism', *Economica*, N. S. XI/3, August 1944, p. 122 (in the book edition, London, 1957, p. 65), where he speaks of 'the undesigned results of human action' and adds in a note that 'undesigned social institutions may emerge as *unintended consequences of rational actions*'; as well as in *The Open Society and its Enemies*, 4th ed., Princeton, 1963, Vol. II, p. 93, where he speaks of 'the indirect, the unintended and often the unwanted byproducts of such actions' (i.e., 'conscious and intentional human actions'). (I cannot agree, however, with the statement, *ibid.*, p. 323, based on a suggestion of Karl Polanyi, that 'it was Marx who first conceived social theory as the study of the *unwanted social repercussions of nearly all our actions*'. The idea was clearly expressed by Adam Ferguson and Adam Smith, to mention only the authors to whom Marx was unquestionably indebted.) The conception is also used (though perhaps not adopted) by Ernest Nagel, 'Problems of Concept and Theory Formation in the Social Sciences', in *Science, Language and Human Rights* (American Philosophical Association, Eastern Division, Vol. 1), Philadelphia, 1952, p. 54, where he says that 'social phenomena are indeed not generally the intended results of individual actions; nevertheless the central task of social science is the explanation of phenomena as the unintended outcome of springs of action'. Similar though not identical is K. R. Merton's conception of 'The unanticipated consequences of purposive social action' (see his article under that title in *American Sociological Review*, 1936, and the further discussion in *Social Theory and Social Structure*, rev. ed. Glencoe, Ill., 1957, pp. 61–2).

case (as in all others) as to promote the public interest by those efforts it shall make towards pursuing its own.'[13]

The point in this which was long not fully understood until at last Carl Menger explained it clearly, was that the problem of the origin or formation and that of the manner of functioning of social institutions was essentially the same: the institutions did develop in a particular way because the co-ordination of the actions of the parts which they secured proved more effective than the alternative institutions with which they had competed and which they had displaced. The theory of evolution of traditions and habits which made the formation of spontaneous orders possible stands therefore in a close relation to the theory of evolution of the particular kinds of spontaneous orders which we call organisms, and has in fact provided the essential concepts on which the latter was built.[14]

But if in the theoretical social sciences these insights appear at last to have firmly established themselves, another branch of knowledge of much greater practical influence, jurisprudence, is still almost wholly unaffected by it. The philosophy dominant in this field, legal positivism, still clings to the essentially anthropomorphic view which regards all rules of justice as the product of deliberate invention or design, and even prides itself to have at last escaped from all influence of that 'metaphysical' conception of 'natural law' from the pursuit of which, as we have seen, all theoretical understanding of social phenomena springs. This may be accounted for by the fact that the natural law concept against which modern jurisprudence reacted was the perverted rationalist conception which interpreted the law of nature as the deductive constructions of 'natural reason' rather than as the undesigned outcome of a process of growth in which the test of what is justice was not anybody's arbitrary will but compatibility with a whole system of inherited but partly inarticulated rules. Yet the fear of contamination by what was regarded as a metaphysical conception has not only driven legal theory into much more unscientific fictions, but these fictions have in effect

[13] Josiah Tucker, *The Elements of Commerce* (1756), reprinted in *Josiah Tucker: A Selection from his Economic and Political Writings*, ed. R. L. Schuyler, New York, 1931, p. 59. Cf. also my *Individualism and Economic Order*, London and Chicago, 1948, p. 7.

[14] Carl Menger, *l.c.*, p. 88: 'Dieses genetische Element ist untrennbar von der Idee theoretischer Wissenschaften'; also C. Nishiyama, *l.c.* It is interesting to compare this with the insight from the biological field stressed by L. von Bertalanffy, *Problems of Life*, New York, 1952, p. 134: 'What are called structures are slow processes of long duration, functions are quick processes of short duration. If we say that a function such as a contraction of a muscle is performed by a structure, it means that a quick and short process-wave is superimposed on a long-lasting and slowly running wave.'

deprived law of all that connection with justice which made it an intelligible instrument for the inducement of a spontaneous order.

The whole conception, however, that law is only what a legislator has willed and that the existence of law presupposes a previous articulation of the will of a legislator is both factually false and cannot even be consistently put into practice. Law is not only much older than legislation or even an organized state: the whole authority of the legislator and of the state derives from pre-existing conceptions of justice, and no system of articulated law can be applied except within a framework of generally recognized but often unarticulated rules of justice.[15] There never has been and there never can be a 'gap-less' (*lückenlos*) system of formulated rules. Not only does all made law *aim* at justice and *not create* justice, not only has no made law ever succeeded in replacing all the already recognized rules of justice which it presupposes or even succeeded in dispensing with explicit references to such unarticulated conceptions of justice; but the whole process of development, change and interpretation of law would become wholly unintelligible if we closed our eyes to the existence of a framework of such unarticulated rules from which the articulated law receives its meaning.[16] The whole of this positivist conception of law derives from that factually untrue anthropomorphic interpretation of grown institutions as the product of design which we owe to constructivist rationalism.

The most serious effect of the dominance of that view has been that it leads necessarily to the destruction of all belief in a justice which can be found and not merely decreed by the will of a legislator. If law is wholly the product of deliberate design, whatever the designer decrees to be law is just by definition and unjust law becomes a contradiction in terms.[17] The will of the duly authorized legislator is then wholly unfettered and guided solely by his concrete interests. As the most consistent representative of contemporary legal positivism has put it, 'From the point of view of rational cognition, there are only interests of human beings and hence conflicts of interests. The solution of these conflicts

---

[15] Cf. Paulus (*Dig.* 50.17.1) 'non ex regula ius sumatur, sed ex iure quod est regula fiat'; and Accursius (Gloss 9 to *Dig.* I.1.1.pr.) 'Est autem ius a iustitia, sicut a matre sua, ergo prius fuit iustitia quam ius.'

[16] Cf. H. Kantorowicz, *The Definition of Law*, ed. A. H. Campbell, London, 1958, p. 35: 'The whole history of legal science, particularly the work of the Italian glossators and the German pandectists, would become unintelligible if law were to be considered as a body of commands of a sovereign.'

[17] Cf. T. Hobbes, *Leviathan*, Ch. 30, ed. M. Oakeshott, London, 1946, p. 227: 'no law can be unjust.'

can be brought about either by satisfying one interest at the expense of another, or by a compromise between the conflicting interests.'[18]

All that is proved by this argument, however, is that the approach of rationalist constructivism cannot arrive at any criterion of justice. If we realize that law is never wholly the product of design but is judged and tested within a framework of rules of justice which nobody has invented and which guided people's thinking and actions even before those rules were ever expressed in words, we obtain, though not a positive, yet still a negative criterion of justice which enables us, by progressively eliminating all rules which are incompatible with the rest of the system,[19] gradually to approach (though perhaps never to reach) absolute justice.[20] This means that those who endeavoured to discover something 'naturally' (i.e., undesignedly) given were nearer the truth and therefore more 'scientific' than those who insisted that all law had been set ('posited') by the deliberate will of men. The task of applying the insight of social theory to the understanding of law has, however, yet to be accomplished, after a century of the dominance of positivism has almost entirely obliterated what had already been accomplished in this direction.

Because there has been a period in which those insights of social theory had begun to affect legal theory; Savigny and his older historical school, largely based on the conception of a grown order elaborated by the Scottish philosophers of the eighteenth century, continued their efforts in what we now call social anthropology and even appear to have been the main channel through which those ideas reached Carl Menger and made the revival of their conceptions possible.[21] That in this respect

---

[18] Hans Kelsen, *What is Justice?*, University of California Press, 1960, pp. 21–2.

[19] On the problem of compatibility of the several rules as test, see now the interesting studies by Jürgen von Kempski, collected in *Recht und Politik*, Stuttgart, 1965, and his essay 'Grundlegung zu einer Strukturtheorie des Rechts', *Abhandlungen der Geistes- und Sozialwissenschaftlichen Klasse der Akademie der Wissenschaften und der Literatur* in Mainz, Jg. 1961, No. 2.

[20] The conception of a negative test of the justice of legal rules (essentially of the kind at which the legal philosophy of I. Kant aimed) which would enable us continuously to approach justice by eliminating all inconsistencies or incompatibilities from the whole body of rules of justice, of which at any one time a large part is always the common and undisputed possession of the members of a given civilization, is one of the central points of a book on which I am at present working.

[21] For the channels through which the ideas of Burke (and through Burke, those of David Hume) appear to have reached Savigny see H. Ahrens, *Die Rechtsphilosophie oder das Naturrecht*, 4th ed. Wien, 1854, p. 64. This book was probably also one of Carl Menger's first sources of information. On Savigny and his school, cf. also the acute observations of E. Ehrlich, *Juristische Logik*, Tübingen, 1918, p. 84: 'Burke, Savigny und Puchta . . . verstehen, was immer verkannt wird, unter Volk oder Nation dasselbe, was wir heute als Gesellschaft im Gegensatz zum Staate bezeichnen, allerdings in nationaler Begrenzung'; and Sir Frederick Pollock, *Oxford Lectures and Other Discourses*, London, 1890, pp. 41–2: 'The

Savigny continued or resumed the aim of the older natural law theorists has been concealed by his rightly directing his argument against the rationalist natural law theories of the seventeenth and eighteenth centuries. But though he thereby helped to discredit that conception of natural law, his whole concern had been to discover how law had arisen largely without design, and even to demonstrate that it was impossible by design adequately to replace the outcome of such natural growth. The natural law which he opposed was not the natural law to be discovered but the natural law which was deductively derived from natural reason.

But if for the older historical school, though they spurned the word 'natural', law and justice were still given objects to be discovered and explained, the whole idea of law as something objectively given was abandoned by positivism, according to which it was regarded as wholly the product of the deliberate will of the legislator. The positivists no longer understood that something might be objectively given although it was not part of material nature but a result of men's actions; and that law indeed could be an object for a science only in so far as at least part of it was given independently of any particular human will: it led to the paradox of a science which explicitly denied that it had an object.[22] Because, if 'there can be no law without a legislative act',[23] there may arise problems for psychology or sociology but not for a science of law.

The attitude found its expression in the slogan which governed the whole positivist period: that 'what man has made he can also alter to suit his desires'. This is, however, a complete *non-sequitur* if 'made' is understood to include what has arisen from man's actions without his design. This whole belief, of which legal positivism is but a particular form, is entirely a product of that Cartesian constructivism which must deny that there are rules of justice to be discovered because it has no

doctrine of evolution is nothing else than the historical method applied to the facts of nature, the historical method is nothing else than the doctrine of evolution applied to human societies and institutions. When Charles Darwin created the philosophy of natural history (. . .), he was working in the same spirit and towards the same ends as the great publicists who, heeding his fields of labour as little as he heeded theirs, had laid in the patient study of historical facts the bases of a solid and rational philosophy of politics and law. Savigny, whom we do not yet know and honour enough, or our own Burke, whom we know and honour but cannot honour too much, were Darwinians before Darwin. In some measure the same may be said of the great Frenchman Montesquieu, whose unequal but illuminating genius was lost in a generation of formalists.' The claim to have been 'Darwinians before Darwin' was, however, first advanced by the theorists of language (see August Schleicher, *Die Darwinsche Theorie und die Sprachwissenschaft*, Weimar, 1869, and Max Müller, 'Lectures on Mr. Darwin's Philosophy of Language', *Frazer's Magazine*, Vol. VII, 1893, p. 662) from whom Pollock seems to have borrowed the phrase.

[22] Cf. Leonard Nelson, *Rechtswissenschaft ohne Recht*, Leipzig, 1917.
[23] John Austin, *Jurisprudence*, third edition, London, 1872, p. 555.

room for anything which is 'the result of human action but not of human design' and therefore no place for social theory. While on the whole we have now successfully expelled this influence from the theoretical sciences of society—and had to, to make them possible—the conceptions which today guide legal theory and legislation still belong almost wholly to this pre-scientific approach. And though it was French social scientists who earlier than others had clearly seen that from the famous *Discours de la Méthode* 'il était sorti autant de déraison sociale et d'aberrations métaphysiques, d'abstractions et d'utopies, que de données positives, que s'il menait à Comte il avait aussi mené à Rousseau',[24] it would seem at least to the outsider that in France, even more than elsewhere, law is still under its influence.

SUPPLEMENTARY NOTES

1. Sten Gagnèr, *Studien zur Ideengeschichte der Gesetzgebung*, Uppsala 1960, pp. 208 and 242, shows that the terms 'natural law' and 'positive law' derive from the introduction by Gellius in the second century A.D. of the latin adjectives *naturalis* and *positivus* to render the meaning of the Greek nouns *physis* and *thesis*. This indicates that the whole confusion involved in the dispute between legal positivism and the theories of the law of nature traces back directly to the false dichotomy here discussed, since it should be obvious that systems of legal rules (and therefore also the individual rules which have meaning only as part of such a system) belong to those cultural phenomena which are 'the result of human action but not of human design'. See on this also chapter 4 above.

2. Herr Christoph Eucken has drawn my attention to the fact that the contrast that is drawn in the opening sentence of Herodotus' *Histories* between what has arisen from [the actions of] men (*ta genomena ex anthrōpōn*) and their great and astounding works (*erga megala kai thōmasta*) suggests that he was more aware of the distinction here made than was true of many of the later ancient Greeks.

[24] Albert Sorel, 'Comment j'ai lu la "Réforme Sociale",' *Réforme Sociale*, 1st November, 1906, p. 614, quoted by A. Schatz, *L'individualisme économique et sociale*, Paris, 1907, p. 41, which together with H. Michel, *L'Idée de l'Etat*, 3rd ed., Paris, 1898, is most instructive on this influence of Cartesianism on French social thought.

CHAPTER SEVEN

The Legal and Political Philosophy of David Hume*

It is always misleading to label an age by a name which suggests that it was ruled by a common set of ideas. It particularly falsifies the picture if we do this for a period which was in such a state of ferment as was the eighteenth century. To lump together under the name of 'enlightenment' (or *Aufklärung*) the French philosophers from Voltaire to Condorcet on the one hand, and the Scottish and English thinkers from Mandeville through Hume and Adam Smith to Edmund Burke on the other, is to gloss over differences which for the influence of these men on the next century was much more important than any superficial similarity which may exist. So far as David Hume in particular is concerned, a much truer view has recently been expressed when it was said that he 'turned

---

* A public lecture delivered at the University of Freiburg on July 18, 1963 and published in *Il Politico*, XXVIII/4, 1963. The reference to the philosophical works of Hume will be throughout to the editions of T. H. Green and T. H. Grose, namely *A Treatise of Human Nature*, two volumes, London, 1890 (which will be referred to as I and II) and *Essays, Moral, Political, and Literary*, two volumes, London, 1875 (which will be referred to as III and IV). The references to Hume's *History of England* will be to the quarto edition in six volumes, London, 1762.

Since the first publication of this essay a number of Continental studies of Hume's Legal Philosophy have come to my notice, of which the most important is Georges Vlachos, *Essai sur la politique de Hume*, Paris (Domat-Monchretien), 1955. Others are: G. Laviosa, *La filosofia scientifica del diritto in Inghilterra, Parte I, Da Bacone a Hume*, Turin, 1897, pp. 697–850; W. Wallenfels, *Die Rechtsphilosophie David Humes*, Doctoral Dissertation at the University of Göttingen, 1938; L. Bagolini, *Esperienza giuridica ed esperienza politica nel pensiero di David Hume*, Siena, 1947; and Silvana Castignone, 'La Dottrina della o giustizia in D. Hume', *Rivista Internationale di Filosofia di Diritto*, XXXVIII, 1960 and 'Diritto naturale e diritto positivo in David Hume', *ibid.*, XXXIX, 1962.

against the enlightenment its own weapons' and undertook 'to whittle down the claims of reason by the use of rational analysis'.[1]

The habit of speaking of the *Aufklärung* as if it represented a homogeneous body of ideas is nowhere so strong as it is in Germany, and there is a definite reason for this. But the reason which has led to this view of eighteenth-century thought had also had very grave and, in my opinion, regrettable consequences. This reason is that the English ideas of the time (which were, of course, mainly expounded by Scotsmen—but I cannot rid myself of the habit of saying 'English' when I mean 'British') became known in Germany largely through French intermediaries and in French interpretations—and often misinterpretations. It appears to me to be one of the great tragedies of intellectual and political history that thus the great ideals of political freedom became known on the Continent almost exclusively in the form in which the French, a people who had never known liberty, interpreted traditions, institutions and ideas which derived from an entirely different intellectual and political climate. They did this in a spirit of constructivist intellectualism, which I shall briefly call rationalism, a spirit which was thoroughly congenial to the atmosphere of an absolute state which endeavoured to design a new centralized structure of government, but entirely alien to the older tradition which ultimately was preserved only in Britain.

The seventeenth century, indeed, had on both sides of the Channel been an age in which this constructivist rationalism dominated. Francis Bacon and Thomas Hobbes were no less spokesmen of this rationalism than Descartes or Leibniz—and even John Locke could not entirely escape its influence. It was a new phenomenon which must not be confused with ways of thought of earlier times which are also described as rationalism. Reason was for the rationalist no longer a capacity to recognize the truth when he found it expressed, but a capacity to arrive at truth by deductive reasoning from explicit premises.[2] The older tradition, which had been represented by the earlier theorists of the law of nature, survived chiefly in England in the works of the great common lawyers, especially Sir Edward Coke and Matthew Hale, the opponents of Bacon and Hobbes, who were able to hand on an understanding of the

---

[1] S. S. Wolin, 'Hume and Conservatism', *American Political Science Review*, XLVIII, 1954, p. 1001.

[2] John Locke seems to have been clearly aware of this change in the meaning of the term 'reason'. In his recently published *Essays on the Law of Nature* (ed. W. von Leyden, Oxford, 1954, p. 111) he wrote: 'By reason, however, I do not think is meant here that faculty of the understanding which forms trains of thought and deduces proofs, but certain definite principles of action from which spring all virtues and whatever is necessary for the proper moulding of morals.'

growth of institutions which was elsewhere displaced by the ruling desire deliberately to remake them.

But when the attempt to create also in England a centralized absolute monarchy with its bureaucratic apparatus had failed, and what in Continental eyes appeared as a weak government coincided with one of the greatest upsurges of national strength and prosperity which are known to history, the interest in the prevailing undesigned, 'grown' institutions led to a revival of this older way of thinking. While the Continent was dominated during the eighteenth century by constructivist rationalism, there grew up in England a tradition which by way of contrast has sometimes been described as 'anti-rationalist'.

The first great eighteenth-century figure in this tradition was Bernard Mandeville, originally a Dutchman, and many of the ideas I shall have to discuss in connection with David Hume can be found *in nuce* already in the writings of the former.[3] That Hume owes much to him seems to be beyond doubt. I shall discuss these ideas, however, in the fully developed form which only Hume gave them.

Almost all these ideas can be found already in the second part of the *Treatise on Human Nature* which he published at the age of twenty-nine in 1740 and which, though it was almost completely overlooked at first, is today universally acknowledged as his greatest achievement. His *Essays*, which began to appear in 1742, the *Enquiry concerning the Principles of Morals*, in which nine years later he attempted to restate those ideas in briefer and more popular form, and his *History of England*, contain sometimes improved formulations and were much more effective in spreading his ideas; but they added little that is new to the first statement.

Hume is of course known mainly for his theory of knowledge, and in Germany largely as the author who stated the problems which Immanuel Kant endeavoured to solve. But to Hume the chief task was from the beginning a general science of human nature, for which morals and politics were as important as the sources of knowledge. And it would seem probable that in those fields he awoke Kant as much from his 'dogmatic slumber' as he had done in epistemology. Certainly Kant, but also the two other great German liberals, Schiller and Humboldt, still knew Hume better than was true of later generations, which were entirely dominated by French thought, and particularly by the influence of Rousseau. But Hume as a political theorist and as a historian has never been properly appreciated on the Continent. It is characteristic of the

[3] See C. Nishiyama, *The Theory of Self-Love: An Essay on the Methodology of the Social Sciences, and Especially of Economics, with Special Reference to Bernard Mandeville*, University of Chicago, Ph.D. Thesis (Mimeographed), Chicago, 1960.

misleading generalizations about the eighteenth century that even today it is still largely regarded as a period which lacked historical sense, a statement which is true enough of the Cartesian rationalism which ruled in France, but certainly not of Britain and least of all of Hume who could describe his as 'the historical age and [his] as the historical nation'.[4]

The neglect of Hume as a legal and political philosopher is, however, not confined to the Continent. Even in England, where it is now at last recognized that he is not merely the founder of the modern theory of knowledge but also one of the founders of economic theory, his political and still more his legal philosophy is curiously neglected. In works on jurisprudence we will look in vain for his name. The systematic philosophy of law begins in England with Jeremy Bentham and John Austin who were both indebted mainly to the Continental rationalist tradition—Bentham to Helvetius and Beccaria, and Austin to German sources. But the greatest legal philosopher whom Britain produced before Bentham and who, incidentally, was trained as a lawyer, had practically no influence on that development.[5]

This is the more remarkable as Hume gives us probably the only comprehensive statement of the legal and political philosophy which later became known as liberalism. It is today fairly generally recognized that the programme of nineteenth-century liberalism contained two distinct and in some ways even antagonistic elements, liberalism proper and the democratic tradition. Of these only the second, democracy, is essentially French in origin and was added in the course of the French revolution to the older, individualistic liberal tradition which came from England. The uneasy partnership which the two ideals kept during the nineteenth century should not lead us to overlook their different character and origin. The liberal ideal of personal liberty was first formulated in England which throughout the eighteenth century had been the envied land of liberty and whose political institutions and doctrines served as models for the theorists elsewhere. These doctrines were those of the Whig party, the doctrines of the Glorious Revolution of 1688. And it is in Hume, and not, as is commonly believed, in Locke, who had provided the justification of that revolution, that we find the fullest statement of that doctrine.

If this is not more widely recognized, it is partly a consequence of the erroneous belief that Hume himself was a Tory rather than a Whig. He

---

[4] *The Letters of David Hume*, ed. by J. Y. T. Greig, London, 1932, Vol. II, p. 444.

[5] My attention was first directed to these parts of Hume's works many years ago by Professor Sir Arnold Plant, whose development of the Humean theory of property we are still eagerly awaiting.

acquired this reputation because in his *History*, as an eminently just man, he defended the Tory leaders against many of the unfair accusations brought against them—and, in the religious field, he chided the Whigs for the intolerance which, contrary to their own doctrine, they showed towards the catholic leanings prevalent among the Tories. He himself explained his position very fairly when he wrote, with reference to his *History*, that 'my views of *things* are more conformable to Whig principles; my representations of *persons* to Tory prejudices'.[6] In this respect such an arch-reactionary as Thomas Carlyle, who once described Hume as 'the father of all succeeding Whigs',[7] saw his position more correctly than most of the democratic liberals of the nineteenth and twentieth centuries.

There are of course some exceptions to the common misunderstanding and neglect of Hume as the outstanding philosopher of liberal political and legal theory. One of these is Friedrich Meinecke who in his *Entstehung des Historismus* clearly describes how for Hume 'der Sinn der englischen Geschichte [war], von einem *government of men* zu einem *government of law* zu werden. Diesen unendlich mühsamen, ja hässlichen, aber zum Guten endenden Prozess in seiner ganzen Komplikation und in allen seinen Phasen anschaulich zu machen, war oder wurde vielmehr sein Vorhaben. . . . Eine politische Grund- und Hauptfrage wurde so zum Generalthema seines Werkes. Nur von ihm aus ist es, was bisher immer übersehen wurde, in seiner Anlage und Stoffauswahl zu verstehen.'[8]

It was not Meinecke's task to trace this interpretation of history back to Hume's philosophical work where he could have found the theoretical foundation of the ideal which guided Hume in the writing of his *History*. It may be true that through his historical work Hume did more to spread this ideal than through his philosophical treatment. Indeed, Hume's *History* did probably as much to spread Whig liberalism throughout Europe in the eighteenth century as Macaulay's *History* did in the nineteenth. But that does not alter the fact that if we want an explicit and reasoned statement of this ideal, we must turn to his philosophical works, the *Treatise* and the easier and more elegant exposition in the *Essays* and *Enquiries*.

It is no accident that Hume develops his political and legal ideas in his philosophical work. They are most intimately connected with his

[6] E. M. Mossner, *Life of David Hume*, London, 1954, p. 311. For a survey of Hume's relations to Whigs and Tories, see Eugene Miller, 'David Hume: Whig or Tory?', *New Individualist Review*, I/4, Chicago, 1962.

[7] Thomas Carlyle, 'Boswell's Life of Johnson'.

[8] Friedrich Meinecke, *Die Entstehung des Historismus*, 1938, Vol. I, p. 234.

general philosophical conceptions, especially with his sceptical views on the 'narrow bounds of human understanding'. His concern was human nature in general, and his theory of knowledge was intended mainly as a step towards an understanding of the conduct of man as a moral being and a member of society. What he produced was above all a theory of the growth of human institutions which became the basis of his case for liberty and the foundation of the work of the great Scottish moral philosophers, of Adam Ferguson, Adam Smith and Dugald Stewart, who are today recognized as the chief ancestors of modern evolutionary anthropology. His work also provided the foundation on which the authors of the American constitution built[9] and in some measure for the political philosophy of Edmund Burke which is much closer to, and more directly indebted to, Hume than is generally recognized.[10]

Hume's starting point is his anti-rationalist theory of morals which shows that, so far as the creation of moral rules is concerned, 'reason of itself is utterly impotent' and that 'the rules of morality, therefore, are not conclusions of our reason'.[11] He demonstrates that our moral beliefs are neither natural in the sense of innate, nor a deliberate invention of human reason, but an 'artifact' in the special sense in which he introduces this term, that is, a product of cultural evolution, as we would call it. In this process of evolution what proved conducive to more effective human effort survived, and the less effective was superseded. As a recent writer put it somewhat pointedly, 'Standards of morality and justice are what Hume calls "artifacts"; they are neither divinely ordained, nor an integral part of original human nature, nor revealed by pure reason. They are an outcome of the practical experience of mankind, and the sole consideration in the slow test of time is the utility each moral rule can demonstrate towards promoting human welfare. Hume may be called a precursor to Darwin in the field of ethics. In effect, he proclaimed a doctrine of the survival of the fittest among human conventions—fittest not in terms of good teeth but in terms of maximum social utility.'[12]

It is, however, in his analysis of the circumstances which determined the evolution of the chief legal institutions, in which he shows why a complex civilization could grow up only where certain types of legal institutions developed, that he makes some of his most important contributions to jurisprudence. In the discussion of these problems his

[9] Douglas Adair, 'That politics may be reduced to a science. David Hume, James Madison and the Federalist', *Huntington Library Quarterly*, XX, 1957

[10] H. B. Acton, 'Prejudice', *Revue Internationale de Philosophie*, XXI, 1952

[11] II, p. 235

[12] C. Bay, *The Structure of Freedom*, Stanford University Press, 1958, p. 33

economic and his legal and political theory are intimately connected. Hume is indeed one of the few social theorists who are clearly aware of the connection between the rules men obey and the order which is formed as a result.

The transition from explanation to ideal does not, however, involve him in any illegitimate confusion of explanation and recommendation. Nobody was more critical of, or explicit about the impossibility of, a logical transition from the *is* to the *ought*,[13] about the fact that 'an active principle can never be founded on an inactive' one.[14] What he undertakes is to show that certain characteristics of modern society which we prize are dependent on conditions which were not created in order to bring about these results, yet are nevertheless their indispensable presuppositions. They are institutions 'advantageous to the public though . . . not intended for that purpose by the inventors'.[15] Hume shows, in effect, that an orderly society can develop only if men learn to obey certain rules of conduct.

The section of the *Treatise* which deals 'Of the Origin of Justice and Property' and which examines 'the manner in which rules of justice are established by the artifice of men'[16] is his most significant contribution in this field. It sets out from the fact that it is life in society which alone gives that weak animal, man, his exceptional powers. He concisely describes the advantages of the 'partition of employments'[17] (what Adam Smith was to make popular under the Mandevillian term 'division of labour') and shows how the obstacles to union in society are gradually overcome. The chief ones among these are firstly every individual's predominant concern with the needs of his own or of his immediate associates, and secondly the scarcity (Hume's term!) of means, i.e., the fact that 'there is not a sufficient quantity of them to supply everyone's desires and necessities'.[18] It is thus 'the concurrence of certain *qualities* of the human mind with the *situation* of external objects'[19] which forms the obstacles to smooth collaboration: 'The qualities of mind are selfishness and *limited generosity*: And the situation of external objects is their *easy change*, joined to their *scarcity* in comparison of the wants and desires for them.'[20] Were it not for those facts, no laws would ever have been necessary or have

[13] II, p. 245.
[14] II, p. 235.
[15] II, p. 296.
[16] II, pp. 258–73. Note Hume's acknowledgement of his indebtedness to H. Grotius, IV, p. 275.
[17] II, p. 259.
[18] II, p. 261.
[19] II, p. 266.
[20] II, pp. 266–7.

been thought of: 'if men were supplied with everything in the same abundance, or if *everyone* had the same affection and tender regard for *everyone* as for himself, justice and injustice would be equally unknown among mankind.'[21] 'For what purpose make a partition of goods, when everyone has already more than enough? . . . Why call this object *mine*, when, upon seizing of it by another, I need but stretch out my hand to possess myself of what is equally valuable? Justice, in that case, being totally *useless*, would be an idle ceremonial.'[22] It is thus 'only from the selfishness and confined generosity of men, along with the scanty provisions nature has made for his wants, that justice derives its origin.'[23]

It is thus the nature of the circumstances, what Hume calls 'the necessity of human society', that gives rise to the 'three fundamental laws of nature':[24] those of 'the stability of possession, of its transference by consent, and of the performance of promises'[25] of which the whole system of law is merely an elaboration. These rules were, however, not deliberately invented by men to solve a problem which they saw (though it has become a task of legislation to improve them). Hume takes great pains to show for each of these rules how self-interest will lead to their being increasingly observed and finally enforced. 'The rule concerning the stability of possession', he writes, for instance, 'arises gradually, and acquires force by slow progression, and our repeated experience of the inconveniences of transgressing it.'[26] Similarly, 'it is evident that if men were to regulate their conduct [as regards the keeping of promises] by the view of a particular *interest*, they would involve themselves in endless confusion.'[27] He points out that, in like manner as rules of justice arise, 'are languages gradually established by human conventions without any promise. In like manner gold and silver become the common measure of exchange.'[28] Law and morals, like language and money, are, as we would say, not deliberate inventions but grown institutions or 'formations'. To guard against the impression that his emphasis on proven utility means that men adopted these institutions because they foresaw their utility, he stresses that in all his

21 II, p. 267.
22 IV, p. 180.
23 II, pp. 267–8. The whole passage is in italics.
24 Cf. II, p. 258: 'Though the rules of justice be *artificial*, they are not *arbitrary*. Nor is the expression improper to call them *Laws of Nature*; if by natural we understand what is common to any species, or even if we confine it to mean what is inseparable from the species.'
25 II, p. 293.
26 II, p. 263.
27 II, p. 318.
28 II, p, 263, cf. IV, p. 275.

references to utility he 'only suppose[s] those reflections to be formed at once which in fact arise insensibly and by degrees'.[29]

Rules of this sort must be recognized before people can come to agree or bind themselves by promise or contract to any form of government. Therefore, 'though it be possible for men to maintain a small un-cultivated society without government, it is impossible they should maintain a society of any kind without justice, and the observance of those three fundamental laws concerning the stability of possession, its translation by consent, and the performance of promises. These are, therefore, *antecedent to government*, though government, *upon its first establishment*, would naturally be supposed to derive its obligation from those laws of nature', and in particular from that concerning the per-formance of promises.[30]

Hume's further concern is chiefly to show that it is only the universal application of the same 'general and inflexible rules of justice' which will secure the establishment of a general order, that this and not any parti-cular aims or results must guide the application of the rules if an order is to be the result. Any concern with particular ends of either the in-dividuals or the community, or a regard for the merits of particular in-dividuals, would entirely spoil that aim. This contention is intimately bound up with Hume's belief in the short-sightedness of men, their propensity to prefer immediate advantage to distant gain, and their incapacity to be guided by a proper appreciation of their true long-run interest unless they bind themselves by general and inflexible rules which in the particular case are applied without regard to consequences.

These ideas, first developed in the *Treatise* from which I have so far mainly quoted, become more prominent in Hume's later writing, in which they are also more clearly connected with his political ideals. The most concise statement of them will be found in the Appendix III to the *Enquiry concerning the Principles of Morals*.[31] I would recommend to all who wish to become acquainted with Hume's legal philosophy to begin with

[29] II, p. 274.

[30] II, p. 306, first group of italics added.

[31] Cf. II, p. 301: men 'prefer any trivial advantage that is present to the maintenance of order in society which so much depends on the observance of justice. . . . You have the same propension that I have, in favour of what is contiguous above what is remote'; and II, p. 303: 'Here then is the origin of civil government au.1 society. Men are not able radically to cure, either in themselves or others, that narrowness of soul which makes them prefer the present to the remote. They cannot change their natures. All they can do is to change their situation, and render the observance of justice the immediate interest of some parti-cular persons. . . . But this execution of justice, though the principal, is not the only ad-vantage of government . . . . . Not contented to protect men in those conventions they make for their mutual interest, it often obliges them to make such conventions, and forces them to seek their own advantage, by concurrence in some common end or purpose.

those six pages (272–8 of Volume II of the standard edition of the *Essays*) and to work backwards from them to the fuller statements in the *Treatise*. But I shall continue to quote mainly from the *Treatise*, where the individual statements often have greater freshness, even though the exposition as a whole is sometimes rather prolix.

The weakness of men's minds (or the 'narrow bounds of human understanding' as Hume would say, or their inevitable ignorance, as I should prefer to express it) would, without fixed rules, have the result that they 'would conduct themselves, on most occasions, by particular judgments, and would take into consideration the characters and circumstances of the persons, as well as the general nature of the question. But it is easy to observe that this would produce an infinite confusion in human society, and that the avidity and partiality of men would quickly bring disorder into the world, if not restrained by some general and inflexible principles.'[32]

The rules of law, however, 'are not derived from any utility or advantage which either the *particular* person or the public may reap from his enjoyment of any *particular* goods. . . . Justice in her decisions never regards the fitness or unfitness of objects to particular persons, but conducts herself by more extensive views.'[33] In particular: 'The relation of fitness or suitableness ought never to enter into consideration, in distributing the properties of mankind.'[34] A single act of justice is even 'frequently contrary to the *public interest*; and were it to stand by itself, without being followed by other acts, may, in itself, be very prejudicial to society. . . . Nor is every single act of justice, considered apart, more conducive to private interest than to public. . . . But, however single acts of justice may be contrary, either to public or to private interest, it is certain that the whole plan or scheme is highly conducive, or indeed absolutely requisite, both to the support of society and the wellbeing of

---

[32] II, pp. 298–9. Cf. also II, p. 318: 'it is evident that if men were to regulate their conduct in this particular [the appointment of magistrates] by the view of a particular *interest*, either public or private, they would involve themselves in endless confusion, and would render all government, in a great measure, ineffectual. The private interest of everyone is different; and though the public interest in itself be always one and the same, yet it becomes the source of great dissensions, by reason of the different opinions of particular persons concerning it . . . . were we to follow the same advantage, in assigning particular possessions to particular persons, we should disappoint our end, and perpetuate the confusion which that rule is intended to prevent. We must, therefore, proceed by general rules, and regulate ourselves by general interests.'

[33] II, p. 273.

[34] II, p. 283.

There is no quality in human nature which causes more fatal errors in our conduct, than that which leads us to prefer whatever is (304) present to the distant and remote.'

every individual.'[35] Or, as Hume puts it in the Appendix to the *Enquiry*, 'the benefit resulting from [the social virtues of justice and fidelity] is not the consequence of every individual single act; but arises from the whole scheme or system, concurred in by the whole, or the greater part of society. . . . The result of the individual act is here, in many instances, directly opposite to that of the whole system of actions; and the former may be extremely hurtful, while the latter is, to the highest degree, advantageous. . . . Its benefit arises only from the observance of the general rule; and it is sufficient, if compensation is thereby made for all the ills and inconveniences which flow from the particular characters and situations.'[36]

Hume sees clearly that it would be contrary to the whole spirit of the system if individual merit rather than those general and inflexible rules of law were to govern justice and government: were mankind to execute a law which . . . 'assigned the largest possession to the most extensive virtue, and gave everyone the power of doing good according to his inclinations . . . so great is the uncertainty of merit, both from its natural obscurity, and from the self-conceit of every individual, that no determinate rule of conduct would ever follow from it, and the total dissolution of society must be the immediate consequence.'[37] This follows necessarily from the fact that law can deal only with 'the external performance [which] has no merit. [While] we must look within to find the moral quality.'[38] In other words, there can be no rules for rewarding merit, or no rules of distributive justice, because there are no circumstances which may not affect merit, while rules always single out some circumstances as the only relevant ones.

I cannot pursue here further the extent to which Hume elaborates the distinction between the general and abstract rules of justice and the particular and concrete aims of individual and public action. I hope what I have already said will suffice to show how central this distinction is for his whole legal philosophy, and how questionable therefore is the prevalent view which I have just found tersely expressed in an otherwise excellent Freiburg doctoral dissertation that 'Die moderne Geschichte des Begriffes des allgemeinen Gesetzes beginnt mit Kant.'[39] What Kant

---

[35] II, p. 269. This passage shows particularly clearly that Hume's utilitarianism was what is now called 'restricted' and not an 'extreme' utilitarianism. Cf. I. I. C. Smart, 'Extreme and Restricted Utilitarianism', *Philosophical Quarterly*, VI, 1956, and H. J. McCloskey, 'An Examination of Restricted Utilitarianism', *Philosophical Review*, LXVI, 1957.

[36] IV, p. 273.

[37] IV, p. 187.

[38] II, p. 252.

[39] Konrad Huber, *Massnahmegesetz und Rechtsgesetz*, Berlin, 1963, p. 133.

had to say about this seems to derive directly from Hume. This becomes even more evident when we turn from the more theoretical to the more practical part of his discussion, especially his conception of the government of laws and not of men[40] and his general idea of freedom under the law. It contains the fullest expression of the Whig or liberal doctrines which was made familiar to Continental thinking by Kant and the later theorists of the *Rechtsstaat*. It is sometimes suggested that Kant developed his theory of the *Rechtsstaat* by applying to public affairs his moral conception of the categorical imperative.[41] It probably was the other way round, and Kant developed his theory of the categorical imperative by applying to morals the concept of the rule of law which he found ready made.

I cannot deal here with Hume's political philosophy in the same detail in which I have considered his legal philosophy. It is extremely rich, but also somewhat better known than the latter. I will completely pass over his important and characteristic discussion of how all government is guided by opinion, of the relations between opinion and interest, and of how opinion is formed. The few points I will consider are those where his political theory rests directly on his legal theory and particularly his views on the relations between law and liberty.

In Hume's last statements on these problems, the essay 'On the origin of Government' which he added in 1770 to his *Essays*, he defines 'the government which, in common appellation, receives the appellation of free [as] that which admits of a partition of power among several members whose united authority is no less, or is commonly greater, than that of a monarch, but who, in the usual course of administration, must act by general and equal laws, that are previously known to all members, and to all their subjects. In this sense, it must be owned that liberty is the perfection of civil society.'[42] Earlier he had in the same series of essays described how in such a government it is necessary 'to maintain a watchful *jealousy* over the magistrates, to remove all discretionary powers, and to secure every one's life and fortune by general and inflexible laws. No action must be deemed a crime, but what the law has plainly determined to be such . . .',[43] and that, while 'all general laws are attended with inconveniences, when applied to particular cases; and it requires great penetration and experience, both to perceive that these inconveniences

[40] III, p. 161.
[41] K. Huber, *l.c.*
[42] III, p. 116.
[43] III, p. 96; Cf. also *History*, V, p. 110: 'in a monarchical constitution where an eternal jealousy must be preserved against the sovereign, and no discretionary power must ever be entrusted to him by which the property or personal liberty of any subject can be affected.'

are fewer than what results from full discretionary powers in every magistrate; and also to discern what general laws are, upon the whole, attended with the fewest inconveniences. This is a matter of so great a difficulty that men have made some advances, even in the sublime art of poetry and eloquence, where a rapidity of genius and imagination assists their progress, before they have arrived at any great refinement in their municipal laws, where frequent trials and diligent observation can alone direct their improvements.'[44] And in his *History of England*, speaking of the Revolution of 1688, he tells us proudly how 'No government, at that time, appeared in the world, nor is perhaps to be found in the records of any history, which subsisted without the mixture of some arbitrary authority, committed to some magistrate; and it might reasonably, beforehand, appear doubtful, whether human society could ever arrive at such a state of perfection, as to support itself with no other control, than the general and rigid maxims of law and equity. But the parliament justly thought, that the King was too eminent a magistrate to be trusted with discretionary power, which he might so easily turn to the destruction of liberty. And in the event it has been found, that, though some inconveniences arise from the maxim of adhering strictly to law, yet the advantages so much overbalance them, as should render the English for ever grateful to the memory of their ancestors, who, after repeated contests, at last established that noble principle.'[45]

I must not tire your patience by more quotations, though the temptation is strong to show in detail how he endeavoured to distinguish sharply between, on the one hand, 'all the laws of nature which regulate property, as well as all civil laws [which] are general, and regard alone some essential circumstance of the case, without taking into consideration the characters, situations, and connections of the persons concerned, or any particular consequences which may result from the determination of these laws, in any particular case which offers'[46] and, on the other hand, those rules which determine the organization of authority;[47] and how even in the preserved manuscript corrections of his printed works he is careful to substitute 'rules of justice' for 'laws

[44] III, p. 178, cf. also p. 185: 'To balance a large state . . . on general laws, is a work of so great difficulty that no human genius, however comprehensive, is able, by the mere dint of reason and reflection, to effect it. The judgment of many must unite in this work: Experience must guide their labour, Time must bring it to perfection: And the feeling of inconveniences must correct the mistakes which they inevitably fall into, in their first trials and experiments.'

[45] *History*, V, p. 280.

[46] IV, p. 274.

[47] Cf. G. H. Sabine, *A History of Political Theory*, rev. ed., New York, 1950, p. 604.

of society'[48] where this seemed advisable to make his meaning clear. I want in conclusion rather to turn to another point to which I referred earlier: the general significance of his 'evolutionary' account of the rise of law and other institutions.

I spoke then of Hume's doctrine as a theory of the growth of an order which provided the basis of his argument for freedom. But this theory did more. Though his primary aim was to account for the evolution of social institutions, he seems to have been clearly aware that the same argument could also be used to explain the evolution of biological organisms. In his posthumously published *Dialogues on Natural Religion* he more than hints at such an application. He points out there that 'matter may be susceptible to many and great revolutions, through the endless periods of eternal duration. The incessant changes to which every part of it is subject, seem to indicate some such general transformation.'[49] The apparent design of the 'parts in the animals or vegetables and their curious adjustment to each other' does not seem to him to require a designer, because he 'would fain know how an animal could subsist unless its parts were so adjusted? Do we not find that it perishes wherever this adjustment ceases, and that its matter corrupting tries some new form?'[50] And 'no form can subsist unless it possess those powers and organs necessary for its subsistence: some new order or œconomy must be tried, and so on, without intermission; till at last some order which can support and maintain itself, is fallen upon.'[51] Man, he insists, cannot 'pretend to an exemption from the lot of all living animals . . . [the] perpetual war . . . kindled among all living creatures'[52] affects also his evolution. It was still another hundred years before Darwin finally described this 'struggle for existence'. But the transmission of ideas from Hume to Darwin is continuous and can be traced in detail.[53]

Let me conclude this discussion of Hume's teaching by a glance on its fate during the last two hundred years. Let me focus particularly on the year 1766 which happens to be the year when the elder Pitt for the last time defended the old Whig principles in support of the demand of the American colonies, and the year before Parliament with the assertion of

---

[48] Cf. the Appendix by R. Klibansky to Hume, *Theory of Politics*, ed. by T. Watkins, London, 1951, p. 246, note to p. 246 and also note to p. 88.

[49] II, p. 419.

[50] II, p. 428.

[51] II, p. 429.

[52] II, p. 436.

[53] The most direct channel seems to have been Erasmus Darwin, who was clearly influenced by Hume and whose influence on his grandson is unquestioned.

its claim to omnipotence not only brought the most glorious period of the development of political principles to an abrupt close but also produced the cause for the eventual break with the American colonies. In this year David Hume, who by then had essentially completed his work and at the age of fifty-five had become one of the most celebrated figures of his age, out of sheer goodness, brought from France to England an equally famous man who was only a few months his junior but who had lived in misery and, as he thought, was generally persecuted: Jean-Jacques Rousseau. This encounter between the serene and even placid philosopher, known to the French as 'le bon David', and the emotionally unstable, unaccountable and half-mad idealist who in his personal life disregarded all moral rules, is one of the most dramatic episodes of intellectual history. It could not but end in a violent clash and there can be no question today, for anyone who reads the full story, which of the two was the greater intellectual and moral figure.

In a way their work had been directed against the same dominant rationalism of their age. But while Hume, to repeat a phrase I have already quoted, had attempted to 'whittle down the claims of reason by rational analysis', Rousseau had to oppose to it only his uncontrolled emotion. Who then observing this encounter would have believed that it would be the ideas of Rousseau and not those of Hume which would govern the political development of the next two hundred years? Yet this is what happened. It was the Rousseauesque idea of democracy, his still thoroughly rationalist conceptions of the social contract and of popular sovereignty, which were to submerge the ideals of liberty under the law and of government limited by law. It was Rousseau and not Hume who fired the enthusiasm of the successive revolutions which created modern government on the Continent and guided the decline of the ideals of the older liberalism and the approach to totalitarian democracy in the whole world. How did this development come about?

I believe the explanation lies largely in an accusation which with some justice has often been levelled against Hume, the accusation that his philosophy was essentially negative. The great sceptic, with his profound conviction of the imperfection of all human reason and knowledge, did not expect much positive good from political organization. He knew that the greatest political goods, peace, liberty, and justice, were in their essence negative, a protection against injury rather than positive gifts. No man strove more ardently for peace, liberty and justice. But Hume clearly saw that the further ambitions which wanted to establish some other positive justice on earth were a threat to those values. As he put it in the *Enquiry*: 'Fanatics may suppose, that *domination is founded on grace,* and *that saints alone inherit the earth*; but the civil magistrate very justly puts these sublime theorists on the same footing with common robbers, and teaches them by the severest discipline, that a rule, which, in speculation, may seem the most advantageous to society, may yet be found, in practice, totally pernicious and destructive.'[54] It was not from the goodness of men but from institutions which 'made it the interest even of bad men, to act for the public good'[55] that he expected peace, liberty, and justice. He knew that in politics *'every man must be supposed a knave'*; though, as he adds, 'it appears somewhat strange, that a maxim should be true in *politics* which is false in fact.'[56]

He was far from denying that government had also positive tasks. Like Adam Smith later, he knew that it is only thanks to the discretionary powers granted to government that 'bridges are built, harbours opened, ramparts raised, canals formed, fleets equipped, and armies disciplined; everywhere, by the care of government, which, though composed of men subject to all human infirmities, becomes, by one of the finest and most subtle inventions imaginable, a composition, which is, in some measure, exempted from all these infirmities.'[57] This invention is that in these tasks in which positive aims and therefore expediency rule government was given no power of coercion and was subject to the same general and inflexible rules which aim at an overall order by creating its negative conditions: peace, liberty, and justice.

[54] IV, p. 187.
[55] III, p. 99.
[56] III, p. 118.
[57] II, p. 304.

CHAPTER EIGHT

*The Dilemma of Specialization**

We have been commemorating the foundation of a research centre within our University, and our thoughts have inevitably often touched upon the problems of the relation between research and education, and of education for research. It may therefore be fitting if this last evening is devoted to a problem in this field which must give concern to many of us. Research, of necessity, requires specialization, often in a very minute field. It is probably also true that those exacting standards which fruitful scientific work demands can be acquired only through the complete mastery of at least one field, which today means that it must be a narrow field and, also, that it ought to be one which has its own firmly established standards. Thus a progressive tendency toward specialization seems to be inevitable, bound to continue and to grow, both in research and in university education.

This applies, of course, to all branches of science and is not peculiar to the study of society, which is our particular concern. It is so conspicuous a fact that the sad joke about the scientific specialist who knows more and more about less and less has become about the one thing which everybody believes to know about science. There seem to me to exist, however, in this respect important differences among the various fields, special circumstances which ought to warn us not to accept too readily in the social sciences a tendency which natural scientists can treat as a regrettable necessity to which they may submit with impunity. It may well be that the chemist or physiologist is right when he decides that he will become a better chemist or physiologist if he concentrates on his subject at the expense of his general education.

* A lecture delivered at the celebration of the twenty-fifth anniversary of the opening of the Social Science Research Building of the University of Chicago and now reprinted from Leonard D. White (ed.): *The State of the Social Sciences* (University of Chicago Press, 1956).

But in the study of society exclusive concentration on a speciality has a peculiarly baneful effect: it will not merely prevent us from being attractive company or good citizens but may impair our competence in our proper field—or at least for some of the most important tasks we have to perform. The physicist who is only a physicist can still be a first-class physicist and a most valuable member of society. But nobody can be a great economist who is only an economist—and I am even tempted to add that the economist who is only an economist is likely to become a nuisance if not a positive danger.

I do not wish to exaggerate a difference which in the last resort, of course, is one of degree; but it still seems to me so great that what in one field is a venal offence is a cardinal sin in the other. What we face is a true dilemma imposed upon us by the nature of our subject or, perhaps I should say, by the different significance we must attach to the concrete and particular as against the general and theoretical. Although the logical relation between theory and its application, of course, is the same in all sciences and although theory is quite as indispensable in our field as anywhere, there is no denying that the interest of the natural scientist is concentrated on the general laws, while our interest in the end is mainly in the particular, individual, and unique event, and that in a sense our theories are more remote from reality—requiring much more additional knowledge before they can be applied to particular instances.

One result of this is that in the natural sciences specialization is predominantly what might be called systematic specialization—specialization in a theoretical discipline—while at least in research in the social sciences topical specialization is more common. Of course this contrast is again not absolute. The expert in the topography of Mars, in the ecology of Nyasaland, or in the fauna of the Triassic is as much a topical specialist as anyone in the social sciences; yet even there the share of general knowledge which qualifies the specialist is probably much greater in the natural sciences than in the social. The ecologist will need to learn less when he shifts from Nyasaland to Alaska than the archaeologist when he shifts from Crete to Peru. The former is readily done, while the latter requires almost a new training.

A further consequence is that the disparity between the age at which the human mind works at its best and the age at which one can have accumulated the knowledge demanded from the competent specialist becomes greater and greater as we move from the purely theoretical subjects to those in which the concern with the concrete is the main part. Every one of us probably lives for most of his life on the original ideas which he conceived when very young. But while this means for the mathematician or logician that he may do his most brilliant work at eighteen, the historian, to go to the other extreme, may do his best work at eighty.

I trust I shall not be misunderstood as identifying the difference between the natural and the social sciences with that between the theoretical and the historical. This is certainly not my view. I am not defending what I regard as the erroneous view that the study of society is nothing but history, but I merely want to stress that the need for understanding history arises in every application of our knowledge. The degree of abstraction which the theoretical disciplines in our field require makes them at least as theoretical, if not more so, than any in the natural sciences. This, however, is precisely the source of our difficulty. Not only is the individual concrete instance much more important to us than it is in the natural sciences, but the way from the theoretical construction to the explanation of the particular is also much longer.

For almost any application of our knowledge to concrete instances, the knowledge of one discipline, and even of all the scientific knowledge we can bring to bear on the topic, will be only a small part of the foundations of our opinions. Let me speak first of the need of using the results of scientific disciplines other than our own, though this is far from all that is required. That concrete reality is not divisible into distinct objects corresponding to the various scientific disciplines is a commonplace, yet a commonplace which severely limits our competence to pronounce as scientists on any particular event. There is scarcely an individual phenomenon or event in society with which we can deal adequately without knowing a great deal of several disciplines, not to speak of the knowledge of particular facts that will be required. None of us can feel but very humble when he reflects what he really ought to know in order to account for even the simplest social process or to be able to give sensible advice on almost any political issue. We are probably so used to this impossibility of knowing what we ideally ought to know that we are rarely fully aware of the magnitude of our shortcomings. In an ideal world an economist who knows no law, an anthropologist who knows no economics, a psychologist who knows no philosophy, or a historian who does not know almost every subject should be inconceivable; yet the fact is, of course, that the limitations of our capacities make such deficiencies the rule. We can do no better than be guided by the particular topic which we take up for research and gradually acquire whatever special technical equipment is demanded by it. Indeed, most successful research work will require a very particular combination of diverse kinds of knowledge and accomplishments, and it may take half a lifetime before we are better than amateurs in three-quarters of the knowledge demanded by the task we have set ourselves. In this sense, fruitful research undoubtedly demands the most intense specialization—so intense, indeed, that those who practise it may soon cease to be of much use in teaching the whole of any one of the conventional subjects. That such specialists are badly needed, that today the advance of knowledge depends largely on them, and that a great university cannot have enough of them is as true in our fields as it is in the natural sciences.

Yet professors, curiously enough, want students, and preferably students all of whose work they direct. Thus the multiplicity of research specializations tends to produce a proliferation of teaching departments. It is here that the educational aspects of our problem begin. Not every legitimate research speciality is equally suitable as a scientific education. Even if we look at it entirely as education for research, it must be doubtful whether the composite knowledge demanded by a particular empirical object ought to be taught as a whole in those decisive years during which a student must learn what real competence is, during which his standards are set and the conscience of a scholar is formed. It seems to me that at this stage the complete mastery of one clearly circumscribed field, of the whole of a systematically coherent subject, should be acquired. It cannot always be, as I am a little inclined to wish, a theoretical field, because some of the descriptive and historical disciplines have, of course, their own highly developed techniques which it takes years to master. But it ought to be a field that has its own firmly established standards and where it is not true that most workers, except those who have already spent a lifetime in it, are inevitably more or less amateurs in much of the field.

Let me illustrate what I mean from a subject which, for my present purpose, has the advantage of not being represented in this University, so that I shall not offend any susceptibilities. It is ancient economic history, which to me has always seemed not only a particularly fascinating subject but also one of great importance for the understanding of our own civilization. I very much wish it were represented and taught here. But by this I do not mean that there ought to exist a separate department of ancient economic history in which students should from the beginning of their graduate career divide their energies among the variety of disciplines and accomplishments which a competent ancient economic historian must command. I believe, rather, that the men who will do good work in such a field will do much better if, in the first instance, they get a thorough training in the classics, or in ancient history, or in archaeology, or in economics; and, only when they are really competent in that one field and start to work largely on their own, begin to work seriously on the other subjects.

When I stress here the need of intense systematic specialization during a certain phase of education, I do not, of course, approve of the system of prescribed courses or lectures which leaves the student no time for exploring anything else and which often prevents him from following that intellectual curiosity which ought to gain him more education than anything which is formally offered. If there is anything I somewhat miss in the great American universities, it is that attitude of intellectual adventure among the students, an attitude which leads them, concurrently with their specialized work, to range over wide fields, to sample a great variety of courses, and to make them feel that the university and not their department is their intellectual home. I do not believe that this is so much the fault of the students as of university organization, which keeps the students largely ignorant of what happens outside their departments in the form of extra fees or rigid departmental schedules, and tends even to put obstacles in the way of their inclinations. It is only by the greatest freedom in this respect that the student will discover his true vocation.

What I do mean is that there must be a period or phase in his education when the chief object is to acquire complete mastery of one well-defined subject and when he will learn to distrust superficial knowledge and facile generalizations. But I am speaking only of one necessary phase in the process of education for research. My chief point is that different things are true of different phases. If it seems to me to be untrue that all the recognized research specialities are equally suitable as a basic training, it seems to be no less untrue that the advanced work usually leading to a Ph.D. thesis must fit into any one of the already established research specialities. What I am arguing is that only certain kinds of specializations deserve the name of 'disciplines' in the original sense of a discipline of the mind, and even that it is not so important which discipline of this kind a mind has undergone as that it has experienced all the rigour and strictness of such a schooling. I can even see some merit in the belief on which English higher education used to be based that a man who has thoroughly studied either mathematics or the classics can be presumed to be capable of learning on his own almost any other subject. The number of true disciplines which achieve this object may today be much larger; but I do not think that it has become co-extensive with the number of research specialities.

There is another side to this which I can best explain with reference to my own field. I happen to believe that economic theory is one of those true disciplines of the mind, but I regret that most of those whose basic training is in pure economic theory tend to remain specialists in this field. What I have said implies that those of us who teach such subjects ought to do so in the awareness and the hope, and even with the deliberate aim, that those whom we train as specialists ought not to remain specialists in this field but should use their competence for some other, realistic or topical, specialization. I would be happier to see even the majority of the economic theorists we turn out become economic historians, or specialists in labour economics or agricultural economics —though I must admit to some doubts about the suitability of these topics as a basic training.

Please note that what I have said about such composite subjects is said in no slighting spirit but rather from an appreciation of the very high demands which they put on our mental equipment. It is based on the recognition that for most worthwhile research subjects we ought to be masters of more than one systematic subject, and on the belief that we are more likely to achieve this if we use the short period during which we work under close guidance to become real masters of one. I am also pleading for such a period of intense specialization only on the assumption that it is preceded by a good general education which, I am afraid, American schools hardly provide and which our College so manfully struggles to supply. But my main emphasis, of course, is on how far we still are, at the end of such an indispensable period of specialization, from being competent to deal with most of the problems the study of human civilization raises. So far I have spoken only of the limited and modest tasks which most of us can reasonably set ourselves and where still the ideal after which we must strive far exceeds our powers. I have not spoken of the need for synthesis, of efforts to understand our civilization, or any other civilization, as a whole, and still less of the even more ambitious conception of a comparative study of civilizations. I will not comment on such efforts beyond saying that it is fortunate that there do still occasionally arise exceptional men who have the power and the courage to make the human universe their province. You will have the privilege, later this evening, of listening to a great scholar who has probably come nearer than any other living man to achieve the seemingly impossible in this field.[1]

We certainly ought to feel nothing but admiration for the mature scholar who is willing to run the serious risk of disregarding all the boundaries of specialization in order to venture on tasks for which perhaps no man can claim full competence. While I sympathize with the

[1] This lecture was followed by one by Arnold J. Toynbee.

healthy prejudice which brings it about that the scholar who produces a best seller thereby rather lowers himself in the estimation of his peers—and sometimes even wish that there were more of it in this country—the suspicion of boundary violations as such must not go so far as to discourage attempts which are beyond the scope of any specialist. I would go even further, although the economist suffers perhaps more from—and tends, therefore, also to be more intolerant of—intrusions into his preserve than other social scientists. It is perhaps not unjust to suggest that in other subjects, too, there is a little too much of a clannish spirit among the representatives of the recognized specialities, which makes them almost resent an attempt at a serious contribution even from a man in a neighbouring field—although the basic kinship of all our disciplines makes it more than likely that ideas conceived in one field may prove fertile in another.

The grand efforts toward a comprehension of civilization as a whole, of which I have just spoken, are specially significant in our context in one respect: they raise particularly clearly one difficulty which to a lesser degree affects all our efforts. I have so far spoken only of the constant need to draw on knowledge belonging to specializations other than our own. But, though the need to know many disciplines presents a formidable difficulty, it is only part of our problem. Even where we study only some part or aspect of a civilization of which we and our whole way of thinking are a part, this means, of course, that we cannot take for granted much that in the normal course of life we must unquestioningly accept if we are to get our work done, or even if we are to remain sane; it means that we must question systematically all the presuppositions which in acting we accept unreflectingly; it means, in short, that in order to be strictly scientific we ought to see, as it were, from the outside what we can never see as a whole in such a manner; and, in practice, it means that we have constantly to deal with many important questions to which we have no scientific answer, where the knowledge on which we must draw is either the kind of knowledge of men and the world which only rich and varied experience can give, or the accumulated wisdom of the past, the inherited cultural treasures of our civilization, which to us must thus at the same time be tools which we use in orienting ourselves in our world and objects of critical study. This means that in most of our tasks we need not only be competent scientists and scholars but ought also to be experienced men of the world and, in some measure, philosophers.

Before I develop these points, let me briefly remind you of one respect where with us specialization goes less far than in the natural sciences: we do not know as sharp a division between the theoretician and the practitioner as there exists between the physicist and the engineer or between the physiologist and the doctor. This is not an accident or merely an earlier stage of development but a necessary consequence of the nature of our subject. It is due to the fact that the task of recognizing the presence in the real world of the conditions corresponding to the various assumptions of our theoretical schemes is often more difficult than the theory itself, an art which only those will acquire to whom the theoretical schemes have become second nature. We cannot state simple, almost mechanical criteria by which a certain type of theoretical situation can be identified, but we have to develop something like a sense for the physiognomy of events. We can, therefore, only rarely delegate the application of our knowledge to others, but must be our own practitioners, doctors as well as physiologists.

The factual knowledge, the familiarity with particular circumstances, which we cannot leave to our 'engineers' but must ourselves acquire, is, moreover, only in part of the kind which can be ascertained by established techniques. Although we endeavour to add by systematic effort to the knowledge of the world and of man, this effort can neither displace nor make unnecessary that knowledge of the world which is acquired only by extensive experience and a steepening in the wisdom contained in great literature and in our whole cultural tradition.

I need not say more about the necessity of a knowledge of the world in the usual sense, of the variety of human situations and characters with which we ought to be familiar. But I must say a word about what seems to me the unfortunate effect of the separation of what we now call the social *sciences* from the other human studies. By this I do not mean merely such paradoxical results as that so scientific a discipline as linguistics, from whose method and approach the other social sciences might well profit, should, for purely historical reasons, be counted among the humanities. What I have in mind is mainly a question of the climate in which our work will prosper; the question whether the atmosphere created by the pursuit of the humanities proper, of literature and the arts, is not quite as indispensable to us as the austerity of the scientific one. I am not sure that the results of the ambition to share in the prestige, and the funds, available for scientific research have always been fortunate, and that the separation of the social sciences from the humanities, of which this building is a symbol, was altogether a gain. I do not wish to overstress this point, and I will readily admit that, if I were speaking to a European rather than to an American audience, I might well stress the opposite view. But that here the separation of the humanities from what we mean to dignify by the name of social sciences may have gone too far ought not to be forgotten when we are looking back at twenty-five years of existence in a separate home.

We must admit, however, that there is one respect in which our attitude does differ from that of the humanities and in which we may even be disturbing and unwelcome in their circle. It is that our approach to the traditions which they cultivate must in some measure always be a critical and dissecting one; that there is no value which we must not on occasion question and analyse, though we can, of course, never do so for all values at the same time. Since our aim must be to discover what role particular institutions and traditions play in the functioning of society, we must constantly put the dissolving acid of reason to values and customs which not only are dear to others but are also so largely the cement which keeps society together. Especially in the study of that experience of the human race which is not preserved as explicit human knowledge but rather implicit in habits and institutions, in morals and mores—in short, in the study of those adaptations of the human race which act as non-conscious factors, of whose significance we are not normally aware, and which we may never fully understand, we are bound all the time to question fundamentals. This, I need hardly add, is, of course, the opposite to following intellectual fashions. While it must be our privilege to be radical, this ought not to mean 'advanced' in the sense that we claim to know which is the only forward direction.

Such constant practice is a heady wine which, if not paired with modesty, may make us little better than a nuisance. If we are not to become a mainly destructive element, we must also be wise enough to understand that we cannot do without beliefs and institutions whose significance we do not understand and which, therefore, may seem meaningless to us. If life is to proceed, we must, in practice, accept much which we cannot justify, and resign ourselves to the fact that reason cannot always be the ultimate judge in human affairs. This is, though not the only, yet perhaps the main, point where, whether we want it or not, we must in some measure be philosophers. By philosophy I mean here, in the first instance, not so much those problems which, like those of logic, have themselves already become the subjects of highly specialized and technical disciplines, but rather that remaining body of inchoate knowledge from which the distinct disciplines only gradually detach themselves and which has always been the province of philosophers. But there are also two fully developed branches of philosophy to which we cannot afford to be total strangers. The problems of ethics are constantly with us, and questions of scientific method are bound to be more troublesome for us than in most other fields. What Einstein once said about science, 'Without epistemology—insofar as it is thinkable at all—it is primitive and muddled', applies even more to our subjects.

Rather than be slightly ashamed of this connection, I feel we ought to be proud of the intimate relation which for centuries has existed between the social sciences and philosophy. It is certainly no accident that, so far as economics is concerned, in England, the country which has so long been leading in the subject, a list of her great economists, if we leave out only two major figures, might readily be taken for a list of her great philosophers: Locke, Hume, Adam Smith, Bentham, James and John Stuart Mill, Samuel Bailey, W. S. Jevons, Henry Sidgwick, to John Neville and John Maynard Keynes—all occupy equally honoured places in the history of economics as in that of philosophy or of scientific method. I see little reason to doubt that other social sciences would equally profit if they could attract a similar array of philosophic talent.

I have said enough, however, to describe our dilemma and must hasten to my conclusion. A true dilemma, of course, has no perfect solution, and my main point has been that we *are* faced by a true dilemma —that our task puts conflicting demands upon us which we cannot all satisfy. The choice imposed upon us by our imperfections remains a choice between evils. The main conclusion must thus probably be that there is no single best way and that our main hope is to preserve room for that multiplicity of efforts which true academic freedom makes possible.

But as a norm for academic education some general principles seem to emerge. We probably all agree that the main need for students who enter upon their graduate careers is a good general education. I have been arguing for the need for a following period of intense specialization in one of a somewhat limited number of subjects. But this, I feel, ought not regularly to continue to the end of the graduate work—and, if my contention is accepted that not all topical specializations are equally suitable as basic training, cannot always mean the end. Many students will of course continue to do their specialized research in the field of their basic training. But they should not have to do so or in their majority do so. At least for those who are willing to shoulder the extra burden, there ought to be opportunities to work, wherever possible under the guidance of competent specialists, on any suitable combination of knowledge. There ought to be opportunities for men who want to strike out in their own new field on some new combination of specialism or some other border-line problem. There is clearly an urgent need for a place in the University where the specialisms again meet, which provides the facilities and the climate for work which is not on well-established lines, and where requirements are flexible enough to be adapted to the individual tasks. The whole position in the field which I have been surveying seems to me to call for a sort of College of Advanced Human Studies as a recognized part of the organization of the social sciences and the humanities, some such institution as our chairman[2] has so devotedly and judiciously striven to provide with his pathbreaking conception of the Committee on Social Thought.

[2]Professor John U. Nef.

PART TWO

Politics

Upon this first, and in one sense this sole, rule of reason, that in order to learn, and in so desiring not to be satisfied with what you already incline to think, there follows one corollary which deserves to be inscribed upon every wall of the city of philosophy:

Do not block the way of inquiry.

Charles S. Peirce

CHAPTER NINE

Historians and
the Future of Europe*

Whether we shall be able to rebuild something like a common European civilization after this war will be decided mainly by what happens in the years immediately following it. It is possible that the events that will accompany the collapse of Germany will cause such destruction as to remove the whole of Central Europe for generations or perhaps permanently from the orbit of European civilization. It seems unlikely that, if this happens, the developments can be confined to Central Europe; and if the fate of Europe should be to relapse into barbarism, though ultimately a new civilization may emerge from it, it is not likely that this country would escape the consequences. The future of England is tied up with the future of Europe, and, whether we like it or not, the future of Europe will be largely decided by what will happen in Germany. Our efforts at least must be directed towards regaining Germany for those values on which European civilization was built and which alone can form the basis from which we can move towards the realization of the ideals which guide us.

Before we consider what we can do to that end, we must try to form a realistic picture of the kind of intellectual and moral situation we must expect to find in a defeated Germany. If anything is certain it is that even after victory we shall not have it in our power to make the defeated think just as we would wish them to; that we shall not be able to do more than assist any promising development; and that any clumsy efforts to proselytize may well produce results opposite to those at which we aim.

* A paper read to The Political Society at King's College, Cambridge, on February 28, 1944. The chair was taken by Sir John Clapham. Not published before.

[135]

Two extreme views can still be heard which are equally naïve and mis-leading: on the one hand, that all the Germans are equally corrupted and that therefore only the complete education of a new generation imposed from outside can change them, or, on the other hand, that the masses of the Germans, once they are freed from their present masters, will quickly and readily embrace political and moral views similar to our own. The position will certainly be more complicated than either of these views suggests. We shall almost certainly find a moral and intellectual desert, but one with many oases, some very fine, but almost completely isolated from each other. The outstanding feature will be the absence of any common tradition—beyond that of opposition to the Nazis and, probably, also to Communism—of any common beliefs, a great dis-illusionment about all political ideals, and a certain scepticism and even cynicism about what can be positively achieved by political action. There will, at first at any rate, be any amount of good will; but nothing will probably be more conspicuous than the powerlessness of good in-tentions without the uniting element of those common moral and political traditions which we take for granted, but which in Germany a complete break of a dozen years has destroyed, with a thoroughness which few people in this country can imagine.

On the other hand, we must be prepared not only to find an extra-ordinarily high intellectual level in some of the oases that have been preserved, but even to find that many of the Germans have learnt lessons which we have not yet understood, and that some of our conceptions will appear to their experience-hardened minds very naïve and *simpliste*. Hampered as discussion is under the Nazi regime, it has by no means stopped; and from the few samples of German war-time works I have seen (and from the complete list of books published in Germany which I have recently been able to peruse) I have the impression that the in-tellectual level of the academic discussion of social and political problems in war-time is at least not lower than in this country—probably because many of the best Germans either are precluded, or have voluntarily excluded themselves, from immediate participation in the war effort.

It will be on the Germans who have carried on in this manner—not numerous in proportion to the population of Germany, but numerous enough compared with the number of people who think independently in any country—that our hopes must rest, and to them that we must give any assistance we can. The task of finding them and assisting them with-out at the same time discrediting them with their own people will be a most difficult and delicate one. If these men are to succeed in making their views prevail, they will need some measure of moral and material support from outside. But they will need almost as much protection against well-intentioned but injudicious attempts to use them by the governmental machinery set up by the victorious powers. While they will probably be anxious to re-establish connections with, and to obtain the goodwill of, persons in other countries with whom they share common ideals, they will be rightly reluctant to become in any form instruments of the governmental apparatus of the victors. Unless opportunities are deliberately created for the meeting as equal individuals of persons from both sides who share certain basic ideals, it is not likely that such contacts will soon be re-established. But for a long time such opportunities can be created only by initiative from this side. And it seems to me certain that it must come through the efforts of private individuals and not through governmental agencies if such efforts are to have beneficial effects.

There will be many directions in which international contacts between individuals and groups might be deliberately re-established with beneficial effects. It will probably be easiest, and take place quickest, between the political groups of the Left. But such contacts should clearly not be limited to party groups, and if they were to be confined for some time to the political groups of the Left, this would be very unfortunate from every point of view. If in Germany a more cosmopolitan outlook should once more become, as has largely been true in the past, a prerogative of the Left, this might well contribute to drive the large groups of the Centre again into a nationalist attitude. It will be a more difficult, but in some ways even more important, task to assist the resumption of contacts between those groups where existing alignments in internal politics will not at once provide the channels. And there are tasks for which any grouping on the lines of party politics would be a definite obstacle, though a certain minimum of agreement on political ideals will be essential for any collaboration.

What I want to talk about tonight is more specifically the role which the historians can play in this connection—where by historians I mean really all students of society, past or present. There can be no doubt that in what is called the 're-education of the German people' the historians will in the long run play a decisive part, just as they did in creating the ideas that rule Germany today. I know that it is difficult for English people to appreciate how great and immediate the influence of academic work of this kind is in Germany, and how seriously the Germans take their professors—almost as seriously as the German professors take themselves. The role which the German political historians of the nineteenth century have played in creating the veneration for the power-state and the expansionist ideas which created modern Germany can scarcely be overrated. It was indeed 'that garrison of distinguished historians', of which Lord Acton wrote in 1886, 'who had prepared the Prussian supremacy together with their own, and now hold Berlin like a fortress', who created the ideas 'by which the rude strength centred in a region more ungenial than Latium was employed to absorb and to stiffen the diffused sentimental, and strangely impolitical talent of the studious Germans'. There was indeed, to quote Lord Acton again, 'probably no considerable group less in harmony with our sentiments in approaching history than that ... mainly represented by Sybel, Droysen, and Treitschke, with Mommsen and Gneist, Bernhardi and Duncker on their flanks', and so much given 'to maxims which it has cost the world so much effort to reverse'. And it was no accident that it was also Acton the historian who, in spite of all his admiration for much in Germany, foresaw fifty years ago that that tremendous power built up by very able minds, chiefly in Berlin, was 'the greatest danger that remains to be encountered by the Anglo-Saxon race'.

Though I cannot attempt here to trace in any detail the ways in which the teaching of the historians has helped to produce the doctrines which rule Germany today, you will probably agree with me that this influence was very great. Even some of the most repulsive features of the Nazi ideology trace back to German historians whom Hitler has probably never read but whose ideas have dominated the atmosphere in which he grew up. This is true especially of all the race doctrines, which, though I believe the German historians took them first from the French, were mainly developed in Germany. If I had time I could show how in other respects as well scholars of international fame like Werner Sombart taught a generation ago what to all intents and purposes is the same as the later Nazi doctrines. And I could add, in order not to leave all the blame on the historians, how in a related field my own professional colleagues, the economists, became willingly the instruments of extreme nationalist aspirations so that, e.g., Admiral Tirpitz, when forty or fifty years ago he found the big industrialists rather lukewarm in their reception of his naval policy, could enlist the support of the economists in order to persuade the capitalists of the advantages of his imperialistic ambitions.[1]

There can be little doubt, however, that the influence of the historians

---

[1] In his *Memoirs* Tirpitz records how one of the officers of the information department of the Admiralty was sent 'the round of the universities, where all the political economists, including Brentano, were ready to give splendid support. Schmoller, Wagner, Sering, Schumacher, and many others showed that the expenditure on the fleet would be a productive outlay, etc., etc.'

proper was the most important; and there is more than one reason why it seems likely that in the future the influence of history for good or bad will be even greater than it was in the past. The complete break in the continuity of most traditions will probably itself produce a turning back to history in search of traditions which provide a foundation for future developments. There will be a great deal of history to be written on the way in which all the misfortunes came about, questions in which the public will take a passionate interest and which are almost bound to become the subject of political disputes.

From our point of view, there is an additional reason why it is urgently to be desired that the Germans should be led to re-examine recent history and to take account of certain facts of which the majority of them are still unaware. The picture of recent history which not only the masses of the German people, but almost everybody in that country still start from, will indeed be the effect of Nazi propaganda which it will be most difficult to remove. It is of great importance that we should remember that many of the facts which have been decisive in forming our opinion of German responsibility and German character will be either unknown to most Germans, or so lightly fixed in their recollections as to carry little weight. Though many Germans will at first be ready to admit that the Allies have reason to distrust them and to insist on far-reaching precautions against another German aggression, even the most reasonable among them will soon be alienated by what to them will appear excessive restrictions imposed upon them, unless they come to see the full extent of the harm they have inflicted on Europe. After the last war, the gulf which separated the respective views of the two belligerent groups about the facts with which they most reproached each other was never really closed. The admirable willingness to forget, shown at least by the English, brought it about that soon after the last war almost everything which did not fit into the German picture was dismissed as 'atrocity stories'. We may quite possibly find again that not all the reports about the Germans which reached us during the war were true. But this is merely another reason for a careful re-examination of all the facts, a sorting out of what is definitely established from the mere rumours. To follow the natural tendency of letting bygones be bygones and not raking up the mud of the Nazi period would be fatal to the prospect of any real understanding with the Germans. The point at which the more unpleasant facts of recent German history are forgotten must not be allowed to come before the Germans have acknowledged their truth to themselves. The air of injured innocence, with which most Germans reacted to the settlement after the last war, was very largely due to real ignorance of the charges of which at that time they were regarded as guilty by nearly everybody in the victorious countries.

These things will have to be discussed—and they certainly will be discussed by ill-informed politicians and by way of recrimination. But if, instead of new causes of future conflict, something like a common view is to emerge, this will depend on these matters not being left entirely to party discussion and nationalist passions, but on their being considered in a more dispassionate spirit by men who wish above all to find the truth. Whether, in Germany in particular, the result of these discussions shall be new political myths or something like the truth, will to a great extent depend on the school of historians which will gain the ear of the people. Personally, I can have no doubt that the work which will determine future German opinion will come from inside Germany and not from outside. The suggestion one can now often hear that the victors should produce the textbooks on which future generations of Germans should be brought up appears to me pitifully silly. Such an attempt would be certain to produce the opposite of what is desired. No officially imposed creed, no history written to please another authority in the place of that in the interest of which so much German history was written in the past, least of all one inspired by foreign governments (or by emigrants) can hope to gain credence or lasting influence with the German people. The best we can hope, and all we from the outside can usefully work for, is that the history which is to influence the course of German opinions will be written in a sincere effort to find out the truth, subservient to no authority, no nation, race or class. History must above all cease to be an instrument of national policy.

The most difficult thing to re-create in Germany will be the belief in the existence of an objective truth, of the possibility of a history which is not written in the service of a particular interest. This is where, I believe, international collaboration, if it is collaboration between free individuals, may be of immense value. It would demonstrate the possibility of agreement independent of national allegiance. It would be particularly effective if the historians of the more fortunate countries set the example of not boggling at criticism of their own governments whenever called for. The desire for recognition by and encouragement from his own peers in other countries is perhaps the strongest safeguard against the corruption of the historian by nationalist sentiments, and the closer the international contacts the less will be the danger—just as isolation is almost certain to have the opposite effect. I remember only too well how after the last war the expulsion of all Germans from certain learned societies and their exclusion from certain international scientific congresses was among the strongest of the forces which drove many German scholars into the nationalist camp.

Thus, even in so far as the mere supremacy of truth in the historical teaching of future generations of Germans is concerned, the restoration of contacts with other historians would be of value, and any facilities we can create for this purpose will have a useful role to play. But, supremely important as strict adherence to truth is, I do not believe that it is enough to prevent history from being perverted in its teaching. We must distinguish here between historical research proper and historiography, the exposition of history for the people at large. I am now coming to a very delicate and much disputed subject, and I shall probably be accused of contradicting much of what I have just said. I am convinced, however, that no historical teaching can be effective without passing implicit or explicit judgments, and that its effects will depend very largely on the moral standards which it applies. Even if the academic historian tried to keep his history 'pure' and strictly 'scientific', there will be written for the general public histories which will judge and for that reason will have a greater influence. I believe, indeed, that if those German historians who did value truth above everything had so much less influence than their more political colleagues, and if even what influence the former had was in a direction not so very different from that of the latter, it was largely because of their extreme ethical neutrality, which tended to 'explain'— and thereby seemed to justify—everything by the 'circumstances of the time', and which was afraid ever to call black black or white white. It was these scientific historians as much as their political colleagues who inculcated the Germans with the belief that political acts cannot be measured by moral standards, and even that the ends justify the means. I cannot see that the most perfect respect for truth is in any way incompatible with the application of very rigorous moral standards in our judgment of historical events; and it seems to me that what the Germans need, and what in the past would have done them all the good in the world, is a strong dose of what it is now the fashion to call 'Whig history', history of the kind of which Lord Acton is one of the last great representatives. The future historian must have the courage to say that Hitler was a bad man, or else the time he spends on 'explaining' him will only serve to the glorification of his misdeeds.

It is probable that in the cultivation of certain common standards of moral judgment collaboration across frontiers could contribute a great deal—particularly where we have to deal with a country where traditions have been so disrupted and standards so lowered as in Germany of recent years. Even more important, however, is that collaboration will be possible only with those—or at least, that we ought to be willing to collaborate only with those—who are ready to subscribe to certain moral standards, and who in their work have adhered to them. There must be certain common values beyond the sacredness of truth: an agreement, at least, that the ordinary rules of moral decency must apply to political action, and beyond that also a certain minimum agreement on the most general political ideals. The latter need probably be no more than a common belief in the value of individual freedom, an affirmative attitude towards democracy without any superstitious deference to all its dogmatic applications, particularly without condoning the oppression of minorities any more than that of majorities, and, finally, an equal opposition to all forms of totalitarianism, whether it be from the Right or from the Left.

But while it seems that no collaboration would be possible unless it was based on agreement on a common set of values, a kind of agreed programme, it may be doubted whether any programme drawn up for the purpose would be likely to serve this end. No brief statement, however skilfully drawn up, is likely to give satisfactory expression to the set of ideals I have in mind, or would have much chance of uniting a considerable body of scholars. It seems that much more effective than any such programme designed *ad hoc* would be some great figure who embodies in an especially high degree the virtues and ideals which such an association would have to serve, and whose name could serve as a flag under which men who agree could unite.

I believe that there is one great name available who fits the bill as perfectly as if he had been created for the purpose: I am thinking of Lord Acton. The suggestion I want to put before you is indeed that an 'Acton Society' might form the most suitable agency to assist in the tasks of the historians of this country and of Germany, and perhaps of other countries, which I have attempted to sketch. There are many features united in the figure of Lord Acton that make him almost uniquely suitable as such a symbol. He was, of course, half German by education and more than half German in his training as a historian, and the Germans, for that reason, regard him almost as one of themselves. At the same time he unites, as perhaps no other recent figure, the great English liberal tradition with the best there is in the liberal tradition of the Continent—always using 'liberal' in its true and comprehensive sense, not, as Lord Acton expressed it, for the 'defenders of secondary liberties', but for one to whom individual liberty is of supreme value and 'not a means to a higher political end'.

If to us Lord Acton perhaps sometimes appears to err by the extreme rigour with which he applies universal moral standards to all times and conditions, this is all to the good, when sympathy with his general outlook is to be a test of selection. I do not know of another figure with regard to whom we can say with equal confidence that, if after the war we find that a German scholar sincerely agrees with his ideals, he is the type of German with whom no Englishman need feel reluctant to shake hands. In spite of all he took from Germany, I think it can be said that he was not only more free of all we hate in the Germans than many a pure Englishman, but also that he had discerned the dangerous aspects of German developments earlier and more clearly than most other people.

Before I say more about Acton's political philosophy, let me mention one or two other advantages his name seems to combine for our purpose. One is that Acton was a Catholic, even a devout Catholic, yet one who in political matters always preserved complete independence of Rome and never shrank from using the whole austerity of his moral standards in judging the history of the institution he most revered, the Roman Catholic Church. This seems to me very important: not only because, if a more liberal outlook is to be fostered among the great masses who are neither definitely 'Right' or 'Left', any such effort must carefully avoid that hostile attitude towards religion characteristic of much of Continental liberalism, which has done a great deal to drive hosts of decent people into opposition to any kind of liberalism. More important even it is that among the real opposition to Hitler in Germany the Catholics have played such an important part that no organization which, without being itself Roman Catholic, is not at least of such a character as to make it possible for a devout Catholic to collaborate, can hope to gain influence among the great middle groups on which the success of its efforts will so much depend. From what little one can see of German war literature it almost seems as if what spirit of liberalism can still be found in Germany is mainly to be found among the Catholic groups. So far as the historians more especially are concerned, it is almost certainly true that at least some of the Roman Catholic historians (I am thinking particularly of Franz Schnabel and his *Deutsche Geschichte im 19. Jahrhundert*) have kept more free from the poison of nationalism and the veneration of the power state than most other German historians.

Another reason which makes it seem probable that the political philosophy of Lord Acton would have a great appeal to many Germans in the state of mind in which they will be after this war is the extraordinary vogue which, according to all signs, the writings of Jakob Burckhardt are enjoying in Germany today. Burckhardt, though he differs from Acton by his deep pessimism, has much in common with him, above all the ever-reiterated emphasis on power as the arch-evil, the opposition to centralism, and the sympathy for the small and multi-national state. It might indeed be desirable to couple with the name of Acton, though not in the name, yet in the programme of the society, not only the name of Burckhardt, but also that of the great French historian who has so much in common with both of them, de Tocqueville. Jointly, these three names indicate probably even better than the single name of Acton the kind of basic political ideals under whose inspiration history might give the future Europe the political re-education which it needs—perhaps because, more than almost anybody else, these three men continued the tradition of the great political philosopher who, as Acton said, 'at his best was England at its best'—Edmund Burke.

If I were to attempt fully to justify my choice of Lord Acton as the main name under which such an effort might be attempted, I should have to give you an outline of his historical maxims and of his political philosophy. But though this would be a task worth attempting (and, significantly, recently attempted by a German scholar), it can hardly be done in a few minutes. All I can do is to read to you from my private Acton anthology some passages which express briefly a few characteristic convictions—though any such selection will give a somewhat one-sided and, in the undesirable sense, too 'political' impression.

I can be very brief about Acton's notion of history. 'My notion of history', he wrote, 'is of a thing the same for all men, not open to treatment from special and exclusive standpoints.' This implies, of course, not only the singleness of truth, but also Acton's belief in the universal validity of moral standards. I will remind you in this connection of the famous passage from the Inaugural Lecture in which he says that

> The weight of opinion is against me when I exhort you never to debase the moral currency or to lower the standards of rectitude but to try others by the final maxims that govern your own lives, and to suffer no man and no cause to escape the undying penalty which history has power to inflict on wrong. The plea in extenuation of guilt and mitigation of punishment is perpetual. . . .

an argument which Acton develops more fully in a well-known letter to a fellow historian, which I should like to quote at length, but from which I can read only a sentence or two. He argues there against the thesis that great historical figures must be judged

> unlike other men, with a favourable assumption that they did no wrong. If there is any presumption, it is the other way, against the holders of power, increasing as the power increases. Historic responsibility has to make up for

[144]

the want of legal responsibility. Power tends to corrupt and absolute power tends to corrupt absolutely. Great men are almost always bad men, even when they exercise influence and not authority, still more when you super-add the tendency or certainty of corruption by authority. There is no worse heresy than that the office sanctifies the holder of it. That is the point at which the negation of Catholicism and the negation of Liberalism meet and keep high festival.

And he concludes: 'The inflexible integrity of the moral code is, to me, the secret of the authority, the dignity, the utility of history.'

My illustrations of Acton's political philosophy must be even more unsystematic and incomplete, selected mainly for their relevance to the present situation and to what I have already said. I shall give the few quotations without comment, and only hope that they will have more freshness than the somewhat hackneyed passages I have just quoted. But perhaps recent events make it easier to appreciate the significance of some of these statements, such as the following discussion of what we now call 'totalitarianism':

> Whenever a single definite object is made the supreme end of the State, be it the advantage of a class, the safety or the power of the country, the greatest happiness of the greatest number, or the support of any speculative idea, the State becomes for a time inevitably absolute. Liberty alone demands for its realization the limitation of the public authority, for liberty is the only object which benefits all alike, and provokes no sincere opposition.

Or take the following:

> The true democratic principle, that none shall have power over the people, is taken to mean that none shall be able to restrain or elude its power. The true democratic principle, that the people shall not be made to do what it does not like, is taken to mean that it shall never be required to tolerate what it does not like. The true democratic principle, that every man's free will shall be as unfettered as possible, is taken to mean that the free will of the collective people shall be fettered in nothing.

Or:

> A theory that identified liberty with a single right, the right of doing all that you have the actual power to do, and a theory which secures liberty by certain unalterable rights, and founds it on truth which men did not invent and cannot abjure, cannot both be formative principles in the same Constitution. Absolute power and restrictions on its exercise cannot exist together. It is but a new form of the old contest between the spirit of true freedom and despotism in its most dexterous disguise.

And finally:

Liberty depends on the division of power. Democracy tends to unity of power. To keep asunder the agents, one must divide the source; that is, one must maintain, or create, separate administrative bodies. In the view of increasing democracy, a restricted federalism is the one possible check on concentration and centralism.

Perhaps the most important argument, too long to quote, is that of the essay on nationality where Acton courageously opposed to the dominant doctrine that (as expressed by J. S. Mill) 'it is in general a necessary condition of free institutions that the boundaries of governments should coincide with those of nationalities' the opposite view that the 'co-existence of several nations under the same State is a test, as well as the best security of freedom. It is also one of the chief instruments of civilization, and, as such, it is in the natural and providential order, and indicates a greater advancement than the national unity which is the ideal of modern liberalism.' Nobody who knows central Europe will deny that we cannot hope there for lasting peace and advance of civilization unless these ideas become at last victorious, nor that the most practical solution of the problems of that part of the world is a federalism of the kind Acton advocated.

Do not say that these ideals are utopian and therefore not worth working for. It is *because* they are ideals which can only be realized in the more or less distant future that they are the kind of ideals by which the historian can allow himself to be guided without the risk of becoming involved in party passions. As a teacher, and the historian cannot help being the political teacher of the future generations, he must not allow himself to be influenced by considerations of what is now possible, but ought to be concerned with making possible what decent people agree to be desirable, but what seems impracticable in view of the existing state of opinion. It is because, whether he wills it or not, the historian shapes the political ideals of the future, that he himself must be guided by the highest ideals and keep free from the political disputes of the day. The higher the ideals which guide him, and the more he can keep independent from political movements aiming at immediate goals, the more he may hope in the long run to make possible many things for which the world may not yet be ready. I am not even sure that we may not, by keeping distant ends in view, exercise a greater influence than the 'hard-boiled realist' of the kind that is now fashionable.

I have little doubt that a considerable group of historians, or, I should rather say, students of society, pledged to the ideals embodied in the work of Lord Acton, could become a great force for good. But what, you will ask, can any formal organization, such as the Acton Society I have suggested, contribute towards this end? To this my answer is, first, that I should not expect so much from its action as a body, but a great deal from it as an instrument for making possible in the near future the resumption of numerous individual contacts across the boundaries. I need not again emphasize why it is so important that what help or encouragement we can give should not come mainly through official or governmental channels. But for the individual it will for a long time be very difficult to do anything in isolation. The purely technical difficulties of seeking out individually the persons on the other side with whom one would wish to collaborate will be even greater. In all this such a society (or it would rather have to be a kind of club with selected membership) would be of great help.

But though I regard this facilitating of contacts between individuals as the more important purpose, and though it is scarcely possible now to sketch in any detail what the collective activities of the society might be, I believe that there will be not inconsiderable scope for such activities, mainly of an editorial kind. A good deal could be done to revive and popularize the works of those German political writers who in the past have represented a political philosophy more in accord with the ideals we wish to foster than those who had the greatest influence during the past seventy years. Even a journal largely devoted to the common discussion of problems of recent history might well prove beneficial, and might canalize discussion into a direction more profitable than the 'war-guilt' bickerings after the last war. It is possible that both in this country and in Germany a journal devoted not to the results of historical research proper, but to the exposition of history to the general public might prove both successful and have a real role to play if conducted by responsible historians. The society as such would, of course, never presume to decide any of the controversial questions, but in providing a forum for discussion and opportunity for collaboration between historians from different countries it would probably perform a very useful service.

But I must not let myself be led into any discussion of detail. My purpose has been not to solicit support for a definite project, but rather to submit a tentative suggestion to your criticism. While the more I think about the potential good such a society might do, the more I am attracted by the idea, it does not seem worth pursuing it further without first trying it out on other people. So if you will tell me whether you think that some attempt in the direction indicated seems to you worth while, and whether the name of Lord Acton appears to you a suitable symbol under which such an association might be formed, this will be of great help to me in deciding whether to pursue the idea further or to drop it.

CHAPTER TEN

Opening Address to a Conference at Mont Pèlerin*

I must confess that now, when the moment has arrived to which I have looked forward so long, my feeling of intense gratitude to all of you is much tempered by an acute sense of astonishment at my temerity in setting all this in motion, and of alarm about the responsibility I have assumed in asking you to give up so much of your time and energy to what you might well have regarded as a wild experiment. I will, however, confine myself at this stage to a simple but profoundly sincere 'thank you'.

It is my duty, before I step down from the position I have so immodestly assumed, and gladly hand over to you the task of carrying on what fortunate circumstances have enabled me to initiate, to give you a somewhat fuller account of the aims which have guided me in proposing this meeting and suggesting its programme. I shall endeavour not to tax your patience too much, but even the minimum of explanation which I

* April 1, 1947. Not before published. The members of the Conference were the following: Maurice Allais, Paris; Carlo Antoni, Rome; Hans Barth, Zürich; Karl Brandt, Stanford, Calif.; John Davenport, New York, N.Y.; Stanley R. Dennison, Cambridge; Aaron Director, Chicago, Ill.; Walter Eucken, Freiburg i.B.; Erich Eyck, Oxford; Milton Friedman, Chicago, Ill.; H. D. Gideonse, Brooklyn, N.Y.; F. D. Graham, Princeton, N.J.; F. A. Harper, Irvington-on-Hudson, N.Y.; Henry Hazlitt, New York, N.Y.; T. J. B. Hoff, Oslo; Albert Hunold, Zürich; Bertrand de Jouvenel, Chexbres, Vaud; Carl Iversen, Copenhagen; John Jewkes, Manchester; F. H. Knight, Chicago, Ill.; Fritz Machlup, Buffalo, N.Y.; L. B. Miller, Detroit, Mich.; Ludwig von Mises, New York, N.Y.; Felix Morley, Washington, D.C.; Michael Polanyi, Manchester; Karl R. Popper, London; William E. Rappard, Geneva; L. E. Read, Irvington-on-Hudson, N.Y.; Lionel Robbins, London; Wilhelm Röpke, Geneva; George J. Stigler, Providence, R.I.; Herbert Tingsten, Stockholm; François Trevoux, Lyon; V. O. Watts, Irvington-on-Hudson, N.Y.; C. V. Wedgwood, London.

owe you will take some little time. The basic conviction which has guided me in my efforts is that, if the ideals which I believe unite us, and for which, in spite of so much abuse of the term, there is still no better name than liberal, are to have any chance of revival, a great intellectual task must be performed. This task involves both purging traditional liberal theory of certain accidental accretions which have become attached to it in the course of time, and also facing up to some real problems which an over-simplified liberalism has shirked or which have become apparent only since it has turned into a somewhat stationary and rigid creed.

The belief that this is the prevailing condition has been strongly confirmed to me by the observation that in many different fields and in many different parts of the world, individuals who have been brought up in different beliefs and to whom party liberalism had little attraction, have been rediscovering for themselves the basic principles of liberalism and been trying to reconstruct a liberal philosophy which can meet the objections which in the eyes of most of our contemporaries have defeated the promise the earlier liberalism offered.

During the last two years I have had the good fortune to visit several parts of Europe and America and I have been surprised by the number of isolated men whom I found in different places, working on essentially the same problems and on very similar lines. Working in isolation or in very small groups they are, however, constantly forced to defend the basic elements of their beliefs and rarely have opportunity for an interchange of opinion on the more technical problems which arise only if a certain common basis of conviction and ideals is present.

It seems to me that effective endeavours to elaborate the general principles of a liberal order are practicable only among a group of people who are in agreement on fundamentals, and among whom certain basic conceptions are not questioned at every step. But not only is, at this time, the number of those who in any one country agree on what seems to me the basic liberal principles small, but the task is a very big one, and there is much need for drawing on as wide an experience under varying conditions as possible.

One of the most instructive observations to me was that, the farther one moves to the West, to countries where liberal institutions are still comparatively firm, and people professing liberal convictions still comparatively numerous, the less are these people prepared really to re-examine their own conviction and the more are they inclined to compromise, and to take the accidental historical form of a liberal society which they have known as the ultimate standard. I found on the other hand that in those countries which either had directly experienced a totalitarian regime, or had closely approached it, a few men had from this experience gained a clearer conception of the conditions and value of a free society. The more I discussed these problems with people in different countries, the more I was driven to the conviction that the wisdom is not all on one side, and that the observation of the actual decay of a civilization has taught some independent thinkers on the European Continent lessons which I believe have yet to be learnt in England and America if these countries are to avoid a similar fate.

Yet it is not only the students of economics and politics in various countries who have much to profit from each other and who, by joining their forces across the national frontiers, could do much to advance their common cause. I was no less impressed by the fact of how much more fruitful the discussion of the great problems of our time could be between, say, an economist and a historian, or a lawyer and a political philosopher, if they shared certain common premises, than the discussion is between students of the same subjects who differed on these basic values. Of course, a political philosophy can never be based exclusively on economics or expressed mainly in economic terms. It seems that the dangers which we are facing are the result of an intellectual movement which has expressed itself in, and affected the attitude towards, all aspects of human affairs. Yet while in his own subject every one of us may have learnt to recognize the beliefs which are part and parcel of the movement that leads to totalitarianism, we cannot be sure that, e.g., as economists, we do not, under the influence of the atmosphere of our time, accept as uncritically as anyone else ideas in the field of history or philosophy, morals or law, which are part and parcel of the very system of ideas which we have learnt to oppose in our own field.

The need for an international meeting of representatives of these different subjects seemed to me especially great as a result of the war which not only has for so long disrupted many of the normal contacts but also inevitably, and in the best of us, created a self-centredness and nationalist outlook which ill accords with a truly liberal approach to our problems. Worst of all, the war and its effects have created new obstacles to the resumption of international contacts which to those in the less fortunate countries are still practically unsurmountable without outside help, and are serious enough for the rest of us. There seemed clearly to exist a case for some sort of organization which would help to reopen communications between people with a common outlook. Unless some sort of private organization was created, there would be serious danger that contacts beyond national frontiers would become increasingly the monopoly of those who were in one way or another tied up in the existing governmental or political machinery and were bound to serve the dominating ideologies.

It was evident from the beginning that no permanent organization of this kind could be created without some experimental meeting at which the usefulness of the idea could be tried out. But as this, in the present circumstances, seemed hardly possible to arrange without considerable funds, I did little but talk about this plan to as many people as would listen, until, to my own surprise, a fortunate accident suddenly placed this within the range of possibility. One of our Swiss friends here, Dr. Hunold, had raised funds for a cognate but different project which for accidental reasons had to be abandoned, and he succeeded in persuading the donors to turn the amount over for this new purpose.

It was only when thus a unique opportunity offered itself that I fully realized what a responsibility I had taken on, and that, if the chance was not to be missed, I must undertake to propose this conference and, worst of all, to decide who was to be invited. You will perhaps sympathize enough with the difficulty and the embarrassing nature of such a task to make it unnecessary for me to apologize at length for the manner in which I have discharged it.

There is only one point in this connection which I ought to explain: as I see our task, it is not sufficient that our members should have what used to be called 'sound' views. The old liberal who adheres to a traditional creed *merely* out of tradition, however admirable his views, is not of much use for our purpose. What we need are people who have faced the arguments from the other side, who have struggled with them and fought themselves through to a position from which they can both critically meet the objection against it and justify their views. Such people are even less numerous than good liberals in the old sense, and there are now few enough even of them. But when it came to drawing up a list I discovered to my pleasant surprise that the number of people whom I thought had a title to be included in such a list was a good deal larger than I had expected or than could be asked to the conference. And the final selection had inevitably to a large extent to be arbitrary.

It is a matter of great regret to me that, largely as a result of my personal shortcomings, the membership of the present conference is somewhat unevenly balanced and that the historians and political philosophers, instead of being as strongly represented as the economists, are a comparatively small minority. This is partly due to the fact that my personal contacts among this group are more limited, and to the fact that even among those who were on the original list a particularly high proportion of the non-economists was unable to attend, but partly also to the fact that at this particular juncture economists seem perhaps to be more generally aware of the immediate dangers and of the urgency of the intellectual problems which we must solve if we are to have a chance to guide developments in a more desirable direction. There are similar disproportions in the national distribution of the membership of this conference and I particularly regret that both Belgium and Holland are entirely unrepresented. I have no doubt that, apart from these faults of which I am conscious, there are other and perhaps more serious blunders which I have unwittingly committed, and all I can do is to ask for your indulgence, and to beg your help so that in future we shall possess a more complete list of all those from whom we may expect sympathetic and active support in our efforts.

It has given me much encouragement that not a single one of all those to whom I sent invitations did not express his sympathies with the aim of the conference and the wish to be able to take part. If nevertheless many of them are not here this is due to physical difficulties of one kind or another. You will probably like to hear the names of those who have expressed their wish that they could be with us and their sympathy with the aims of this conference.[1]

In mentioning those who cannot be with us for temporary reasons I must also mention others on whose support I had particularly counted but who will never again be with us. Indeed the two men with whom I had most fully discussed the plan for this meeting both have not lived to see its realization. I had first sketched the plan three years ago to a small group in Cambridge presided over by Sir John Clapham who took a great interest in it but who died suddenly a year ago. And it is now less than a year since I discussed the plan in all its detail with another man whose whole life had been devoted to the ideals and problems with which we shall be concerned: Henry Simons of Chicago. A few weeks later he was no more. If with their names I mention that of a much

---

[1] I then read out the following list of names: Costatino Bresciani-Turroni, Rome; William H. Chamberlin, New York; René Courtin, Paris; Max Eastman, New York; Luigi Einaudi, Rome; Howard Ellis, Berkeley, Calif.; A. G. B. Fisher, London; Eli Heckscher, Stockholm; Hans Kohn, Northampton, Mass.; Walter Lippmann, New York; Friedrich Lutz, Princeton; Salvador de Madariaga, Oxford; Charles Morgan, London; W. A. Orton, Northampton, Mass.; Arnold Plant, London; Charles Rist, Paris; Michael Roberts, London; Jacques Rueff, Paris; Alexander Rüstow, Istanbul; F. Schnabel, Heidelberg; W. J. H. Sprott, Nottingham; Roger Truptil, Paris; D. Villey, Poitiers; E. L. Woodward, Oxford; H. M. Wriston, Providence, R.I.; G. M. Young, London. Though not present at the meeting at Mont Pélèrin, all those named later agreed to join the society there formed as original members.

younger man who had also taken a great interest in my plans and whom, if he had lived, I should have hoped to see as our Permanent Secretary, a post for which Etienne Mantoux would have been ideally suited, you will understand how heavy are the losses which our group has suffered even before it first had an opportunity to meet.

If it had not been for these tragic deaths I should not have had to act alone in summoning this conference. I confess that at one time these blows had completely shaken my resolution to pursue the plan further. But when the opportunity came I felt it a duty to make of it what I could.

There is another point connected with the membership of our meeting which I should briefly mention. We have among us a fair number of regular writers for the periodical press, not in order that the meeting should be reported, but because they have the best opportunity to spread the ideas to which we are devoted. But to reassure other members it may be useful to mention that unless and until you should decide otherwise, I think this should be regarded as a private meeting and all that is said here in the discussion as 'off the record'.

Let me now turn to the programme I have suggested for this meeting. It is obviously the first thing you will have to consider and I need hardly say that the proposals which I sent out and will now explain are no more than suggestions which this meeting may or may not approve.

Of the subjects which I have suggested for systematic examination by this conference, and of which most members seem to have approved, the first is the relation between what is called 'Free Enterprise' and a really competitive order. It seems to me to be much the biggest and in some ways the most important problem and I hope that a considerable part of our discussion will be devoted to its exploration. It is the field where it is most important that we should become clear in our own minds, and arrive at an agreement about the kind of programme of economic policy which we should wish to see generally accepted. It is probably the set of problems in which the largest proportion among us are actively interested and where it is most urgent that the work which has been conducted independently in parallel directions in many parts of the world should be brought together. Its ramifications are practically endless, since an adequate treatment involves a complete programme of a liberal economic policy. It is likely that after a survey of the general problem you may prefer to split it up into more special questions to be discussed in separate sessions. We could probably in this manner find room for one or more of the additional topics which I mentioned in one of my circulars, or for such further problems as that of the inflationary high-pressure economy which, as has been justly observed by more than one member, is at the moment the main tool by which a collectivist development is forced on the majority of countries. Perhaps the best plan will be that, after devoting one or two sessions to the general issue, we set aside half an hour or so at the end of one of these discussions to decide on the further course of our deliberations. I propose that we devote the whole of this afternoon and evening to a general survey of this topic and perhaps you will allow me to say a few words more about it this afternoon. I have taken the liberty to ask Professor Aaron Director of Chicago, Professor Walter Eucken of Freiburg and Professor Allais of Paris to introduce the debate on this subject and I have no doubt that we shall then have more than enough food for discussion.

Profoundly important as the problems of the principles of economic order are, there are several reasons why I hope that we will, still during the first part of the conference, have time also for some of the other topics. We are probably all agreed that the roots of the political and social dangers which we face are not purely economic and that, if we are to preserve a free society, a revision not only of the strictly economic concepts which rule our generation is required. I believe it will also help to make us more rapidly acquainted if during the early part of the conference we range over a rather wider field and look at our problems from several angles before we attempt to proceed to more technical aspects or problems of detail.

You will probably agree that the interpretation and teaching of history has during the past two generations been one of the main instruments through which essentially anti-liberal conceptions of human affairs have spread; the widespread fatalism which regards all developments that have in fact taken place as inevitable consequences of great laws of necessary historical development, the historical relativism which denies any moral standards except those of success and non-success, the emphasis on mass movements as distinguished from individual achievements, and not least the general emphasis on material necessity as against the power of ideas to shape our future, are all different facets of a problem as important and almost as wide as the economic problem. I have suggested as a separate subject for discussion merely one aspect of this wide field, the relation between historiography and political education, but it is an aspect which should soon lead us to the wider problem. I am very glad that Miss Wedgwood and Professor Antoni have consented to open the discussion on this question.

It is, I think, important that we fully realize that the popular liberal creed, on the Continent and in America more than in England, contained many elements which on the one hand often led its adherents directly into the folds of socialism or nationalism, and on the other hand antagonized many who shared the basic values of individual freedom but were repelled by the aggressive rationalism which would recognize no values except those whose utility (for an ultimate purpose never disclosed) could be demonstrated by individual reason, and which presumed that science was competent to tell us not only what is but also what ought to be. Personally I believe that this false rationalism, which gained influence in the French Revolution and which during the past hundred years has exercised its influence mainly through the twin movements of Positivism and Hegelianism, is an expression of an intellectual hubris which is the opposite of that intellectual humility which is the essence of the true liberalism that regards with reverence those spontaneous social forces through which the individual creates things greater than he knows. It is this intolerant and fierce rationalism which is mainly responsible for the gulf which, particularly on the Continent, has often driven religious people from the liberal movement into reactionary camps in which they felt little at home. I am convinced that unless this breach between true liberal and religious convictions can be healed there is no hope for a revival of liberal forces. There are many signs in Europe that such a reconciliation is today nearer than it has been for a long time, and that many people see in it the one hope of preserving the ideals of Western civilization. It was for this reason that I was specially anxious that the subject of the relation between Liberalism and Christianity should be made one of the separate topics of our discussion; and although we cannot hope to get far in exploring this topic in a single meeting, it seems to me essential that we should explicitly face the problem.

The two further topics which I have suggested for discussion are questions of the practical application of our principles to the problems of our time rather than questions of principles themselves. But both the problem of the future of Germany, and that of the possibilities and prospects of a European federation, seemed to me problems of such immediate urgency that no international group of students of politics should meet without considering them, even if we cannot hope to do more than clear our own minds a little by an exchange of views. They are both questions on which the present state of public opinion more than anything else is the great obstacle to any reasonable discussion and I feel that it is a special duty not to shirk their consideration. It is a symptom of their complexity that I have had the greatest difficulty in persuading any members of this conference to open the discussion on these two subjects.

There is one other topic which I should have liked to see discussed because it seems to me central to our problem, namely the meaning and conditions of the Rule of Law. If I did not actually suggest it it was because, in order to discuss this problem adequately, it would have been necessary to extend our membership even further and to include lawyers. It was again largely lack of knowledge on my part which prevented this, and I mention it largely in order to make it clear how wide we shall have to cast our net if in any permanent organization we are to be competent adequately to deal with all the different aspects of our task. But the programme I have suggested is probably ambitious enough for this one conference and I will now leave this point and turn to one or two other matters on which I ought to comment briefly.

So far as the first of these, the formal organization of this conference, is concerned, I don't think we need to burden ourselves with any elaborate machinery. We could not have wished for a person better qualified to preside over us at this first meeting than Professor Rappard and I am sure you will allow me to thank him on your behalf for having consented. But we should not expect him or anyone else to carry this burden throughout the conference. The most appropriate arrangement will probably be to have this task rotate and, if you agree, one of the acts of this first meeting will be to elect chairmen for the next few meetings. If the meeting will agree on a programme at least for the first part of the conference, little formal business should arise until we have to consider the agenda for the second part which I have suggested we might do at a special meeting on Monday evening. It would probably be wise if in addition we set up, at this meeting, a small standing committee of five or six members to fill in any details of the programme on which we agree now or to make any changes which circumstances may show to be desirable. You may also feel it desirable to appoint a secretary to the conference, or perhaps still better, two secretaries, one to look after the programme and another to be in charge of general arrangements. I believe this would be amply sufficient at this stage to regularize our proceedings.

There is another point of organization which I should probably mention at this stage. I shall of course see that proper minutes will be kept of the business part of our discussions. But no arrangements have been made or seemed practicable for obtaining a shorthand record of our discussions. Apart from the technical difficulties, this would also have impaired the private and informal character of our discussions. But I hope that the members will themselves keep some notes of their major contributions so that, if the conference should decide to embody its main results in some kind of written record, it will be easy for them to put on paper the essence of their remarks.

There is also the question of language. In my preliminary correspondence I have tacitly assumed that all the members are familiar with English, and as this is certainly true of the majority of us, it would greatly facilitate our deliberations if English were mainly used. We are not in the fortunate position of official international bodies which command a staff of interpreters. It seems to me that the rule should be that every member should use the language in which he can hope to make himself most widely understood.

The immediate purpose of this conference is, of course, to provide an opportunity for a comparatively small group of those who in different parts of the world are striving for the same ideals, to get personally acquainted, to profit from one another's experience, and perhaps also to give mutual encouragement. I am confident that at the end of these ten days you will agree that this meeting will have been well worth while if it has achieved no more than this. But I rather hope that this experiment in collaboration will prove so successful that we shall want to continue it in one form or another.

However small the total number of people of our general outlook may be, there are of course among them many more competent scholars actively interested in the problems I have outlined than the small number present. I could myself have drawn up a list two or three times as long, and from the suggestions I have already received I have no doubt that together we could without difficulty compile a list of several hundred men and women in the various countries who share our general beliefs and would be willing to work for them. I hope we will compile such a list, selecting the names rather carefully, and design some means of continued contacts between these people. A beginning of such a list I am placing on the table and I hope you will add to it as many names as you think desirable, indicate by your signatures which of the other proposals you wish to support, and also perhaps let me know privately if any of the persons appearing on the list seem to you to be unsuitable for inclusion among the members of a permanent organization. We should probably not include any name unless it receives the support of two or three members of our present group and it may be desirable, later during the conference, to set up a small scrutiny committee to edit a final list. I assume that all those who were invited to this conference but were unable to attend will as a matter of course be included in this list.

There are of course many forms in which such regular contacts might be provided. When in one of my circulars I employed the somewhat highflown expression of an 'International Academy for Political Philosophy' I meant to emphasize by the term 'Academy' one aspect which seems to me essential if such a permanent organization is to fulfil its purpose: it must remain a closed society, not open to all and sundry, but only to people who share with us certain common convictions. This character can only be preserved if membership can be acquired only by election, and if we treat admission into our circle as seriously as the great learned academies. I did not mean to suggest that we call ourselves an Academy. It will be for you, if you decide to form a Society, to choose a name for it. I have been rather attracted by the idea of calling it The Acton-Tocqueville Society, and somebody has suggested that it might be appropriate to add Jakob Burckhardt as a third patron saint. But this is a question we need not yet consider at this stage.

Beyond the important point that, as it seems to me, whatever permanent body we form must be a closed society, I have no strong view about its organization. Much is to be said for giving it, at first at least, the loosest possible form and making it, perhaps, no more than a kind of correspondence society in which the list of members serves no other purpose than to enable them to keep in direct contact with each other. If it were practicable, as I fear it is not, to arrange that all the members provided one another with reprints or mimeographed copies of their relevant writings, this would in many ways be one of the most useful things we could do. It would, on the one hand, avoid the danger, which a specialized journal would create, that we would talk only to those already converted, but it would, on the other, keep us informed of the parallel or complementary activities of others. But the two desiderata, that the efforts of the members of our group should reach a great variety of audiences and not be confined to those who are already converted, and that at the same time the members of our group should be kept fully informed of one another's contributions, should somehow be reconciled, and we shall at least have to consider the possibility of sooner or later issuing a journal.

But it may well be that for some time to come such a loose and informal arrangement as I have suggested is all that we can achieve, since more would require greater financial means than we shall be able to raise from our midst. If there were larger funds available, all sorts of possibilities might open up. But, desirable as this might be, I shall be content with such a modest beginning if that is all we can do without in any manner compromising our complete independence.

This conference itself of course illustrates how the pursuit of our aims is dependent on the availability of some financial means, and we cannot expect to be often so fortunate as we have been this time in securing the necessary funds for it mainly from Swiss and, so far as the travelling expenses of the American members are concerned, from American sources, without any strings or conditions being attached to the offer. I wanted to take the earliest opportunity explicitly to reassure you on this point and at the same time to say how grateful we must be to Dr. Hunold who has raised the Swiss funds, and to Mr. W. H. Luhnow of the William Volker Charities Trust in Kansas City, who has made possible the participation of our American friends, for their help in this respect. To Dr. Hunold we are further indebted for undertaking all the local arrangements; and all the pleasures and comforts we are now enjoying we owe to his efforts and foresight.

I feel that it will be best if we do not turn to any discussion of the practical task I have mentioned until we are much better acquainted with one another and have more experience of the possibilities of collaboration than we have now. I hope there will be a good deal of private conversation on these questions during the next few days and that in the course of these our ideas will gradually crystallize. When after three days of work and another three days of more informal companionship we resume our regular business meetings, one of those meetings should probably be set aside for a systematic examination of the possibilities. I will defer till then any attempt to justify the name which I have tentatively suggested for the permanent Society or any discussion of the principles and aims which would have to govern its activity.

For the time being we are just the Mont Pèlèrin Conference to which you will have to give your own laws and whose procedure and destiny is now entirely in your hands.

CHAPTER ELEVEN

The Principles of a Liberal Social Order

1. By 'liberalism' I shall understand here the conception of a desirable political order which in the first instance was developed in England from the time of the Old Whigs in the later part of the seventeenth century to that of Gladstone at the end of the nineteenth. David Hume, Adam Smith, Edmund Burke, T. B. Macaulay and Lord Acton may be regarded as its typical representatives in England. It was this conception of individual liberty under the law which in the first instance inspired the liberal movements on the Continent and which became the basis of the American political tradition. A few of the leading political thinkers in those countries like B. Constant and A. de Tocqueville in France, Immanuel Kant, Friedrich von Schiller and Wilhelm von Humboldt in Germany, and James Madison, John Marshall and Daniel Webster in the United States belong wholly to it.

2. This liberalism must be clearly distinguished from another, originally Continental European tradition, also called 'liberalism' of which what now claims this name in the United States is a direct descendant. This latter view, though beginning with an attempt to imitate the first tradition, interpreted it in the spirit of a constructivist rationalism prevalent in France and thereby made of it something very different, and in the end, instead of advocating limitations on the powers of government, ended up with the ideal of the unlimited powers of the majority. This is the tradition of Voltaire, Rousseau, Condorcet and the French Revolution which became the ancestor of modern socialism.

---

*A paper submitted to the Tokyo Meeting of the Mont Pèlèrin Society, September 1966, and published in *Il Politico*, December 1966.

English utilitarianism has taken over much of this Continental tradition and the late-nineteenth-century British liberal party, resulting from a fusion of the liberal Whigs and the utilitarian Radicals, was also a product of this mixture.

3. Liberalism and democracy, although compatible, are not the same. The first is concerned with the extent of governmental power, the second with who holds this power. The difference is best seen if we consider their opposites: the opposite of liberalism is totalitarianism, while the opposite of democracy is authoritarianism. In consequence, it is at least possible in principle that a democratic government may be totalitarian and that an authoritarian government may act on liberal principles. The second kind of 'liberalism' mentioned before has in effect become democratism rather than liberalism and, demanding *unlimited* power of the majority, has become essentially anti-liberal.

4. It should be specially emphasized that the two political philosophies which both describe themselves as 'liberalism' and lead in a few respects to similar conclusions, rest on altogether different philosophical foundations. The first is based on an evolutionary interpretation of all phenomena of culture and mind and on an insight into the limits of the powers of the human reason. The second rests on what I have called 'constructivist' rationalism, a conception which leads to the treatment of all cultural phenomena as the product of deliberate design, and on the belief that it is both possible and desirable to reconstruct all grown institutions in accordance with a preconceived plan. The first kind is consequently reverent of tradition and recognizes that all knowledge and all civilization rests on tradition, while the second type is contemptuous of tradition because it regards an independently existing reason as capable of designing civilization. (Cf. the statement by Voltaire: 'If you want good laws, burn those you have and make new ones.') The first is also an essentially modest creed, relying on abstraction as the only available means to extend the limited powers of reason, while the second refuses to recognize any such limits and believes that reason alone can prove the desirability of particular concrete arrangements.

(It is a result of this difference that the first kind of liberalism is at least not incompatible with religious beliefs and has often been held and even been developed by men holding strong religious beliefs, while the 'Continental' type of liberalism has always been antagonistic to all religion and politically in constant conflict with organized religions.)

5. The first kind of liberalism, which we shall henceforth alone consider, is itself not the result of a theoretical construction but arose from the desire to extend and generalize the beneficial effects which un-

[161]

expectedly had followed on the limitations placed on the powers of government out of sheer distrust of the rulers. Only after it was found that the unquestioned greater personal liberty which the Englishman enjoyed in the eighteenth century had produced an unprecedented material prosperity were attempts made to develop a systematic theory of liberalism, attempts which in England never were carried very far while the Continental interpretations largely changed the meaning of the English tradition.

6. Liberalism thus derives from the discovery of a self-generating or spontaneous order in social affairs (the same discovery which led to the recognition that there existed an object for theoretical social sciences), an order which made it possible to utilize the knowledge and skill of all members of society to a much greater extent than would be possible in any order created by central direction, and the consequent desire to make as full use of these powerful spontaneous ordering forces as possible.

7. It was thus in their efforts to make explicit the principles of an order already existing but only in an imperfect form that Adam Smith and his followers developed the basic principles of liberalism in order to demonstrate the desirability of their general application. In doing this they were able to presuppose familiarity with the common law conception of justice and with the ideals of the rule of law and of government under the law which were little understood outside the Anglo-Saxon world; with the result that not only were their ideas not fully understood outside the English-speaking countries, but that they ceased to be fully understood even in England when Bentham and his followers replaced the English legal tradition by a constructivist utilitarianism derived more from Continental rationalism than from the evolutionary conception of the English tradition.

8. The central concept of liberalism is that under the enforcement of universal rules of just conduct, protecting a recognizable private domain of individuals, a spontaneous order of human activities of much greater complexity will form itself than could ever be produced by deliberate arrangement, and that in consequence the coercive activities of government should be limited to the enforcement of such rules, whatever other services government may at the same time render by administering those particular resources which have been placed at its disposal for those purposes.

9. The distinction between a *spontaneous order* based on abstract rules which leave individuals free to use their own knowledge for their own purposes, and an *organization or arrangement* based on commands, is of central importance for the understanding of the principles of a free

society and must in the following paragraphs be explained in some detail, especially as the spontaneous order of a free society will contain many organizations (including the biggest organization, government), but the two principles of order cannot be mixed in any manner we may wish.

10. The first peculiarity of a spontaneous order is that by using its ordering forces (the regularity of the conduct of its members) we can achieve an order of a much more complex set of facts than we could ever achieve by deliberate arrangement, but that, while availing ourselves of this possibility of inducing an order of much greater extent than we otherwise could, we at the same time limit our power over the details of that order. We shall say that when using the former principle we shall have power only over the abstract character but not over the concrete detail of that order.

11. No less important is the fact that, in contrast to an organization, neither has a spontaneous order a purpose nor need there be agreement on the concrete results it will produce in order to agree on the desirability of such an order, because, being independent of any particular purpose, it can be used for, and will assist in the pursuit of, a great many different, divergent and even conflicting individual purposes. Thus the order of the market, in particular, rests not on common purposes but on reciprocity, that is on the reconciliation of different purposes for the mutual benefit of the participants.

12. The conception of the common welfare or of the public good of a free society can therefore never be defined as a sum of known particular results to be achieved, but only as an abstract order which as a whole is not oriented on any particular concrete ends but provides merely the best chance for any member selected at random successfully to use his knowledge for his purposes. Adopting a term of Professor Michael Oakeshott (London), we may call such a free society a *nomocratic* (law-governed) as distinguished from an unfree *telocratic* (purpose-governed) social order.

13. The great importance of the spontaneous order or nomocracy rests on the fact that it extends the possibility of peaceful co-existence of men for their mutual benefit beyond the small group whose members have concrete common purposes, or were subject to a common superior, and that it thus made the appearance of the *Great* or *Open Society* possible. This order which has progressively grown beyond the organizations of the family, the horde, the clan and the tribe, the principalities and even the empire or national state, and has produced at least the beginning of a world society, is based on the adoption—without and often against the

desire of political authority—of rules which came to prevail because the groups who observed them were more successful; and it has existed and grown in extent long before men were aware of its existence or understood its operation.

14. The spontaneous order of the market, based on reciprocity or mutual benefits, is commonly described as an economic order; and in the vulgar sense of the term 'economic' the Great Society is indeed held together entirely by what are commonly called economic forces. But it is exceedingly misleading, and has become one of the chief sources of confusion and misunderstanding, to call this order an economy as we do when we speak of a national, social, or world economy. This is at least one of the chief sources of most socialist endeavour to turn the spontaneous order of the market into a deliberately run organization serving an agreed system of common ends.

15. An economy in the strict sense of the word in which we can call a household, a farm, an enterprise or even the financial administration of government an economy, is indeed an organization or a deliberate arrangement of a given stock of resources in the service of a unitary order of purposes. It rests on a system of coherent decisions in which a single view of the relative importance of the different competing purposes determines the uses to be made of the different resources.

16. The spontaneous order of the market resulting from the interaction of many such economies is something so fundamentally different from an economy proper that it must be regarded as a great misfortune that it has ever been called by the same name. I have become convinced that this practice so constantly misleads people that it is necessary to invent a new technical term for it. I propose that we call this spontaneous order of the market a *catallaxy* in analogy to the term 'catallactics', which has often been proposed as a substitute for the term 'economics'. (Both 'catallaxy' and 'catallactics' derive from the ancient Greek verb *katallattein* which, significantly, means not only 'to barter' and 'to exchange' but also 'to admit into the community' and 'to turn from enemy into friend'.)

17. The chief point about the catallaxy is that, as a spontaneous order, its orderliness does *not* rest on its orientation on a single hierarchy of ends, and that, therefore, it will *not* secure that for it as a whole the more important comes before the less important. This is the chief cause of its condemnation by its opponents, and it could be said that most of the socialist demands amount to nothing less than that the catallaxy should be turned into an economy proper (i.e., the purposeless spontaneous order into a purpose-oriented organization) in order to assure that the more important be never sacrificed to the less important. The defence of

the free society must therefore show that it is due to the fact that we do not enforce a unitary scale of concrete ends, nor attempt to secure that some particular view about what is more and what is less important governs the whole of society, that the members of such a free society have as good a chance successfully to use their individual knowledge for the achievement of their individual purposes as they in fact have.

18. The extension of an order of peace beyond the small purpose-oriented organization became thus possible by the extension of purpose-independent ('formal') rules of just conduct to the relations with other men who did not pursue the same concrete ends or hold the same values except those abstract rules—rules which did not impose obligations for particular actions (which always presuppose a concrete end) but consisted solely in prohibitions from infringing the protected domain of each which these rules enable us to determine. Liberalism is therefore inseparable from the institution of private property which is the name we usually give to the material part of this protected individual domain.

19. But if liberalism presupposes the enforcement of rules of just conduct and expects a desirable spontaneous order to form itself only if appropriate rules of just conduct are in fact observed, it also wants to restrict the *coercive* powers of government to the enforcement of such rules of just conduct, including at least one prescribing a positive duty, namely, the rule requiring citizens to contribute according to uniform principles not only to the cost of enforcing those rules but also to the costs of the non-coercive service functions of government which we shall presently consider. Liberalism is therefore the same as the demand for the rule of law in the classical sense of the term according to which the coercive functions of government are strictly limited to the enforcement of uniform rules of law, meaning uniform rules of just conduct towards one's fellows. (The 'rule of law' corresponds here to what in German is called *materieller Rechtsstaat* as distinguished from the mere *formelle Rechtsstaat* which requires only that each act of government is authorized by legislation, whether such a law consists of a general rule of just conduct or not.)

20. Liberalism recognizes that there are certain other services which for various reasons the spontaneous forces of the market may not produce or may not produce adequately, and that for this reason it is desirable to put at the disposal of government a clearly circumscribed body of resources with which it can render such services to the citizens in general. This requires a sharp distinction between the coercive powers of government, in which its actions are strictly limited to the enforcement of rules of just conduct and in the exercise of which all discretion is

excluded, and the provision of services by government, for which it can use only the resources put at its disposal for this purpose, has no coercive power or monopoly, but in the use of which resources it enjoys wide discretion.

21. It is significant that such a conception of a liberal order has arisen only in countries in which, in ancient Greece and Rome no less than in modern Britain, justice was conceived as something to be discovered by the efforts of judges or scholars and not as determined by the arbitrary will of any authority; that it always had difficulty in taking roots in countries in which law was conceived primarily as the product of deliberate legislation, and that it has everywhere declined under the joint influence of legal positivism and of democratic doctrine, both of which know no other criterion of justice than the will of the legislator.

22. Liberalism has indeed inherited from the theories of the common law and from the older (pre-rationalist) theories of the law of nature, and also presupposes, a conception of justice which allows us to distinguish between such rules of just individual conduct as are implied in the conception of the 'rule of law' and are required for the formation of a spontaneous order on the one hand, and all the particular commands issued by authority for the purpose of organization on the other. This essential distinction has been made explicit in the legal theories of two of the greatest philosophers of modern times, David Hume and Immanuel Kant, but has not been adequately restated since and is wholly uncongenial to the governing legal theories of our day.

23. The essential points of this conception of justice are (a) that justice can be meaningfully attributed only to human action and not to any state of affairs as such without reference to the question whether it has been, or could have been, deliberately brought about by somebody; (b) that the rules of justice have essentially the nature of prohibitions, or, in other words, that injustice is really the primary concept and the aim of rules of just conduct is to prevent unjust action; (c) that the injustice to be prevented is the infringement of the protected domain of one's fellow men, a domain which is to be ascertained by means of these rules of justice; and (d) that these rules of just conduct which are in themselves negative can be developed by consistently applying to whatever such rules a society has inherited the equally negative test of universal applicability—a test which, in the last resort, is nothing else than the self-consistency of the actions which these rules allow if applied to the circumstances of the real world. These four crucial points must be developed further in the following paragraphs.

24. *Ad (a)*: Rules of just conduct can require the individual to take into account in his decisions only such consequences of his actions as he himself can foresee. The concrete results of the catallaxy for particular people are, however, essentially unpredictable; and since they are not the effect of anyone's design or intentions, it is meaningless to describe the manner in which the market distributed the good things of this world among particular people as just or unjust. This, however, is what the so-called 'social' or 'distributive' justice aims at in the name of which the liberal order of law is progressively destroyed. We shall later see that no test or criteria have been found or can be found by which such rules of 'social justice' can be assessed, and that, in consequence, and in contrast to the rules of just conduct, they would have to be determined by the arbitrary will of the holders of power.

25. *Ad(b)*: No particular human action is fully determined without a concrete purpose it is meant to achieve. Free men who are to be allowed to use their own means and their own knowledge for their own purposes must therefore not be subject to rules which tell them what they must positively do, but only to rules which tell them what they must not do; except for the discharge of obligations an individual has voluntarily incurred, the rules of just conduct thus merely delimit the range of permissible actions but do not determine the particular actions a man must take at a particular moment. (There are certain rare exceptions to this, like actions to save or protect life, prevent catastrophes, and the like, where either rules of justice actually do require, or would at least generally be accepted as just rules if they required, some positive action. It would lead far to discuss here the position of such rules in the system.) The generally negative character of the rules of just conduct, and the corresponding primacy of the injustice which is prohibited, has often been noticed but scarcely ever been thought through to its logical consequences.

26. *Ad(c)*: The injustice which is prohibited by rules of just conduct is any encroachment on the protected domain of other individuals, and they must therefore enable us to ascertain what is the protected sphere of others. Since the time of John Locke it is customary to describe this protected domain as property (which Locke himself had defined as 'the life, liberty, and possessions of a man'). This term suggests, however, a much too narrow and purely material conception of the protected domain which includes not only material goods but also various claims on others and certain expectations. If the concept of property is, however, (with Locke) interpreted in this wide sense, it is true that law, in the sense of rules of justice, and the institution of property are inseparable.

27. *Ad (d)*: It is impossible to decide about the justice of any one particular rule of just conduct except within the framework of a whole system of such rules, most of which must for this purpose be regarded as unquestioned: values can always be tested only in terms of other values. The test of the justice of a rule is usually (since Kant) described as that of its 'universalizability', i.e., of the possibility of willing that the rules should be applied to all instances that correspond to the conditions stated in it (the 'categorical imperative'). What this amounts to is that in applying it to any concrete circumstances it will not conflict with any other accepted rules. The test is thus in the last resort one of the compatibility or non-contradictoriness of the whole system of rules, not merely in a logical sense but in the sense that the system of actions which the rules permit will not lead to conflict.

28. It will be noticed that only purpose-independent ('formal') rules pass this test because, as rules which have originally been developed in small, purpose-connected groups ('organizations') are progressively extended to larger and larger groups and finally universalized to apply to the relations between any members of an Open Society who have no concrete purposes in common and merely submit to the same abstract rules, they will in this process have to shed all references to particular purposes.

29. The growth from the tribal organization, all of whose members served common purposes, to the spontaneous order of the Open Society in which people are allowed to pursue their own purposes in peace, may thus be said to have commenced when for the first time a savage placed some goods at the boundary of his tribe in the hope that some member of another tribe would find them and leave in turn behind some other goods to secure the repetition of the offer. From the first establishment of such a practice which served reciprocal but not common purposes, a process has been going on for millennia which, by making rules of conduct independent of the particular purposes of those concerned, made it possible to extend these rules to ever wider circles of undetermined persons and eventually might make possible a universal peaceful order of the world.

30. The character of those universal rules of just individual conduct, which liberalism presupposes and wishes to improve as much as possible, has been obscured by confusion with that other part of law which determines the organization of government and guides it in the administration of the resources placed at its disposal. It is a characteristic of liberal society that the private individual can be coerced to obey only the rules of private and criminal law; and the progressive permeation of

private law by public law in the course of the last eighty or hundred years, which means a progressive replacement of rules of conduct by rules of organization, is one of the main ways in which the destruction of the liberal order has been effected. A German scholar (Franz Böhm) has for this reason recently described the liberal order very justly as the *Privatrechtsgesellschaft* (private law society).

31. The difference between the order at which the rules of conduct of private and criminal law aim, and the order at which the rules of organization of public law aim, comes out most clearly if we consider that rules of conduct will determine an order of action only in combination with the particular knowledge and aims of the acting individuals, while the rules of organization of public law determine directly such concrete action in the light of particular purposes, or, rather, give some authority power to do so. The confusion between rules of conduct and rules of organization has been assisted by an erroneous identification of what is often called the 'order of law' with the order of actions, which in a free system is not fully determined by the system of laws but merely presupposes such system of laws as one of the conditions required for its formation. Not every system of rules of conduct which secures uniformity of action (which is how the 'order of law' is frequently interpreted) will, however, secure an order of action in the sense that the actions permitted by the rules will not conflict.

32. The progressive displacement of the rules of conduct of private and criminal law by a conception derived from public law is the process by which existing liberal societies are progressively transformed into totalitarian societies. This tendency has been most explicitly seen and supported by Adolf Hitler's 'crown jurist' Carl Schmitt who consistently advocated the replacement of the 'normative' thinking of liberal law by a conception of law which regards as its purpose the 'concrete order formation' (*konkretes Ordnungsdenken*).

33. Historically this development has become possible as a result of the fact that the same representative assemblies have been charged with the two different tasks of laying down rules of individual conduct and laying down rules and giving orders concerning the organization and conduct of government. The consequence of this has been that the term 'law' itself, which in the older conception of the 'rule of law' had meant only rules of conduct equally applicable to all, came to mean any rule of organization or even any particular command approved by the constitutionally appointed legislature. Such a conception of the rule of law which merely demands that a command be legitimately issued and not that it be a rule of justice equally applicable to all (what the Germans call

the merely *formelle Rechsstaat*), of course no longer provides any protection of individual freedom.

34. If it was the nature of the constitutional arrangements prevailing in all Western democracies which made this development possible, the driving force which guided it in the particular direction was the growing recognition that the application of uniform or equal rules to the conduct of individuals who were in fact very different in many respects, inevitably produced very different results for the different individuals; and that in order to bring about by government action a reduction in these unintended but inevitable differences in the material position of different people, it would be necessary to treat them not according to the same but according to different rules. This gave rise to a new and altogether different conception of justice, namely that usually described as 'social' or 'distributive' justice, a conception of justice which did not confine itself to rules of conduct for the individual but aimed at particular results for particular people, and which therefore could be achieved only in a purpose-governed organization but not in a purpose-independent spontaneous order.

35. The concepts of a 'just price', a 'just remuneration' or a 'just distribution of incomes' are of course very old; it deserves notice, however, that in the course of the efforts of two thousand years in which philosophers have speculated about the meaning of these concepts, not a single rule has been discovered which would allow us to determine what is in this sense just in a market order. Indeed the one group of scholars which have most persistently pursued the question, the schoolmen of the later middle ages and early modern times, were finally driven to define the just price or wage as that price or wage which would form itself on a market in the absence of fraud, violence or privilege—thus referring back to the rules of just conduct and accepting as a just result whatever was brought about by the just conduct of all individuals concerned. This negative conclusion of all the speculations about 'social' or 'distributive' justice was, as we shall see, inevitable, because a just remuneration or distribution has meaning only within an organization whose members act under command in the service of a common system of ends, but can have no meaning whatever in a catallaxy or spontaneous order which can have no such common system of ends.

36. A state of affairs as such, as we have seen, cannot be just or unjust as a mere fact. Only in so far as it has been brought about designedly or could be so brought about does it make sense to call just or unjust the actions of those who have created it or permitted it to arise. In the catallaxy, the spontaneous order of the market, nobody can foresee,

however, what each participant will get, and the results for particular people are not determined by anyone's intentions; nor is anyone responsible for particular people getting particular things. We might therefore question whether a deliberate choice of the market order as the method for guiding economic activities, with the unpredictable and in a great measure chance incidence of its benefits, is a just decision, but certainly not whether, once we have decided to avail ourselves of the catallaxy for that purpose, the particular results it produces for particular people are just or unjust.

37. That the concept of justice is nevertheless so commonly and readily applied to the distribution of incomes is entirely the effect of an erroneous anthropomorphic interpretation of society as an organization rather than as a spontaneous order. The term 'distribution' is in this sense quite as misleading as the term 'economy', since it also suggests that something is the result of deliberate action which in fact is the result of spontaneous ordering forces. Nobody distributes income in a market order (as would have to be done in an organization) and to speak, with respect to the former, of a just or unjust distribution is therefore simple nonsense. It would be less misleading to speak in this respect of a 'dispersion' rather than a 'distribution' of incomes.

38. All endeavours to secure a 'just' distribution must thus be directed towards turning the spontaneous order of the market into an organization or, in other words, into a totalitarian order. It was this striving after a new conception of justice which produced the various steps by which rules of organization ('public law'), which were designed to make people aim at particular results, came to supersede the purpose-independent rules of just individual conduct, and which thereby gradually destroyed the foundations on which a spontaneous order must rest.

39. The ideal of using the coercive powers of government to achieve 'positive' (i.e., social or distributive) justice leads, however, not only necessarily to the destruction of individual freedom, which some might not think too high a price, but it also proves on examination a mirage or an illusion which cannot be achieved in any circumstances, because it presupposes an agreement on the relative importance of the different concrete ends which cannot exist in a great society whose members do not know each other or the same particular facts. It is sometimes believed that the fact that most people today desire social justice demonstrates that this ideal has a determinable content. But it is unfortunately only too possible to chase a mirage, and the consequence of this is always that the result of one's striving will be utterly different from what one had intended.

[171]

40. There can be no rules which determine how much everybody 'ought' to have unless we make some unitary conception of relative 'merits' or 'needs' of the different individuals, for which there exists no objective measure, the basis of a central allocation of all goods and services—which would make it necessary that each individual, instead of using *his* knowledge for *his* purposes, were made to fulfil a duty imposed upon him by somebody else, and were remunerated according to how well he has, in the opinion of others, performed this duty. This is the method of remuneration appropriate to a closed organization, such as an army, but irreconcilable with the forces which maintain a spontaneous order.

41. It ought to be freely admitted that the market order does not bring about any close correspondence between subjective merit or individual needs and rewards. It operates on the principle of a combined game of skill and chance in which the results for each individual may be as much determined by circumstances wholly beyond his control as by his skill or effort. Each is remunerated according to the value his particular services have to the particular people to whom he renders them, and this value of his services stands in no necessary relation to anything which we could appropriately call his merits and still less to his needs.

42. It deserves special emphasis that, strictly speaking, it is meaningless to speak of a value 'to society' when what is in question is the value of some services to certain people, services which may be of no interest to anybody else. A violin virtuoso presumably renders services to entirely different people from those whom a football star entertains, and the maker of pipes altogether different people from the maker of perfumes. The whole conception of a 'value to society' is in a free order as illegitimate an anthropomorphic term as its description as 'one economy' in the strict sense, as an entity which 'treats' people justly or unjustly, or 'distributes' among them. The results of the market process for particular individuals are neither the result of anybody's will that they should have so much, nor even foreseeable by those who have decided upon or support the maintenance of this kind of order.

43. Of all the complaints about the injustice of the results of the market order the one which appears to have had the greatest effect on actual policy, and to have produced a progressive destruction of the equal rules of just conduct and their replacement by a 'social' law aiming at 'social justice', however, was not the extent of the inequality of the rewards, nor their disproportion with recognizable merits, needs, efforts, pains incurred, or whatever else has been chiefly stressed by social philosophers, but the demands for protection against an undeserved descent from an

already achieved position. More than by anything else the market order has been distorted by efforts to protect groups from a decline from their former position; and when government interference is demanded in the name of 'social justice' this now means, more often than not, the demand for the protection of the existing relative position of some group. 'Social justice' has thus become little more than a demand for the protection of vested interests and the creation of new privilege, such as when in the name of social justice the farmer is assured 'parity' with the industrial worker.

44. The important facts to be stressed here are that the positions thus protected were the result of the same sort of forces as those which now reduce the relative position of the same people, that their position for which they now demand protection was no more deserved or earned than the diminished position now in prospect for them, and that their former position could in the changed position be secured to them only by denying to others the same chances of ascent to which they owed their former position. In a market order the fact that a group of persons has achieved a certain relative position cannot give them a claim in justice to maintain it, because this cannot be defended by a rule which could be equally applied to all.

45. The aim of economic policy of a free society can therefore never be to assure particular results to particular people, and its success cannot be measured by any attempt at adding up the value of such particular results. In this respect the aim of what is called 'welfare economics' is fundamentally mistaken, not only because no meaningful sum can be formed of the satisfactions provided for different people, but because its basic idea of a maximum of need-fulfilment (or a maximum social product) is appropriate only to an economy proper which serves a single hierarchy of ends, but not to the spontaneous order of a catallaxy which has no common concrete ends.

46. Though it is widely believed that the conception of an optimal economic policy (or any judgment whether one economic policy is better than another) presupposes such a conception of maximizing aggregate real social income (which is possible only in value terms and therefore implies an illegitimate comparison of the utility to different persons), this is in fact not so. An optimal policy in a catallaxy may aim, and ought to aim, at increasing the chances of any member of society taken at random of having a high income, or, what amounts to the same thing, the chance that, whatever his share in total income may be, the real equivalent of this share will be as large as we know how to make it.

47. This condition will be approached as closely as we can manage,

irrespective of the dispersion of incomes, if everything which is produced is being produced by persons or organizations who can produce it more cheaply than (or at least as cheaply as) anybody who does not produce it, and is sold at a price lower than that at which it would be possible to offer it for anybody who does not in fact so offer it. (This allows for persons or organizations to whom the costs of producing one commodity or service are lower than they are for those who actually produce it and who still produce something else instead, because their comparative advantage in that other production is still greater; in this case the total costs of their producing the first commodity would have to include the loss of the one which is not produced.)

48. It will be noticed that this optimum does not presuppose what economic theory calls 'perfect competition' but only that there are no obstacles to the entry into each trade and that the market functions adequately in spreading information about opportunities. It should also be specially observed that this modest and achievable goal has never yet been fully achieved because at all times and everywhere governments have both restricted access to some occupations and tolerated persons and organizations deterring others from entering occupations when this would have been to the advantage of the latter.

49. This optimum position means that as much will be produced of whatever combination of products and services is in fact produced as can be produced by any method that we know, because we can through such a use of the market mechanism bring more of the dispersed knowledge of the members of society into play than by any other. But it will be achieved only if we leave the share in the total, which each member will get, to be determined by the market mechanism and all its accidents, because it is only through the market determination of incomes that each is led to do what this result requires.

50. We owe, in other words, our chances that our unpredictable share in the total product of society represents as large an aggregate of goods and services as it does to the fact that thousands of others constantly submit to the adjustments which the market forces on them; and it is consequently also our duty to accept the same kind of changes in our income and position, even if it means a decline in our accustomed position and is due to circumstances we could not have foreseen and for which we are not responsible. The conception that we have 'earned' (in the sense of morally deserved) the income we had when we were more fortunate, and that we are therefore entitled to it so long as we strive as honestly as before and had no warning to turn elsewhere, is wholly mistaken. Everybody, rich or poor, owes his income to the outcome of a

mixed game of skill and chance, the aggregate result of which and the shares in which are as high as they are only because we have agreed to play that game. And once we have agreed to play the game and profited from its results, it is a moral obligation on us to abide by the results even if they turn against us.

51. There can be little doubt that in modern society all but the most unfortunate and those who in a different kind of society might have enjoyed a legal privilege, owe to the adoption of that method an income much larger than they could otherwise enjoy. There is of course no reason why a society which, thanks to the market, is as rich as modern society should not provide *outside the market* a minimum security for all who in the market fall below a certain standard. Our point was merely that considerations of justice provide no justification for 'correcting' the results of the market and that justice, in the sense of treatment under the same rules, requires that each takes what a market provides in which every participant behaves fairly. There is only a justice of individual conduct but not a separate 'social justice'.

52. We cannot consider here the legitimate tasks of government in the administration of the resources placed at its disposal for the rendering of services to the citizens. With regard to these functions, for the discharge of which the government is given money, we will here only say that in exercising them government should be under the same rules as every private citizen, that it should possess no monopoly for a particular service of the kind, that it should discharge these functions in such a manner as not to disturb the much more comprehensive spontaneously ordered efforts of society, and that the means should be raised according to a rule which applies uniformly to all. (This, in my opinion, precludes an overall progression of the burden of taxation of the individuals, since such a use of taxation for purposes of redistribution could be justified only by such arguments as we have just excluded.) In the remaining paragraphs we shall be concerned only with some of the functions of government for the discharge of which it is given not merely money but power to enforce rules of private conduct.

53. The only part of these coercive functions of government which we can further consider in this outline are those which are concerned with the preservation of a functioning market order. They concern primarily the conditions which must be provided by law to secure the degree of competition required to steer the market efficiently. We shall briefly consider this question first with regard to enterprise and then with regard to labour.

54. With regard to enterprise the first point which needs underlining

is that it is more important that government refrain from assisting monopolies than that it combat monopoly. If today the market order is confined only to a part of the economic activities of men, this is largely the result of deliberate government restrictions of competition. It is indeed doubtful whether, if government consistently refrained from creating monopolies and from assisting them through protective tariffs and the character of the law of patents for inventions and of the law of corporations, there would remain an element of monopoly significant enough to require special measures. What must be chiefly remembered in this connection is, firstly, that monopolistic positions are always undesirable but often unavoidable for objective reasons which we cannot or do not wish to alter; and, secondly, that all government-supervised monopolies tend to become government-protected monopolies which will persist when their justification has disappeared.

55. Current conceptions of anti-monopoly policy are largely misguided by the application of certain conceptions developed by the theory of perfect competition which are irrelevant to conditions where the factual presuppositions of the theory of perfect competition are absent. The theory of perfect competition shows that if on a market the number of buyers and sellers is sufficiently large to make it impossible for any one of them deliberately to influence prices, such quantities will be sold at prices which will equal marginal costs. This does not mean, however, that it is either possible or even necessarily desirable everywhere to bring about a state of affairs where large numbers buy and sell the same uniform commodity. The idea that in situations where we cannot, or do not wish to, bring about such a state, the producers should be held to conduct themselves as if perfect competition existed, or to sell at a price which would rule under perfect competition, is meaningless, because we do not know what would be the particular conduct required, or the price which would be formed, if perfect competition existed.

56. Where the conditions for perfect competition do not exist, what competition still can and ought to be made to achieve is nevertheless very remarkable and important, namely the conditions described in paragraphs 46–49 above. It was pointed out then that this state will tend to be approached if nobody can be prevented by government or others to enter any trade or occupation he desired.

57. This condition would, I believe, be approached as closely as it is possible to secure this if, *firstly*, all agreements to restrain trade were without exception (not prohibited, but merely) made void and unenforceable, and, *secondly*, all discriminatory or other aimed actions towards an actual or potential competitor intended to make him observe

certain rules of market conduct were to make liable for multiple damages. It seems to me that such a modest aim would produce a much more effective law than actual prohibitions under penalties, because no exceptions need to be made from such a declaration as invalid or unenforceable of all contracts in restraint of trade, while, as experience has shown, the more ambitious attempts are bound to be qualified by so many exceptions as to make them much less effective.

58. The application of this same principle that all agreements in restraint of trade should be invalid and unenforceable and that every individual should be protected against all attempts to enforce them by violence or aimed discrimination, is even more important with regard to labour. The monopolistic practices which threaten the functioning of the market are today much more serious on the side of labour than on the side of enterpise, and the preservation of the market order will depend, more than on anything else, on whether we succeed in curbing the latter

59. The reason for this is that the developments in this field are bound to force government, and are already forcing many governments, into two kinds of measures which are wholly destructive of the market order: attempts authoritatively to determine the appropriate incomes of the various groups (by what is called an 'incomes policy') and efforts to overcome the wage 'rigidities' by an inflationary monetary policy. But since this evasion of the real issue by only temporarily effective monetary means must have the effect that those 'rigidities' will constantly increase, they are a mere palliative which can only postpone but not solve the central problem.

60. Monetary and financial policy is outside the scope of this paper. Its problems were mentioned only to point out that its fundamental and in the present situation insoluble dilemmas cannot be solved by any monetary means but only by a restoration of the market as an effective instrument for determining wages.

61. In conclusion, the basic principles of a liberal society may be summed up by saying that in such a society all coercive functions of government must be guided by the overruling importance of what I like to call THE THREE GREAT NEGATIVES: PEACE, JUSTICE AND LIBERTY. Their achievement requires that in its coercive functions government shall be confined to the enforcement of such prohibitions (stated as abstract rules) as can be equally applied to all, and to exacting under the same uniform rules from all a share of the costs of the other, noncoercive services it may decide to render to the citizens with the material and personal means thereby placed at its disposal.

CHAPTER TWELVE

*The Intellectuals and Socialism**

I

In all democratic countries, in the United States even more than else-where, a strong belief prevails that the influence of the intellectuals on politics is negligible. This is no doubt true of the power of intellectuals to make their peculiar opinions of the moment influence decisions, of the extent to which they can sway the popular vote on questions on which they differ from the current views of the masses. Yet over some-what longer periods they have probably never exercised so great an influence as they do today in those countries. This power they wield by shaping public opinion.

In the light of recent history it is somewhat curious that this decisive power of the professional secondhand dealers in ideas should not yet be more generally recognized. The political development of the Western world during the last hundred years furnishes the clearest demon-stration. Socialism has never and nowhere been at first a working-class movement. It is by no means an obvious remedy for an obvious evil which the interests of that class will necessarily demand. It is a con-struction of theorists, deriving from certain tendencies of abstract thought with which for a long time only the intellectuals were familiar; and it required long efforts by the intellectuals before the working classes could be persuaded to adopt it as their programme.

In every country that has moved towards socialism the phase of the development in which socialism becomes a determining influence on politics has been preceded for many years by a period during which socialist ideals governed the thinking of the more active intellectuals. In Germany this stage had been reached towards the end of the last century; in England and France, about the time of the First World War.

* Reprinted from *The University of Chicago Law Review*, Vol. 16, No. 3, Spring 1949.

To the casual observer it would seem as if the United States had reached this phase after the Second World War and that the attraction of a planned and directed economic system is now as strong among the American intellectuals as it ever was among their German or English fellows. Experience suggests that once this phase has been reached it is merely a question of time until the views now held by the intellectuals become the governing force of politics.

The character of the process by which the views of the intellectuals influence the politics of tomorrow is therefore of much more than academic interest. Whether we wish merely to foresee, or to attempt to influence, the course of events, it is a factor of much greater importance than is generally understood. What to the contemporary observer appears as the battle of conflicting interests has indeed often been decided long before in a clash of ideas confined to narrow circles. Paradoxically enough, however, in general the parties of the Left have done most to spread the belief that it was the numerical strength of the opposing material interests which decided political issues, whereas in practice these same parties have regularly and successfully acted as if they understood the key position of the intellectuals. Whether by design or driven by the force of circumstances, they have always directed their main effort towards gaining the support of this *élite*, while the more conservative groups have acted, as regularly but unsuccessfully, on a more naïve view of mass democracy and have usually vainly tried directly to reach and to persuade the individual voter.

II

The term intellectuals, however, does not at once convey a true picture of the large class to which we refer and the fact that we have no better name by which to describe what we have called the secondhand dealers in ideas is not the least of the reasons why their power is not better understood. Even persons who use the word 'intellectual' mainly as a term of abuse are still inclined to withhold it from many who undoubtedly perform that characteristic function. This is neither that of the original thinker nor that of the scholar or expert in a particular field of thought. The typical intellectual need be neither: he need not possess special knowledge of anything in particular, nor need he even be particularly intelligent, to perform his role as intermediary in the spreading of ideas. What qualifies him for his job is the wide range of subjects on which he can readily talk and write, and a position or habits through which he becomes acquainted with new ideas sooner than those to whom he addresses himself.

Until one begins to list all the professions and activities which belong to this class, it is difficult to realize how numerous it is, how the scope for its activities constantly increases in modern society, and how dependent on it we have all become. The class does not consist only of journalists, teachers, ministers, lecturers, publicists, radio commentators, writers of fiction, cartoonists, and artists—all of whom may be masters of the technique of conveying ideas but are usually amateurs so far as the substance of what they convey is concerned. The class also includes many professional men and technicians, such as scientists and doctors, who through their habitual intercourse with the printed word become carriers of new ideas outside their own fields and who, because of their expert knowledge on their own subjects, are listened to with respect on most others. There is little that the ordinary man of today learns about events or ideas except through the medium of this class; and outside our special fields of work we are in this respect almost all ordinary men, dependent for our information and instruction on those who make it their job to keep abreast of opinion. It is the intellectuals in this sense who decide what views and opinions are to reach us, which facts are important enough to be told to us, and in what form and from what angle they are to be presented. Whether we shall ever learn of the results of the work of the expert and the original thinker depends mainly on their decision.

The layman, perhaps, is not fully aware to what extent even the popular reputations of scientists and scholars are made by that class and are inevitably affected by its views on subjects which have little to do with the merits of the real achievements. And it is specially significant for our problem that every scholar can probably name several instances from his field of men who have undeservedly achieved a popular reputation as great scientists solely because they hold what the intellectuals regard as 'progressive' political views; but I have yet to come across a single instance where such a scientific pseudo-reputation has been bestowed for political reason on a scholar of more conservative leanings. This creation of reputations by the intellectuals is particularly important in the fields where the results of expert studies are not used by other specialists but depend on the political decision of the public at large. There is indeed scarcely a better illustration of this than the attitude which professional economists have taken to the growth of such doctrines as socialism or protectionism. There was probably at no time a majority of economists, who were recognized as such by their peers, favourable to socialism (or, for that matter, to protection). In all probability it is even true to say that no other similar group of students contains so high a proportion of its members decidedly opposed to socialism (or protection). This is the more significant as in recent times it is as likely as not that it was an early interest in socialist schemes for reform which led a man to choose economics for his profession. Yet it is not the predominant views of the experts but the views of a minority, often of rather doubtful standing in their profession, which are taken up and spread by the intellectuals.

The all-pervasive influence of the intellectuals in contemporary society is still further strengthened by the growing importance of 'organization'. It is a common but probably mistaken belief that the increase of organization increases the influence of the expert or specialist. This may be true of the expert administrator and organizer, if there are such people, but hardly of the expert in any particular field of knowledge. It is rather the person whose general knowledge is supposed to qualify him to appreciate expert testimony, and to judge between the experts from different fields, whose power is enhanced. The point which is important for us, however, is that the scholar who becomes a university president, the scientist who takes charge of an institute or foundation, the scholar who becomes an editor or the active promoter of an organization serving a particular cause, all rapidly cease to be scholars or experts and become intellectuals in our sense, people who judge all issues not by their specific merits but, in the characteristic manner of intellectuals, solely in the light of certain fashionable general ideas. The number of such institutions which breed intellectuals and increase their number and power grows every day. Almost all the 'experts' in the mere technique of getting knowledge over are, with respect to the subject matter which they handle, intellectuals and not experts.

In the sense in which we are using the term, the intellectuals are in fact a fairly new phenomenon of history. Though nobody will regret that education has ceased to be a privilege of the propertied classes, the fact that the propertied classes are no longer the best educated, and the fact that the large number of people who owe their position solely to their general education do not possess that experience of the working of the economic system which the administration of property gives, are important for understanding the role of the intellectual. Professor Schumpeter, who has devoted an illuminating chapter of his *Capitalism, Socialism and Democracy* to some aspects of our problem, has not unfairly stressed that it is the absence of direct responsibility for practical affairs and the consequent absence of firsthand knowledge of them which distinguishes the typical intellectual from other people who also wield the power of the spoken and written word. It would lead too far, however, to examine here further the development of this class and the curious claim which has recently been advanced by one of its theorists that it was the only one whose views were not decidedly influenced by its own economic interests. One of the important points that would have to be examined in such a discussion would be how far the growth of this class has been artificially stimulated by the law of copyright.[1]

III

It is not surprising that the real scholar or expert and the practical man of affairs often feel contemptuous about the intellectual, are disinclined to recognize his power, and are resentful when they discover it. Individually they find the intellectuals mostly to be people who understand nothing in particular especially well, and whose judgment on matters they themselves understand shows little sign of special wisdom. But it would be a fatal mistake to underestimate their power for this reason. Even though their knowledge may be often superficial, and their intelligence limited, this does not alter the fact that it is their judgment which mainly determines the views on which society will act in the not too distant future. It is no exaggeration to say that once the more active part of the intellectuals have been converted to a set of beliefs, the process by which these become generally accepted is almost automatic and irresistible. They are the organs which modern society has developed for spreading knowledge and ideas, and it is their convictions and opinions which operate as the sieve through which all new conceptions must pass before they can reach the masses.

It is of the nature of the intellectual's job that he must use his own knowledge and convictions in performing his daily task. He occupies his position because he possesses, or has had to deal from day to day with, knowledge which his employer in general does not possess, and his activities can therefore be directed by others only to a limited extent. And just because the intellectuals are mostly intellectually honest it is inevitable that they should follow their own convictions whenever they have discretion, and that they should give a corresponding slant to everything that passes through their hands. Even where the direction of

[1] It would be interesting to discover how far a seriously critical view of the benefits to society of the law of copyright, or the expression of doubts about the public interest in the existence of a class which makes its living from the writing of books, would have a chance of being publicly stated in a society in which the channels of expression are so largely controlled by people who have a vested interest in the existing situation.

policy is in the hands of men of affairs of different views, the execution of policy will in general be in the hands of intellectuals, and it is frequently the decision on the detail which determines the net effect. We find this illustrated in almost all fields of contemporary society. Newspapers in 'capitalist' ownership, universities presided over by 'reactionary' governing bodies, broadcasting systems owned by conservative governments, have all been known to influence public opinion in the direction of socialism, because this was the conviction of the personnel. This has often happened not only in spite of but perhaps even because of the attempts of those at the top to control opinion and to impose principles of orthodoxy.

The effect of this filtering of ideas through the convictions of a class which is constitutionally disposed to certain views is by no means confined to the masses. Outside his special field the expert is generally no less dependent on this class and scarcely less influenced by their selection. The result of this is that today in most parts of the Western world even the most determined opponents of socialism derive from socialist sources their knowledge on most subjects on which they have no firsthand information. With many of the more general preconceptions of socialist thought the connection with their more practical proposals is by no means at once obvious, and in consequence many men who believe themselves to be determined opponents of that system of thought become in fact effective spreaders of its ideas. Who does not know the practical man who in his own field denounces socialism as 'pernicious rot', but when he steps outside his subject spouts socialism like any Left journalist?

In no other field has the predominant influence of the socialist intellectuals been felt more strongly during the last hundred years than in the contacts between different national civilizations. It would go far beyond the limits of this article to trace the causes and significance of the highly important fact that in the modern world the intellectuals provide almost the only approach to an international community. It is this which mainly accounts for the extraordinary spectacle that for generations the supposedly 'capitalist' West has been lending its moral and material support almost exclusively to those ideological movements in the countries farther east which have aimed at undermining Western civilization; and that at the same time the information which the Western public has obtained about events in Central and Eastern Europe has almost inevitably been coloured by a socialist bias. Many of the 'educational' activities of the American forces of occupation in Germany have furnished clear and recent examples of this tendency.

IV

A proper understanding of the reasons which tend to incline so many of the intellectuals towards socialism is thus most important. The first point here which those who do not share this bias ought to face frankly is that it is neither selfish interests nor evil intentions but mostly honest convictions and good intentions which determine the intellectuals' views. In fact it is necessary to recognize that on the whole the typical intellectual is today more likely to be a socialist the more he is guided by good will and intelligence, and that on the plane of purely intellectual argument he will generally be able to make out a better case than the majority of his opponents within his class. If we still think him wrong we must recognize that it may be genuine error which leads the well-meaning and intelligent people who occupy those key positions in our society to spread views which to us appear a threat to our civilization.[2] Nothing could be more important than to try to understand the sources of this error in order that we should be able to counter it. Yet those who are generally regarded as the representatives of the existing order and who believe that they comprehend the dangers of socialism are usually very far from such understanding. They tend to regard the socialist intellectuals as nothing more than a pernicious bunch of high-brow radicals without appreciating their influence, and, by their whole attitude to them, tend to drive them even further into opposition to the existing order.

If we are to understand this peculiar bias of a large section of the intellectuals we must be clear about two points. The first is that they generally judge all particular issues exclusively in the light of certain general ideas; the second that the characteristic errors of any age are frequently derived from some genuine new truths it has discovered, and that they are erroneous applications of new generalizations which have proved their value in other fields. The conclusion to which we shall be led by a full consideration of these facts will be that the effective refutation of such errors will frequently require further intellectual advance, and often advance on points which are very abstract and may seem very remote from the practical issues.

It is perhaps the most characteristic feature of the intellectual that he

---

[2] It was therefore not (as has been suggested by one reviewer of *The Road to Serfdom*, Professor J. Schumpeter) 'politeness to a fault' but profound conviction of the importance of this which made me, in Professor Schumpeter's words, 'hardly ever attribute to opponents anything beyond intellectual error'.

judges new ideas not by their specific merits but by the readiness with which they fit into his general conceptions, into the picture of the world which he regards as modern or advanced. It is through their influence on him and on his choice of opinions on particular issues that the power of ideas for good and evil grows in proportion with their generality, abstractness, and even vagueness. As he knows little about the particular issues, his criterion must be consistency with his other views, suitability to combine them into a coherent picture of the world. Yet this selection from the multitude of new ideas presenting themselves at every moment creates the characteristic climate of opinion, the dominant *Weltanschauung*, of a period which will be favourable to the reception of some opinions and unfavourable to others, and which will make the intellectual readily accept one conclusion and reject another without a real understanding of the issues.

In some respects the intellectual is indeed closer to the philosopher than to any specialist, and the philosopher is in more than one sense a sort of prince among the intellectuals. Although his influence is further removed from practical affairs and correspondingly slower and more difficult to trace than that of the ordinary intellectual, it is of the same kind and in the long run even more powerful than that of the latter. It is the same endeavour towards a synthesis, pursued more methodically, the same judgment of particular views in so far as they fit into a general system of thought rather than by their specific merits, the same striving after a consistent world view, which for both forms the main basis for accepting or rejecting ideas. For this reason the philosopher has probably a greater influence over the intellectuals than any other scholar or scientist, and more than anyone else determines the manner in which the intellectuals exercise their censorship function. The popular influence of the scientific specialist begins to rival that of the philosopher only when he ceases to be a specialist and commences to philosophize about the progress of his subject—and usually only after he has been taken up by the intellectuals for reasons which have little to do with his scientific eminence.

The 'climate of opinion' of any period is thus essentially a set of very general preconceptions by which the intellectual judges the importance of new facts and opinions. These preconceptions are mainly applications to what seem to him the most significant aspects of scientific achievements, a transfer to other fields of what has particularly impressed him in the work of the specialists. One could give a long list of such intellectual fashions and catchwords which in the course of two or three generations have in turn dominated the thinking of the intellectuals. Whether it was

[185]

the 'historical approach' or the theory of evolution, nineteenth-century determinism and the belief in the predominant influence of environment as against heredity, the theory of relativity or the belief in the power of the unconscious—every one of these general conceptions has been made the touchstone by which innovations in different fields have been tested. It seems as if the less specific or precise (or the less understood) these ideas are, the wider may be their influence. Sometimes it is no more than a vague impression rarely put into words which thus wields a profound influence. Such beliefs as that deliberate control or conscious organization is also in social affairs always superior to the results of spontaneous processes which are not directed by a human mind, or that any order based on a plan laid down beforehand must be better than one formed by the balancing of opposing forces, have in this way profoundly affected political development.

Only apparently different is the role of the intellectuals where the development of more properly social ideals is concerned. Here their peculiar propensities manifest themselves in making shibboleths of abstractions, in rationalizing and carrying to extremes certain ambitions which spring from the normal intercourse of men. Since democracy is a good thing, the further the democratic principle can be carried, the better it appears to them. The most powerful of these general ideas which have shaped political development in recent times is of course the ideal of material equality. It is, characteristically, not one of the spontaneously grown moral convictions, first applied in the relations between particular individuals, but an intellectual construction originally conceived in the abstract and of doubtful meaning or application in particular instances. Nevertheless, it has operated strongly as a principle of selection among the alternative courses of social policy, exercising a persistent pressure towards an arrangement of social affairs which nobody clearly conceives. That a particular measure tends to bring about greater equality has come to be regarded as so strong a recommendation that little else will be considered. Since on each particular issue it is this one aspect on which those who guide opinion have a definite conviction, the ideal of equality has determined social change even more strongly than its advocates intended.

Not only moral ideals act in this manner, however. Sometimes the attitudes of the intellectuals towards the problems of social order may be the consequence of advances in purely scientific knowledge; and it is in such instances that their erroneous views on particular issues may for a time seem to have all the prestige of the latest scientific achievements behind them. It is not in itself surprising that a genuine advance of knowledge should in this manner become on occasion a source of new error. If no false conclusions followed from new generalizations they would be final truths which would never need revision. Although as a rule such a new generalization will merely share the false consequences which can be drawn from it with the views which were held before, and thus not lead to *new* error, it is quite likely that a new theory, just as its value is shown by the valid new conclusions to which it leads, will produce other new conclusions which further advance will show to have been erroneous. But in such an instance a false belief will appear with all the prestige of a result of the latest scientific knowledge. Although in the particular field to which this belief is applied, all the scientific evidence may be against it, it will nevertheless, before the tribunal of the intellectuals and in the light of the ideas which govern their thinking, be selected as the view which is best in accord with the spirit of the time. The specialists who will thus achieve public fame and wide influence will thus not be those who have gained recognition by their peers, but will often be men whom the other experts regard as cranks, amateurs, or even frauds, but who in the eyes of the general public nevertheless become the best-known exponents of their subject.

In particular, there can be little doubt that the manner in which during the last hundred years man has learned to organize the forces of nature has contributed a great deal towards the creation of the belief that a similar control of the forces of society would bring comparable improvements in human conditions. That, with the application of engineering techniques, the direction of all forms of human activity according to a single coherent plan should prove to be as successful in society as it has been in innumerable engineering tasks, is too plausible a conclusion not to seduce most of those who are elated by the achievement of the natural sciences. It must indeed be admitted both that it would require powerful arguments to counter the strong presumption in favour of such a conclusion and that these arguments have not yet been adequately stated. It is not sufficient to point out the defects of particular proposals based on this kind of reasoning. The argument will not lose its force until it has been conclusively shown why what has proved so eminently successful in producing advances in so many fields should have limits to its usefulness and become positively harmful if extended beyond those limits. This is a task which has not yet been satisfactorily performed and which will have to be achieved before this particular impulse towards socialism can be removed.

This, of course, is only one of many instances where further intellectual advance is needed if the harmful ideas at present current are to be refuted, and where the course which we shall travel will ultimately be decided by the discussion of very abstract issues. It is not enough for the man of affairs to be sure, from his intimate knowledge of a particular field, that the theories of socialism which are derived from more general ideas will prove impracticable. He may be perfectly right, and yet his resistance will be overwhelmed and all the sorry consequences which he foresees will follow if he is not supported by an effective refutation of the *idées mères*. So long as the intellectual gets the better of the general argument, the most valid objections to the specific issue will be brushed aside.

V

This is not the whole story, however. The forces which influence recruitment to the ranks of the intellectuals operate in the same direction and help to explain why so many of the most able among them lean towards socialism. There are of course as many differences of opinion among intellectuals as among other groups of people; but it seems to be true that it is on the whole the more active, intelligent, and original men among the intellectuals who most frequently incline towards socialism, while its opponents are often of an inferior calibre. This is true particularly during the early stages of the infiltration of socialist ideas; later, although outside intellectual circles it may still be an act of courage to profess socialist convictions, the pressure of opinion among intellectuals will often be so strongly in favour of socialism that it requires more strength and independence of mind to resist it than to join in what one's fellows regard as modern views. Nobody, for instance, who is familiar with large numbers of university faculties (and from this point of view the majority of university teachers probably have to be classed as intellectuals rather than as experts) can be oblivious of the fact that the most brilliant and successful teachers are today more likely than not to be socialists, while those who hold more conservative political views are as frequently mediocrities. This is of course by itself an important factor leading the younger generation into the socialist camp.

The socialist will, of course, see in this merely a proof that the more intelligent person is today bound to become a socialist. But this is far from being the necessary or even the most likely explanation. The main reason for this state of affairs is probably that, for the exceptionally able man who accepts the present order of society, a multitude of other avenues to influence and power are open, while to the disaffected and dissatisfied an intellectual career is the path both to influence and to power that promises to contribute most to the achievement of his ideals. Even more than that: the more conservatively inclined man of first-class ability will in general choose intellectual work (and the sacrifice in material reward which this choice usually entails) only if he enjoys it for its own sake. He is in consequence more likely to become an expert scholar rather than an intellectual in the specific sense of the word; while to the more radically minded the intellectual pursuit is more often than not a means rather than an end, a path to exactly that kind of wide influence which the professional intellectual exercises. It is therefore probably a fact, not that the more intelligent people are generally socialists, but that a much higher proportion of socialists among the best minds devote themselves to those intellectual pursuits which in modern society give them a decisive influence on public opinion.[3]

The selection of the personnel of the intellectuals is also closely connected with the predominant interest which they show in general and abstract ideas. Speculations about a possible entire reconstruction of society give the intellectual a fare much more to his taste than the more practical and short-run considerations of those who aim at a piecemeal improvement of the existing order. In particular, socialist thought owes its appeal to the young largely to its visionary character; the very courage to indulge in Utopian thought is in this respect a source of strength to the socialists which traditional liberalism sadly lacks. This difference operates in favour of socialism, not only because speculation about general principles provides an opportunity for the play of the imagination of those who are unencumbered by much knowledge of the facts of present-day life, but also because it satisfies a legitimate desire for the understanding of the rational basis of any social order and gives scope for the exercise of that constructive urge for which liberalism, after it had won its great victories, left few outlets. The intellectual, by his whole disposition, is uninterested in technical details or practical difficulties. What appeals to him are the broad visions, the specious comprehension of the social order as a whole which a planned system promises.

This fact that the tastes of the intellectual are better satisfied by the speculations of the socialists proved fatal to the influence of the liberal

[3] Related to this is another familar phenomenon: there is little reason to believe that really first-class intellectual ability for original work is any rarer among Gentiles than among Jews. Yet there can be little doubt that men of Jewish stock almost everywhere constitute a disproportionately large number of the intellectuals in our sense, that is of the ranks of the professional interpreters of ideas. This may be their special gift and certainly is their main opportunity in countries where prejudice puts obstacles in their way in other fields. It is probably more because they constitute so large a proportion of the intellectuals than for any other reason that they seem to be so much more receptive to socialist ideas than people of different stocks.

tradition. Once the basic demands of the liberal programmes seemed satisfied, the liberal thinkers of the old type turned to problems of detail and tended to neglect the development of the general philosophy of liberalism, which in consequence ceased to be a live issue offering scope for general speculation. Thus, for something over half a century, it has been only the socialists who have offered anything like an explicit programme of social development, a picture of the kind of future society at which they were aiming, and a set of general principles to guide decisions on particular issues. Even though, if I am right, their ideals suffer from inherent contradictions, and any attempt to put them into practice must produce something utterly different from what they expect, this does not alter the fact that their programme for change is the only one which in recent times has actually influenced the development of social institutions. It is because theirs has become the only explicit general philosophy of social policy held by a large group, the only system or theory which raises new problems and opens new horizons, that they have succeeded in inspiring the imagination of the intellectuals.

The actual developments of society during this period were determined, not by a battle of conflicting ideals, but by the contrast between an existing state of affairs and that one ideal of a possible future society which the socialists were the only ones to hold up before the public. Very few of the other programmes which offered themselves provided genuine alternatives. Most of them were mere compromises or half-way houses between the more extreme types of socialism and the existing order. All that was needed to make almost any socialist proposal appear reasonable to those 'judicious' minds who were constitutionally convinced that the truth must always lie in the middle between the extremes, was for someone to advocate a sufficiently more extreme proposal. There seemed to exist only one direction in which we could move, and the only question seemed to be how fast and how far the movement should proceed.

VI

The significance of the special appeal to the intellectuals which socialism derives from its speculative character will become clearer if we contrast further the position of the socialist theorist with that of his counterpart who is a liberal in the old sense of the word. This comparison will also lead us to whatever lesson we can draw from an adequate appreciation of the intellectual forces which are undermining the foundations of a free society.

Paradoxically enough, one of the main handicaps which deprive the liberal thinker of popular influence is closely connected with the fact that until socialism had actually arrived he had more opportunity of directly influencing decisions on current policy and that in consequence he was not only not tempted into that long-run speculation which is the strength of the socialists, but was actually discouraged from it, because any effort of this kind is likely to reduce the immediate good he can do. Whatever power he has to influence practical decisions he owes to his standing with the representatives of the existing order, and this standing he would endanger if he devoted himself to the kind of speculation which would appeal to the intellectuals and which through them could influence developments over longer periods. In order to carry weight with the powers that be he has to be 'practical', 'sensible', and 'realistic'. So long as he concerns himself with immediate issues he is rewarded with influence, material success, and popularity with those who up to a point share his general outlook. But these men have little respect for those speculations on general principles which shape the intellectual climate. Indeed, if he seriously indulges in such long-run speculation he is apt to acquire the reputation of being 'unsound' or even half a socialist, because he is unwilling to identify the existing order with the free system at which he aims.[4]

If, in spite of this, his efforts continue in the direction of general speculation, he soon discovers that it is unsafe to associate too closely with those who seem to share most of his convictions and he is soon driven into isolation. Indeed, there can be few more thankless tasks at present than the essential one of developing the philosophical foundation on which the further development of a free society must be based. Since the man who undertakes it must accept much of the framework of the existing order, he will appear to many of the more speculatively minded intellectuals merely as a timid apologist of things as they are; at the same time he will be dismissed by the men of affairs as an unpractical theorist. He is not radical enough for those who know only the world where 'with ease together dwell the thoughts' and much too radical for those who see only how 'hard in space together clash the things'. If he takes advantage of such support as he can get from the men of affairs, he will

---

[4] The most glaring recent example of such condemnation of a somewhat unorthodox liberal work as 'socialist' has been provided by some comments on the late Henry Simons' *Economic Policy for a Free Society* (1948). One need not agree with the whole of this work, and one may even regard some of the suggestions made in it as incompatible with a free society, and yet recognize it as one of the most important contributions made in recent times to our problem and as just the kind of work which is required to get discussion started on the fundamental issues. Even those who violently disagree with some of its suggestions should welcome it as a contribution which clearly and courageously raises the central problems of our time.

almost certainly discredit himself with those on whom he depends for the spreading of his ideas. At the same time he will need most carefully to avoid anything resembling extravagance or over-statement. While no socialist theorist has ever been known to discredit himself with his fellows even by the silliest of proposals, the old-fashioned liberal will damn himself by an impracticable suggestion. Yet for the intellectuals he will still not be speculative or adventurous enough, and the changes and improvements in the social structure he will have to offer will seem limited in comparison with what their less restrained imagination conceives.

At least in a society in which the main requisites of freedom have already been won and further improvements must concern points of comparative detail, the liberal programme can have none of the glamour of a new invention. The appreciation of the improvements it has to offer requires more knowledge of the working of the existing society than the average intellectual possesses. The discussion of these improvements must proceed on a more practical level than that of the more revolutionary programmes, thus giving it a complexion which has little appeal for the intellectual and tending to bring in elements to whom he feels directly antagonistic. Those who are most familiar with the working of the present society are also usually interested in the preservation of particular features of that society which may not be defensible on general principles. Unlike the person who looks for an entirely new future order and who naturally turns for guidance to the theorist, the men who believe in the existing order also usually think that they understand it much better than any theorist and in consequence are likely to reject whatever is unfamiliar and theoretical.

The difficulty of finding genuine and disinterested support for a systematic policy for freedom is not new. In a passage of which the reception of a recent book of mine has often reminded me, Lord Acton long ago described how 'at all times sincere friends of freedom have been rare, and its triumphs have been due to minorities, that have prevailed by associating themselves with auxiliaries whose objects differed from their own; and this association, which is always dangerous, has been sometimes disastrous, by giving to opponents just grounds of opposition . . .'[5] More recently, one of the most distinguished living American economists has complained in a similar vein that the main task of those who believe in the basic principles of the capitalist system must frequently be to defend this system against the capitalists—indeed the great liberal economists, from Adam Smith to the present, have always known this.

[5] Acton, *The History of Freedom*, London, 1922

The most serious obstacle which separates the practical men who have the cause of freedom genuinely at heart from those forces which in the realm of ideas decide the course of development is their deep distrust of theoretical speculation and their tendency to orthodoxy; this, more than anything else, creates an almost impassable barrier between them and those intellectuals who are devoted to the same cause and whose assistance is indispensable if the cause is to prevail. Although this tendency is perhaps natural among men who defend a system because it has justified itself in practice, and to whom its intellectual justification seems immaterial, it is fatal to its survival because it deprives it of the support it most needs. Orthodoxy of any kind, any pretence that a system of ideas is final and must be unquestioningly accepted as a whole, is the one view which of necessity antagonizes all intellectuals, whatever their views on particular issues. Any system which judges men by the completeness of their conformity to a fixed set of opinions, by their 'soundness' or the extent to which they can be relied upon to hold approved views on all points, deprives itself of a support without which no set of ideas can maintain its influence in modern society. The ability to criticize accepted views, to explore new vistas and to experiment with new conceptions, provides the atmosphere without which the intellectual cannot breathe. A cause which offers no scope for these traits can have no support from him and is thereby doomed in any society which, like ours, rests on his services.

VII

It may be that a free society as we have known it carries in itself the forces of its own destruction, that once freedom has been achieved it is taken for granted and ceases to be valued, and that the free growth of ideas which is the essence of a free society will bring about the destruction of the foundations on which it depends. There can be little doubt that in countries like the United States the ideal of freedom has today less real appeal for the young than it has in countries where they have learnt what its loss means. On the other hand, there is every sign that in Germany and elsewhere, to the young men who have never known a free society, the task of constructing one can become as exciting and fascinating as any socialist scheme which has appeared during the last hundred years. It is an extraordinary fact, though one which many visitors have experienced, that in speaking to German students about the principles of a liberal society one finds a more responsive and even enthusiastic audience than one can hope to find in any of the Western democracies.

[193]

In Britain also there is already appearing among the young a new interest in the principles of true liberalism which certainly did not exist a few years ago.

Does this mean that freedom is valued only when it is lost, that the world must everywhere go through a dark phase of socialist totalitarianism before the forces of freedom can gather strength anew? It may be so, but I hope it need not be. Yet so long as the people who over longer periods determine public opinion continue to be attracted by the ideals of socialism, the trend will continue. If we are to avoid such a development we must be able to offer a new liberal programme which appeals to the imagination. We must make the building of a free society once more an intellectual adventure, a deed of courage. What we lack is a liberal Utopia, a programme which seems neither a mere defence of things as they are nor a diluted kind of socialism, but a truly liberal radicalism which does not spare the susceptibilities of the mighty (including the trade unions), which is not too severely practical and which does not confine itself to what appears today as politically possible. We need intellectual leaders who are prepared to resist the blandishments of power and influence and who are willing to work for an ideal, however small may be the prospects of its early realization. They must be men who are willing to stick to principles and to fight for their full realization, however remote. The practical compromises they must leave to the politicians. Free trade and freedom of opportunity are ideals which still may arouse the imaginations of large numbers, but a mere 'reasonable freedom of trade' or a mere 'relaxation of controls' is neither intellectually respectable nor likely to inspire any enthusiasm.

The main lesson which the true liberal must learn from the success of the socialists is that it was their courage to be Utopian which gained them the support of the intellectuals and thereby an influence on public opinion which is daily making possible what only recently seemed utterly remote. Those who have concerned themselves exclusively with what seemed practicable in the existing state of opinion have constantly found that even this has rapidly become politically impossible as the result of changes in a public opinion which they have done nothing to guide. Unless we can make the philosophic foundations of a free society once more a living intellectual issue, and its implementation a task which challenges the ingenuity and imagination of our liveliest minds, the prospects of freedom are indeed dark. But if we can regain that belief in the power of ideas which was the mark of liberalism at its best, the battle is not lost. The intellectual revival of liberalism is already under way in many parts of the world. Will it be in time?

CHAPTER THIRTEEN

*The Transmission of the Ideals of Economic Freedom**

At the end of the First World War the spiritual tradition of liberalism was all but dead. True, it was still uppermost in the thoughts of many a leading figure of public and business life, many of whom belonged to a generation which took liberal thought for granted. Their public pronouncements sometimes led the general public to believe that a return to a liberal economy was the ultimate goal desired by the majority of leading men. But the intellectual forces then at work had begun to point in quite a different direction. Anyone familiar, thirty years ago, with the thought of the coming generation and especially with the views propounded to the students in their universities, could foresee developments very different from those still hoped for by some of the public figures and the press of the time. There was no longer, at that time, a living world of liberal thought which could have fired the imagination of the young.

Nonetheless, the main body of liberal thought has been safeguarded through that eclipse in the intellectual history of liberalism which lasted throughout the fifteen or twenty years following the First World War; indeed, during that very period the foundations were laid for a new development. This was due, almost exclusively, to the activities of a handful of men about whom I wish to say something here. No doubt, they were not the only ones striving to uphold the liberal tradition. But it seems to me that these men, each working alone and independently of the others, were the only ones who succeeded, by their teaching, in

* First published in German as a tribute to L. v. Mises on his seventieth birthday, which it was known he did not wish to see formally noticed, in the *Schweizer Monatshefte*, Vol. 31, No. 6, 1951, and later in an English translation in *The Owl*, London, 1951. I should not have wished to reprint this somewhat hastily written occasional piece, if with all its imperfections and errors of translation it had not already been used as a historical source, so that it seems desirable to make a corrected version available.

creating the new traditions which more recently have again united in one common stream. The circumstances surrounding the lives of the past generation make it hardly surprising that it should have taken so long for the like-minded efforts of an Englishman, an Austrian and an American to be recognized as such and to be built into the common foundation for the following generation's work. But the new liberal school which does now exist and about which there will be more to say, consciously builds upon the work of these men.

The oldest, and perhaps the least known outside his own country, was the Englishman, Edwin Cannan, who died nearly twenty years ago. The part he played is little known beyond a rather narrow circle. The reason for this may be that his main interests really lay elsewhere and that he dealt with questions of economic policy only in occasional writings; or it may be, perhaps, that he was more interested in practical details than in the basic philosophical questions. Many of his economic essays which he published in two volumes, *The Economic Outlook* (1912) and *An Economist's Protest* (1927), deserve, even now, renewed and wider attention, and translation into other languages. Their simplicity, clarity and sound common sense make them models for the treatment of economic problems, and even some that were written before 1914 are still astonishingly topical. Cannan's greatest merit, however, was the training, over many years, of a group of pupils at the London School of Economics: it was they who later formed what probably became the most important centre of the new liberalism—though, it is true, at a time when such a development had already been got under way by the work of the Austrian economist of whom we shall presently speak. But first let us say a little more about Cannan's pupils. The oldest is the well-known financial expert, Sir Theodore Gregory. For many years, when holding a chair at the London School of Economics, he too wielded great influence on academic youth; but he gave up teaching a good many years ago. It was Lionel Robbins, who now has held Cannan's chair for twenty-two years, who became the real nucleus of a group of younger economists all very nearly the same age, which emerged at the London School of Economics during the 'thirties. Owing to a rare combination of literary talent and a gift for organizing his material, his writings have found a very wide circulation. Robbins' colleague, Sir Arnold Plant, has been teaching at the School nearly as long. He, even more than Cannan himself, is wont to hide away his most important contributions in little-known occasional publications, and all his friends have long been looking forward eagerly to a book about the foundations and significance of private property. If he ever publishes it, it should become one of the most important contributions to the theory of modern liberalism. We cannot here list all Cannan's pupils who have contributed to the discussion of our problems; just to give an impression of the scope of his influence, let us add the names of F. C. Benham, W. H. Hutt and F. W. Paish—even though the latter was not Cannan's student, he belongs to the same circle.

It could be said with some justification that Cannan really prepared the ground, in England, for the reception of the ideas of a much younger Austrian who has been working since the early 'twenties on the reconstruction of a solid edifice of liberal thought in a more determined, systematic and successful way than anyone else. This is Ludwig von Mises who worked first in Vienna, then in Geneva, and who is still very actively at work now in New York. Even before the First World War Mises had become known for his work on monetary theory. Immediately after the war, his prophetic book *Nation, Staat und Wirtschaft* (1919) initiated a development which reached its first peak as early as 1922 in *Die Gemeinwirtschaft*,[1] a comprehensive critique of socialism—and at that time, that meant a critique of all the ideologies of any serious consequence in the literature of economic policy.

There is no space here to give the long list of important writings which intervened between this and Mises's second main work which appeared in 1941 in Geneva. This was written in German and was originally called *Nationalökonomie*; its revised American edition, *Human Action*, has achieved almost unique success for a theoretical treatise of such size. Mises's work as a whole covers far more than economics in the narrower sense. His penetrating studies of the philosophical foundations of the social sciences and his remarkable historical knowledge place his work much closer to that of the great eighteenth-century moral philosophers than to the writings of contemporary economists. Mises was strongly attacked from the very beginning because of his relentlessly uncompromising attitude; he made enemies and, above all, did not find academic recognition until late. Yet his work has wielded an influence which is the more lasting and the more extensive for all its slow beginnings. Even some of Mises's own pupils were often inclined to consider as 'exaggerated' that unfaltering tenacity with which he pursued his reasoning to its utmost conclusions; but the apparent pessimism which he habitually displayed in his judgment of the consequences of the economic policies of his time has proved right over and over again, and eventually an ever-widening circle came to appreciate

[1] Translated into English by Jacques Kahane, under the title *Socialism*, London, Jonathan Cape, 1936.

the fundamental importance of his writings which ran counter to the main stream of contemporary thought in nearly every respect. Even when still in Vienna, Mises did not lack close disciples most of whom are now in the United States, like Mises himself; they include Gottfried Haberler (Harvard University), Fritz Machlup (Johns Hopkins University), and the present writer. But Mises's influence now reaches beyond the personal sphere to a far greater extent than does that of the other two main personalities with whom we are here concerned. He alone of them has given us a comprehensive treatment ranging over the whole economic and social field. We may or may not agree with him on details, but there is hardly an important question in these fields about which his readers would fail to find real instruction and stimulation.

Mises' influence became important not only for the London group, but equally so for the third, the Chicago, group. This group owes its origins to Professor Frank H. Knight of the University of Chicago, who is Mises's junior by a few years. Like Mises, Knight owes his original reputation to a theoretical monograph; notwithstanding an early lack of recognition, the latter's *Risk, Uncertainty and Profit* (1921) eventually became, and for many years continued to be, one of the most influential textbooks on economic theory, although it had not originally been designed as such. Knight has since written a great deal on questions of economic policy and social philosophy—mostly in articles the majority of which have since been republished in book form. The best-known, and perhaps also the most characteristic, volume is *The Ethics of Competition and other Essays* (1935). Knight's personal influence, through his teaching, exceeds even the influence of his writings. It is hardly an exaggeration to state that nearly all the younger American economists who really understand and advocate a competitive economic system have at one time been Knight's students. From the point of view which interests us here the most important of these was Henry C. Simons, whose untimely and early death we mourn. In the 'thirties his pamphlet, *A Positive Program for Laissez Faire*, offered a new and common basis for the aspirations of America's young liberals. Hopes for a systematic and comprehensive work from Simons were disappointed; instead, he left a collection of essays which appeared in 1948 under the title *Economic Policy for a Free Society*. This book became very influential owing to its wealth of ideas and to the courage with which Simons discussed such delicate problems as trade unionism. Today, the nucleus of a group of like-minded economists—no longer confined to Chicago—is formed by Simons' closest friend, Aaron Director, and two of the best-known younger American theoreticians, George Stigler and Milton

Friedman. Director has edited Simons' papers and carried on his work.

Alas, good manners make it impossible to claim a great nation's head of State for any particular economic school;[2] I should, otherwise, name a fourth scientist whose influence in his own country is of comparable consequence. Instead, I shall complete the picture by turning at once to the last group which interests us here.[3] It is a German group, and differs from the others in that its origin cannot be traced back directly to any great figure of the preceding generation. It came into being through the association of a number of younger men whose common interest in a liberal economic system brought them together during the years preceding Hitler's seizure of power. There can be no doubt that this group too received decisive stimulus from Mises' writings. This group had not yet made its mark in economic literature by 1933, and at that time some of its members had to leave Germany. There remained, however, one of the group's oldest members, Walter Eucken, who was then as yet relatively little known. Today we realize that his sudden death a little over a year ago robbed the liberal revival of one of its really great men. He had matured slowly, had long refrained from publication and had mainly devoted himself to teaching and to practical problems. It was not until after Germany's collapse that it became apparent how fruitful and beneficial his quiet activities had been during the National Socialist period; for only then was the circle of his friends and students in Germany revealed as the most important bulwark of rational economic thinking. That was also the time when Eucken's first major work began to spread its influence and when he undertook the exposition of his whole economic thought in several other works. The future will show how much of this remains to be recovered from the papers he left at his

[2] The reference is, of course, to the late Luigi Einaudi, at the time when this article appeared President of the Italian Republic.

[3] In the original version of this sketch I unpardonably omitted to mention a promising beginning of this liberal renaissance which, though cut short by the outbreak of war in 1939, provided many of the personal contacts which after the war were to form the basis of a renewed effort on an international scale. In 1937 Walter Lippmann had delighted and encouraged all liberals by the publication of his brilliant restatement of the fundamental ideals of classic liberalism in his book *The Good Society*. Recognizing the importance of this work as a possible rallying point of dispersed efforts, Professor Louis Rougier of the University of Paris called a symposium at which at the end of August 1938 about twenty-five students of public affairs from several European countries and the United States met at Paris to discuss the principles stated by Lippmann. They included Louis Baudin, Walter Lippmann, Ludwig von Mises, Michael Polanyi, Lionel Robbins, Wilhelm Röpke, Alexander Rüstow, Marcel van Zeeland and the present author. The meeting approved the proposal for the creation of a Centre International des Etudes pour la Rénovation du Libéralisme—but when its report appeared in print (*Colloque Walter Lippmann*, Paris, 1939), only a few weeks were left before the outbreak of the Second World War and the consequent suspension of all efforts of this kind.

death. The annual *Ordo* which he founded continues to be the most important publication of the entire movement.

The second leading figure of this German group, Wilhelm Röpke, had been in close contact with Eucken from the beginning. By 1933, Röpke had made such a mark in public life that his stay in Hitler's Germany immediately became impossible. He went to Istanbul first, and has now been in Switzerland for many years. He is the most active and the most prolific writer of the whole group and has become known to a wide public.

If the existence of a neo-liberal movement is known far beyond the narrow circles of experts, the credit belongs mainly to Röpke, at least so far as the German-speaking public is concerned.

It has been said above that all these groups which came into being in the course of the last quarter of a century did not really get to know each other until after the Second World War. We then witnessed a lively exchange of ideas. Today, it has almost become a matter of history to speak of separate national groups. For that very reason, this is perhaps the right moment to give a brief outline of this development. Gone is the day when the few remaining liberals each went his own way in solitude and derision; gone the day when they found no response among the young. On the contrary, they bear a heavy responsibility now, because the new generation demands to be told of liberalism's answers to the great problems of our time. An integrated structure of liberal thought is required and its application to the problems of different countries needs to be worked out. This will only be possible by a meeting of minds within a large group. There remain serious difficulties, in many countries, with regard to the dissemination of the available literature, and the lack of translations of some of the most important works still stands in the way of a more rapid propagation of these ideas. But there is, today, personal contact between most of their supporters. Twice already Switzerland has been host to the informal, yet cohesive group which met there for the common study of its problems and whose name derives from a Swiss place-name. Another meeting took place in Holland in 1950, and a fourth conference in France in 1951.

The period which we have discussed in this paper can, then, be regarded as closed. Thirty years ago liberalism may still have had some influence among public men, but it had well-nigh disappeared as a spiritual movement. Today its practical influence may be scant, but its problems have once more become a living body of thought. We may feel justified in looking forward with renewed faith to the future of liberalism.

CHAPTER FOURTEEN

*History and Politics**

Political opinion and views about historical events ever have been and always must be closely connected. Past experience is the foundation on which our beliefs about the desirability of different policies and institutions are mainly based, and our present political views inevitably affect and colour our interpretation of the past. Yet, if it is too pessimistic a view that man learns nothing from history, it may well be questioned whether he always learns the truth. While the events of the past are the source of the experience of the human race, their opinions are determined not by the objective facts but by the records and interpretations to which they have access. Few men will deny that our views about the goodness or badness of different institutions are largely determined by what we believe to have been their effects in the past. There is scarcely a political ideal or concept which does not involve opinions about a whole series of past events, and there are few historical memories which do not serve as a symbol of some political aim. Yet the historical beliefs which guide us in the present are not always in accord with the facts; sometimes they are even the effects rather than the cause of political beliefs. Historical myths have perhaps played nearly as great a role in shaping opinion as historical facts. Yet we can hardly hope to profit from past experience unless the facts from which we draw our conclusions are correct.

The influence which the writers of history thus exercise on public opinion is probably more immediate and extensive than that of the political theorists who launch new ideas. It seems as though even such new ideas reach wider circles usually not in their abstract form but as the

---

* Introduction to *Capitalism and the Historians*. Essays by T. S. Ashton, L. M. Hacker, W. H. Hutt, and B. de Jouvenel. London and Chicago, 1954.

interpretations of particular events. The historian is in this respect at least one step nearer to direct power over public opinion than is the theorist. And long before the professional historian takes up his pen, current controversy about recent events will have created a definite picture, or perhaps several different pictures, of these events which will affect contemporary discussion as much as any division on the merits of new issues.

This profound influence which current views about history have on political opinion is today perhaps less understood than it was in the past. One reason for this probably is the pretension of many modern historians to be purely scientific and completely free from all political prejudice. There can be no question, of course, that this is an imperative duty of the scholar in so far as historical research, that is, the ascertainment of the facts, is concerned. There is indeed no legitimate reason why, in answering questions of fact, historians of different political opinions should not be able to agree. But at the very beginning, in deciding which questions are worth asking, individual value judgments are bound to come in. And it is more than doubtful whether a connected history of a period or of a set of events could be written without interpreting these in the light, not only of theories about the interconnection of social processes, but also of definite values—or at least whether such a history would be worth reading. Historiography, as distinguished from historical research, is not only at least as much an art as a science; the writer who attempts it without being aware that his task is one of interpretation in the light of definite values also will succeed merely in deceiving himself and will become the victim of his unconscious prejudices.

There is perhaps no better illustration of the manner in which for more than a century the whole political ethos of a nation, and for a shorter time of most of the Western world, was shaped by the writings of a group of historians than the influence exercised by the English 'Whig interpretation of history'. It is probably no exaggeration to say that, for every person who had firsthand acquaintance with the writings of the political philosophers who founded the liberal tradition, there were fifty or a hundred who had absorbed it from the writings of men like Hallam and Macaulay, or Grote and Lord Acton. It is significant that the modern English historian who more than any other has endeavoured to discredit this Whig tradition later came to write that 'those who, perhaps in the misguided austerity of youth, wish to drive out that Whig interpretation . . . are sweeping a room which humanly speaking cannot long remain empty. They are opening the doors for seven devils which, precisely because they are newcomers, are bound to be worse than this first.'[1] And, although he still suggests that 'Whig history' was 'wrong' history, he emphasizes that it 'was one of our assets' and that 'it had a wonderful effect on English politics'.[2]

Whether in any relevant sense 'Whig history' really was wrong history is a matter on which the last word has probably not yet been said but which we cannot discuss here. Its beneficial effect in creating the essentially liberal atmosphere of the nineteenth century is beyond doubt and was certainly not due to any misrepresentation of facts. It was mainly political history, and the chief facts on which it was based were known beyond question. It may not stand up in all respects to modern standards of historical research, but it certainly gave the generations brought up on it a true sense of the value of the political liberty which their ancestors had achieved for them, and it served them as a guide in preserving that achievement.

The Whig interpretation of history has gone out of fashion with the decline of liberalism. But it is more than doubtful whether, because history now claims to be more scientific, it has become a more reliable or trustworthy guide in those fields where it has exercised most influence on political views. Political history indeed has lost much of the power and fascination it had in the nineteenth century; and it is doubtful whether any historical work of our time has had a circulation or direct influence comparable with, say, T. B. Macaulay's *History of England*. Yet the extent to which our present political views are coloured by historical beliefs has certainly not diminished. As interest has shifted from the constitutional to the social and economic field, so the historical beliefs which act as driving forces are now mainly beliefs about economic history. It is probably justifiable to speak of a socialist interpretation of history which has governed political thinking for the last two or three generations and which consists mainly of a particular view of economic history. The remarkable thing about this view is that most of the assertions to which it has given the status of 'facts which everybody knows' have long been proved not to have been facts at all; yet they still continue, outside the circle of professional economic historians, to be almost universally accepted as the basis for the estimate of the existing economic order.

Most people, when being told that their political convictions have been affected by particular views on economic history, will answer that they never have been interested in it and never have read a book on the

---

[1] Herbert Butterfield, *The Englishman and His History* (Cambridge: Cambridge University Press, 1944), p. 3.
[2] *Ibid.*, p. 7.

subject. This, however, does not mean that they do not, with the rest, regard as established facts many of the legends which at one time or another have been given currency by writers on economic history. Although in the indirect and circuitous process by which new political ideas reach the general public the historian holds a key position, even he operates chiefly through many further relays. It is only at several removes that the picture which he provides becomes general property; it is *via* the novel and the newspaper, the cinema and political speeches, and ultimately the school and common talk, that the ordinary person acquires his conceptions of history. But in the end even those who never read a book and probably have never heard the names of the historians whose views have influenced them come to see the past through their spectacles. Certain beliefs, for instance, about the evolution and effects of trade unions, the alleged progressive growth of monopoly, the deliberate destruction of commodity stock as the result of competition (an event which, in fact, whenever it happened, was always the result of monopoly and usually of government-organized monopoly), about the suppression of beneficial inventions, the causes and effects of 'imperialism', and the role of the armament industries or of 'capitalists' in general in causing war, have become part of the folklore of our time. Most people would be greatly surprised to learn that most of what they believe about these subjects are not safely established facts but myths, launched from political motives and then spread by people of good will into whose general beliefs they fitted. It would require several books like the present one to show how most of what is commonly believed on these questions, not merely by radicals but also by many conservatives, is not history but political legend. All we can do here with regard to these topics is to refer the reader to a few works from which he can inform himself about the present state of knowledge on the more important of them. [3]

There is, however, one supreme myth which more than any other has served to discredit the economic system to which we owe our present-

[3] Cf. M. Dorothy George, 'The Combination Laws Reconsidered', *Economic History* (supplement to the *Economic Journal*), I (May 1927), 214–28; W. H. Hutt, *The Theory of Collective Bargaining* (London: P. S. King & Son, 1930) and *Economists and the Public* (London: J. Cape, 1936); L. C. Robbins, *The Economic Basis of Class Conflict* (London: Macmillan & Co., 1939) and *The Economic Causes of War* (London: J. Cape, 1939); Walter Sulzbach, *'Capitalistic Warmongers': A Modern Superstition* ('Public Policy Pamphlets', No. 35 (Chicago: University of Chicago Press, 1942)); G. J. Stigler, 'Competition in the United States', in *Five Lectures on Economic Problems* (London and New York: Longmans, Green & Co., 1949); G. Warren Nutter, *The Extent of Enterprise Monopoly in the United States, 1899–1939* (Chicago: University of Chicago Press, 1951); and, on most of these problems, the writings of Ludwig von Mises, especially his *Socialism* (London: J. Cape, 1936).

day civilization and to the examination of which the present volume is devoted. It is the legend of the deterioration of the position of the working classes in consequence of the rise of 'capitalism' (or of the 'manufacturing' or 'industrial system'). Who has not heard of the 'horrors of early capitalism' and gained the impression that the advent of this system brought untold new suffering to large classes who before were tolerably content and comfortable? We might justly hold in disrepute a system to which the blame attached that even for a time it worsened the position of the poorest and most numerous class of the population. The widespread emotional aversion to 'capitalism' is closely connected with this belief that the undeniable growth of wealth which the competitive order has produced was purchased at the price of depressing the standard of life of the weakest elements of society.

That this was the case was at one time indeed widely taught by economic historians. A more careful examination of the facts has, however, led to a thorough refutation of this belief. Yet, a generation after the controversy has been decided, popular opinion still continues as though the older belief had been true. How this belief should ever have arisen and why it should continue to determine the general view long after it has been disproved are both problems which deserve serious examination.

This kind of opinion can be frequently found not only in the political literature hostile to capitalism but even in works which on the whole are sympathetic to the political tradition of the nineteenth century. It is well represented by the following passage from Ruggiero's justly esteemed *History of European Liberalism*:

> Thus it was precisely at the period of intensest industrial growth that the condition of the labourer changed for the worse. Hours of labour multiplied out of all measure; the employment of women and children in factories lowered wages: the keen competition between the workers themselves, no longer tied to their parishes but free to travel and congregate where they were most in demand, further cheapened the labour they placed on the market: numerous and frequent industrial crises, inevitable at a period of growth, when population and consumption are not yet stabilized, swelled from time to time the ranks of the unemployed, the reserves in the army of starvation.[4]

[4] Guido de Ruggiero, *Storia del liberalismo europeo* (Bari, 1925), trans. R. G. Collingwood under the title *The History of European Liberalism* (London: Oxford University Press, 1927), p. 47, esp. p. 85. It is interesting that Ruggiero seems to derive his facts mainly from another supposedly liberal historian, Élie Halévy, although Halévy never expressed them so crudely.

There was little excuse for such a statement even when it appeared a quarter-century ago. A year after it was first published, the most eminent student of modern economic history, Sir John Clapham, rightly complained:

> The legend that everything was getting worse for the working man, down to some unspecified date between the drafting of the People's Charter and the Great Exhibition, dies hard. The fact that, after the price fall of 1820-1, the purchasing power of wages in general—not, of course, of everyone's wages—was definitely greater than it had been just before the revolutionary and Napoleonic wars, fits so ill with the tradition that it is very seldom mentioned, the works of statisticians of wages and prices being constantly disregarded by social historians.[5]

In so far as general public opinion is concerned, the position is scarcely better today, although the facts have had to be conceded even by most of those who had been mainly responsible for spreading the contrary opinion. Few authors have done more to create the belief that the early nineteenth century had been a time in which the position of the working class had become particularly bad than Mr. and Mrs. J. L. Hammond; their books are frequently quoted to illustrate this. But towards the end of their lives they admitted candidly that

> statisticians tell us that when they have put in order such data as they can find, they are satisfied that earnings increased and that most men and women were less poor when this discontent was loud and active than they were when the eighteenth century was beginning to grow old in a silence like that of autumn. The evidence, of course, is scanty, and its interpretation not too simple, but this general view is probably more or less correct.[6]

This did little to change the general effect their writing had on public opinion. In one of the latest competent studies of the history of the Western political tradition, for instance, we can still read that, 'like all the great social experiments, however, the invention of the labour market was expensive. It involved, in the first instance, a swift and drastic decline in the material standard of living of the working classes.'[7]

I was going to continue here that this is still the view which is almost exclusively represented in the popular literature when the latest book by

[5] J. H. Clapham, *An Economic History of Modern Britain* (Cambridge, 1926), I, 7.

[6] J. L. and Barbara Hammond, *The Bleak Age* (1934) (rev. ed., London: Pelican Books, 1947), p. 15.

[7] Frederick Watkins, *The Political Tradition of the West* (Cambridge, Mass.: Harvard University Press, 1948), p. 213.

Bertrand Russell came to my hands in which, as if to confirm this, he blandly asserts:

> The industrial revolution caused unspeakable misery both in England and in America. I do not think any student of economic history can doubt that the average happiness in England in the early nineteenth century was lower than it had been a hundred years earlier; and this was due almost entirely to scientific technique.[8]

The intelligent layman can hardly be blamed if he believes that such a categorical statement from a writer of this rank must be true. If a Bertrand Russell believes this, we must not be surprised that the versions of economic history which today are spread in hundreds of thousands of volumes of pocket editions are mostly of the kind which spread this old myth. It is also still a rare exception when we meet a work of historical fiction which dispenses with the dramatic touch which the story of the sudden worsening of the position of large groups of workers provides.

The true fact of the slow and irregular progress of the working class which we now know to have taken place is of course rather unsensational and uninteresting to the layman. It is no more than he has learned to expect as the normal state of affairs; and it hardly occurs to him that this is by no means an inevitable progress, that it was preceded by centuries of virtual stagnation of the position of the poorest, and that we have come to expect continuous improvement only as a result of the experience of several generations with the system which he still thinks to be the cause of the misery of the poor.

Discussions of the effects of the rise of modern industry on the working classes refer almost always to the conditions in England in the first half of the nineteenth century; yet the great change to which they refer had commenced much earlier and by then had quite a long history and had spread far beyond England. The freedom of economic activity which in England had proved so favourable to the rapid growth of wealth was probably in the first instance an almost accidental by-product of the limitations which the revolution of the seventeenth century had placed on the powers of government; and only after its beneficial effects had come to be widely noticed did the economists later undertake to explain the connection and to argue for the removal of the remaining barriers to commercial freedom. In many ways it is misleading to speak of 'capitalism' as though this had been a new and altogether different system which suddenly came into being towards the end of the eigh-

---

[8] Bertrand Russell, *The Impact of Science on Society* (New York: Columbia University Press, 1951), pp. 19–20.

teenth century; we use this term here because it is the most familiar name, but only with great reluctance, since with its modern connotations it is itself largely a creation of that socialist interpretation of economic history with which we are concerned. The term is especially misleading when, as is often the case, it is connected with the idea of the rise of the propertyless proletariat which by some devious process have been deprived of their rightful ownership of the tools for their work.

The actual history of the connection between capitalism and the rise of the proletariat is almost the opposite of that which these theories of the expropriation of the masses suggest. The truth is that, for the greater part of history, for most men the possession of the tools for their work was an essential condition for survival or at least for being able to rear a family. The number of those who could maintain themselves by working for others, although they did not themselves possess the necessary equipment, was limited to a small proportion of the population. The amount of arable land and of tools handed down from one generation to the next limited the total number who could survive. To be left without them meant in most instances death by starvation or at least the impossibility of procreation. There was little incentive and little possibility for one generation to accumulate the additional tools which would have made possible the survival of a larger number to the next, so long as the advantage of employing additional hands was limited mainly to the instances where the division of the tasks increased the efficiency of the work of the owner of the tools. It was only when the larger gains from the employment of machinery provided both the means and the opportunity for their investment that what in the past had been a recurring surplus of population doomed to early death was in an increasing measure given the possibility of survival. Numbers which had been practically stationary for many centuries began to increase rapidly. The proletariat which capitalism can be said to have 'created' was thus not a proportion of the population which would have existed without it and which it had degraded to a lower level; it was an additional population which was enabled to grow up by the new opportunities for employment which capitalism provided. In so far as it is true that the growth of capital made the appearance of the proletariat possible, it was in the sense that it raised the productivity of labour so that much larger numbers of those who had not been equipped by their parents with the necessary tools were enabled to maintain themselves by their labour alone; but the capital had to be supplied first before those were enabled to survive who afterwards claimed as a right a share in its ownership. Although it was certainly not from charitable motives, it still was the first time in history that one group of people found it in their interest to use their earnings on a large scale to provide new instruments of production to be operated by those who without them could not have produced their own sustenance.

Of the effect of the rise of modern industry on the growth of population, statistics tell a vivid tale. That this in itself largely contradicts the common belief about the harmful effect of the rise of the factory system on the large masses is not the point with which we are at present concerned. Nor need we more than mention the fact that, so long as this increase of the numbers of those whose output reached a certain level brought forward a fully corresponding increase in population, the level of the poorest fringe could not be substantially improved, however much the average might rise. The point of immediate relevance is that this increase of population and particularly of the manufacturing population had proceeded in England at least for two or three generations before the period of which it is alleged that the position of the workers seriously deteriorated.

The period to which this refers is also the period when the problem of the position of the working class became for the first time one of general concern. And the opinions of some of the contemporaries are indeed the main sources of the present beliefs. Our first question must therefore be how it came about that such an impression contrary to the facts should have become widely held among the people then living.

One of the chief reasons was evidently an increasing awareness of facts which before had passed unnoticed. The very increase of wealth and well-being which had been achieved raised standards and aspirations. What for ages had seemed a natural and inevitable situation, or even as an improvement upon the past, came to be regarded as incongruous with the opportunities which the new age appeared to offer. Economic suffering both became more conspicuous and seemed less justified, because general wealth was increasing faster than ever before. But this, of course, does not prove that the people whose fate was beginning to cause indignation and alarm were worse off than their parents or grandparents had been. While there is every evidence that great misery existed, there is none that it was greater than or even as great as it had been before. The aggregations of large numbers of cheap houses of industrial workers were probably more ugly than the picturesque cottages in which some of the agricultural labourers or domestic workers had lived; and they were certainly more alarming to the landowner or to the city patrician than the poor dispersed over the country had been. But for those who had moved from country to town it meant an improvement;

and even though the rapid growth of the industrial centres created sanitary problems with which people had yet slowly and painfully to learn to cope, statistics leave little doubt that even general health was on the whole benefited rather than harmed.[9]

More important, however, for the explanation of the change from an optimistic to a pessimistic view of the effects of industrialization than this awakening of social conscience was probably the fact that this change of opinion appears to have commenced, not in the manufacturing districts which had firsthand knowledge of what was happening, but in the political discussion of the English metropolis which was somewhat remote from, and had little part in, the new development. It is evident that the belief about the 'horrible' conditions prevailing among the manufacturing populations of the Midlands and the north of England was in the 1830's and 1840's widely held among the upper classes of London and the south. It was one of the main arguments with which the landowning class hit back at the manufacturers to counter the agitation of the latter against the Corn Laws and for free trade. And it was from these arguments of the conservative press that the radical intelligentsia of the time, with little firsthand knowledge of the industrial districts, derived their views which were to become the standard weapons of political propaganda.

This position, to which so much even of the present-day beliefs about the effects of the rise of industrialism on the working classes can be traced, is well illustrated by a letter written about 1843 by a London lady, Mrs. Cooke Taylor, after she had for the first time visited some industrial districts of Lancashire. Her account of the conditions she found is prefaced by some remarks about the general state of opinion in London:

> I need not remind you of the statements put forward in the newspapers, relative to the miserable conditions of the operatives, and the tyranny of their masters, for they made such an impression on me that it was with reluctance that I consented to go to Lancashire; indeed these misrepresentations are quite general, and people believe them without knowing why or wherefore. As an instance: just before starting I was at a large dinner party, at the west end of the town, and seated next a gentleman who is considered a very clever and intelligent man. In the course of the conversation I mentioned that I was going to Lancashire. He stared and asked, 'What on earth could take me there? That he would as soon think of going to St. Giles's; that it was a horrid place—factories all over; that the people,

9 Cf. M. C. Buer, *Health, Wealth and Population in the Early Days of the Industrial Revolution* (London: G. Routledge & Sons, 1926).

from starvation, oppression, and over-work, had almost lost the form of humanity; and that the mill-owners were a bloated, pampered race, feeding on the very vitals of the people.' I answered that this was a dreadful state of things; and asked 'In what part he had seen such misery?' He replied that 'he had never *seen* it, but had been *told* that it existed; and that for his part he never had been in the manufacturing districts, and that he never would.' This gentleman was one of the very numerous body of people who spread reports without ever taking the trouble of inquiring if they be true or false.[10]

Mrs. Cooke Taylor's detailed description of the satisfactory state of affairs which to her surprise she found ends with the remark:

Now that I have seen the factory people at their work, in their cottages and in their schools, I am totally at a loss to account for the outcry that has been made against them. They are better clothed, better fed, and better conducted than many other classes of working people.[11]

But even if at the time itself the opinion which was later taken over by the historians was loudly voiced by one party, it remains to explain why the view of one party among the contemporaries, and that not of the radicals or liberals but of the Tories, should have become the almost uncontradicted view of the economic historians of the second half of the century. The reason for this seems to have been that the new interest in economic history was itself closely associated with the interest in socialism and that at first a large proportion of those who devoted themselves to the study of economic history were inclined towards socialism. It was not merely the great stimulus which Karl Marx's 'materialist interpretation of history' undoubtedly gave to the study of economic history; practically all the socialist schools held a philosophy of history intended to show the relative character of the different economic institutions and the necessity of different economic systems succeeding each other in time. They all tried to prove that the system which they attacked, the system of private property in the means of production, was a perversion of an earlier and more natural system of communal property; and, because the theoretical preconceptions which guided them postulated that the rise of capitalism must have been detrimental to the working classes, it is not surprising that they found what they were looking for.

[10] This letter is quoted in 'Reuben', *A Brief History of the Rise and Progress of the Anti-Corn-Law League* (London [1845]). Mrs. Cooke Taylor, who appears to have been the wife of the radical Dr. Cooke Taylor, had visited the factory of Henry Ashworth at Turton, near Bolton, then still a rural district and therefore probably more attractive than some of the urban industrial districts.
[11] *Ibid.*

But not only those by whom the study of economic history was consciously made a tool of political agitation—as is true in many instances from Marx and Engels to Werner Sombart and Sidney and Beatrice Webb—but also many of the scholars who sincerely believed that they were approaching the facts without prejudice produced results which were scarcely less biased. This was in part due to the fact that the 'historical approach' which they adopted had itself been proclaimed as a counterblast to the theoretical analysis of classical economics, because the latter's verdict on the popular remedies for current complaints had so frequently been unfavourable.[12] It is no accident that the largest and most influential group of students of economic history in the sixty years preceding the First World War, the German Historical School, prided themselves also on the name of the 'socialists of the chair' (*Katheder-sozialisten*); or that their spiritual successors, the American 'institutionalists', were mostly socialists in their inclination. The whole atmosphere of these schools was such that it would have required an exceptional independence of mind for a young scholar not to succumb to the pressure of academic opinion. No reproach was more feared or more fatal to academic prospects than that of being an 'apologist' of the capitalist system; and, even if a scholar dared to contradict dominant opinion on a particular point, he would be careful to safeguard himself against such accusation by joining in the general condemnation of the capitalist system.[13] To treat the existing economic order as merely a 'historical phase' and to be able to predict from the 'laws of historical development' the emergence of a better future system became the hallmark of what was then regarded as the truly scientific spirit.

Much of the misrepresentation of the facts by the earlier economic historians was, in reality, directly traceable to a genuine endeavour to look at these facts without any theoretical preconceptions. The idea that one can trace the causal connections of any events without employing a theory, or that such a theory will emerge automatically from the accumulation of a sufficient amount of facts, is of course sheer illusion. The complexity of social events in particular is such that, without the tools of analysis which a systematic theory provides, one is almost bound

[12] Merely as an illustration of the general attitude of that school a characteristic statement of one of its best-known representatives, Adolf Held, may be quoted. According to him, it was David Ricardo 'in whose hand orthodox economics became the docile servant of the exclusive interests of mobile capital', and his theory of rent 'was simply dictated by the hatred of the moneyed capitalist against the landowners' (*Zwei Bücher zur socialen Geschichte Englands*, Leipzig: Duncker & Humblot, 1881, p. 178).

[13] A good account of the general political atmosphere prevailing among the German Historical School of economists will be found in Ludwig Pohle, *Die gegenwärtige Krise in der deutschen Volkswirtschaftslehre* (Leipzig, 1911).

to misinterpret them; and those who eschew the conscious use of an explicit and tested logical argument usually merely become the victims of the popular beliefs of their time. Common sense is a treacherous guide in this field, and what seem 'obvious' explanations frequently are no more than commonly accepted superstitions. It may seem obvious that the introduction of machinery will produce a general reduction of the demand for labour. But persistent effort to think the problem through shows that this belief is the result of a logical fallacy, of stressing one effect of the assumed change and leaving out others. Nor do the facts give any support to the belief. Yet anyone who thinks it to be true is very likely to find what seems to him confirming evidence. It is easy enough to find in the early nineteenth century instances of extreme poverty and to draw the conclusion that this must have been the effect of the introduction of machinery, without asking whether conditions had been any better or perhaps even worse before. Or one may believe that an increase of production must lead to the impossibility of selling all the product and, when one then finds a stagnation of sales, regard this as a confirmation of the expectations, although there are several more plausible explanations than general 'overproduction' or 'underconsumption'.

There can be no doubt that many of these misrepresentations were put forward in good faith; and there is no reason why we should not respect the motives of some of those who, to arouse public conscience, painted the misery of the poor in the blackest colours. We owe to agitation of this kind, which forced unwilling eyes to face unpleasant facts, some of the finest and most generous acts of public policy—from the abolition of slavery to the removal of taxes on imported food and the destruction of many entrenched privileges and abuses. And there is every reason to remember how miserable the majority of the people still were as recently as a hundred or a hundred and fifty years ago. But we must not, long after the event, allow a distortion of the facts, even if committed out of humanitarian zeal, to affect our view of what we owe to a system which for the first time in history made people feel that this misery might be avoidable. The very claims and ambitions of the working classes were and are the result of the enormous improvement of their position which capitalism brought about. There were, no doubt, many people whose privileged position, whose power to secure a comfortable income by preventing others from doing better what they were being paid for, was destroyed by the advance of freedom of enterprise. There may be various other grounds on which the development of modern industrialism might be deplored by some; certain aesthetic and moral values to which the privileged upper classes attached great importance were no doubt endangered by it. Some people might even question whether the rapid increase of population, or, in other words, the decrease in infant mortality, was a blessing. But if, and in so far as, one takes as one's test the effect on the standard of life of the large number of the toiling classes, there can be little doubt that this effect was to produce a general upward trend.

The recognition of this fact by the students had to wait for the rise of a generation of economic historians who no longer regarded themselves as the opponents of economics, intent upon proving that the economists had been wrong, but who were themselves trained economists who devoted themselves to the study of economic evolution. Yet the results which this modern economic history had largely established a generation ago have still gained little recognition outside professional circles. The process by which the results of research ultimately become general property has in this instance proved to be even slower than usual.[14] The new results in this case have not been of the kind which is avidly picked up by the intellectuals because it readily fits into their general prejudices but, on the contrary, are of a kind which is in conflict with their general beliefs. Yet, if we have been right in our estimate of the importance which erroneous views have had in shaping political opinion, it is high time that the truth should at last displace the legend which has so long governed popular belief. It was the conviction that this revision was long overdue which led to this topic being put on the programme of the meeting at which the first three of the following papers were originally presented and then to the decision that they should be made available to a wider public.

The recognition that the working class as a whole benefited from the rise of modern industry is of course entirely compatible with the fact that some individuals or groups in this as well as other classes may for a time have suffered from its results. The new order meant an increased rapidity of change, and the quick increase of wealth was largely the result of the increased speed of adaptation to change which made it possible. In those spheres where the mobility of a highly competitive market became effective, the increased range of opportunities more than compensated for the greater instability of particular jobs. But the spreading of the new order was gradual and uneven. There remained— and there remain to the present day—pockets which, while fully exposed to the vicissitudes of the markets for their products, are too isolated to

---

[14] On this, cf. my essay, 'The Intellectuals and Socialism', *University of Chicago Law Review*, Vol. XVI (1949), and reprinted as No. 12 in the present volume.

benefit much from the opportunities which the market opened else-where. The various instances of the decline of old crafts which were dis-placed by a mechanical process have been widely publicized (the fate of the hand-loom weavers is the classical example always quoted). But even there it is more than doubtful whether the amount of suffering caused is comparable to that which a series of bad harvests in any region would have caused before capitalism had greatly increased the mobility of goods and of capital. The incidence on a small group among a pros-pering community is probably felt as more of an injustice and a challenge than was the general suffering of earlier times which was considered as unalterable fate.

The understanding of the true sources of the grievances, and still more the manner in which they might be remedied so far as possible, pre-supposes a better comprehension of the working of the market system than most of the earlier historians possessed. Much that has been blamed on the capitalist system is in fact due to remnants or revivals of pre-capitalistic features: to monopolistic elements which were either the direct result of ill-conceived state action or the consequence of a failure to understand that a smooth-working competitive order required an appropriate legal framework. We have already referred to some of the features and tendencies for which capitalism is usually blamed and which are in fact due to its basic mechanism not being allowed to work; and the question, in particular, why and to what extent monopoly has interfered with its beneficial operation is too big a problem for us to attempt to say more about it here.

This introduction is not intended to do more than to indicate the general setting in which the more specific discussion of the following papers must be seen. For its inevitable tendency to run in generalities I trust these special studies will make up by the very concrete treatment of their particular problems. They cover merely part of the wider issue, since they were intended to provide the factual basis for the discussion which they opened. Of the three related questions—What were the facts? How did the historians present them? and Why?—they deal primarily with the first and chiefly by implication with the second. Only the paper by M. de Jouvenel, which therefore possesses a somewhat different character, addresses itself mainly to the third question; and, in so doing, it raises problems which reach even beyond the complex of questions which have been sketched here.

CHAPTER FIFTEEN

The Road to Serfdom *after Twelve Years**

Although this book might in some respects have been different if I had written it in the first instance with American readers primarily in mind, it has by now made for itself too definite, if unexpected, a place in this country to make any rewriting advisable. Its republication in a new form, however, more than ten years after its first appearance, is perhaps an appropriate occasion for explaining its original aim and for a few comments on the altogether unforeseen and in many ways curious success it has had in this country.

The book was written in England during the war years and was designed almost exclusively for English readers. Indeed, it was addressed mainly to a very special class of readers in England. It was in no spirit of mockery that I dedicated it 'To the Socialists of All Parties'. It had its origin in many discussions which, during the preceding ten years, I had with friends and colleagues whose sympathies had been inclined towards the left, and it was in continuation of those arguments that I wrote *The Road to Serfdom*.

When Hitler came into power in Germany, I had already been teaching at the University of London for several years, but I kept in close touch with affairs on the Continent and was able to do so until the outbreak of war. What I had thus seen of the origins and evolution of the various totalitarian movements made me feel that English public opinion, particularly among my friends who held 'advanced' views on social matters, completely misconceived the nature of those movements.

---

* Foreword to the American paperback edition of *The Road to Serfdom*, University of Chicago Press, 1956.

The Road to Serfdom *after Twelve Years*

Even before the war I was led by this to state in a brief essay what became the central argument of this book. But after war broke out I felt that this widespread misunderstanding of the political systems of our enemies, and soon also of our new ally, Russia, constituted a serious danger which had to be met by a more systematic effort. Also, it was already fairly obvious that England herself was likely to experiment after the war with the same kind of policies which I was convinced had contributed so much to destroy liberty elsewhere.

Thus this book gradually took shape as a warning to the socialist intelligentsia of England; with the inevitable delays of wartime production, it finally appeared there early in the spring of 1944. This date will, incidentally, also explain why I felt that in order to get a hearing I had somewhat to restrain myself in my comments on the regime of our wartime ally and to choose my illustrations mainly from developments in Germany.

It seems that the book appeared at a propitious moment, and I can feel only gratification at the success it had in England which, though very different in kind, was quantitatively no smaller than it was to be in the United States. On the whole, the book was taken in the spirit in which it was written, and its argument was seriously examined by those to whom it was mainly addressed. Excepting only certain of the leading politicians of the Labour party—who, as if to provide an illustration for my remarks on the nationalist tendencies of socialism, attacked the book on the ground that it was written by a foreigner—the thoughtful and receptive manner in which it was generally examined by persons who must have found its conclusions running counter to their strongest convictions was deeply impressive.[1]

The same applies also to the other European countries where the book eventually appeared; and its particularly cordial reception by the post-Nazi generation of Germany, when copies of a translation published in Switzerland at last reached that country, was one of the unforeseen pleasures I derived from its publication.

Rather different was the reception the book had in the United States when it was published here a few months after its appearance in England. I had given little thought to its possible appeal to American readers

[1] The most representative example of British criticism of the book from a left-wing point of view is probably Mrs. Barbara Wootton's courteous and frank study, *Freedom under Planning* (London: George Allen & Unwin, 1946). It is often quoted in the United States as an effective refutation of my argument, though I cannot help feeling that more than one reader must have gained the impression that, as one American reviewer expressed it, 'it seems substantially to confirm Hayek's thesis' (Chester I. Barnard, *Southern Economic Journal*, January 1946).

when writing it. It was then twenty years since I had last been in America as a research student, and during that time I had somewhat lost touch with the development of American ideas. I could not be sure how far my argument had direct relevance to the American scene, and I was not in the least surprised when the book was in fact rejected by the first three publishing houses approached.[2]

It was certainly most unexpected when, after the book was brought out by its present publishers, it soon began to sell at a rate almost unprecedented for a book of this kind, not intended for popular consumption.[3] And I was even more surprised by the violence of the reaction from both political wings, by the lavish praise the book received from some quarters no less than by the passionate hatred it appeared to arouse in others.

Contrary to my experience in England, in America the kind of people to whom this book was mainly addressed seem to have rejected it out of hand as a malicious and disingenuous attack on their finest ideals; they appear never to have paused to examine its argument. The language used and the emotion shown in some of the more adverse criticism the book received were indeed rather extraordinary.[4] But scarcely less surprising to me was the enthusiastic welcome accorded to the book by many whom I never expected to read a volume of this type—and from many more of whom I still doubt whether in fact they ever read it. And I must add that occasionally the manner in which it was used vividly brought home to me the truth of Lord Acton's observation that 'at all times sincere friends of freedom have been rare, and its triumphs have been due to minorities that have prevailed by associating themselves with auxiliaries whose objects often differed from their own; and this association, which is always dangerous, has sometimes been disastrous.'

[2] I did not know then, as has since been admitted by a person advising one of the firms, that this appears to have been due not to any doubts of the success of the book but to political prejudice which went to the extent of representing the book as 'unfit for publication by a reputable house' (see on this the statement by William Miller quoted by W. T. Couch in 'The Sainted Book Burners', *The Freeman*, April 1955, p. 423, and also William Miller, *The Book Industry: A Report of the Public Library Inquiry of the Social Science Research Council*, New York: Columbia University Press, 1949, p. 12).

[3] Not a little of this was due to the publication of a condensation of this book in the *Reader's Digest*, and I should like to pay here to the editors of this journal a public tribute for the extremely skilful manner in which this was done without my assistance. It is inevitable that the compression of a complex argument to a fraction of its original length produces some oversimplification, but to have done this without distortion and better than I could have done it myself is a remarkable achievement.

[4] To any reader who would like to see a specimen of abuse and invective which is probably unique in contemporary academic discussion I recommend a reading of Professor Herman Finer's *Road to Reaction* (Boston: Little Brown & Co., 1945).

The Road to Serfdom *after Twelve Years*

It seems hardly likely that this extraordinary difference in the reception of the book on the two sides of the Atlantic is due entirely to a difference in national temperament. I have since become increasingly convinced that the explanation must lie in a difference of intellectual situation at the time when it arrived.

In England, and in Europe generally, the problems with which I dealt had long ceased to be abstract questions. The ideals which I examined had long before come down to earth, and even their most enthusiastic adherents had already seen concretely some of the difficulties and unlooked-for results which their application produced. I was thus writing about phenomena of which almost all my European readers had some more or less close experience, and I was merely arguing systematically and consistently what many had already intuitively felt. There was already a disillusionment about these ideals under way which their critical examination merely made more vocal or explicit.

In the United States, on the other hand, these ideals were still fresh and more virulent. It was only ten or fifteen years earlier—not forty or fifty, as in England—that a large part of the intelligentsia had caught the infection. And, in spite of the experimentation of the New Deal, their enthusiasm for the new kind of rationally constructed society was still largely unsoiled by practical experience. What to most Europeans had in some measure become *vieux jeu* was to the American radicals still the glittering hope of a better world which they had embraced and nourished during the recent years of the Great Depression.

Opinion moves fast in the United States, and even now it is difficult to remember how comparatively short a time it was before *The Road to Serfdom* appeared that the most extreme kind of economic planning had been seriously advocated and the model of Russia held up for imitation by men who were soon to play an important role in public affairs. It would be easy enough to give chapter and verse for this, but it would be invidious now to single out individuals. Be it enough to mention that in 1934 the newly established National Planning Board devoted a good deal of attention to the example of planning provided by these four countries: Germany, Italy, Russia, and Japan. Ten years later we had of course learnt to refer to these same countries as 'totalitarian', had fought a long war with three of them, and were soon to start a 'cold war' with the fourth. Yet the contention of this book that the political development in those countries had something to do with their economic policies was then still indignantly rejected by the advocates of planning in this country. It suddenly became the fashion to deny that the inspiration of planning had come from Russia and to contend, as one of my eminent critics put it, that it was 'a plain fact that Italy, Russia, Japan, and Germany all reached totalitarianism by very different roads'.

The whole intellectual climate in the United States at the time *The Road to Serfdom* appeared was thus one in which it was bound either profoundly to shock or greatly to delight the members of sharply divided groups. In consequence, in spite of its apparent success, the book has not had here the kind of effect I should have wished or which it has had elsewhere. It is true that its main conclusions are today widely accepted. If twelve years ago it seemed to many almost sacrilege to suggest that fascism and communism are merely variants of the same totalitarianism which central control of all economic activity tends to produce, this has become almost a commonplace. It is now even widely recognized that democratic socialism is a very precarious and unstable affair, ridden with internal contradictions and everywhere producing results most distasteful to many of its advocates.

For this sobered mood the lessons of events and more popular discussions of the problem[5] are certainly more responsible than this book. Nor was my general thesis, as such, original when it was published. Although similar but earlier warnings may have been largely forgotten, the dangers inherent in the policies which I criticized had been pointed out again and again. Whatever merits this book possesses consist not in the reiteration of this thesis but in the patient and detailed examination of the reasons why economic planning will produce such unlooked-for results and of the process by which they come about.

It is for this reason that I rather hope that the time may now be more favourable in America for a serious consideration of the true argument of the book than it was when it first appeared. I believe that what is important in it still has to render its service, although I recognize that the hot socialism against which it was mainly directed—that organized movement towards a deliberate organization of economic life by the state as the chief owner of the means of production—is nearly dead in the Western world. The century of socialism in this sense probably came to an end around 1948. Many of its illusions have been discarded even by its leaders, and elsewhere as well as in the United States the very name has lost much of its attraction. Attempts will no doubt be made to rescue the name for movements which are less dogmatic, less doctrinaire, and less systematic. But an argument applicable solely against those clear-cut conceptions of social reform which characterized the socialist movements of the past might today well appear as tilting against windmills.

[5] The most effective of these was undoubtedly George Orwell's *1984*. The author had earlier kindly reviewed *The Road to Serfdom* in *The Observer* of 9 April 1944.

Yet though hot socialism is probably a thing of the past, some of its conceptions have penetrated far too deeply into the whole structure of current thought to justify complacency. If few people in the Western world now want to remake society from the bottom according to some ideal blueprint, a great many still believe in measures which, though not designed completely to remodel the economy, in their aggregate effect may well unintentionally produce this result. And, even more than at the time when I wrote this book, the advocacy of policies which in the long run cannot be reconciled with the preservation of a free society is no longer a party matter. That hodge-podge of ill-assembled and often inconsistent ideals which under the name of the Welfare State has largely replaced socialism as the goal of the reformers needs very careful sorting out if its results are not to be very similar to those of full-fledged socialism. This is not to say that some of its aims are not both practicable and laudable. But there are many ways in which we can work towards the same goal, and in the present state of opinion there is some danger that our impatience for quick results may lead us to choose instruments which, though perhaps more efficient for achieving the particular ends, are not compatible with the preservation of a free society. The increasing tendency to rely on administrative coercion and discrimination where a modification of the general rules of law might, perhaps more slowly, achieve the same object, and to resort to direct state controls or to the creation of monopolistic institutions where judicious use of financial inducements might evoke spontaneous efforts, is still a powerful legacy of the socialist period which is likely to influence policy for a long time to come.

Just because in the years ahead of us political ideology is not likely to aim at a clearly defined goal but towards piecemeal change, a full understanding of the process through which certain kinds of measures can destroy the bases of an economy based on the market and gradually smother the creative powers of a free civilization seems now of the greatest importance. Only if we understand why and how certain kinds of economic controls tend to paralyse the driving forces of a free society, and which kinds of measures are particularly dangerous in this respect, can we hope that social experimentation will not lead us into situations none of us want.

It is as a contribution to this task that this book is intended. I hope that at least in the quieter atmosphere of the present it will be received as what it was meant to be, not as an exhortation to resistance against any improvement or experimentation, but as a warning that we should insist that any modification in our arrangements should pass certain tests (described in the central chapter on the Rule of Law) before we commit ourselves to courses from which withdrawal may be difficult.

The fact that this book was originally written with only the British public in mind does not appear to have seriously affected its intelligibility for the American reader. But there is one point of phraseology which I ought to explain here to forestall any misunderstanding. I use throughout the term 'liberal' in the original, nineteenth-century sense in which it is still current in Britain. In current American usage it often means very nearly the opposite of this. It has been part of the camouflage of leftish movements in this country, helped by the muddleheadedness of many who really believe in liberty, that 'liberal' has come to mean the advocacy of almost every kind of government control. I am still puzzled why those in the United States who truly believe in liberty should not only have allowed the left to appropriate this almost indispensable term but should even have assisted by beginning to use it themselves as a term of opprobrium. This seems to be particularly regrettable because of the consequent tendency of many true liberals to describe themselves as conservatives.

It is true, of course, that in the struggle against the believers in the all-powerful state the true liberal must sometimes make common cause with the conservative, and in some circumstances, as in contemporary Britain, he has hardly any other way of actively working for his ideals. But true liberalism is still distinct from conservativism, and there is danger in the two being confused. Conservativism, though a necessary element in any stable society, is not a social programme; in its paternalistic, nationalistic, and power-adoring tendencies it is often closer to socialism than true liberalism; and with its traditionalistic, anti-intellectual, and often mystical propensities it will never, except in short periods of disillusionment, appeal to the young and all those others who believe that some changes are desirable if this world is to become a better place. A conservative movement, by its very nature, is bound to be a defender of established privilege and to lean on the power of government for the protection of privilege. The essence of the liberal position, however, is the denial of all privilege, if privilege is understood in its proper and original meaning of the state granting and protecting rights to some which are not available on equal terms to others.

Perhaps a further word of apology is required for my allowing this book to reappear in entirely unchanged form after the lapse of almost twelve years. I have many times tried to revise it, and there are numerous points I should like to explain at greater length or to state more cautiously or to fortify by more illustration and proof. But all attempts at rewriting only proved that I could never again produce as short a book covering as much of the field; and it seems to me that, whatever other merits it may have, its relative brevity is its greatest. I have thus been forced to the conclusion that whatever I want to add to the argument I must attempt in separate studies. I have begun to do so in various essays some of which provide a more searching discussion of certain philosophical and economic issues on which the present book only touches.[6] On the special question of the roots of the ideas here criticized and of their connection with some of the most powerful and impressive intellectual movements of this age, I have commented in another volume.[7] And before long I hope to supplement the all-too-brief central chapter of this book by a more extensive treatment of the relation between equality and justice.[8]

There is one particular topic, however, on which the reader will with justice expect me to comment on this occasion, yet which I could even less treat adequately without writing a new book. Little more than a year after *The Road to Serfdom* first appeared, Great Britain had a socialist government which remained in power for six years. And the question of how far this experience has confirmed or refuted my apprehensions is one which I must try to answer at least briefly. If anything, this experience has strengthened my concern and, I believe I may add, has taught the reality of the difficulties I pointed out to many for whom an abstract argument would never have carried conviction. Indeed, it was not long after the Labour government came into power that some of the issues which my critics in America dismissed as bogeys became in Great Britain main topics of political discussion. Soon even official documents were gravely discussing the danger of totalitarianism raised by the policy of economic planning. There is no better illustration of the manner in which the inherent logic of their policies drove an unwilling socialist government into the kind of coercion it disliked than the following passage in the *Economic Survey for 1947* (which the Prime Minister presented to Parliament in February of that year) and its sequel:

> There is an essential difference between totalitarian and democratic planning. The former subordinates all individual desires and preferences to the demand of the State. For this purpose, it uses various methods of compulsion upon the individual which deprive him of his freedom of choice. Such methods may be necessary even in a democratic country during the extreme emergency of a great war. Thus the British people gave their war-

[6] *Individualism and Economic Order* (Chicago, 1948).

[7] *The Counter-Revolution of Science* (Glencoe, Ill., 1952).

[8] An advance sketch of my treatment of this subject has been published by the National Bank of Egypt in the form of four lectures on *The Political Ideal of the Rule of Law* (Cairo, 1955), and the full version was published in 1960 under the title *The Constitution of Liberty*.

time Government the power to direct labour. But in normal times the people of a democratic country will not give up their freedom of choice to their Government. A democratic Government must therefore conduct its economic planning in a manner which preserves the maximum possible freedom of choice to the individual citizen.

The interesting point about this profession of laudable intentions is that six months later the same government found itself in peacetime forced to put the conscription of labour back on the statute book. It hardly diminishes the significance of this when it is pointed out that the power was in fact never used—because, if it is known that the authorities have power to coerce, few will wait for actual coercion. But it is rather difficult to see how the government could have persisted in its illusions when in the same document it claims that it was now for 'the Government to say what is the best use for the resources in the national interest' and to 'lay down the economic task for the nation: it must say which things are the most important and what the objectives of policy ought to be.'

Of course, six years of socialist government in England have not produced anything resembling a totalitarian state. But those who argue that this has disproved the thesis of *The Road to Serfdom* have really missed one of its main points: that the most important change which extensive government control produces is a psychological change, an alteration in the character of the people. This is necessarily a slow affair, a process which extends not over a few years but perhaps over one or two generations. The important point is that the political ideals of a people and its attitude towards authority are as much the effect as the cause of the political institutions under which it lives. This means, among other things, that even a strong tradition of political liberty is no safeguard if the danger is precisely that new institutions and policies will gradually undermine and destroy that spirit. The consequences can of course be averted if that spirit reasserts itself in time and the people not only throw out the party which has been leading them further and further in the dangerous direction, but also recognize the nature of the danger and resolutely change their course. There is not yet much ground to believe that the latter has happened in England.

Yet the change undergone by the character of the British people, not merely under its Labour government but in the course of the much longer period during which it has been enjoying the blessings of a paternalistic welfare state, can hardly be mistaken. These changes are not easily demonstrated but are clearly felt if one lives in the country. In illustration, I will cite a few significant passages from a sociological survey dealing with the impact of the surfeit of regulation on the mental attitudes of the young. It is concerned with the situation before the Labour government came into power, in fact, about the time this book was first published, and deals mainly with the effects of those wartime regulations which the Labour government made permanent:

It is above all in the city that the province of the optional is felt as dwindling away to nothing. At school, in the place of work, on the journey to and fro, even in the very equipment and provisioning of the home, many of the activities normally possible to human beings are either forbidden or enjoined. Special agencies, called Citizens' Advice Bureaux, are set up to steer the bewildered through the forest of rules, and to indicate to the persistent the rare clearings where a private person may still make a choice. . . . [The town lad] is conditioned not to lift a finger without referring mentally to the book of words first. A time-budget of an ordinary city youth for an ordinary working day would show that he spends great stretches of his waking hours going through motions that have been predetermined for him by directives in whose framing he has had no part, whose precise intention he seldom understands, and of whose appropriateness he cannot judge. . . . The inference that what the city lad needs is more discipline and tighter control is too hasty. It would be nearer the mark to say that he is suffering from an overdose of control already. . . . Surveying his parents and his older brothers or sisters he finds them as regulation-bound as himself. He sees them so acclimatized to that state that they seldom plan and carry out under their own steam any new social excursion or enterprise. He thus looks forward to no future period at which a sinewy faculty of responsibility is likely to be of service to himself or others. . . . [The young people] are obliged to stomach so much external and, as it seems to them, meaningless control that they seek escape and recuperation in an absence of discipline as complete as they can make it.[9]

Is it too pessimistic to fear that a generation grown up under these conditions is unlikely to throw off the fetters to which it has grown used? Or does this description not rather fully bear out de Tocqueville's prediction of the 'new kind of servitude' when

after having thus successively taken each member of the community in its powerful grasp, and fashioned him at will, the supreme power then extends its arm over the whole community. It covers the surface of society with a network of small complicated rules, minute and uniform through which the most original minds and the most energetic characters cannot penetrate to rise above the crowd. The will of man is not shattered but softened, bent and guided; men are seldom forced by it to act, but they are constantly restrained

[9] L. J. Barnes, *Youth Service in an English County: A Report Prepared for King George's Jubilee Trust* (London, 1945).

from acting. Such a power does not destroy, but it prevents existence; it does not tyrannize, but it compresses, enervates, extinguishes, and stupefies a people, till each nation is reduced to be nothing better than a flock of timid and industrial animals of which government is the shepherd.—I have always thought that servitude of the regular, quiet, and gentle kind which I have just described might be combined more easily than is commonly believed with some of the outward forms of freedom and that it might even establish itself under the wing of the sovereignty of the people.[10]

What de Tocqueville did not consider was how long such a government would remain in the hands of benevolent despots when it would be so much more easy for any group of ruffians to keep itself indefinitely in power by disregarding all the traditional decencies of political life.

Perhaps I should also remind the reader that I have never accused the socialist parties of deliberately aiming at a totalitarian regime or even suspected that the leaders of the old socialist movements might ever show such inclinations. What I have argued in this book, and what the British experience convinces me even more to be true, is that the unforeseen but inevitable consequences of socialist planning create a state of affairs in which, if the policy is to be pursued, totalitarian forces will get the upper hand. I explicitly stress that 'socialism can be put into practice only by methods of which most socialists disapprove' and even add that in this 'the old socialist parties were inhibited by their democratic ideals' and that 'they did not possess the ruthlessness required for the performance of their chosen task'. I am afraid the impression one gained under the Labour government was that these inhibitions were, if anything, weaker among the British socialists than they had been among their German fellow-socialists twenty-five years earlier. Certainly the German Social Democrats, in the comparable period of the 1920's under equally or more difficult economic conditions, never approached as closely to totalitarian planning as the British Labour government has done.

Since I cannot here examine the effect of these policies in detail, I will rather quote the summary judgments of other observers who may be less suspect of preconceived opinions. Some of the most damning, in fact, come from men who not long before had themselves been members of the Labour party. Thus Mr. Ivor Thomas, in a book apparently intended to explain why he left that party, comes to the conclusion that

---

[10] A. de Tocqueville, *Democracy in America*, Part II, Book IV, Chap. vi. The whole chapter should be read in order to realize with what acute insight de Tocqueville was able to foresee the psychological effects of the modern welfare state. It was, incidentally, de Tocqueville's frequent reference to the 'new servitude' which suggested the title of the present book.

'from the point of view of fundamental human liberties there is little to choose between communism, socialism, and national socialism. They all are examples of the collectivist or totalitarian state . . . in its essentials not only is completed socialism the same as communism but it hardly differs from fascism.'[11]

The most serious development is the growth of a measure of arbitrary administrative coercion and the progressive destruction of the cherished foundation of British liberty, the Rule of Law, for exactly the reasons here discussed in Chapter VI. This process had of course started long before the last Labour government came into power and had been accentuated by the war. But the attempts at economic planning under the Labour government carried it to a point which makes it doubtful whether it can be said that the Rule of Law still prevails in Britain. The 'New Despotism' of which a Lord Chief Justice had warned Britain as long as twenty-five years ago is, as *The Economist* recently observed, no longer a mere danger but an established fact.[12] It is a despotism exercised by a thoroughly conscientious and honest bureaucracy for what they sincerely believe is the good of the country. But it is nevertheless an arbitrary government, in practice free from effective parliamentary control; and its machinery would be as effective for any other than the beneficent purposes for which it is now used. I doubt whether it was much exaggerated when recently an eminent British jurist, in a careful analysis of these trends, came to the conclusions that 'in Britain today, we live on the edge of dictatorship. Transition would be easy, swift, and it could be accomplished with complete legality. Already so many steps have been taken in this direction, due to the completeness of power possessed by the Government of the day, and the absence of any real check such as the terms of a written constitution or the existence of an effective second chamber, that those still to be taken are small in comparison.'[13]

For a more detailed analysis of the economic policies of the British Labour government and its consequences I cannot do better than refer the reader to Professor John Jewkes' *Ordeal by Planning* (London: Macmillan and Co., 1948). It is the best discussion known to me of a concrete instance of the phenomena discussed in general terms in this

---

[11] *The Socialist Tragedy* (London: Latimer House, Ltd., 1949), pp. 241 and 242.

[12] In an article in the issue of June 19, 1954, discussing the *Report on the Public Inquiry Ordered by the Minister of Agriculture into the Disposal of Land at Crichel Down* (Cmd. 9176; London: H.M. Stationery Office, 1954), a document deserving the most careful study by all those interested in the psychology of a planning bureaucracy.

[13] G. W. Keeton, *The Passing of Parliament* (London, 1952).

book. It supplements it better than anything I could add here and spells out a lesson which is of significance far beyond Great Britain.

It seems now unlikely that, even when another Labour government should come into power in Great Britain, it would resume the experiments in large-scale nationalization and planning. But in Britain, as elsewhere in the world, the defeat of the onslaught of systematic socialism has merely given those who are anxious to preserve freedom a breathing space in which to re-examine our ambitions and to discard all those parts of the socialist inheritance which are a danger to a free society. Without such a revised conception of our social aims, we are likely to continue to drift in the same direction in which outright socialism would merely have carried us a little faster.

CHAPTER SIXTEEN

The Moral Element in Free Enterprise*

Economic activity provides the material means for all our ends. At the same time, most of our individual efforts are directed to providing means for the ends of others in order that they, in turn, may provide us with the means for our ends. It is only because we are free in the choice of our means that we are also free in the choice of our ends.

Economic freedom is thus an indispensable condition of all other freedom, and free enterprise both a necessary condition and a consequence of personal freedom. In discussing The Moral Element in Free Enterprise I shall therefore not confine myself to the problems of economic life but consider the general relations between freedom and morals.

By freedom in this connection I mean, in the great Anglo-Saxon tradition, independence of the arbitrary will of another. This is the classical conception of freedom under the law, a state of affairs in which a man may be coerced only where coercion is required by the general rules of law, equally applicable to all, and never by the discretionary decision of administrative authority.

The relationship between this freedom and moral values is mutual and complex. I shall therefore have to confine myself to bringing out the salient points in something like telegram style.

It is, on the one hand, an old discovery that morals and moral values will grow only in an environment of freedom, and that, in general, moral

* An address to the 66th Congress of American Industry organized by The National Association of Manufacturers, New York, December 6, 1961 and first printed with similar addresses by Felix Morley, Herrell De Graff and John Davenport under the title *The Spiritual and Moral Significance of Free Enterprise*, New York, 1962.

standards of people and classes are high only where they have long enjoyed freedom—and proportional to the amount of freedom they have possessed. It is also an old insight that a free society will work well only where free action is guided by strong moral beliefs, and, therefore, that we shall enjoy all the benefits of freedom only where freedom is already well established. To this I want to add that freedom, if it is to work well, requires not only strong moral standards but moral standards of a particular kind, and that it is possible in a free society for moral standards to grow up which, if they become general, will destroy freedom and with it the basis of all moral values.

Before I turn to this point which is not generally understood, I must briefly elaborate upon the two old truths which ought to be familiar but which are often forgotten. That freedom is the matrix required for the growth of moral values—indeed not merely one value among many but the source of all values—is almost self-evident. It is only where the individual has choice, and its inherent responsibility, that he has occasion to affirm existing values, to contribute to their further growth, and to earn moral merit. Obedience has moral value only where it is a matter of choice and not of coercion. It is in the order in which we rank our different ends that our moral sense manifests itself; and in applying the general rules of morals to particular situations each individual is constantly called upon to interpret and apply the general principles and in doing so to create particular values.

I have no time here for showing how this has in fact brought it about that free societies not only have generally been law-abiding societies, but also in modern times have been the source of all the great humanitarian movements aiming at active help to the weak, the ill, and the oppressed. Unfree societies, on the other hand, have as regularly developed a disrespect for the law, a callous attitude to suffering, and even sympathy for the malefactor.

I must turn to the other side of the medal. It should also be obvious that the results of freedom must depend on the values which free individuals pursue. It would be impossible to assert that a free society will always and necessarily develop values of which we would approve, or even, as we shall see, that it will maintain values which are compatible with the preservation of freedom. All that we can say is that the values we hold are the product of freedom, that in particular the Christian values had to assert themselves through men who successfully resisted coercion by government, and that it is to the desire to be able to follow one's own moral convictions that we owe the modern safeguards of individual freedom. Perhaps we can add to this that only societies which hold moral values essentially similar to our own have survived as free societies, while in others freedom has perished.

All this provides strong argument why it is most important that a free society be based on strong moral convictions and why if we want to preserve freedom and morals, we should do all in our power to spread the appropriate moral convictions. But what I am mainly concerned with is the error that men must first be good before they can be granted freedom.

It is true that a free society lacking a moral foundation would be a very unpleasant society in which to live. But it would even so be better than a society which is unfree and immoral; and it at least offers the hope of a gradual emergence of moral convictions which an unfree society prevents. On this point I am afraid I strongly disagree with John Stuart Mill who maintained that until men have attained the capacity of being guided to their own improvement by conviction or persuasion, 'there is nothing for them but implicit obedience to an Akbar or Charlemagne, if they are so fortunate as to find one.' Here I believe T. B. Macaulay expressed the much greater wisdom of an older tradition, when he wrote that 'many politicians of our time are in the habit of laying it down as a self-evident proposition that no people are to be free till they are fit to use their freedom. The maxim is worthy of the fool in the old story who resolved not to go into the water till he had learned to swim. If men are to wait for liberty till they become wise and good, they may indeed wait forever.'

But I must now turn from what is merely the re-affirmation of old wisdom to more critical issues. I have said that liberty, to work well, requires not merely the existence of strong moral convictions but also the acceptance of particular moral views. By this I do not mean that within limits utilitarian considerations will contribute to alter moral views on particular issues. Nor do I mean that, as Edwin Cannan expressed it, 'of the two principles, Equity and Economy, Equity is ultimately the weaker . . . the judgment of mankind about what is equitable is liable to change, and . . . one of the forces that causes it to change is mankind's discovery from time to time that what was supposed to be quite just and equitable in some particular matter has become, or perhaps always was, uneconomical'.

This is also true and important, though it may not be a commendation to all people. I am concerned rather with some more general conceptions which seem to me an essential condition of a free society and without which it cannot survive. The two crucial ones seem to me the belief in individual responsibility and the approval as just of an arrangement by which material rewards are made to correspond to the value which a person's particular services have to his fellows; not to the esteem in which he is held as a whole person for his moral merit.

I must be brief on the first point—which I find very difficult. Modern developments here are part of the story of the destruction of moral value by scientific error which has recently been my chief concern—and what a scholar happens to be working on at the moment tends to appear to him as the most important subject in the world. But I shall try to say what belongs here in a very few words.

Free societies have always been societies in which the belief in individual responsibility has been strong. They have allowed individuals to act on their knowledge and beliefs and have treated the results achieved as due to them. The aim was to make it worth while for people to act rationally and reasonably and to persuade them that what they would achieve depended chiefly on them. This last belief is undoubtedly not entirely correct, but it certainly had a wonderful effect in developing both initiative and circumspection.

By a curious confusion it has come to be thought that this belief in individual responsibility has been refuted by growing insight into the manner in which events generally, and human actions in particular, are determined by certain classes of causes. It is probably true that we have gained increasing understanding of the kinds of circumstances which affect human action—but no more. We can certainly not say that a particular conscious act of any man is the necessary result of particular circumstances that we can specify—leaving out his peculiar individuality built up by the whole of his history. Of our generic knowledge as to how human action can be influenced we make use in assessing praise and blame—which we do for the purpose of making people behave in a desirable fashion. It is on this limited determinism—as much as our knowledge in fact justifies—that the belief in responsibility is based, while only a belief in some metaphysical self which stands outside the chain of cause and effect could justify the contention that it is useless to hold the individual responsible for his actions.

Yet, crude as is the fallacy underlying the opposite and supposedly scientific view, it has had the most profound effect in destroying the chief device which society has developed to assure decent conduct—the pressure of opinion making people observe the rules of the game. And it has ended in that *Myth of Mental Illness* which a distinguished psychiatrist, Dr. T. S. Szasz, has recently justly castigated in a book so titled. We have probably not yet discovered the best way of teaching people to live according to rules which make life in society for them and their fellows not too unpleasant. But in our present state of knowledge I am sure that we shall never build up a successful free society without that pressure of praise and blame which treats the individual as responsible for his conduct and also makes him bear the consequences of even innocent error.

But if it is essential for a free society that the esteem in which a person is held by his fellows depends on how far he lives up to the demand for moral law, it is also essential that material reward should not be determined by the opinion of his fellows of his moral merits but by the value which they attach to the particular services he renders them. This brings me to my second chief point: the conception of social justice which must prevail if a free society is to be preserved. This is the point on which the defenders of a free society and the advocates of a collectivist system are chiefly divided. And on this point, while the advocates of the socialist conception of distributive justice are usually very outspoken, the upholders of freedom are unnecessarily shy about stating bluntly the implications of their ideal.

The simple facts are these: We want the individual to have liberty because only if he can decide what to do can he also use all his unique combination of information, skills and capacities which nobody else can fully appreciate. To enable the individual to fulfil his potential we must also allow him to act on his own estimates of the various chances and probabilities. Since we do not know what he knows, we cannot decide whether his decisions were justified; nor can we know whether his success or failure was due to his efforts and foresight, or to good luck. In other words, we must look at results, not intentions or motives, and can allow him to act on his own knowledge only if we also allow him to keep what his fellows are willing to pay him for his services, irrespective of whether we think this reward appropriate to the moral merit he has earned or the esteem in which we hold him as a person.

Such remuneration, in accordance with the value of a man's services, inevitably is often very different from what we think of his moral merit. This, I believe, is the chief source of the dissatisfaction with a free enterprise system and of the clamour for 'distributive justice'. It is neither honest nor effective to deny that there is such a discrepancy between the moral merit and esteem which a person may earn by his actions and, on the other hand, the value of the services for which we pay him. We place ourselves in an entirely false position if we try to gloss over this fact or to disguise it. Nor have we any need to do so.

It seems to me one of the great merits of a free society that material reward is not dependent on whether the majority of our fellows like or esteem us personally. This means that, so long as we keep within the accepted rules, moral pressure can be brought on us only through the esteem of those whom we ourselves respect and not through the allocation of material reward by a social authority. It is of the essence of a free society that we should be materially rewarded not for doing what others order us to do, but for giving some others what they want. Our conduct ought certainly to be guided by our desire for their esteem. But we are free because the success of our daily efforts does not depend on whether particular people like us, or our principles, or our religion, or our manners, and because we can decide whether the material reward others are prepared to pay for our services makes it worth while for us to render them.

We seldom know whether a brilliant idea which a man suddenly conceives, and which may greatly benefit his fellows, is the result of years of effort and preparatory investment, or whether it is a sudden inspiration induced by an accidental combination of knowledge and circumstance. But we do know that, where in a given instance it has been the former, it would not have been worth while to take the risk if the discoverer were not allowed to reap the benefit. And since we do not know how to distinguish one case from the other, we must also allow a man to get the gain when his good fortune is a matter of luck.

I do not wish to deny, I rather wish to emphasize, that in our society personal esteem and material success are much too closely bound together. We ought to be much more aware that if we regard a man as entitled to a high material reward that in itself does not necessarily entitle him to high esteem. And, though we are often confused on this point, it does not mean that this confusion is a necessary result of the free enterprise system—or that in general the free enterprise system is more materialistic than other social orders. Indeed, and this brings me to the last point I want to make, it seems to me in many respects considerably less so.

In fact, free enterprise has developed the only kind of society which, while it provides us with ample material means, if that is what we mainly want, still leaves the individual free to choose between material and non-material reward. The confusion of which I have been speaking—between the value which a man's services have to his fellows and the esteem he deserves for his moral merit—may well make a free enterprise society materialistic. But the way to prevent this is certainly not to place the control of all material means under a single direction, to make the distribution of material goods the chief concern of all common effort and thus to get politics and economics inextricably mixed.

It is at least possible for a free enterprise society to be in this respect a pluralistic society which knows no single order of rank but has many different principles on which esteem is based; where wordly success is neither the only evidence nor regarded as certain proof of individual merit. It may well be true that periods of a very rapid increase of wealth in which many enjoy the benefits of wealth for the first time, tend to produce for a time a predominant concern with material improvement. Until the recent European upsurge many members of the more comfortable classes there used to decry as materialistic the economically more active periods to which they owed the material comfort which had made it easy for them to devote themselves to other things.

Periods of great cultural and artistic creativity have generally followed, rather than coincided with, the periods of the most rapid increase in wealth. To my mind this shows not that a free society must be dominated by material concerns, but rather that with freedom it is the moral atmosphere in the widest sense, the values which people hold, that will determine the chief direction of their activities. Individuals as well as communities, when they feel that other things have become more important than material advance, can turn to them. It is certainly not by the endeavour to make material reward correspond to all merit, but only by frankly recognizing that there are other and often more important goals than material success, that we can guard ourselves against becoming too materialistic.

Surely it is unjust to blame a system as more materialistic because it leaves it to the individual to decide whether he prefers material gain to other kinds of excellence, instead of having this decided for him. There is indeed little merit in being idealistic if the provision of the material means required for these idealistic aims is left to somebody else. It is only where a person can himself choose to make a material sacrifice for a non-material end that he deserves credit. The desire to be relieved of the choice, and of any need for personal sacrifice, certainly does not seem to me particularly idealistic.

I must say that I find the atmosphere of the advanced Welfare State in every sense more materialistic than that of a free enterprise society. If the latter gives individuals much more scope to serve their fellows by the pursuit of purely materialistic aims, it also gives them the opportunity to pursue any other aim they regard as more important. One must remember, however, that the pure idealism of an aim is questionable whenever the material means necessary for its fulfilment have been created by others.

In conclusion I want for a moment to return to the point from which I started. When we defend the free enterprise system we must always remember that it deals only with means. What we make of our freedom is up to us. We must not confuse efficiency in providing means with the purposes which they serve. A society which has no other standard than efficiency will indeed waste that efficiency. If men are to be free to use their talents to provide us with the means we want, we must remunerate them in accordance with the value these means have to us. Nevertheless, we ought to esteem them only in accordance with the use they make of the means at their disposal.

Let us encourage usefulness to one's fellows by all means, but let us not confuse it with the importance of the ends which men ultimately serve. It is the glory of the free enterprise system that it makes it at least possible that each individual, while serving his fellows, can do so for his own ends. But the system is itself only a means, and its infinite possibilities must be used in the service of ends which exist apart.

CHAPTER SEVENTEEN

What is 'Social'?—What Does it Mean?*

Except in the fields of philology and logic, there are probably few cases in which one would be justified in devoting a whole article to the meaning of a single word. Sometimes, however, such a little word not only throws light upon the process of the evolution of ideas and the story of human error, but often also exercises an irrational power which becomes apparent only when, by analysis, we lay bare its true meaning. I doubt whether there exists a better example of the little understood influence that may be exercised by a single word than that afforded by the role which for a hundred years the word 'social' has played in the whole sphere of political problems—and is still playing. We are so familiar with it, we accept it so much as a matter of course, that we are hardly conscious of any problem regarding its meaning. We have accepted it for so long as the natural description of good behaviour and sincere thinking, that it seems almost sacrilege even to ask what this word really means which so many men consider as the guiding star of their moral aspirations. Indeed, I rather suspect that the majority of my readers, though they may not be quite sure what 'social' means, nevertheless have little doubt that it does indicate an ideal by which all good men should regulate their conduct, and that they will hope that I shall now tell them exactly what it does mean. Let me say at once that in this respect I shall disappoint them; for the primary conclusion to which a meticulous scrutiny of the word and its meaning has led me is that even so exceptionally potent a word as this

* First published in German in *Masse und Demokratie* (ed. A. Hunold), Zürich, 1957 and then in an unauthorized translation in *Freedom and Serfdom* (ed. A. Hunold), Dordrecht, 1961. The present reprint is a revised version of that translation which in parts gravely misrepresented the meaning of the original.

[237]

can be incredibly empty of meaning and offer us no answer to our question.

Generally speaking, I am no friend of the new sport of semantics which derives particular satisfaction from dissecting the meaning of words that are familiar to us all. Equally I have no desire to turn the tables and, for once, to employ against the concepts of the radical reformers the technique which has hitherto been used almost exclusively against the traditional values of the free world. Nevertheless, I see in the ambiguity of the word and the slovenly manner in which it is normally used a very real danger to any clear thinking, to any possibility of reasoned discussion with regard to a great number of our most serious problems. It is, I admit, no pleasant task to have to brush aside the roseate veil in which such a 'good' word has been able to envelop all our discussions on problems of internal policy; but it is a very important task, and one that must be undertaken. The fact that for three or four generations it has been regarded almost as the hall-mark of good men that they make constant use of it, must not be allowed to disguise the other fact that very soon avoidance of its use will inevitably come to be regarded as the hall-mark of clear thinking.

Perhaps it would be as well if, at this juncture, I explained how it came about that, as far as I myself am concerned, a certain *malaise* regarding the use of the word 'social' was transformed into open hostility that caused me to regard it as a real danger. It was the fact that not only did many of my friends in Germany deem it appropriate and desirable to qualify the term 'free market economy' by calling it 'social market economy', but that even the constitution of the Federal German Republic, instead of adhering to the clear and traditional conception of a *Rechtsstaat*, used the new and ambiguous phrase 'a social *Rechtsstaat*'. I doubt very much whether anyone could really explain what the addition of this adjectival frill is supposed to denote. But in any case, it gave me a great deal to think about, and the second of the two instances I have quoted will furnish lawyers in the future with plenty of hard nuts to crack.

Be that as it may, the final conclusion emerging from my deliberations has been that the word 'social' has become an adjective which robs of its clear meaning every phrase it qualifies and transforms it into a phrase of unlimited elasticity, the implications of which can always be distorted if they are unacceptable, and the use of which, as a general rule, serves merely to conceal the lack of real agreement between men regarding a formula upon which, in appearance, they are supposed to be agreed. To a large extent it seems to me that it is to the result of this attempt to dress up political slogans in a guise acceptable to all tastes that phrases like 'social market economy' and the like owe their existence. When we all use a word which always confuses and never clarifies the issue, which pretends to give an answer where no answer exists and, even worse, which is so often used as camouflage for aspirations that certainly have nothing to do with the common interest, then the time has obviously come for a radical operation which will free us from the confusing influence of this magical incantation.

Nothing brings more clearly to light the role played in our thinking by our interpretation of the meaning of 'social' than the significant fact that in the course of the last few decades the word has, in all languages known to me, to an ever increasing degree taken the place of the word 'moral' or simply 'good'. An interesting light is thrown on the whole issue if we ask ourselves what, exactly, does it mean when we speak of 'social' feeling or conduct, where our grandparents or great-grand-parents would simply have said that a man was a good man or that his conduct was ethical? Once upon a time a man was good if he obeyed the ethical rules, or was a good citizen when he acted faithfully according to the laws of his country. What, then, was implied in this new demand, which the freshly awakened 'social conscience' made of us and which has led to a distinction being drawn between 'mere' morality and a 'social' sense?

Primarily, it was doubtless a praiseworthy appeal that we should carry our thinking further than we had been in the habit of doing, that in our actions and our attitude we should take into consideration the situation and the problems of *all* the members of our society. In order, however, fully to understand what was meant by this, we must go back to the situation as it was when the 'social question' first became the subject of public discussion. This, in the middle of the last century, was, roughly speaking, a situation in which both political discussion and the taking of political decisions were confined to a small upper class; and there were good grounds for reminding this upper class that they were responsible for the fate of 'the most numerous and poorest' sections of the community, who themselves had little or no part in the government of the country. It was at that time—when the civilized world had discovered that there existed an 'underworld', which it felt itself called upon to 'raise', if it were not to be engulfed by it, and before the era of modern democracy and universal suffrage—that 'social' came to assume the meaning of the taking care of those who were incapable of grasping where their own interests lay—a concept which seems somewhat of an anachronism in an age when it is the masses who wield political power.

Side by side with this challenge to deal with problems of whose existence many had until then been unaware, there was, however, another, though kindred, school of thought, which drew a distinction between the necessity for 'social' thinking and conduct and the demands of the traditionally accepted ethical standards. The rules of the latter referred to the concrete and recognized situation in which a man found himself, and prescribed the things he should in bounden duty do or refrain from doing, regardless of the consequences. (A man, for example, did not lie or cheat, even though it might be to his or someone else's advantage that he should do so.) But the demand for 'social' thinking contained also the demand that we should consciously take into consideration even the very remote consequences of our actions and should order our conduct accordingly.

In this respect the demand for social conduct differed fundamentally from the traditionally accepted tenets of morality and justice, which, on principle, expect a man to give due consideration only to those consequences of his actions which in normal circumstances would be readily apparent to him; from this it easily followed that a man came to regard it as desirable that he should be instructed as to what he should or could do in any given case by someone endowed with greater knowledge and judgment than himself. This whole conception of social conduct is most closely linked, therefore, with a desire for a comprehensive blueprint of the social scene as a whole and a code of social conduct based upon it in accordance with a uniform and orderly plan. Implicit in this conception is also the desire to see all individual activity directed towards defined 'social' aims and tasks and subordinated to the interests of the 'community'. These tasks and aims may or may not be recognizable to the individual, but they will not, in any case, be achieved if the individual, even though his actions may consistently be governed by the traditional rules of conduct and justice, devotes his activities solely to the promotion of his own aspirations.

As long as forty years ago, the Cologne sociologist, Leopold von Wiese, drew attention to this somewhat peculiar interpretation of the social idea. In an essay published in January 1919[1] he remarked: 'Only those who were young men in the "social age"—the decades immediately before the war—can appreciate how strong was the inclination to regard the social sphere as a substitute for the religious. In those days there existed a dramatic manifestation—the social pastors. Even the philosophers fell under their spell. One particularly loquacious gentleman wrote a voluminous book, entitled *The Social Question in the Light of*

---

[1] *Der Liberalismus in Vergangenheit und Zukunft*, Berlin, 1917, p. 115.

Philosophy. . . . In the meanwhile, throughout Europe, and particularly in Germany, social work had been crowned with a halo. Rationally assessed, the relative value of all social policies and charitable activities is very considerable; but their limitations must be very clearly recognized. To be "social" is not the same as being good or "righteous in the eyes of the Lord".'

That this use of the word 'social' instead of simply saying 'moral' constitutes a complete change, indeed, almost a complete reversal, of its original meaning becomes apparent only when we go back some two hundred years to the era in which the concept of society was first discovered—or at any rate first became the subject of scientific discussion—and ask ourselves what, exactly, it was supposed to denote. It was, of course, introduced to describe that order of human relationships which had developed spontaneously, as distinct from the deliberate organization of the State. We still use the word in its original sense when we talk about 'social forces' or 'social structures', such as language and customs, or rights that have gradually come to be recognized in contrast to rights that have been deliberately granted; and the object thereof was to show that these things were not the creations of an individual will, but the unforeseen results of the haphazard activities of countless individuals and generations. The truly social in this sense is, of its very nature, anonymous, non-rational and not the result of logical reasoning, but the outcome of a supra-individual process of evolution and selection, to which the individual, admittedly, makes his contribution, but the component parts of which cannot be mastered by any one single intelligence.

It came to be realized that there existed forces working quite independently of the aspirations of mankind, and that the combination of their activities gave birth to structures which furthered the endeavours of the individual, even though they had not been designed for the purpose; and it was this realization that led to the introduction of the concept of society, as distinct from the deliberately created and directed State.

How quickly the meaning of the word has changed until it has been transformed almost into the very opposite of its original meaning, becomes clear when we consider what it denotes in the very frequently used phrase, 'the social order'. This phrase *can*, of course, be used exclusively in the sense of something created spontaneously *by* society itself. Mostly, however, the word 'social' in this connection denotes nothing more than something or other *connected with* the community, if not, indeed, primarily the only sort of order which so many people are capable of envisaging, namely, a social structure which has been forcibly imposed, as it were, on the community from without. How few there are today who understand Ortega y Gasset's dictum that 'order is not a pressure imposed upon society from without, but an equilibrium which is set up from within'.

If we are content to designate as social not only those co-ordinating forces which come into being as the result of the independent activities of the individual in the community, but also everything else which has in any way anything to do with the community, then the whole essential difference becomes completely obliterated. There then remains little or nothing in life which is not 'social' in one sense or another, and the word becomes, to all practical intents, meaningless. It is therefore high time that these various meanings were sorted out. Let us for the moment adhere to the meaning 'peculiar to society' or 'arising out of a specifically social process'—the sense in which we use it when speaking of social structures and social forces. This is a sense in which we have urgent need of the word, and the true sense, which I should like to see reserved for it. It is obviously quite different from the sense in which we use it in such phrases as 'social awareness', 'social conscience', 'social responsibility', 'social activities', 'social welfare', 'social policy', 'social legislation' or 'social justice', or from the other sense implicit in the terms 'social insurance', 'social rights' or 'social control'. One of the most astonishing, albeit most familiar, combinations of this kind is 'social democracy'—I should very much like to know what aims of a democracy can be said to be not social, and why! That, however, is by the way.

The really important point is, that all these combinations have but little to do with the specific character of social forces, and that, in particular, the difference between that which has developed spontaneously and that which has been deliberately organized by the State has completely disappeared. In so far as 'social' is not taken to mean merely 'communal', the word, obviously, should mean either 'in the interest of society' or 'in accordance with the will of society', i.e., of the majority, or sometimes perhaps 'an obligation on society' as such, *vis-à-vis* the relatively less fortunate minority. I do not propose here to discuss the question why the rather indefinite word 'society' should be preferred to such precise and concrete terms as 'the people', 'the nation' or 'the citizens of a State', although it is these latter that are meant. The important thing, to me, is that in all these uses the word 'social' *presupposes* the existence of known and common aims behind the activities of a community, *but does not define them*. It is simply assumed that 'society' has certain concrete tasks that are known to all and are acknowledged by all, and that 'society' should direct the endeavours of its individual members to the accomplishment of these tasks. 'Society' thus assumes a dual personality: it is firstly a thinking, collective entity with aspirations of its own that are different from those of the individuals of whom it is composed; and secondly, by identifying it with them, it becomes the personification of the views held on these social aspirations by certain individuals who claim to be endowed with a more profound insight or to possess a stronger sense of moral values. Frequently enough a speaker will claim that his own views and aspirations are 'social', while those of his opponent are brushed aside as 'anti-social'. There is, I think, no need for me further to emphasize that, when 'social' is used in the sense of 'serving the interests of society', it certainly raises a problem, but provides no solution. It concedes precedence to certain values to which society should adhere, but it does not describe them. Were the word strictly used in this sense, there would, I think, be but little objection. In point of fact, however, not only does it compete in many ways with existing ethical values, but it has also undermined their prestige and influence. Indeed, I am coming more and more to the belief that the substitution of this rubber word, 'social', to denote values we have always described as 'moral', may well be one of the main causes of the general degeneration of moral sense in the world.

The first great difference, at which I have already hinted, stems from the fact that the tenets of ethical behaviour consist of abstract, general rules which we are called upon to obey, regardless of what the consequences may be and very often without our even knowing why it is desirable that we should act in one particular way and in no other. These rules have never been invented, and no one, so far, has ever succeeded in producing a rational foundation of the whole of the existing system of ethical behaviour. As I see them, these rules are genuine social growths, the results of a process of evolution and selection, the distilled essence of experiences of which we ourselves have no knowledge. They have acquired general authority because the groups in which they held sway have proved themselves to be more effective than other groups. Their claim to be observed is not based upon the fact that the individual is aware of the consequences of disregarding them, but they exemplify a recognition of the fundamental fact that the majority of these concrete consequences are beyond our ken and that our actions will not lead to constant conflict with our fellow men only when they are guided by rules which pay due regard to the circumstances under which we commit them. But it is against the very nature of *all* these rules of ethical behaviour and justice that this bogus rationalism to which the concept of 'social interest' owes its origin, transgresses. Rationalism refuses to be guided by anything it does not completely understand; it reserves to itself the right to decide what is desirable in each individual case, because it claims to be fully aware of all possible consequences; it refuses to obey any rules, but insists on pursuing definite, concrete aims. But by so doing, it transgresses against every fundamental principle of ethical behaviour, for agreement regarding the importance of any aspiration is only possible if it is reached in unison and in accordance with accepted general rules which themselves are impervious to rationalization. Thus, by undermining respect for rules and 'plain' ethical behaviour, this demand for 'social behaviour' is destroying the foundations on which it is itself built.

This dependence of the conception of what is 'social' on ethical rules which are not explicitly stated or simply disregarded is shown most clearly by the fact that it leads to an extension of the concept of justice to fields to which it is not applicable.[2] The demand for a just or more equal distribution of the world's goods has today become one of the primary 'social' demands. The application of the concept of justice to distribution requires, however, reward according to merit or desert, and merit cannot be measured by achievement but only by the extent to which known rules of ethics have been observed. Reward according to merit thus presupposes that we know all the circumstances which led to a particular performance. But in a free society we allow the individual to decide himself about his actions because we do not know those very circumstances which determine how meritorious his achievement is. It is therefore necessary in a free society to reward the individuals according to the value of the services actually rendered to their fellows, a value which has often little relation to the subjective merit they have earned in rendering them. The concept of justice has application only in so far as all will be equally rewarded according to the value of the objective results of their efforts and not according to someone's judgment of the merit they have thereby acquired. The demand for the latter, for a reward according to merit, is a demand which cannot be met in a free society, because we cannot know or isolate all the circumstances which determine merit. The attempt at a partial application of the principle of reward according to merit can, however, lead only to general injustice, because it would mean that different people were rewarded

---

[2] The extent to which the misuse of the word 'social' has been pushed in this connection seems at last to have provoked protests in other quarters; and it was with great satisfaction that, shortly after delivering this lecture, I read in a book review by Charles Curran in *The Spectator* of July 6, 1958 (p. 8) the sentence: 'Social Justice is a semantic fraud from the same stable as People's Democracy.'

according to different principles. Such abuse of the concept of justice must ultimately lead to a destruction of the sense of justice.

In reality, things in this connection are even worse. Since in questions of distribution there exists no yardstick of justice, other and less noble feelings inevitably and unexpectedly insinuate themselves when decisions come to be taken. That the social concept in this context is only too frequently used as a cloak for envy, that a sentiment which John Stuart Mill has rightly described as the most anti-social of all passions,[3] should be able to make its appearance, decked in the beautifying form of an ethical demand, is one of the worst consequences for which we have to thank the unthinking use of the word 'social'.

The third point in which the predominance of the idea of the 'social' has had an anti-ethical effect is the destruction of the feeling of personal responsibility to which it has led. Originally, the appeal to the social sense was expected to lead to a more widely spread acceptance of personal responsibility. But the confusion that arose between the further aims to which the individual man should aspire, between the taking-into-consideration of social repercussions and social—in the sense of collective—behaviour, and between the moral obligations of the individual to the community and his claims upon it, has gradually undermined that sense of personal responsibility which is the foundation of all ethics. To this, all kinds of intellectual movements have made their contributions, into which I cannot go in any detail, but which, like 'social psychology', in most cases sail under the 'social' flag. Indeed, there seems to me to be very little doubt that this whole process which has thoroughly confused the issue as regards personal responsibility, absolving the individual on the one hand of all responsibility as regards his immediate environment and, on the other hand, placing upon him vague and undefined responsibilities for things that are not clearly apparent, has, by and large, led to a marked diminution of man's sense of personal responsibility. Without placing upon the individual any new and clear obligations which he has to fulfil by his own personal endeavours, it has expunged the boundaries of all responsibility and has become a standing invitation to make further demands or to do good at the expense of others.

Fourthly, with their emphasis on concrete aims and on the claims of expediency, these 'social movements' have hindered more than they have promoted the very essential emergence of genuine principles of political ethics. All ethics and justice are based, surely, on the application of general, abstract principles to concrete cases; and the dictum that the

[3] John Stuart Mill, *On Liberty*, 1859 (p. 10).

end justifies the means has for a long time been justly regarded as a negation of all that is ethical. It is, however, just this that is, in fact, very often meant by the plea, so frequently heard nowadays, that due consideration must be given to 'the social aspect'. As regards the genuine products of social evolution, such as justice and ethics, it is claimed on behalf of the social will of the moment that it is justified in neglecting those principles in favour of its own immediate aims.

I have, unfortunately, insufficient space to go in any detail into the reasons why the rules of political ethics, like all other rules of ethics, are, of their nature, long-term principles, and for that reason must not be judged on the evidence of their effect upon an individual case. More important from our point of view is the fact that it is only as the result of a long and unfettered process of evolution that these rules are able to come into being and to acquire authority. Only when adherence to a principle comes, as a matter of course, to be regarded as more important than success in any individual case, and only when we acknowledge that the use of compulsion is justifiable solely when it is applied in accordance with general principles, and never when it is used as an expedient in the pursuit of a concrete aim, can we hope that a general principle of political ethics will gradually come to be accepted by all. Any 'social' code of ethics must be based upon rules which are binding on the collective behaviour of society, and to me it seems that we are further from a recognition of this fact today than we were in the past.

For there certainly *was* a time when a conscious sense of what was just and right imposed ethical limits on the use of compulsion by society for its own ends. The ideal of the freedom of the individual was one, and, indeed, the most important, of these ethical rules of political behaviour which, at one time, enjoyed universal recognition. But it is just this ideal that those who march under the 'social' standard have been attacking with ever increasing vehemence. The ideals of freedom and independence, of being answerable to one's own conscience and of respect for the individual, have all gone by the board under the dominant pressure of the conception of the 'social'. But in reality, it is the nurturing of the spontaneous forces of freedom that truly constitutes a service to society —to that which has grown, as distinct from that which has been deliberately created—and to the further strengthening of the creative forces of the social process. What we have experienced under the banner of the social concept has been a metamorphosis from service *to* society to a demand for an absolute control *of* society, from a demand for the subordination of the State to the free forces of society to a demand for the subordination of society to the State. If the human intellect is allowed to impose a preconceived pattern on society, if our powers of reasoning are allowed to lay claim to a monopoly of creative effort (and hence to recognition only of premeditated results), then we must not be surprised if society, as such, ceases to function as a creative force. And in particular we must not be surprised if, from a policy based upon the ideal of material equality, there emerges a mass society, admittedly more thoroughly organized, but devoid of any spontaneous articulation. True service to the social concept is not rendered by the imposition of absolute authority or leadership, nor does it even consist of common endeavour towards a common aim, but rather of the contribution that each and every one of us makes to a process which is greater than any one of us, from which there constantly emerges something new, something unforeseen, and which can flourish only in freedom. In the last resort we find ourselves constrained to repudiate the ideal of the social concept because it has become the ideal of those who, on principle, deny the existence of a true society and whose longing is for the artificially constructed and the rationally controlled. In this context, it seems to me that a great deal of what today professes to be social is, in the deeper and truer sense of the word, thoroughly and completely anti-social.

PART THREE

Economics

CHAPTER EIGHTEEN

The Economy, Science, and Politics*

I

The assumption of new duties and the entry into a new sphere of activities are for the academic teacher a salutary occasion for giving an account of the aims of his efforts. This is even more true when, after long years of study in various parts of the world which were devoted more to research than to teaching, he speaks for his first time from the place at which he hopes during the remainder of his active life to pass on the fruits of his experience.

I do not know to what good star I owe it that for the third time in the course of one life that faculty has honoured me with the offer of a chair which I would have chosen if an absolutely free choice in such things were possible. Not only is the move to this place in the heart of Europe, exactly half-way between Vienna and London, the two places which have shaped me intellectually, and in addition in *Vorder-Österreich*,[1] after a dozen years in the New World, for me something like coming home—even though my acquaintance with Freiburg counts only in days. I also value particularly the opportunity to teach again in a faculty of law, in the atmosphere to which I owe my own schooling. After one has endeavoured for thirty years to teach economics to students possessing no knowledge of law or the history of legal institutions, one is sometimes

* Inaugural lecture delivered (in German) at the assumption of the professorship of Political Economy at the University of Freiburg i.B., June 18, 1962, and published under the title, *Wirtschaft, Wissenschaft und Politik*, Freiburg i.B., 1963. Footnotes have been added to the translation.

[1] Hither-Austria: The Breisgau in which Freiburg is situated and some connected territories used to be called *Vorder-Österreich* during the centuries when they were part of the domain of the Habsburgs.

tempted to ask whether the separation of legal and economic studies was not perhaps, after all, a mistake. For my own person, although I have retained little knowledge of positive law, I have at any rate always been grateful that when I commenced the study of economics, this was possible only as part of the study of law.

Special mention is due to the personal contacts with professional colleagues which have for decades provided for me a connection with this university. Unfortunately these ties have been severed by the premature death of those contemporaries to whom community of convictions had drawn me. With Adolf Lampe and with my predecessor in this chair, Alfons Schmitt, whom I unfortunately never met in person, I have long been connected by common interests which occasionally had led to an exchange of views by correspondence. With Leonhard Miksch I shared in addition common efforts for the elaboration of an economic philosophy for a free society. By far the most important for me was, however, the friendship of many years' standing, based on the closest agreement on scientific as well as on political questions, with the unforgettable Walter Eucken. During the last four years of his life this friendship had led to close collaboration; and I would like to use this opportunity to tell you of the extraordinary reputation which Eucken had gained in the world during this period.

More than fifteen years ago—less than two years after the end of the war—I had undertaken to call an international conference of some economists, lawyers and historians of the Western world who were passionately concerned about the preservation of personal freedom. The conference was held in Switzerland and it was at that time not only still incredibly difficult to make it possible for a German to enter Switzerland, but also the problem of a meeting between scholars from what so recently had been enemy camps was at that time, curious as this fortunately sounds fifteen years later, a cause of some apprehension and hesitation. My friends and I had initially hoped to get the historian, Franz Schnabel, and Walter Eucken to Switzerland, but we succeeded in overcoming all the technical difficulties only with regard to Eucken, who, in consequence, was the only participant from Germany at the conference on Mont Pélèrin. This made it the more significant that he became the great personal success of the conference and that his moral stature made the most profound impression on all participants. He has thereby contributed much to restore in the West the belief in the existence of liberal thinkers in Germany, and he has further strengthened this impression at a further conference of the Mont Pélèrin Society and on a visit to London in 1950 from which he was not to return.

You know better than I what Eucken has achieved in Germany. I need therefore not explain further what it means if I say here today that I shall regard it as one of my chief tasks to resume and continue the tradition which Eucken and his friends have created at Freiburg and in Germany. It is a tradition of the greatest scientific integrity and at the same time of outspoken conviction on the great issues of public life. The extent to which, and the conditions under which, these two aims can be combined in the academic work of an economist will be the main subject of my further observations.

II

In spite of the fact that at least the first half of my career as an economist has been wholly devoted to pure theory, and because I have since devoted much time to subjects entirely outside the field of economics, I do welcome the prospect that my teaching is to concern in future mainly problems of economic policy. I am very anxious, however, to state clearly and publicly, even before I start on my regular courses, what seem to me the aims and the limits of the contributions of science and the tasks of academic instruction in the field of economic policy.

In this I will not dwell longer than necessary on the much discussed problem which arises here in the first instance and which I cannot wholly pass over even though I have nothing new to say about it: the role of value judgments in the social sciences in general and in the discussion of questions of economic and social policy in particular. It is now almost fifty years since Max Weber stated the essentials of this issue, and if one now re-reads his careful formulations one finds little that one wishes to add. The effects of his admonitions may perhaps sometimes have gone too far. But we must not be surprised that at a time when economics threatened to degenerate in Germany into a doctrine of social reform, and a school of economics could describe itself as the 'ethical school', he pushed his argument to a point where it could also have been misunderstood. This unfortunately has often produced a fear of expressing any value judgments and even to an avoidance of some of the most important problems which the economist ought frankly to face in his teaching.

The general principles which we ought to follow in this respect are really very simple—however difficult may often be their application in a particular case. It is of course an elementary duty of intellectual honesty to distinguish clearly between connections of cause and effect, on which science is competent to pronounce, and the desirability or undesirability of particular results. Science as such has of course nothing to say on the relative values of ultimate aims. It is equally obvious that the very selection of our problems for scientific examination implies valuations and that therefore the clear separation of scientific knowledge and valuations cannot be achieved by avoiding all valuations, but only by an unmistakable statement of the guiding values. It seems equally incontestable that the academic teacher should not pretend to be neutral or indifferent but should make it easier for his audience to recognize the dependence of his practical conclusions on value judgment by openly stating his personal ideals as such.

It appears to me today as if, at the time when I was a student and for some time thereafter, under the influence of Max Weber's powerful argument, we had been more restrained in this respect than was desirable. When, more than thirty years ago, and somewhat more than a year after I had assumed a professorship at the University of London, I gave my first inaugural lecture and used the opportunity to explain my general economic philosophy,[2] I still felt gratified when I discovered that the students were surprised and disappointed to find that I did not share their predominantly socialist views. It is true that my lectures until then had been confined to questions of pure theory and that I had had no special occasion to deal explicitly with political questions. Today I ask myself whether, rather than being proud of my impartiality, I ought not to have had a bad conscience when I discovered how successfully I had hidden the presuppositions which had guided me at least in the choice of problems I thought to be important.

It was partly that experience which made me desire that on the present occasion my inaugural lecture should really be my first lecture to you, and made me desire to state in it certain views which will be presupposed in much that I shall have to say in the discussion of particular issues.

Concerning the question of the role of value judgments and the appropriateness of taking in academic teaching a position on politically contested issues, I want to add two more observations. The first is that I believe that if Max Weber had lived twenty years longer he would probably have changed his emphasis a little. When in his day he represented intellectual honesty as the only virtue which the academic teacher has to support, it might still have seemed as if this demand had nothing to do with politics. We have since learnt that there exist political systems which make very difficult even such intellectual honesty as is a basic condition for all genuine science. It is certainly possible to preserve intellectual honesty in the most difficult conditions. But we are not all heroes, and if we value science we must also advocate a social

[2] 'The Trend of Economic Thinking', *Economica*, May 1933.

order which does not make such intellectual honesty too difficult. There seems to me to exist in this respect a close connection between the ideals of science and the ideals of personal liberty.

The second point is that it seems to me a clear duty of the social scientist to ask certain questions the mere raising of which will seem to imply the taking of a political position. One illustration will suffice to explain what I have in mind. It is probably sufficient to mark a scholar in many circles as an enemy of the working class if he merely asks whether it is true, as is almost universally believed, that the wage policies of the trade unions have resulted in raising the real wages of the workers as a whole to a level higher than it would otherwise be. There exist in fact not only good reasons to doubt this but even a fair probability that the opposite is true and that as a necessary consequence of the wage policy of the unions the real wages—or at least the real income—of the whole working class is lower than it would have been without it.

The considerations which lead to this apparently paradoxical and certainly not generally understood conclusion are fairly simple and rest on theorems which are scarcely disputed. The power of any particular union to push up the wages of its members, that is, to make them higher than they would be without the activity of the union, rests entirely on its ability to prevent the entry into the trade of workers willing to work for a lower wage. This will have the effect that the latter either must work elsewhere at still lower wages or that they will remain unemployed. It is, of course, in general true that the unions will be strong in prospering and rapidly developing trades and less powerful in stagnating or declining trades. This means that the power of any one union to raise the wages of its members rests on their preventing the movement of workers from points where their marginal productivity is low to points where their marginal productivity is high. This must result in the overall marginal productivity of labour and therefore the level of real wages being kept lower than it would otherwise be.

If we represent this as only a probable and not a certain effect the reason for this is that we cannot exclude the possibility that the gain of that group of workers whose wages are pushed up beyond the level which would establish itself on a free market may be greater than the loss of the group whose wages will be lower than they would be if they had access to the prospering trade. The increased wages of one group will thus certainly be bought at the expense of greater inequality and probably also at the price of a lower real income of the working class as a whole.

I need hardly stress that all these considerations apply only to real wages and not to money wages—and that the fact that the wage policy of the unions may lead to a general rise of money wages, and to inflation, is the reason for the persistence of the illusion that thanks to the unions wages in general are higher than they would otherwise be.

You will observe that the answer to this problem, although likely to arouse intense political passion, depends in no way on value judgments. The answer I have sketched may be true or false—and it is certainly not as simple as such a brief sketch makes it appear—but its truth or falsity depends on the correctness of the theory and perhaps on some particular facts of the concrete situation, but not on our opinion of the desirability or undesirability of the aims we pursue. This is fortunately true of a very great part of the problems of economic policy—I believe of far the greater part. But even where at first there appears to exist unbridgeable contrasts of moral valuations, it usually proves that if the disputing parties can agree on the alternatives between which they have to choose, their differences tend to disappear.

III

Let me show this in somewhat greater detail with respect to the central problem on which socialists and the supporters of a free economy are still in disagreement. I speak of their *still* being in disagreement, because one argument which at one time was seriously advanced in support of socialism has been pretty generally abandoned as a result of the scientific discussion of the problem. This is the contention that a centrally directed economy would be more productive than one guided by the market. I shall later, in another context, return to this question and mention it here only in order to point out that, even if the falsity of this belief were conceded, this does not yet dispose of the argument in support of socialism. Because for most socialists as important as, if not even more important than, the increased general supply of goods is the distribution of those we get. It would be wholly consistent, even though perhaps not very expedient politically, if a socialist guided solely by ethical considerations were to maintain that even a considerable reduction of the aggregate real social income would not be too high a price to pay for achieving a more just distribution of that income.

Even the advocate of a free economy must concede that the conception of justice which inspires socialism can be realized, if at all, only in a centrally directed economy. Yet the question remains whether the socialist would really be prepared to accept *all* the effects which a realization of his ideal of justice would bring about and of which the reduction of material productivity may not be the most important. If that were the case we could indeed only admit a difference on ultimate values which no rational discussion could remove. This, however, seems to me by no means to be the case, and a somewhat more searching analysis of the different but usually vague conceptions which the disputing parties have of what they call 'social justice' will soon show this. In the terminology current since Aristotle we can express the difference by saying that a free economy can always achieve only commutative justice, while socialism—and in a great measure the popular ideal of social justice—demands distributive justice. Commutative justice means here a reward according to the value which a person's services actually have to those of his fellows to whom he renders them, and which finds expression in the price the latter are willing to pay. This value has, as we must concede, no necessary connection with moral merit. It will be the same, irrespective of whether a given performance was in the case of one man the result of great effort and painful sacrifice while it is rendered by another with playful ease and perhaps even for his own enjoyment, or whether he was able to meet a need at the right moment as a result of prudent foresight or by sheer chance. Commutative justice takes no account of personal or subjective circumstances, of needs or good intentions, but solely of how the results of a man's activities are valued by those who make use of them.

The results of such remuneration according to the value of the product must appear as highly unjust from the point of view of distributive justice. It will rarely correspond to what we regard as the subjective merit of a performance. That the speculator who by chance has guessed correctly may earn a fortune in a few hours while the life-long efforts of an inventor who has been anticipated by another by a few days remains unremunerated, or that the hard work of the peasant who clings to his soil barely brings him enough to keep going, while a man who enjoys writing detective stories thereby earns enough to afford a luxurious life, will appear unjust to most people. I understand the dissatisfaction produced by the daily observation of such cases and honour the feeling which calls for distributive justice. If it were a question whether fate or some omnipotent and omniscient power should reward people according to the principles of commutative or according to those of distributive justice, we would probably all choose the latter.

This, however, is not the position in the existing world. In the first instance, we cannot assume that, if the system of remuneration were altogether different, the individual men would still do what they do now. Indeed we can now leave them to decide for themselves what they want to do because they bear the risk of their choice and because we remunerate them not according to their effort and the honesty of their intentions but solely according to the value of the results of their activity. Free choice of occupation and free decision by each of what he wants to produce or what services he wants to render are irreconcilable with distributive justice. The latter is a justice which remunerates each according as he discharges duties which he owes in the opinions of others. It is the kind of justice which may and perhaps must prevail within a military or bureaucratic organization in which each member is judged according to the measure in which in the opinion of his superiors he discharges tasks set to him; and it can extend no further than the group that acts under one authority for the same purposes. It is the justice of a command-society or command-economy and irreconcilable with the freedom of each to decide what he wants to do.

It is irreconcilable, moreover, not only with freedom of action but also with freedom of opinion—because it requires that all men are made to serve a unitary hierarchy of values. In fact, of course, neither do we agree on what represents greater or lesser merit, nor can we objectively ascertain the facts on which such a judgment is based. The merit of an action is in its nature something subjective and rests in a large measure on circumstances which only the acting person can know and the importance of which different people will assess very differently. Does it constitute greater merit to overcome personal loathing or pain, physical weakness or illness? Does it constitute greater merit to have risked one's life or to have damaged one's reputation? Individually each of us may have very definite answers to such questions, but there is little probability that we shall all agree and evidently no possibility to prove to others that our opinion is right. This means, however, that for an attempt to remunerate men according to their subjective merit it must always be the opinion of a few which must be imposed upon the rest. Distributive justice therefore demands not only personal unfreedom but the enforcement of an indisputable hierarchy of values, in other words, a strictly totalitarian regime.

Whether this conclusion is inevitable is of course, again, a matter which one might discuss at considerable length. But for my present purpose the point is solely that it depends only on scientific analysis and not on any value judgments. Only after we have agreed what would be the consequences of enforcing either kind of justice will the choice between them depend on valuations. Personally it seems to me that scarcely anyone who has understood and admits that distributive justice can be realized generally only in a system of personal unfreedom and personal arbitrariness is likely to decide in favour of distributive justice. There are of course many people to whom my argument does not appear cogent, and with them discussion may be instructive and worthwhile. But if anybody concedes the conclusion and asserts that he still prefers a system which realizes an ideal of distributive justice at the price of personal unfreedom and unlimited authority of a few to a system in which personal freedom is combined with merely commutative justice which to him may appear as supreme injustice, science indeed has nothing further to say.

In many instances, in fact, after we have brought out the consequences of alternative decisions, it will appear not only as very pedantic but almost a mockery to add that it is now left to the listener or reader to choose. Already in the first great theoretical work of our science, Richard Cantillon's *Essai sur la nature du commerce en général*, in which more than two hundred years ago the distinction was clearly drawn, it is sometimes difficult not to feel that the author has no doubt about the answer when, for example, he breaks off his discussion of the population problem with the remark that it cannot be the task of science to decide whether it is better to have a numerous but poor or a small but rich population. But we should probably not be afraid of this sort of pedantry which is often resented as a kind of *reductio ad absurdum* and does not tend to make popular those who employ it.

IV

It is necessary now to turn to another limitation of the possibility of a scientific justification of particular political measures which is less familiar but probably more important. This is a consequence of the fundamental difficulty of any complete explanation of highly complex phenomena and not merely of an insufficient development of economic theory. Although there are undoubtedly still many open questions of this theory, it seems to me that it is on the whole in a fairly satisfactory state. My opinion is that the source of our difficulties lies elsewhere than in an insufficiently advanced state of theory which, I sometimes feel, has been refined to a point where in fact we can no longer apply it to the real world.

I take it that I need not defend here the view that only theory can be regarded as science in the strict sense. Knowledge of facts as such is not science and does not help us to control or influence the course of things. But even theoretical insight, even where it enables us to understand in a large measure why things happen as they do, does not always make it possible to predict particular events or to shape things as we desire—if we do not *also* know the particular facts which constitute the data which we must insert into the formulae of our theory. This is where the great obstacle to a full explanation or to effective control of really complex phenomena appears. It seems to me as if in this respect economists often forget the limits of their power and give the unjustified impression that their advanced theoretical insight enables them in concrete instances to predict the particular consequences of given events or measures.

The difficulty I am going to discuss arises not only in economics but in all subjects which deal with processes in highly complex structures. It exists as much in theoretical biology and psychology as in all the social sciences and for this reason deserves somewhat careful consideration, particularly as the example of the physical sciences has often led to a false approach in those fields.

All theory consists in the statement of abstract and schematic orders or patterns. The kinds of order which are characteristic for different groups of phenomena may be relatively simple or relatively complex, by which I mean that the characteristic principle which gives the class of phenomena their distinct character can be exhibited by models which consist of comparatively few elements or only by models which consist of comparatively large numbers of elements. In this sense the phenomena of mechanics are comparatively simple—or, rather, we call mechanical those processes whose principles can be represented by relatively simple models. This does not mean that in particular cases those simple relations cannot be combined into extremely complex structures. But the mere multiplication of the elements does here not produce something new, however difficult may be the application of the simple theory to some of those complex structures.

Because in those fields the theoretical formulae (the description of the characteristic kind of order or pattern) are relatively simple, it will as a rule also be possible to insert into them all the concrete data which must be known to make particular events predictable. For the physicist or chemist the theory, the general description of the kind of order, is for this reason generally of interest only to the extent that, by the insertion of concrete data, he can derive from it specific predictions of individual events. And though he has of course also his difficulties in thus applying his theory, he will generally assume that the particular data which he has to insert into his mathematical formulae can be ascertained to any degree of exactness required to make precise predictions. To him it often appears therefore as incomprehensible that the economist should bother to construct theories which look very much like physical theories and may for instance be stated in the form of systems of simultaneous equations, although the latter admits that he can never ascertain all the data which he would have to insert into the equations before he can solve them.

It is, however, by no means evident that the prediction (or the explanation of the appearance) of an abstract order or pattern of a certain kind is useful or interesting only if we can explain also its concrete manifestation. In the case of simple orders the difference between their general character and their particular manifestation is indeed not very significant. But the more complex the order is, and particularly as several ordering principles are superimposed over each other, the more important this distinction becomes. The prediction merely of the fact that we shall find a certain arrangement of elements will often be an interesting, and above all a refutable and therefore empirical prediction, even if we can say little about the particular properties of those elements, their magnitude or distance, etc. Even in the physical sciences there occur many instances in which our knowledge justifies only the prediction of a general arrangement. The mineralogist, for example, who knows that a certain substance will form hexagonal crystals, will often not be in a position to predict what the size of these crystals will be. But what is rather the exception in the physical sciences is the rule in the sciences of the more highly organized structures. We often know enough to determine the general character of the order which we shall find. Our theory may even be adequate to derive from it the particular events which will occur, provided that we assume that the particular circumstances are known. The difficulty is merely that these particular circumstances are so numerous that we can never ascertain them all!

This, I believe, is true of a large part of theoretical biology, especially of the biological theory of evolution, and certainly of the theoretical social sciences. One of the best examples is the systems of equations of the mathematical theory of prices. They show in an impressive and on the whole probably true manner how the whole system of prices of goods and services is determined by the desires, the resources and the knowledge of all the individuals and enterprises. But, as the creators of the theory perfectly understood, the purpose of those equations is *not* to arrive at a numerical determination of those prices, since, as Vilfredo Pareto put it, it would be 'absurd' to assume that we could ever ascertain all the particular data. Their purpose is exclusively to describe the general character of the order that will form itself. Since this order implies the existence of certain relations between the elements, and the actual presence or absence of such relations can be ascertained, the prediction of such an order can be shown to be false, and the theory will thus be empirically testable. But we shall always be able to predict only the general character of the order and not its detail. So far as I know, no economist has yet succeeded in using his knowledge of theory to make a fortune by a prediction of future prices. (This applies even to Lord Keynes who is sometimes thought to have done so. But so long as he speculated in the field in which one might have thought that his theoretical knowledge would have helped him, namely in foreign exchange, he lost more than he possessed; and only later, when he turned to speculation in commodities where admittedly his theoretical knowledge was of no use to him, did he succeed in acquiring a substantial fortune.)

That our theory does not enable us to predict particular prices, etc., says nothing against its validity. It means merely that we never know all the particular circumstances on which, according to that theory, the several prices depend. These circumstances are in the first instance the desires and the knowledge of all the persons taking part in the economic process.

That we never can know all that the people know whose actions determine the formation of prices and the methods and direction of production is, of course, of decisive importance not only for theory. It has also the greatest significance for political action. The fact that much more knowledge contributes to form the order of a market economy than can be known to any one mind or used by any one organization is the decisive reason why a market economy is more effective than any other known type of economic order.

Before I take up this subject, however, I want to mention that it seems to me that the whole modern development of what is called macroeconomic theory is a result of the erroneous belief that theory will be useful only if it puts us in a position to predict particular events. As it appeared obvious that the data necessary for such a use of macroeconomic theory could never be ascertained, it was attempted to overcome this difficulty by so reconstructing theory that the data which had to be inserted into its formulae were no longer information about individuals but statistical magnitudes, sums or averages. Most of these efforts seem to me to be mistaken. The result is merely that we lose insights we can gain into the structure of the relations between men, and that, as those statistical magnitudes inform us only about the past and provide no justification for the assumption that they will remain constant, we still do not achieve successful prediction of particular events. Apart perhaps from certain problems of the theory of money, those endeavours seem to me to promise little. They certainly offer no escape from the difficulties I have discussed, because the prices and quantities produced of particular commodities are not determined by any averages but by particular circumstances, the knowledge of which is dispersed among hundreds of thousands of men.

V

One of the chief results of the theory of the market economy is thus that in certain conditions, which I cannot further consider here, competition produces an adaptation to countless circumstances which in their totality are not known and cannot be known to any person or authority, and that therefore this adaptation cannot be brought about by a central direction of all economic activity. This means in the first instance that, contrary to a widely held opinion, economic theory has much of importance to say about the effectiveness of different kinds of economic systems, that is, on the very questions of the discussion of which scholars are sometimes afraid because they are so closely connected with opposing political opinions; and that it has comparatively little to say on the concrete effects of particular measures in given circumstances. We know the general character of the self-regulating forces of the economy and the general conditions in which these forces will function or not function, but we do not know all the particular circumstances to which they bring about an adaptation. This is impossible because of the general interdependence of all parts of the economic process, that is because, in order to interfere successfully on any point, we would have to know all the details of the whole economy, not only of our own country but of the whole world.

In so far as we want to avail ourselves of the forces of the market—and there can probably be no doubt that we must do so if we want even approximately to preserve our standard of life—it would seem that a rational economic policy should confine itself to creating the conditions in which the market will function as well as possible, but should not regard it as its task deliberately to influence or guide the individual activities. The chief task of economic policy would thus appear to be the creation of a framework within which the individual not only can freely decide for himself what he wants to do, but in which also this decision based on his particular knowlegde will contribute as much as possible to aggregate output. And our evaluation of any particular measure of policy will have to depend not so much on its particular results, all of which in most instances we shall in any case not know, but on its being in conformity with the whole system (what I believe W. Eucken was the first to describe as *systemgerecht*). This also means that we shall often have to act in all cases on assumptions which in fact are true only of most but not of all instances: a good example of this is the fact that all the exceptions from the rule that free international exchange will benefit both partners have been discovered by convinced advocates of free trade, which did not prevent them from continuing to advocate universal free trade, because they also understood that it is hardly ever possible to establish the actual presence of those unusual circumstances which would justify an exception. Perhaps even more instructive is the case of the late Professor A. C. Pigou, the founder of the theory of welfare economics—who at the end of a long life devoted almost entirely to the task of defining the conditions in which government interference might be used to improve upon the results of the market, had to concede that the practical value of these theoretical considerations was somewhat doubtful because we are rarely in a position to ascertain whether the particular circumstances to which the theory refers exist in fact in any given situation.[3] Not because he knows so much, but because he knows how much he would have to know in order to interfere successfully, and because he knows that he will never know all the relevant circumstances, it would seem that the economist should refrain from recommending isolated acts of interference even in conditions in which the theory tells him that they may sometimes be beneficial.

The recognition of this limitation of our knowledge is important if we do not want to become responsible for measures which will do more harm than good. The general conclusion we ought to draw from the insight seems to me to be that in our evaluation of measures of economic policy we should allow ourselves to be guided only by their general character and not by their particular effects on certain persons or groups. That a certain measure assists somebody deserving is by itself no sufficient justification of it if we are not prepared generally to recommend measures of the kind in question.

This attitude is likely to be criticized as a dogmatic adherence to rigid principles. This, however, is a reproach which ought not to deter us but which we should proudly accept, because principles are the most important contributions we can make to questions of policy. It is no accident that in our subject the term 'principles' is so often used in the titles of general treatises. Especially so far as economic policy is concerned, principles are practically all that we have to contribute.

[3] Cf. his article on 'Some Aspects of the Welfare State', *Diogenes*, No. 7, 1954, p. 6.

Principles are particularly important, however, when the one political aim which we may take for granted is personal freedom. I have attempted in a recent work to show that the ultimate reason why personal freedom is so important is the unavoidable ignorance of most of the circumstances which determine the conduct of all others from which we nevertheless constantly benefit. And I have already used the last opportunity I had on a visit to Freiburg to explain in a lecture[4] how greatly this freedom must be constantly endangered if in our political decisions we consider exclusively their foreseeable effects, because the immediate effects which indicate a measure will necessarily be predictable, while the developments which have been prevented by the restriction of freedom will in their very nature be unforeseeable. I need not therefore dwell further on this point.

VI

I wish rather to use the remaining minutes to forestall two possible misunderstandings of what I have said so far. The first is that the clear position which I feel it is both appropriate and desirable that an academic teacher should take on certain great principles by no means implies that he should commit himself on particular current issues of politics, and still less that he should tie himself to a political party. The latter seems to me to be most undesirable and hardly compatible with the duties of an academic teacher in the social sciences. I quite understand the urge to take a part in the solution of the pressing problems of the public policy of the day, and if special circumstances had not prevented me from doing so I should probably myself have succumbed to the temptation to devote a great part of my energy to such tasks.

Already in my young days in Austria, however, we used to joke that we were better theorists than our colleagues in Germany because we had so little influence on practical affairs. I have later observed the same difference between the English and the American economists: at least in the 1930's the English economists were undoubtedly the better theoreticians and at the same time were much less involved in the conduct of current policy. This has somewhat changed since and I am not sure that the effect has been altogether beneficial for the state of scientific economics in England.

If I look back on the last thirty years I become, at any rate, very much aware of how much I owe to the fact that during the greater part

[4] 'Die Ursachen der ständigen Gefährdung der Freiheit', published in *Ordo*, Vol. 12, 1960–1.

of this time I was a foreigner in the countries in which I worked and for this reason felt it inappropriate to pronounce on the political problems of the day. If I have succeeded during this period in building up something like a fairly systematic body of opinion on economic policy this is not least due to the circumstance that all this time I had to be content with the role of a spectator and had never to ask what was politically possible or would assist any group with which I was connected. This will not be different in the future.

The second point on which I want to prevent possible misunderstandings is my emphasis on the limitations of our theoretical knowledge. I hope none of you has interpreted this to mean that I feel that because the utility of theory is so restricted we had better concentrate on facts. This was certainly not what I meant to convey. Although it is one of the tasks of an academic teacher to show how to ascertain and interpret facts, knowledge of facts does not make a science, and that knowledge of facts which you will some day need in order to apply your scientific knowledge you will constantly have to learn anew on the job. The chief gain from your study at the university must be an understanding of theory, and it is the only profit which you can gain nowhere else. The knowledge of the particular facts to which you will have to apply your scientific knowledge will come soon enough. I hope it has never too seriously detracted from my effectiveness as a teacher that for the reason already mentioned I generally knew less about the particular conditions of the country in which I taught than my students did, and I hope that you will not be too disappointed when you soon discover that for some time at any rate the same will again be true.

The real conflict which arises today in the study of economics—and I do in this not refer to particular curricula or examination requirements about which I know little, but to the ideal aims of study—does not exist between the knowledge of facts and the understanding of theory. If that were the whole problem I should not hesitate to advise you to devote the precious years of study to entire concentration on theory and to let the learning of the concrete facts wait until you meet them in your professional work. And, in spite of certain qualifications which I am going to add, this indeed seems to me desirable at least for a part of one's years at the university. Only those who have really mastered one science—and in spite of all the respect I have for history I am inclined to say one theoretical science—know what science is. Such mastery of a theoretical discipline can, however, today be acquired only in the course of a period of narrow specialization on its problems.

The difficulties lie elsewhere. They are a consequence of the fact that in order to arrive at an answer to those questions of principle on which, on the one hand, we have most to say, economic theory is, on the other, a necessary but not a sufficient equipment. I have said on another occasion, and it seems to me important enough to repeat it here, that he who is only an economist cannot be a good economist. Much more than in the natural sciences, it is true in the social sciences that there is hardly a concrete problem which can be adequately answered on the basis of a single special discipline. Not only are political science and jurisprudence, anthropology and psychology, and of course history, subjects of which we all ought to know much more than any man can know. Even more do all our problems touch on questions of philosophy. It is certainly no accident that in the country which has so long been leading in economics, England, almost all the great economists were also philosophers and, at least in the past, all the great philosophers also economists. There are indeed among the economists two conspicuous exceptions: two of the greatest, David Ricardo and Alfred Marshall. But I am not sure that this does not account for certain shortcomings in their work. If we leave them aside, however, and mention only the most important names, John Locke, George Berkeley and David Hume, Adam Smith and Jeremy Bentham, Samuel Bailey, James and John Stuart Mill, William Stanley Jevons, Henry Sidgwick and finally John Neville and John Maynard Keynes, such a list will appear to the philosophers as a list of important philosophers or logicians, and to the economists as a list of leading economists.

Although the instances of such combinations of philosophy and economics which I encountered as a student in German literature[5] might rather have been a deterrent, I have come to the conclusion that it can be very fertile—and I do not think this belief is merely a result of the often noticed propensity of the old to turn from their special subject to philosophy. Most of the problems upon which I have touched today raise economic as well as philosophical problems. While it is somewhat doubtful whether such a thing as a single theoretical science of society is possible, all the sciences of society certainly do raise the same philosophical problems—many of them problems which have occupied philosophers for two thousand years before they were considered by more specialized disciplines. The problems of the formation of our civilization and institutions are closely connected with the problems of the development of our mind and its tools. The economist can only gain, for instance, if he occasionally looks into the problem of theoretical

---

[5] Especially such figures as Othmar Spann, F. von Gottl-Ottlilienfeld, R. Stolzmann or Werner Sombart.

linguistics, and the common problems which he then discovers are in the last instance philosophical problems.

I mention this not only in order to justify the occasional excursions into philosophy into which I shall certainly be tempted. I speak of it also because I hope to find again this spirit of general intellectual curiosity and spiritual adventure which I remember from my student days in Vienna and which, if not unknown, is at least much more rare in American universities. However much the mastery of the discipline must be the chief aim of study, in the social sciences technical competence in one subject should not be the only purpose. For those who feel that the problems in our field are really important, the specialized study ought to be the beginning of a struggle for achieving a comprehensive philosophy of society—a struggle which will be fruitful only if one's studies have opened one's eyes not merely for the problems of one's special discipline.

It was my wish to talk on these general questions before I commenced my regular course of lectures. I am very conscious, however, that such a *confessio fidei* publicly made before one has become familiar with the peculiar atmosphere of a place incurs certain risks. It is one of the lessons I have learnt in moving from country to country that the intellectual frontiers on which one has to fight shift in the process. I have noticed this for the first time in what was then my special field, the theory of industrial fluctuations, when I moved to England. In the German discussion I was regarded as a pronounced representative of monetary explanations of the trade cycle, and my efforts had indeed been directed to emphasizing the role money played in these processes. But in England I encountered a much more extreme form of a purely monetary explanation which regarded the fluctuations of the general price level as the essence of the phenomena. The consequence was that my arguments had soon to be directed against the dominant kind of monetary theory of the trade cycles and to aim at stressing the importance of the real factors, perhaps somewhat to the bewilderment of those who regarded me as a typical representative of monetary explanations.

Something similar happened to me in the philosophical field. At Vienna I had at least been close to the logical positivism of the Vienna circle, even though I could not accept some of the application of their views to the social sciences. In England, and still more later in the U.S., I found it, however, soon necessary to oppose certain more extreme forms of empiricism which I found there to be prevalent. I should not be surprised if longer acquaintance with the present state of thinking in Germany should again seem to make it appear that such a change of front is indicated. It may well be, for instance, that I shall find that such an emphasis on the importance of theory as I felt today to be desirable was not really appropriate. My general impression, however, is that American fashions are spreading so rapidly that what I intended to say is not altogether out of place. But in case my emphasis should have been misplaced, I wanted in conclusion at least to mention the special difficulty which any one encounters who after a long absence returns to an environment which was at one time familiar to him.

CHAPTER NINETEEN

Full Employment, Planning and Inflation[*]

I

In the years that have elapsed since the war, central planning, 'full employment', and inflationary pressure have been the three features which have dominated economic policy in the greater part of the world. Of these only full employment can be regarded as desirable in itself. Central planning, direction, or government controls, however we care to call it, is at best a means which must be judged by the results. Inflation, even 'repressed inflation', is undoubtedly an evil, though some would say a necessary evil if other desirable aims are to be achieved. It is part of the price we pay for having committed ourselves to a policy of full employment and central planning.

The new fact which has brought about this situation is not a greater desire to avoid unemployment than existed before the war. It is the new belief that a higher level of employment can be permanently maintained by monetary pressure than would be possible without it. The pursuit of a policy based on these beliefs has somewhat unexpectedly shown that inflation and government controls are its necessary accompaniments—unexpected not by all, but by probably the majority of those who advocated those policies.

Full employment policies as now understood are thus the dominant factor of which the other characteristic features of contemporary economic policy are mainly the consequence. Before we can further examine the manner in which central planning, full employment, and

* Reprinted from the *Institute of Public Affairs Review*, Melbourne, Vol. IV, 1950.

inflation interact, we must become clear about what precisely the full employment policies as now practised mean.

II

Full employment has come to mean that maximum of employment that can be brought about in the short run by monetary pressure. This may not be the original meaning of the theoretical concept, but it was inevitable that it should have come to mean this in practice. Once it was admitted that the momentary state of employment should form the main guide to monetary policy, it was inevitable that any degree of unemployment which might be removed by monetary pressure should be regarded as sufficient justification for applying such pressure. That in most situations employment can be temporarily increased by monetary expansion has long been known. If this possibility has not always been used, this was because it was thought that by such measures not only other dangers were created, but that long-term stability of employment itself might be endangered by them. What is new about present beliefs is that it is now widely held that so long as monetary expansion creates additional employment, it is innocuous or at least will cause more benefit than harm.

Yet while in practice full employment policies merely mean that in the short run employment is kept somewhat higher than it would otherwise be, it is at least doubtful whether over longer periods they will not in fact lower the level of employment which can be permanently maintained without progressive monetary expansion. These policies are, however, constantly represented as if the practical problem were not this, but as if the choice were between full employment thus defined and the lasting mass unemployment of the 1930's.

The habit of thinking in terms of an alternative between 'full employment' and a state of affairs in which there are unemployed factors of all kinds available is perhaps the most dangerous legacy which we owe to the great influence of the late Lord Keynes. That so long as a state of general unemployment prevails, in the sense that unused resources of *all* kinds exist, monetary expansion can be only beneficial, few people will deny. But such a state of general unemployment is something rather exceptional, and it is by no means evident that a policy which will be beneficial in such a state will also always and necessarily be so in the kind of intermediate position in which an economic system finds itself most of the time, when significant unemployment is confined to certain industries, occupations or localities.

Of a system in a state of general unemployment it is roughly true that employment will fluctuate in proportion with money income, and that if we succeed in increasing money income we shall also in the same proportion increase employment. But it is just not true that all unemployment is in this manner due to an insufficiency of aggregate demand and can be lastingly cured by increasing demand. The causal connection between income and employment is not a simple one-way connection so that by raising income by a certain ratio we can always raise employment by the same ratio. It is all too naïve a way of thinking to believe that, since, if all workmen were employed at current wages, total income would reach such and such a figure, therefore, if we can bring income to that figure, we shall also necessarily have full employment. Where unemployment is not evenly spread, there is no certainty that additional expenditure will go where it will create additional employment. At least the amount of extra expenditure which would have to be incurred before the demand for the kind of services is raised which the unemployed offer may have to be of such a magnitude as to produce major inflationary effects before it substantially increases employment.

If expenditure is distributed between industries and occupations in a proportion different from that in which labour is distributed, a mere increase in expenditure need not increase employment. Unemployment can evidently be the consequence of the fact that the distribution of labour is different from the distribution of demand. In this case the low aggregate money income would have to be considered as a consequence rather than as a cause of unemployment. Even though, during the process of increasing incomes, enough expenditure may 'spill over' into the depressed sectors temporarily there to cure unemployment, as soon as the expansion comes to an end the discrepancy between the distribution of demand and the distribution of supply will again show itself. Where the cause of unemployment and of low aggregate incomes is such a discrepancy, only a re-allocation of labour can lastingly solve the problem in a free economy.

III

This raises one of the most crucial and most difficult problems in the whole field: is an inappropriate distribution of labour more likely to be corrected under more or less stable or under expanding monetary conditions? This involves in fact two separate problems: the first is whether demand conditions during a process of expansion are such that, if the distribution of labour adjusted itself to the then existing distribution of demand, this would create employment which would continue after expansion has stopped; the second problem is whether the distribution of labour is more likely to adapt itself promptly to any given distribution of demand under stable or under expansionary monetary conditions, or, in other words, whether labour is more mobile under expanding or under stable monetary conditions.

The answer to the first of these questions is fairly clear. During a process of expansion the direction of demand is to some extent necessarily different from what it will be after expansion has stopped. Labour will be attracted to the particular occupations on which the extra expenditure is made in the first instance. So long as expansion lasts, demand there will always run a step ahead of the consequential increases of demand elsewhere. And in so far as this temporary stimulus to demand in particular sectors leads to a movement of labour, it may well become the cause of unemployment as soon as the expansion comes to an end.

Some people may feel doubt about the importance of this phenomenon. To the present writer it seems the main cause of the recurrent waves of unemployment. That during every boom period a greater quantity of factors of production is drawn into the capital goods industries than can be permanently employed there, and that as a result we have normally a greater proportion of our resources specialized in the production of capital goods than corresponds to the share of income which, under full employment, will be saved and be available for investment, seems to him the cause of the collapse which has regularly followed a boom. Any attempt to create full employment by drawing labour into occupations where they will remain employed only so long as credit expansion continues creates the dilemma that either credit expansion must be continued indefinitely (which means inflation), or that, when it stops, unemployment will be greater than it would be if the temporary increase in employment had never taken place.

If the real cause of unemployment is that the distribution of labour does not correspond with the distribution of demand, the only way to create stable conditions of high employment which is not dependent on continued inflation (or physical controls) is to bring about a distribution of labour which matches the manner in which a stable money income will be spent. This depends of course not only on whether during the process of adaptation the distribution of demand is approximately what it will remain, but also on whether conditions in general are conducive to easy and rapid movements of labour.

IV

This leads to the second and more difficult part of our question to which, perhaps, no certain answer can be given, though the probability seems to us to point clearly in one direction. This is the question whether workers will on the whole be more willing to move to new occupations or new localities when general demand is rising, or whether mobility is likely to be greater when total demand is approximately constant. The main difference between the two cases is that in the former the inducement to move will be the attraction of a higher wage elsewhere, while in the second case it will be the inability to earn the accustomed wages or to find any employment in the former occupation which will exercise a push. The former method is, of course, the more pleasant, and it is usually also represented as the more effective. It is this latter belief which I am inclined to question.

That the same wage differentials which in the long run would attract the necessary greater number of new recruits to one industry rather than another will not suffice to tempt workers already established in the latter to move is in itself not surprising. As a rule the movement from job to job involves expenditure and sacrifices which may not be justified by a mere increase in wages. So long as the worker can count on his accustomed money wage in his current job, he will be understandably reluctant to move. Even if, as would be inevitable under an expansionist policy which aimed at bringing about the adjustment entirely by raising some wages without allowing others to fall, the constant money wages meant a lower real wage, the habit of thinking in terms of money wages would deprive such a fall of real wages of most of its effectiveness. It is curious that those disciples of Lord Keynes who in other connections make such constant use of this consideration regularly fail to see its significance in this context.

To aim at securing to men who in the social interest ought to move elsewhere the continued receipt of their former wages can only delay movements which ultimately must take place. It should also not be forgotten that in order to give all the men formerly employed continued employment in a relatively declining industry, the general level of wages in that industry will have to fall more than would be necessary if some of the workers moved away from it.

What is so difficult here for the layman to understand is that to protect the individual against the loss of his job may not be a way to decrease unemployment but may over longer periods rather decrease the number which can be employed at given wages. If a policy is pursued over a long period which postpones and delays movements, which keeps people in their old jobs who ought to move elsewhere, the result must be that what ought to have been a gradual process of change becomes in the end a problem of the necessity of mass transfers within a short period. Continued monetary pressure which has helped people to earn an unchanged money wage in jobs which they ought to have left will have created accumulated arrears of necessary changes which, as soon as monetary pressure ceases, will have to be made up in a much shorter space of time and then result in a period of acute mass unemployment which might have been avoided.

All this applies not only to those maldistributions of labour which arise in the course of ordinary industrial fluctuations, but even more to the task of large-scale re-allocations of labour such as arise after a great war or as a result of a major change in the channels of international trade. It seems highly doubtful whether the expansionist policies pursued since the war in most countries have helped and not rather hindered that adjustment to radically changed conditions of world trade which have become necessary. Especially in the case of Great Britain the low unemployment figures during recent years may be more a sign of a delay in necessary change than of true economic balance.

The great problem in all those instances is whether such a policy, once it has been pursued for years, can still be reversed without serious political and social disturbances. As a result of these policies, what not very long ago might merely have meant a slightly higher unemployment figure, might now, when the employment of large numbers has become dependent on the continuation of these policies, be indeed an experiment which politically is unbearable.

V

Full employment policies, as at present practised, attempt the quick and easy way of giving men employment where they happen to be, while the real problem is to bring about a distribution of labour which makes continuous high employment without artificial stimulus possible. What this distribution is we can never know beforehand. The only way to find out is to let the unhampered market act under conditions which will bring about a stable equilibrium between demand and supply. But the very full employment policies make it almost inevitable that we must constantly interfere with the free play of the forces of the market and that the prices which rule during such an expansionary policy, and to which supply will adapt itself, will not represent a lasting condition. These difficulties, as we have seen, arise from the fact that unemployment is never evenly spread throughout the economic system, but that, at the time when there may still be substantial unemployment in some sectors, there may exist acute scarcities in others. The purely fiscal and monetary measures on which current full employment policies rely are, however, by themselves indiscriminate in their effects on the different parts of the economic system. The same monetary pressure which in some parts of the system might merely reduce unemployment will in others produce definite inflationary effects. If not checked by other measures, such monetary pressure might well set up an inflationary spiral of prices and wages long before unemployment has disappeared, and—with present nation-wide wage bargaining—the rise of wages may threaten the results of the full employment policy even before it has been achieved.

As is regularly the case in such circumstances, the governments will then find themselves forced to take measures to counteract the effects of their own policy. The effects of the inflation have to be contained or 'repressed' by direct controls of prices and of quantities produced and sold: the rise of prices has to be prevented by imposing maximum prices and the resulting scarcities must be met by a system of rationing, priorities and allocations.

The manner in which inflation leads a government into a system of overall controls and central planning is by now too well known to need elaboration. It is usually a particularly pernicious kind of planning, because not thought out beforehand but applied piecemeal as the unwelcome results of inflation manifest themselves. A government which uses inflation as an instrument of policy but wants it to produce only the desired effects is soon driven to control ever increasing parts of the economy.

VI

The connection between inflation and controls and central planning is, however, not only a one-way connection. That inflation leads to controls is nowadays widely seen. But that once an economic system has become cluttered up and encumbered with all sorts of controls and restrictions, continued inflationary pressure is required to keep it going is not yet generally understood but no less important. It is indeed a fact of crucial importance for the understanding of the self-perpetuating and self-accentuating character of the modern tendencies in economic policy.

Since the measures intended to counteract inflation are designed to damp the uplift which the inflationary stimulus would cause, it is inevitable that they should also act as a damper to the spontaneous forces of recovery as soon as the inflationary pressure is relaxed. If most of the post-war economies do not show a greater resilience and spontaneous strength, this is largely due to the fact that they are smothered by controls and that, whenever improvement flags, instead of a removal of all those hindrances an even stronger dose of inflation is demanded which sooner or later leads to further controls.

This tendency of the existing controls to produce a further demand for inflationary pressure is especially important in view of the widely held opinion that, if only the inflationary tendencies can be brought under control, the restrictive measures will subsequently prove unnecessary and be readily removed. If the connection between inflation and controls is a mutual one as here suggested, this view would prove to be erroneous, and to act on it would necessarily lead to failure. Unless the controls are removed at the same time that expansion is discontinued, the pressure for its resumption will probably be irresistible as soon as the deadening effect of the controls makes itself felt.

An economy paralysed by controls needs the extra stimulus of inflation to keep going at anything near full rate. Where the controls deprive the entrepreneur of all scope for initiative, freedom of choice and the assumption of responsibility, where the government in effect decides what and how much he is to produce, he must at least be assured of a certain sale if it is to be worth his while to carry on. It is because extensive government controls have almost always been accompanied by more or less inflationary conditions that they have not as completely paralysed economic activity as seems inevitable to the outside observer who learns of the maze of permits and licences through which any manufacturer who wants to do anything has to find his way.

To such an observer it seems at first impossible that an entrepreneur so largely deprived of the control of his costs and the nature and the quantity of his products should still be willing to run any risks. The answer is that he is in fact relieved of the main risk by the creation of conditions in which almost anything which can be produced can also be sold. The inefficiency of such a 'planned economy' is concealed by the effects of inflation.

But as soon as inflationary pressure disappears, the whole force of all these impediments to successful production makes itself felt. The very controls which in the first instance were imposed to keep the effects of inflation under control make it thus more difficult to stop inflation. If, while the controls remain, stable monetary conditions were restored, unemployment would at once reappear. The impression would be created that continued expansion is an indispensable condition for maintaining a high level of employment, while in fact what is needed is the removal of the controls which hamper trade, even if as a result some of the hitherto concealed effects of inflation should become apparent.

VII

If these considerations are correct, they cannot but make one feel very pessimistic about the prospects of a reasonable economic policy being adopted in the foreseeable future. In the present state of public opinion they are most unlikely to be listened to. The habit of inflation has often been compared to the addiction to a stimulating drug. But the position of a society which has become addicted to the drug of inflation is even worse than that of an individual in the corresponding case. One has to conceive of a position in which the administration of, say, morphia to sufferers were to be decided under the influence of mass psychology and where every demagogue who knows just a little more about these things than the crowd would be able to offer an effective means of relieving present suffering while the more remote harm his remedy causes is understood only by few.

The rapidity with which the full employment ideology has taken hold of the public imagination, the manner in which in the process a subtle although probably mistaken theoretical reasoning has been turned into a crude dogma, and not least the way in which certain bigots of the new doctrine who ought to know better represent the issue as if it were a choice between long-lasting mass unemployment and the wholesale application of their prescriptions, make one sometimes despair about one of the gravest issues of our time: the capacity of democratic institutions to handle the tremendous powers for good and evil which the new instruments of economic policy place in their hands.

If the outcome of economic policy is not to be altogether different from what has been desired, if we are not to be driven from one expedient to another, economic policy, more even than any other, must be long-range policy, governed less by the pressing needs of the moment than by an understanding of the long-period effects. It was certainly wise that at a time when the scope and objectives of monetary policy were much more limited, its direction was placed in the hands of bodies not directly subject to political control. It is understandable and perhaps inevitable that once the much greater use of these powers is recognized, it should become a major political issue. But it must appear more than doubtful whether in the nature of democratic institutions it is possible that democratic governments will ever learn to exercise that restraint which is the essence of economic wisdom of not using palliatives for present evils which not only create worse problems later but also constantly restrict the freedom of further action.

CHAPTER TWENTY

Unions, Inflation and Profits*

Tendencies are observable in the field of labour economics which most seriously threaten our future prosperity. The developments which are bringing this about are not of recent date. They extend at least over the last twenty-five years. But for most of that time, and particularly during the long period of great prosperity through which we have recently passed, it may have seemed as if the United States could take in its stride even those new hurdles which only a few alarmists regarded as serious. But there are strong reasons for thinking that things will soon be coming to a head. It may be that already those new demands of labour which I want later to examine in some detail will prove to be the critical point. Or Walter Reuther may decide that this is not a favourable moment for a decisive test of strength and the fatal struggle will be deferred a little further. Whichever it will be, I have little doubt that we shall soon have to face fundamental issues which we have managed to avoid for so long and which have not become easier to solve because the practices and institutions which raise them have been allowed to continue for such a long time.

Before turning to the more specific problems which the new union demands raise, I must explain how I see the more general problem of policy which the powers of modern labour unions create, and describe the character of the particular phase of business fluctuations in which it seems those problems will now have to be decided.

The first of these tasks divides itself into two distinct yet closely connected ones: the character which labour organizations have gradually assumed, and the new powers they have obtained, not as a result of any-

* Reprinted from *The Public Stake in Union Power*, edited by Philip D. Bradley, New York, 1959.

thing *they* can do, but as a result of the new conceptions of the tasks of credit and fiscal policy. With regard to the first, though it contains the crux of the union problem, I can be very brief. The essential facts are here so well known that I need merely mention the chief points. Unions have not achieved their present magnitude and power by merely achieving the right of association. They have become what they are largely in consequence of the grant, by legislation and jurisdiction, of unique privileges which no other associations or individuals enjoy. They are the one institution where government has signally failed in its first task, that of preventing coercion of men by other men—and by coercion I do not mean primarily the coercion of employers but the coercion of workers by their fellow workers. It is only because of the coercive powers unions have been allowed to exercise over those willing to work at terms not approved by the union, that the latter has become able to exercise harmful coercion of the employer. All this has become possible because in the field of labour relations it has come to be accepted belief that the ends justify the means, and that, because of the public approval of the aims of union effort, they ought to be exempted from the ordinary rules of law. The whole modern development of unionism has been made possible mainly by the fact that public policy was guided by the belief that it was in the public interest that labour should be as comprehensively and completely organized as possible, and that in the pursuit of this aim the unions should be as little restricted as possible. This is certainly not in the public interest. But all this has been so admirably treated by Professor Sylvester Petro of New York University in his recent book *The Labor Policy of the Free Society*[1] that I need merely refer to that work.

I must take a little longer in discussing the particular circumstances which have made the power of unions over wages so especially dangerous in the present world. It is often said that successful general union pressure for higher wages necessarily produces inflation. This is not correct as a general proposition. It is, however, only too true under the particular conditions under which we now live. Since it has become the generally accepted doctrine that it is the duty of the monetary authorities to provide enough credit to secure full employment, whatever the wage level, and this duty has in fact been imposed upon the monetary authorities by statute, the power of the unions to push up money wages cannot but lead to continuous, progressive inflation. It is the blessing that J. M. Keynes has showered on us which we enjoy in this respect.

We are not concerned here with the niceties of his theory. What we are

[1] New York, 1957.

concerned with is the factual assumption on which his whole argument rests: that it is easier to cheat workers out of a gain in real wages by a reduction in the value of money than to reduce money wages; and his contention that this method ought to be employed every time real wages have become too high to allow of 'full employment'. Where Lord Keynes went wrong was in the naïve belief that workers would let themselves be deceived by this for any length of time, and that the lowering of the purchasing power of wages would not at once produce new demands for higher wages—demands which would be even more irresistible when it was recognized that they would not be allowed to have any effect on employment.

What we have achieved is a division of responsibilities under which one group can enforce a wage level without regard to the effects on employment, and another agency is responsible for providing whatever amount of money is needed to secure full employment at that wage level. So long as this is the accepted principle, it is true that the monetary authorities have no choice but to pursue a policy resulting in continuous inflation, however little they may like it. But the fact that in the existing state of opinion they cannot do anything else does not alter the fact that, as always, it is monetary policy and nothing else which is the cause of inflation.

We have behind us the first long period of such cost-push inflation, as it has come to be called. It has been one of the longest periods of high prosperity on record. But, though the upward trend of wages has not yet stopped, the forces which have been making for prosperity have been flagging for some time. We have probably reached the point when we must reap the inevitable harvest of a period of inflation. Nobody can be certain about this. It may well be that another massive dose of inflation may once more get us rapidly out of the recession. But that, in my opinion, would merely postpone the evil day—and make the ultimate result much worse. Inflation-born prosperity has never been and never will be lasting prosperity. It depends on factors which are nourished, not simply by inflation, but by an increase in the rate of inflation. And though we may have permanent inflation, we clearly cannot for very long have inflation at a progressive rate.

Such inflation-fed prosperity neither comes to an end because final demand becomes insufficient to take the whole product off the market, nor can be perpetuated by simply keeping final demand at a sufficiently high level. The decline always begins, and did begin this time, in the field of investment, and it is only as a consequence of the decline of incomes in the investment goods industries that final demand is later affected. It is true that this secondary shrinkage in final demand may become cumulative and tend to become the controlling factor; it may then turn what would otherwise be merely a period of recession and readjustment into a major depression. There is, therefore, every reason to counteract these tendencies and to prevent them from setting up a deflationary spiral. But this does not mean that by merely maintaining final demand at a sufficiently high level we can secure continued full employment and avoid the readjustment and incidental unemployment made necessary by the transition from inflationary to stable monetary conditions. The reason for this is that investment is not, as is often naïvely believed, coupled in any simple manner with final demand; a given volume of final demand does not always evoke a proportional, or perhaps even more than proportional, change in investment in the same direction. There are other factors operating within the whole price-cost structure which determine what rate of investment will be evoked by a given level of demand. It is a change in these factors which brings about the primary decline in investment and incomes which then produces a decline of final demand.

I cannot here examine this highly complex and very controversial mechanism in detail. I will confine myself to two considerations which seem to me to prove that the predominant 'lack of buying power' theory of depression is just wrong. One is the empirical fact that not only have declines of investment often started when final demand and prices are rising rapidly, but also that attempts to revive investment by stimulating final demand have almost invariably failed. The great depression of the 'thirties was indeed the first occasion when, under the influence of such 'purchasing power theories', deliberate efforts were made from the very beginning to maintain wages and purchasing power; and we managed to turn it into the longest and most severe depression on record. The second point is that the whole argument on which the purchasing power view rests suffers from an inherent contradiction. It proceeds as if, even under conditions of full or nearly full employment, an increase in the demand for final products would lead to a switching of resources from producing final goods to producing investment goods. Indeed, it suggests that if at any one time the demand for consumers' goods should become very urgent, the immediate effect would be that fewer consumers' goods and more investment goods would be produced. I suppose it means that in the extreme case, because people want more consumers' goods very urgently, no consumers' goods and only investment goods would be produced. Clearly there must be a mechanism which will bring it about that the opposite happens. But unless we understand that mechanism, we cannot be sure that it may not also operate under conditions of less than full employment. We evidently cannot accept the current popular view on these matters, which not only offers no answer to that crucial problem, but which, if consistently pursued, leads into absurdities.

I now come to my main subject. The reason why I have spent so much time in diagnosing the economic situation in which the new demands of labour are presented is partly that they are presented both as non-inflationary and as a safeguard against (or a remedy for) depression, but mainly because in the present situation the greatest pressure will be brought on the employers to avoid a labour dispute, which at this juncture may have very serious consequences. But the decisions which the corporations facing the new demands will have to make are decisions of principle which may have tremendous long-term effects, indeed, may do much to shape the future of our society. They should be made entirely in consideration of their long-run significance and not be affected by the desire to get out of our momentary difficulties. But with the power the unions have acquired, the capacity of the corporations to resist any harmful demands depends on what support they get from public opinion. It is therefore of the greatest importance that we clearly understand what these demands really imply, what their satisfaction and the general acceptance of the principle underlying them would mean for the future character of our economy.

As will be remembered, Mr. Reuther has presented the demands of the United Automobile Workers for 1958 as a 'two-package' programme, consisting of a set of 'minimum basic demands which will be common for all employers' and of supplementary demands 'in addition to the minimum for those corporations or companies in a more favoured economic position'—or, in other words, one set of demands applying to the automobile industry generally, and further demands directed to the Big Three. The first package constitutes in general only 'more of the same as before'—although we have been told that it will be the biggest wage increase demanded in the history of the automobile industry—and I shall consider it only briefly as an illustration of what I have already said about the inflationary character of these demands and especially about their significance in the present phase of business conditions. It is the second package which raises the interesting new problems and, I believe, constitutes a real threat to the future of our economy.

Of the first part of the demands, I want to examine only the claims that wage increases proportional to the increase in average output per head of the employed are non-inflationary, and that 'increasing mass purchasing power' through wage increases is an effective means of combating depression. They are easy to dispose of. Changes in output per head are, of course, not the same as changes in the productivity of labour. To see this clearly we need merely consider an extreme but by no means impracticable case, such as the replacement of present power stations by highly automatized atomic energy stations. Once one of these modern stations is erected, a handful of men would appear to be the sole producers of a colossal amount of electric energy and their output per head may have increased hundreds of times. But that does not mean that the productivity of labour in that industry has significantly increased in any sense relevant to our problem, or that in that industry the marginal product of a given number of workers has increased at all. The increase in average productivity of labour in the industry is the result of the investment made and in no way reflects the value which a man's work contributes to its product. To raise wages in proportion to the increase in average productivity in that industry would raise them to many times their marginal product in other industries of the economy. Unless we assume that the particular men employed in that industry acquire a vested right in a share of the product of that investment and are entitled to earn much more than exactly similar labour earns elsewhere, it will mean a general rise in money wages far in excess of what can be paid without a general rise in money incomes, that is, without inflation.

This does not mean, of course, that labour may not succeed in pushing up money wages to that level, but it means that this would be highly inflationary and could not mean a significant increase of the real wages for the workers of this kind as a whole. Since the illustration just given throws much light on one of the crucial aspects of the power of modern labour monopoly, I will dwell on it just a little longer. Where very large and very durable investments have once been made, it is today the owner of these investments who is almost completely at the mercy of an effective monopoly of the supply of labour. Once such plants have been created, and so long as they can be kept going without substantial renewal or re-investment, labour is in a position to appropriate almost any share of the returns due to the investment of the capital. The demand for a definite share in the increase in the average productivity of labour due to the investment of capital amounts, in fact, to nothing less than an attempt to expropriate that capital. There is no reason why a really powerful union monopoly should not succeed in this to a large extent so far as investments irrevocably committed to a particular purpose are concerned.

This, however, is only a relatively short-run effect and the advantages that labour as a whole can derive from such policies look very different when we consider what effects such policies must have on the attractiveness of new investment once they come to be anticipated. Personally, I am convinced that this power of union monopolies is, together with contemporary methods of taxation, the chief deterrent to private investment in productive equipment which we have allowed to grow up. We must not be surprised that private investment dries up as soon as uncertainty about the future increases after we have created a situation in which most of the gain of a large, risky and successful investment goes to the unions and the government, while any loss has to be borne by the investor. Man is so made that in times of great prosperity he still tends to forget about these deterrents. But we must not be surprised that as soon as prospects darken a little, these reasonable fears revive in full strength and we face another apparent 'exhaustion of investment opportunities' which is entirely the result of our own follies.

This brings me to the second aspect of the general demands of the U.A.W.: their significance at a time of threatening depression. It is contended that an increase of wages at this juncture will result in an overall increase in purchasing power and thereby reverse the tendency towards a shrinkage of incomes. I do not wish to deny that, at a time when there is danger that we may be entering a deflationary spiral, it is desirable that aggregate spending power should be prevented from falling further. What I question is that raising wages is a sensible or effective method of achieving this. What we need in the first instance is not that some people should earn more, but that more people should earn an income, and particularly that employment should revive in the capital goods industries. There is every likelihood that in the present phase of business an increase of wages will lead immediately to a decrease of employment in the industries concerned—even if it is not achieved through a labour dispute and work stoppage which, at present, would react even more rapidly on employment. And it seems certain to have even more harmful indirect effects on employment in the investment industries. I believe that under conditions of more or less full employment an increase of real wages of the final producers may act as an incentive to investment—crudely speaking because it induces the producer to substitute machinery for labour. But this is certainly *not* true in a situation where a large part of the capacity of the existing equipment is unused. In such a situation, investment does depend solely on how much of the final product can be sold at a profit, and that prospect can only be worsened by raising money costs first.

I must not enlarge any further, however, on the first part of Mr.

Reuther's 'packages' since, after all, they do not raise any problems with which we have not been long familiar. Even if some of the considerations I have mentioned cannot be stated often enough, or emphasized strongly enough, there is nothing new in them.

The interesting part of the proposals is the second 'package', the special discriminatory terms for the more successful enterprises in the automobile industry. It is not quite easy to say what their aim is or what Mr. Reuther expects to achieve by them. But it is well worth while to ask what the consequences would be if they were successful.

It will doubtless be remembered that before the U.A.W. put forward this demand they had asked that the Big Three reduce the price of their cars by $100.00 and promised that if this were done, the U.A.W. would take this into account in formulating their new demands. The fact that this suggestion has not been acted upon is now advanced as a justification for the new demands. I do not believe that that demand for price reduction ought to be taken very seriously, and it is probably more correctly seen as a public relations job—intended to prepare public opinion for the demands subsequently to be put forward. The union had, in fact, used exactly the same tactics twelve years earlier. But it will help to understand the present issue if we examine for a moment the significance of that demand.

For the purposes of the argument, let us assume that General Motors and perhaps also the two other big automobile manufacturers could, in fact, profitably sell their cars at the reduced price, and that perhaps over a limited period this would even turn out to their advantage. There seems very little question but that this would rapidly mean the end of the remaining independent producers and leave the Big Three alone in the field. If that is so, the first question on which we must form an opinion is why they do not go ahead and reduce their prices. One obvious answer is, of course, that such action would probably bring them soon into conflict with the anti-trust authorities. We have reached the ridiculous position where an attempt to act competitively will lay a particularly efficient organization open to the charge of aiming at monopoly. I do not know what advantages Mr. Reuther imagines his workers would reap from this result, if he really wanted it. I merely mention this to point out that it would almost certainly bring about results which are contrary to one of the accepted objects of public policy.

In fact, it seems very doubtful whether the Big Three regard it as really in their interest that the independent producers should be eliminated. If any one of them did think it desirable, he could quickly force the others into a course of action which would have that result. But it seems to me much more likely that a concern like General Motors, which takes such pains to preserve active competition between its divisions, would for the same reasons regard it in its long-run interest to preserve the independent experimentation of the smaller producers. After all, the men inside the big corporations probably understand better than many outside observers that the exceptional efficiency of a particular organization is not the necessary result of size, but rather that size is the result of the exceptional efficiency of a particular organization. They doubtless know also that such exceptional efficiency does not only not follow automatically from size, or from any device or design which can be established once and for all, but only from a constant and ever-renewed effort to do better than can be done by any other known method. I feel very strongly that in this sphere the simplified schemes which the economic theorist legitimately uses as a first approach, which treat costs as a function of size and approach the problem in terms of economics of scale, have become an obstacle to a realistic understanding of the important factors. Many of the individual and unique features of a particular corporation which make for its success are of the same character as the similar features of an individual person; they exist largely as an intangible tradition of an approach to problems, based on a tradition which is handed on but ever changing, and which, though it may secure superiority for long periods, may be challenged at any time by a new and even more effective corporate personality. I must say that if I were responsible for the fate of one of these corporations, I would not only feel that I was acting in the best interest of the corporation if I sacrificed the temporary gain from the control of an even larger share of the market in order to preserve the stimulus which has kept the organization on tip-toe so long; I should also feel that, in my efforts to prolong this leadership as long as possible, and use for this purpose part of the differential profits which this greater efficiency allowed my corporation to earn, I was acting in the interest of the community at large. An advantage of an individual or a corporation which cannot be duplicated remains an advantage to society even though nobody else has it; it ought to be made full use of, so long as nobody else is prevented from bettering the result by different and even greater advantages. To think of such positions in terms which are appropriate to monopolies based on obstacles to entry into an industry leads to an altogether distorted approach to the problems of policy.

It will be useful to remember this when we now turn to the specific demand of the automobile workers directed only to the three dominant corporations. I am not a little puzzled to understand what Mr. Reuther really expects to achieve by them, and from what parts of them he expects to derive any real benefit for the employees, and what part has been put in rather for its optical effect, that is, to gain the support of public opinion. The result of the acceptance of these demands would depend on certain decisions on the part of the management of the corporations, the character of which is by no means obvious. I shall, therefore, have to consider the consequences of these demands being accepted on the basis of alternative assumptions concerning how the corporations respond to the new conditions.

The 'supplementary economic demands' directed to the Big Three are that one half of all profits in excess of 10 per cent on what is called 'net capital' should be divided equally between employees and the consumers so that one quarter of these 'excess profits' during any one year should be given as a rebate to the buyers of cars, while another quarter should be handed over *to the unions* to do with it as they please. It is this last feature which distinguishes the proposal from all other profit-sharing plans and particularly from the profit-sharing plan which was offered by some automobile manufacturers to the workers and was turned down by them. It is not a plan to give the individual worker a determinable share in the ownership of the enterprise and therefore in its profits, but rather a plan to give the union, or the representatives of the workers employed in the corporation at a given time, control over, in the first instance, one quarter of the profits in excess of 10 per cent on net capital.

There are various grounds why the idea seems attractive that the workers in a corporation should be given a favoured opportunity to invest their savings in the corporation, and there are also good reasons why the great hopes which some people have set on such plans have scarcely ever been borne out by the result. Though the worker may find greater satisfaction in working for a corporation where he has a share in the profits, however small, and may take a greater interest in the prosperity of the corporation, it is also natural that, if he has any savings to invest, he will normally prefer not to stake them on the same enterprise on the prosperity of which all the rest of his income depends.

It is, however, an entirely different matter if it is demanded that the body of workers employed by a firm at any one time, without having contributed to its capital, be given a share in the profits. The effect will in part depend on how this share is to be distributed among the workers or otherwise used for their benefit. On this the proposal, as published, leaves us largely in the dark. It merely tells us that the workers of any company 'would determine democratically how they chose to allocate the money available from their companies through this supplementary package', and adds a list of purposes for which they may be used which ends with 'any other purpose which they deem advisable'. I sometimes wonder whether this is not the most ominous sentence in the whole document, since it leaves open the possibility that the individual worker may get little, if anything, for his free disposal, and that the money will be used mainly for the collective purposes of the union, i.e., further to increase its power.

So far as the effects on the position of the companies affected are concerned, we must distinguish between the short- and the long-run effects. In the relatively short run, the companies would have the choice between absorbing the loss of net profits and continuing essentially the same price policies as before, or at once trying to recoup themselves by an adjustment of prices. The former would mean that they would both be in a stronger position in the labour market compared with their weaker competitors, and would also offer the consumers what amounts to a lower price—though how significant the expectation of an uncertain and at best small rebate at the end of the year would be in affecting the choice of the purchaser seems doubtful. At any rate, so long as they followed this policy, the tendency would necessarily be to strengthen their superiority over the less successful companies and to increase the likelihood of the elimination of the latter. If, on the other hand, the companies concerned decided that they could not afford the reduction of profits but that it was expedient to raise prices sufficiently so as to restore them (so far as practicable), the car buyers would not only have no advantage at all— they would have to pay more than before, because they would have to provide the additional profits which would have to be obtained to satisfy the demands of labour.

In the long run, however, the managements of the corporations would have no such choice. Mr. Reuther is here obscuring the main issue by calling all profits in excess of 10 per cent on 'net capital' before taxation (i.e., 4.8 per cent after taxation) 'excess profits'. I will not examine here the difficulties which the vague concept of 'net capital' raises in this connection but, for the purposes of the argument, shall assume that it can be given a sufficiently definite meaning. Whatever this basis of calculation, it is difficult to see in what sense the profits actually earned by the successful industries can be called 'excessive'. It is true they are high in comparison with those companies in the industry that are struggling for survival, but hardly in any other sense. The commonly accepted measures of profitability scarcely suggest that the profits earned by the three companies are more than is necessary in such a highly risky field to make the investment of new capital attractive: at the end of last year the value of the shares of both Ford and Chrysler was below the book value of the assets of these companies, and only the price of General Motors shares exceeded the book value of the assets by more than the average for all the companies included in the Dow-Jones index number of the prices of industrial stocks.[2] But even if it could be seriously maintained that the profits of these companies were in some meaningful sense 'excessive', surely this would only constitute a case that, in the general interest, more capital should be invested in the companies concerned, and not a case for making investment in them less profitable. Or, assuming there were any grounds on which it could be contended that the big firms in the automobile industry were making 'monopoly profits', this would seem to me the strongest possible case against giving the workers a vested interest in the preservation of such monopoly profits.

This brings me at last to the general principle involved in those demands, the question of what would be the significance for the character of our whole economic system if the principle underlying them were applied generally. This is a question which must be examined without any regard to the particular figures mentioned in Mr. Reuther's 'packages'. If it is in any sense right that the employees of a particular firm should get one quarter of the profits in excess of 10 per cent, it would seem equally right that next time they should demand one half, or that they should claim some even larger percentage of all profits. It is, of course, a familiar and an only too often successful practice to establish a new principle by putting forward at first what may quantitatively seem a not very important demand, and only when the principle has been established to push its application further and further. It may be that Mr. Reuther was not very wise in asking in the first instance as much as one quarter of what he calls excess profits. The danger that he would gain his point would probably be much greater if in the first instance he had asked a modest 10 per cent and only after the principle had been established had pushed for a higher participation. Perhaps because he has on the first occasion asked for as much as he did, the public will be more ready to grasp what the establishment of the principle would mean.

The recognition of the right of the worker of a firm, *qua* worker, to participate in a share of the profits, irrespective of any contribution he has made to its capital, establishes him as a part owner of this firm. In this

[2] See the Statement by Theodore O. Yntema, Vice-President-Finance, Ford Motor Company, before the Subcommittee on Anti-trust and Monopoly of the Committee on the Judiciary, United States Senate, Washington D.C., February 4–5, 1958.

sense the demand is, of course, purely socialistic and, what is more, not based on any socialist theory of the more sophisticated and rational kind, but on the crudest type of socialism, commonly known as syndicalism. It is the form in which socialist demands usually first appear but which, because of their absurd consequences, have been abandoned by all of the theorists of socialism. It is at least possible to put up a rational argument in favour of nationalizing all industrial capital (though I believe it can be demonstrated—and is confirmed by all experience—that the consequences of such a policy would be disastrous). But it is not even possible to construct a rational argument in support of the contention that the workers employed at any one time in a firm or industry should collectively own the equipment of that industry. Any attempt to think through the consequences of such an arrangement soon shows that it is utterly incompatible with any rational use of the resources of society, and would soon lead to complete disorganization of the economic system. The final outcome would, no doubt, merely be that some new closed group of established workers would entrench themselves as the new proprietors and endeavour to get out of the seized property as much for their benefit as they could. The expropriation of one group of capitalists would have been achieved, but only to give some other group an equally exclusive (and probably equally temporary) right to the particular assets.

This is not the proper place to demonstrate the unworkability of a syndicalist system, nor should it be necessary once more to attempt to do so. What needs to be brought out is that the fulfilment of Mr. Reuther's demand would be a step towards syndicalism and that, once the first step was taken, it is difficult to see how further demands in the same direction could be resisted. If the U.A.W. have now the power to appropriate part of the capital of some of the biggest enterprises in the country, there is no reason why the same power should not next time be used to appropriate more and in the end all of it, and why the same should not happen in other industries. Nothing, indeed, brings home more vividly the dangers of the situation we have allowed to grow up over the last twenty-five years than the fact that it is necessary to examine such demands seriously and to explain at length why they must on no account be accepted if we are to preserve the fundamental character of our economy. I hope it is owing to the fact that most people believe that these demands will not be pressed seriously and that, at least this time, they have been put forward as a bargaining manœuvre, that they have not caused more concern. But I fear that it may be more owing to the fact that the public have not yet realized that much more is at stake than the prosperity of three big corporations. What will be tested when these demands are seriously put forward is the crucial issue of how far the organized groups of industrial workers are to be allowed to use the coercive power they have acquired to force on the rest of this country a change in the basic institutions on which our social and economic system rests. This is no longer a situation where we can afford the detached view which assumes that in a conflict of interests there is always something to be said for both sides and a compromise to be desired. It is a situation in which even the fear of the grave consequences which at this juncture a prolonged labour dispute and perhaps a long stoppage of production might have must not be allowed to influence our position. It is, it seems to me, a moment at which all who desire the preservation of the market system based on free enterprise must unambiguously desire and support an outright rejection of these demands without flinching at the short-run consequences this may produce.

Many people probably still feel that the great automobile manufacturers are able to take care of themselves and that we need not concern ourselves about their problems. This is scarcely any longer true. The fact is that we have permitted a situation to develop in which the unions have grown so powerful, and at the same time the employers have been deprived of any effective defence, that there must be grave doubt about the outcome if Mr. Reuther, according to his favourite practice, singles out one of the Big Three for attack. We have reached a point when the question of how we can still enable one such corporation effectively to resist demands which, if satisfied, would place us straight on the road to syndicalism must be a major public concern. Mr. Reuther may, indeed, be in a position to bring most severe pressure, not only on that corporation but on the public at large, because it may depend on him whether the present decline is turned into a major depression. It should be clearly recognized that the responsibility is entirely his and that no threat will frighten the public into a compromise which in the long run could be even more fatal. It seems to me that in this situation the economist must not shirk this duty of speaking plainly. This is not a pleasant task for one who as a scientist must aim at being impartial and whose inclination is either not to take sides in a particular dispute of interests or, if he has to, to favour the side on which are the relatively poorer. I have to admit that I have my doubts whether the predominant concern of so many economists with what they regard as justice in the particular case rather than with the consequences of a measure for the structure of society in general has on the whole been beneficial. But I am quite sure that the present issue has nothing at all to do with questions of justice between the particular parties involved but raises a question of principle which should be decided in the light of the consequences which its general adoption would have for our society. If this means that the economist, whose chief duty it is to think through and explain the long-run consequences, has to take what may be the unpopular side, particularly the side which is likely to be unpopular among the general class of intellectuals to which he belongs, I feel it becomes even more his duty to do so unreservedly and unequivocally. Perhaps I may conclude with the words of one of the wisest and most detached of economists, which have been quoted before at the head of a well-known essay called 'Reflections on Syndicalism' and which is now proving to have been dreadfully prophetic. The passage by Alfred Marshall which Henry Simons quoted at the head of that essay runs as follows: 'Students of social science must fear popular approval; evil is with them when all men speak well of them. If there is any set of opinions by the advocacy of which a newspaper can increase its sales, the student, who wishes to leave the world in general and his country in particular better than it would be if he had not been born, is bound to dwell on the limitations and defects and errors, if any, in that set of opinions: and never to advocate unconditionally even in an *ad hoc* discussion. It is almost impossible for a student to be a true patriot and to have the reputation of being one in his own time.'[3] It is probably equally impossible in our time for a student to be a true friend of labour and to have the reputation of being one.

[3] Henry C. Simons, 'Some Reflections on Syndicalism', *Journal of Political Economy*, Vol. LII, No. 1 (March 1944), p. 1.

CHAPTER TWENTY-ONE

Inflation Resulting from the Downward Inflexibility of Wages*

Contrary to what is widely believed, the crucial result of the 'Keynesian Revolution' is the general acceptance of a factual assumption and, what is more, of an assumption which becomes true as a result of its being generally accepted. The Keynesian theory, as it has developed during the last twenty years, has become a formal apparatus which may or may not be more convenient to deal with the facts than classical monetary theory; this is not our concern here. The decisive assumption on which Keynes' original argument rested and which has since ruled policy is that it is impossible ever to reduce the money wages of a substantial group of workers without causing extensive unemployment. The conclusion which Lord Keynes drew from this, and which the whole of his theoretical system was intended to justify, was that since money wages can in practice not be lowered, the adjustment necessary, whenever wages have become too high to allow 'full employment', must be effected by the devious process of reducing the value of money. A society which accepts this is bound for a continuous process of inflation.

This consequence is not at once apparent within the Keynesian system because Keynes and most of his followers are arguing in terms of a general wage level while the chief problem appears only if we think in terms of the relative wages of the different (sectional or regional) groups of workers. Relative wages of the different groups are bound to change substantially in the course of economic development. But if the money wage of no important group is to fall, the adjustment of the relative

* Reprinted from *Problems of United States Economic Development*, ed. by the Committee for Economic Development, New York, 1958, Vol. I, pp. 147–52.

position must be brought about exclusively by raising all other money wages. The effect must be a continuous rise in the level of money wages greater than the rise of real wages, i.e., inflation. One need only consider the normal year-by-year dispersion of wage changes of the different groups in order to realize how important this factor must be.

The twelve years since the end of the war have in fact in the whole Western world been a period of more or less continuous inflation. It does not matter how far this was entirely the result of deliberate policy or the product of the exigencies of government finance. It certainly has been a very popular policy since it has been accompanied by great prosperity over a period of probably unprecedented length. The great problem is whether by the same means prosperity can be maintained indefinitely—or whether an attempt to do so is not bound sooner or later to produce other results which in the end must become unbearable.

The point which tends to be overlooked in current discussion is that inflation acts as a stimulus to business only in so far as it is unforeseen, or greater than expected. Rising prices by themselves, as has often been seen, are not necessarily a guarantee of prosperity. Prices must turn out to be higher than they were expected to be, in order to produce profits larger than normal. Once a further rise of prices is expected with certainty, competition for the factors of production will drive up costs in anticipation. If prices rise no more than expected there will be no extra profits, and if they rise less, the effect will be the same as if prices fell when they had been expected to be stable.

On the whole the post-war inflation has been unexpected or has lasted longer than expected. But the longer inflation lasts, the more it will be generally expected to continue; and the more people count on a continued rise of prices, the more must prices rise in order to secure adequate profits not only to those who would earn them without inflation but also to those who would not. Inflation greater than expected secures general prosperity only because those who without it would make no profit and be forced to turn to something else are enabled to continue with their present activities. A cumulative inflation at a progressive rate will probably secure prosperity for a fairly long time, but not inflation at a constant rate. We need hardly inquire why inflation at a progressive rate cannot be continued indefinitely: long before it becomes so fast as to make any reasonable calculation in the expanding currency impracticable and before it will be spontaneously replaced by some other medium of exchange, the inconvenience and injustice of the rapidly falling value of all fixed payments will produce irresistible demands for a halt— irresistible, at least, when people understand what is happening and realize that a government can always stop inflation. (The hyper-inflations after the First World War were tolerated only because people were deluded into believing that the increase of the quantity of money was not a cause but a necessary consequence of the rise of prices.)

We can therefore not expect inflation-born prosperity to last indefinitely. We are bound to reach a point at which the source of prosperity which inflation now constitutes will no longer be available. Nobody can predict when this point will be reached, but come it will. Few things should give us greater concern than the need to secure an arrangement of our productive resources which we can hope to maintain at a reasonable level of activity and employment when the stimulus of inflation ceases to operate.

Yet the longer we have relied on inflationary expansion to secure prosperity, the more difficult that task will be. We shall be faced not only with an accumulated backlog of delayed adjustments—all those businesses which have been kept above water only by continued inflation. Inflation also becomes the active cause of new 'misdirections' of production, i.e., it induces new activities which will continue to be profitable only so long as inflation lasts. Especially when the additional money first becomes available for investment activities, these will be increased to a volume which cannot be maintained once only current savings are available to feed them.

The conception that we can maintain prosperity by keeping final demand always increasing a jump ahead of costs must sooner or later prove an illusion, because costs are not an independent magnitude but are in the long run determined by the expectations of what final demand will be. And to secure 'full employment' even an excess of 'aggregate demand' over 'aggregate costs' may not lastingly be sufficient, since the volume of employment depends largely on the magnitude of investment and beyond a certain point an excessive final demand may act as a deterrent rather than as a stimulus to investment.

I fear that those who believe that we have solved the problem of permanent full employment are in for a serious disillusionment. This is not to say that we need have a major depression. A transition to more stable monetary conditions by gradually slowing down inflation is probably still possible. But it will hardly be possible without a significant decrease of employment of some duration. The difficulty is that in the present state of opinion any noticeable increase of unemployment will at once be met by renewed inflation. Such attempts to cure unemployment by further doses of inflation will probably be temporarily successful and may even succeed several times if the inflationary pressure is massive enough. But this will merely postpone the problem and in the meantime aggravate the inherent instability of the situation.

In a short paper on the twenty years' outlook there is no space to consider the serious but essentially short-term problem of how to get out of a particular inflationary spell without producing a major depression. The long-term problem is how we are to stop the long-term and periodically accelerated inflationary trend which will again and again raise that problem. The essential point is that it must be once more realized that the employment problem is a wage problem and that the Keynesian device of lowering real wages by reducing the value of money when wages have become too high for full employment will work only so long as the workers let themselves be deceived by it. It was an attempt to get round what is called the 'rigidity' of wages which could work for a time but which in the long run has only made this obstacle to a stable monetary system greater than it had been. What is needed is that the responsibility for a wage level which is compatible with a high and stable level of employment should again be squarely placed where it belongs: with the trade unions. The present division of responsibility where each union is concerned only with obtaining the maximum rate of money wages without regard to the effect on employment, and the monetary authorities are expected to supply whatever increases of money income are required to secure full employment at the resulting wage level, must lead to continuous and progressive inflation. We are discovering that by refusing to face the wage problem and temporarily evading the consequences by monetary deception, we have merely made the whole problem much more difficult. The long-run problem remains the restoration of a labour market which will produce wages which are compatible with stable money. This means that the full and exclusive responsibility of the monetary authorities for inflation must once more be recognized. Though it is true that, so long as it is regarded as their duty to supply enough money to secure full employment at any wage level, they have no choice and their role becomes a purely passive one, it is this very conception which is bound to produce continuous inflation. Stable monetary conditions require that the stream of money expenditure is the fixed datum to which prices and wages have to adapt themselves, and not the other way round.

Such a change of policy as would be required to prevent progressive inflation, and the instability and recurrent crises it is bound to produce, presupposes, however, a change in the still predominant state of opinion. Though a 7 per cent bank rate in the country where they originated and were most consistently practised proclaims loudly the bankruptcy of Keynesian principles, there is yet little sign that they have lost their sway over the generation that grew up in their heyday. But quite apart from this intellectual power that they still exercise, they have contributed so much to strengthen the position of one of the politically most powerful elements in the country, that their abandonment is not likely to come without a severe political struggle. The desire to avoid this will probably again and again lead politicians to put off the necessity by resorting once more to the temporary way out which inflation offers as the path of least resistance. It will probably be only when the dangers of this path have become much more obvious than they are now that the fundamental underlying problem of union power will really be faced.

CHAPTER TWENTY-TWO

The Corporation in a Democratic Society: In Whose Interest Ought It To and Will It Be Run?*

I

For the questions on which I intend to concentrate here the 'ought' and the 'will' cannot be separated. Twenty-five years is a period long enough for the outcome of the developments to depend on what we will do to shape it. I believe that we have the power to avert some of the unpleasant prospects which current tendencies seem to create. Whether we will succeed in doing so depends on whether we clearly recognize the problem and take appropriate action. All I can attempt here is to indicate the channels into which we ought to try to steer developments.

My thesis will be that if we want effectively to limit the powers of corporations to where they are beneficial, we shall have to confine them much more than we have yet done to one specific goal, that of the profitable use of the capital entrusted to the management by the stockholders. I shall argue that it is precisely the tendency to allow and even to impel the corporations to use their resources for specific ends other than those of a long-run maximization of the return on the capital placed under their control that tends to confer upon them undesirable and socially dangerous powers, and that the fashionable doctrine that their policy should be guided by 'social considerations' is likely to produce most undesirable results.

I should like, however, to emphasize at once that when I contend that

* Reprinted from M. Anshen and G. L. Bach (edts.), *Management and Corporations, 1985*. New York (McGraw-Hill Company), 1960.

the only specific purpose which corporations ought to serve is to secure the highest long-term return on their capital, this does not mean that in the pursuit of this end they ought not to be restrained by general legal *and* moral rules. There is an important distinction to be drawn between specific goals and the framework of rules within which the specific aims are to be pursued. In this respect certain generally accepted rules of decency and perhaps even charitableness should probably be regarded as no less binding on corporations than the strict rules of law. But while these rules limit what corporations may do in the pursuit of their concrete aims, this does not mean that they are entitled to use their resources for particular purposes which have nothing to do with their proper aim.

Power, in the objectionable sense of the word, is the capacity to direct the energy and resources of others to the service of values which those others do not share. The corporation that has the sole task of putting assets to the most profitable use has no power to choose between values: it administers resources in the service of the values of others. It is perhaps only natural that management should desire to be able to pursue values which they think are important and that they need little encouragement from public opinion to indulge in these 'idealistic' aims. But it is just in this that the danger rests of their acquiring real and uncontrollable power. Even the largest aggregation of potential power, the largest accumulation of resources under a single control, is comparatively innocuous so long as those who exercise such power are entitled to use it only for one specific purpose and have no right to use it for other aims, however desirable in themselves. I shall maintain, therefore, that the old-fashioned conception which regards management as the trustee of the stockholders and leaves to the individual stockholder the decision whether any of the proceeds of the activities of the corporation are to be used in the service of higher values is the most important safeguard against the acquisition of arbitrary and politically dangerous powers by corporations.

I need hardly stop to point out how much in recent times policy (especially tax policy), public opinion, and the traditions growing inside the corporations, have tended in the opposite direction, and to what extent most of the agitation for reform is actually directed towards making corporations act more deliberately in 'the public interest'. These demands appear to me to be radically mistaken and their satisfaction more likely to aggravate than to reduce the dangers against which they are directed. There can be little doubt, however, that the conception that corporations ought to pursue public as well as private aims has become so widely accepted even by managements that it seems doubtful whether Adam Smith's comment still applies that the affectation to trade for the public good 'is not very common among merchants, and very few words need be employed in dissuading them from it'.

II

There are four groups on whose behalf it might be claimed that the corporations ought to be run in their interest: management, labour, stockholders, and 'the public' at large. So far as management is concerned we can dismiss it briefly with the observation that, though it is perhaps a danger to be guarded against, nobody would probably seriously contend that it is desirable that corporations should be run primarily in their interest.

The interest of 'labour' demands only a little longer consideration. As soon as it is made clear that it is not a question of the interest of workers in general but of the special interests of the employees of a particular corporation, it is fairly obvious that it would not be in the interest of 'society' or even of labour in general that the corporation should be run mainly for the benefit of any particular closed group of people employed by it. Though it may be in the interest of the corporation to tie its employees as closely to it as possible, the tendencies in this direction give ground for serious concern. It is the increasing dependence on the particular corporation by which a person is employed which gives the corporations increasing power over the employees, a power against which there can be no other safeguard than the facility the individual has of changing his employment.

That corporations tend to develop from an aggregation of material resources directed and operated by a body of men hired for that purpose into what is primarily a group of men held together by common experience and traditions, and even developing something like a distinct personality, is an important and probably inevitable fact. Nor can it be denied that some of the features which make a particular corporation especially efficient do not rest entirely with the management but would be destroyed if its whole operating personnel were at a given moment replaced by new men. The performance and very existence of a corporation is thus often bound up with the preservation of a certain continuity in its personnel, the preservation of at least an inner core of men right down the line who are familiar with its peculiar traditions and concrete tasks. The 'going concern' differs from the material structure which will still exist after operations have ceased mainly by the mutually adjusted knowledge and habits of those who operate it.

Nevertheless, in a free system (i.e., in a system of free labour) it is necessary in the interest of the efficient use of resources that the corporation be regarded primarily as an aggregate of material assets. It is they and not the men whom the management can at will allocate to different purposes, they which alone are the means which it is the task of corporations to put to the best use, while the individual must in the last resort himself remain free to decide whether the best use of his energies is within the particular corporation or elsewhere.

The fact is that an enterprise cannot be conducted in the interest of some permanent distinct body of workers if it is at the same time to serve the interest of the consumers. The management will take the decisions it ought to take in the interest of society only if its primary concern is the right use of those resources which it entirely controls, on which the risk of their decisions permanently falls, i.e., the equity capital, and if it treats all other resources it buys or hires as items which it must use only so long as it can make better use of them than anybody else. So long as the individual is free to decide whether he wants to serve this or that corporation, the corporation itself must primarily be concerned with the best use of those resources which are permanently associated with it.

The conception that a corporation ought to be run in the interest of the distinct body of people working in it raises all the problems discussed in connection with the syndicalist type of socialism. I have no space here to enter into a full discussion of these and will merely mention that these could be satisfactorily solved only if not merely this body of people became owners of the material resources of the corporation but if they were also able to hire other workers at the going rate of wages. The result would thus in effect be merely a change in the persons owning the enterprise but not an elimination of the class of wage earners. Whether it is really in the interest of the workers that, if they are also to be capitalists, their investment should be in the same concern which gives them employment is at least questionable.

III

There remain then as possible claimants for the position of the dominating interest in whose service the individual corporation ought to be conducted the owners of the equity and the public at large. (I pass over such other possible claimants as the creditors or the local community to whom the arguments discussed in connection with labour apply *a fortiori*.) The traditional reconciliation of those two interests rested on the assumption that the general rules of law can be given such form that an enterprise, by aiming at long-run maximum return, will also serve the public interest best. There are certain familiar difficulties which arise where property rights cannot be readily so delimited that the direct benefits or disadvantages consequent upon the use made of a particular piece of property will fall exclusively on the owner. These special difficulties, which we must try to remedy as far as possible by a gradual improvement of the law, I shall here disregard as not connected with the special problem of corporations.

Apart from these special instances, the general case for free enterprise and the division of labour rests on a recognition of the fact that, so long as each item of resources gets into the control of the enterprise willing to pay the highest price for it, it will, on the whole, also be used where it will make the largest contribution to the aggregate product of society.

This contention is based on the assumption that each firm will in its decisions consider only such results as will affect, directly or indirectly, the value of its assets and that it will not directly concern itself with the question of whether a particular use is 'socially beneficial'. I believe this is both necessary and right under a regime based on the division of labour, and that the aggregation of assets brought together for the specific purpose of putting them to the most productive use is not a proper source for expenditure which is thought to be generally socially desirable. Such expenditure should be defrayed either by the voluntary payment of individuals out of their income or capital or out of funds raised by taxation.

Rather than further argue this case positively I will briefly consider the consequences which would follow if it were to become the accepted view that the managements of corporations are entitled to spend corporation funds on what they regard as socially desirable purposes. The range of such purposes which might come to be regarded as legitimate objects of corporation expenditure is very wide: political, charitable, educational and in fact everything which can be brought under the vague and almost meaningless term 'social'. I propose to consider this question mainly with reference to the use of corporation funds in the support of higher education and research, since in this instance my personal interest is most likely biased in favour of such practices. All that is to be said in this connection applies equally to all the other fields mentioned.

The popular view of these matters is, of course, connected with the idea that corporations are 'rich' and therefore have special duties. What ought to be stressed here is that in the sense in which an individual may be rich, that is in the sense of having a large disposable income or capital he is free to devote to what seems to him most important, a corporation cannot be rich. In the strict sense the corporation has no more an income of its own than a trustee has in his capacity of trustee. That its management has been entrusted with large resources for a particular purpose does not mean that it is entitled to use it for other purposes. This is, of course, relevant in many other connections than that which concerns me here, especially in connection with taxation.

In fact, the only argument I can discover in favour of allowing corporations to devote their funds to such purposes as higher education and research—not in instances where this is likely to make it a profitable investment for their stockholders, but because this is regarded as a generally desirable purpose—is that in existing circumstances this seems to be the easiest way to raise adequate funds for what many influential people regard as important ends. This, however, seems to me not to be an adequate argument when we consider the consequences that would follow if it were to become generally recognized that managements have such power. If the large aggregations of capital which the corporations represent could, at the discretion of the management, be used for any purpose approved as morally or socially good, if the opinion of the management that a certain end was intellectually or aesthetically, scientifically or artistically desirable, were to justify expenditure by the corporation for such purposes, this would turn corporations from institutions serving the expressed needs of individual men into institutions determining which ends the efforts of individual men should serve. To allow the management to be guided in the use of funds, entrusted to them for the purpose of putting them to the materially most productive use, by what they regard as their social responsibility, would create centres of uncontrollable power never intended by those who provided the capital. It seems to me therefore clearly not desirable that generally higher education or research should be regarded as legitimate purposes of corporation expenditure, because this would not only vest powers over cultural decisions in men selected for capacities in an entirely different field, but would also establish a principle which, if generally applied, would enormously enhance the actual powers of corporations.

This, at least, would be the immediate effect. Yet not the least serious consequence of such a development would be that such powers would not long be left uncontrolled. So long as the management is supposed to serve the interest of the stockholders, it is reasonable to leave the control of its action to the stockholders. But if the management is supposed to serve wider public interests, it becomes merely a logical consequence of this conception that the appointed representatives of the public interest should control the management. The argument against specific interference of government into the conduct of business corporations rests on the assumption that they are constrained to use the resources under their control for a specific purpose. If this assumption becomes invalid, the argument for exemption from specific direction by the representatives of the public interest also lapses.

IV

If ideally corporations ought to be conducted primarily in the interest of the stockholders, this does not mean that the law as it stands fully achieves this, or even that, if they were left unregulated by law, the market would necessarily produce such developments as to make the interest of the stockholders prevail. The general philosophy of government from which I am approaching these problems makes it probably expedient that, before I proceed to ask what particular legal arrangements would seem desirable, I devote a few paragraphs to the question why there should be a need for any special regulation of corporations and why we should not be content to let the market develop appropriate institutions under the general principle of freedom of contract.

Historically, the need for the deliberate creation of special legal institutions in this field arose, of course, out of the problem of limited liability and the desire to protect the creditors. The creation of a legal person capable of entering contracts, for which only the separate property of the corporation and not all the property of the owners was liable, required special legislative action. In this sense limited liability is a privilege and it is a valid argument to say that it is for the law to decide on which conditions this privilege is to be granted.

I shall also state only briefly what I have argued at length in another connection,[1] that 'freedom of contracts', like most freedoms of this kind, does not mean that any contract must be permitted or be made enforceable, but merely that the permissibility or enforceability of a contract is to be decided by the general rules of law and that no authority has power to allow or disallow a contract on the basis of the merits of its specific contents. I am not at all sure that in the field of corporations any kind of contract should be generally prohibited or declared generally invalid. But I am firmly convinced that modern use of the corporate form of organization requires that there should be a standard type of rules

[1] *The Constitution of Liberty*, 1960, pp. 230–1.

applying to all corporations bearing a description reserved to this type so that, for example, any corporation designated by the addition of 'Inc.' to its name should thereby subject itself to a known standard type of rules. I see little reason for making such rules strictly mandatory, or not allowing other types of corporations explicitly described as 'special'. If the public is thus warned that in the particular case the standard rules do not apply, it will probably look very carefully at the provisions of any corporate charter which differs from the standard type.

The problem I want to consider is, thus, whether the rules for the standard type of corporation should, to a much greater degree than is the case at present, be governed by regulations which assure that the interest of the stockholder shall be paramount. I believe this to be the case and wish here to indulge in some bold mental experimentation with regard to the means of giving the stockholders greater powers in this respect. It seems to me that in this field the possibilities of arrangements different from those to which we are accustomed are all too little considered, and that the 'apathy' and lack of influence of the stockholder is largely the result of an institutional set-up which we have wrongly come to regard as the obvious or only possible one. I shall not be surprised if the experts on corporation law should at first regard my suggestions as wildly impracticable and am even prepared to admit that, under the present system of taxation and under current monetary policies, at least the first of the two possibilities I shall consider may do more harm than good. This, however, is no reason for not seriously examining these possibilities, even if it were only in order to free ourselves from the belief that the developments which have taken place were inevitable. It is probable that, on the two chief points I want to consider, the existing arrangements were adopted, not by deliberate choice and in awareness of the consequences, but because the alternatives were never seriously considered.

V

If today the actual influence of the stockholder on the conduct of the corporation is small and often negligible, this is probably due, more than to any other fact, to the circumstance that he has no legally enforceable claim to his share in the whole profits of the corporation. We have come to regard it as natural that a majority decides for all what part of the profits is to be distributed and what part to be reinvested in the corporation, and that on this question the stockholders will normally act on the recommendation of the management. It seems to me that nothing would produce so active an interest of the individual stockholder in the conduct of a corporation, and at the same time give him so much effective power, as to be annually called upon individually to decide what part of his share in the net profits he was willing to reinvest in the corporation.[2] It would still be for the management to say what part of the profits it thought it could profitably use as additional capital and to recommend that additional shares be offered to stockholders who wish to reinvest part or all of their profits in the corporation. But it should normally be for the individual stockholder to decide whether he wants to make use of this opportunity or not.

It is evident that this would be desirable only in conditions of a stable currency where paper profits corresponded to real profits and under a system of taxation different from the present. But disregarding for the moment these obstacles to the present adoption of the principle, it seems to me that this one change would go very far towards making stockholder control of the corporation a reality, and that it would at the same time limit the growth (and probably even the existence) of individual corporations to what is economically desirable. I need not ask here how far the allegations about an excessive expansion of corporations through ploughing back of profits are in fact justified. That with the existing arrangements this is at least a distinct possibility and that the natural bias of the management will tend in this direction can hardly be denied.

It might at first be thought that the striving for the power which an increase of total assets confers on management will also make it aim at maximizing profits. This, however, is true only in a sense of this term different from that in which we have used it and in which it can be maintained that maximizing profits is socially desirable. The interest of a management striving for control of more resources will be to maximize aggregate profits of the corporation, not profits per unit of capital invested. It is the latter, however, which should be maximized if the best use of the resources is to be secured.

VI

So far as the individual stockholder is concerned, it is in general to be assumed that his interest is solely to obtain the maximum direct return from his holdings of the shares of a particular corporation, whether this be in the form of dividends or of appreciation, or in the short or in the long run. It is conceivable that even an individual stockholder may use a controlling influence to direct the activities of a corporation so that the

2 Cf. Louis O. Kelso and Mortimer Adler, *The Capitalist Manifesto*, New York (Random House), 1958, p. 210.

gain will accrue mainly, not to that corporation, but to another corporation or firm where his share of the profit thus obtained would be even greater. Though possible, this is not a very likely situation to occur in the case of individual stockholders, not only because it would require very large resources but even more because such a manœuvre would probably be rather transparent and would be regarded as dishonest.

The situation is different, however, where the shares of one corporation are owned by another corporation, and nobody seriously questions that any control thus exercised by the second corporation over the first can legitimately be employed to increase the profits of the second. In such a situation it is clearly possible, and not unlikely, that the control over the policy of the first corporation will be used to channel the gains from its operations to the second, and that the first would be run, not in the interest of all its stockholders but only in the interest of the controlling majority. When the other stockholders discover this it will be too late for them to apply any remedy. The only possibility they will have is to sell out—which may be just what the corporate stockholder wants.

I must admit that I have never quite understood the *rationale* or justification of allowing corporations to have voting rights in other corporations of which they own shares. So far as I can discover, this was never deliberately decided upon in full awareness of all its applications, but came about simply as a result of the conception that, if legal personality was conferred upon the corporation, it was natural to confer upon it all powers which natural persons possessed. But this seems to me by no means a natural or obvious consequence. On the contrary, it turns the institution of property into something quite different from what it is normally supposed to be. The corporation thereby becomes, instead of an association of partners with a common interest, an association of groups whose interest may be in strong conflict; and the possibility appears that a group which directly owns assets amounting only to a small fraction of those of the corporation, may, through a pyramiding of holdings, acquire control of assets amounting to a multiple of what they own themselves. By owning a controlling interest in a corporation which owns a controlling interest in another corporation and so on, a comparatively small amount owned by a person or group may control a very much bigger aggregation of capital.

There seems to me to exist no reason why a corporation should not be allowed to own stock of another corporation purely as an investment. But it also seems to me that such stock, so long as it is owned by another corporation, should cease to confer a right to vote. Technically this could perhaps be effectively enforced only by permanently setting aside some part of the stock as non-voting shares and permitting only those to be held by other corporations. I am not concerned, here, however, with the practical details. The point I want to bring out is simply that the possibility of the control of one corporation by another opens up the possibility of the complete and perfectly legal control of large resources by persons who own only a small fraction of them, and of the use of such control in the interest of that group only.

The possibility of such an indirect, chainwise ownership of the stock of corporations is probably the second factor which has accentuated the separation of ownership from control and has given management, i.e., a few individuals, powers far exceeding those which their individually owned property could ever confer upon them. This development has nothing to do with the essence of the institution of the corporation as such, or with the reasons for which the privilege of limited liability was conferred upon them. In fact, if anything, it seems to me to be contrary to, rather than a consequence of, the conceptions on which the system of private property rests—an artificial separation of ownership and control which may place the individual owner in the position where his capital is used for purposes conflicting with his own and without his even being able to ascertain who, in fact, possesses the majority of votes. With the grant of voting rights to corporate stockholders the general presumption that the corporation will be run by persons whose interests are the same as those of the individual stockholder is no longer valid.

I will not pursue this possibility further to ask whether these considerations suggest that merely industrial corporations should be deprived of the voting power on the stock of other industrial corporations which they hold, or whether the principle should be extended also to financial corporations. Offhand I can see no reason for allowing such a distinction. Whatever desirable financial activities require that a firm should exercise the voting rights in a corporation could probably be performed without the privilege of limited liability.

Perhaps I should add that it seems to me that in recent years economists have been looking at corporation law (so far as they did so at all!) much too exclusively from the angle of whether it favoured the creation of monopoly positions. No doubt this is one important consideration which we ought to keep in mind. But it is certainly not the only one and perhaps not even the most important. The justification of the corporation is based on the conception that its managers will have to run it in such a manner that the whole of the capital it raises will be used in the most profitable way, and the public at large is certainly under the impression that the law is designed to assure this. So long as the corporations are run by representatives of the majority of the true owners, there is at least a strong probability that this will be the case. But somebody who represents merely the majority of a majority, and whose interests may well be better served if he does not have to share the profit from his control of the corporation with those who have provided the greater part of the capital, may well pursue different aims. A legal situation which makes it theoretically possible that this position may arise in any corporation after the stockholders have committed their capital to it and have no remedy cannot be regarded as satisfactory.

VII

I have considered these two possibilities of changes in corporation law not so much because of their specific merit but as illustrations of the degree to which future developments depend on the legal framework we provide for them. They were meant to show that the complete separation of management from ownership, the lack of real power of the stockholders, and the tendency of corporations to develop into self-willed and possibly irresponsible empires, aggregates of enormous and largely uncontrollable power, is not a fact which we must accept as inevitable, but largely the result of special conditions which the law has created and the law can change. We have it in our power to halt and reverse this process if we want to. Even the two changes in the law I have considered would probably be much more far-reaching in this respect than is at first apparent or could be indicated in a few paragraphs.

Let me repeat, in conclusion, that to me the chief merit of these changes would seem to be that they would tie management much more effectively than is now the case to the single task of employing the capital of their stockholders in the most profitable manner and would deprive them of the power of using it in the service of some 'public interest'. The present tendency not only to allow but to encourage such use of corporate resources appears to me as dangerous in its short-run as in its long-run consequences. The immediate effect is greatly to extend the powers of the management of corporations over cultural, political, and moral issues for which proven ability to use resources efficiently in production does not necessarily confer special competence; and at the same time to substitute a vague and indefinable 'social responsibility' for a specific and controllable task. But while in the short run the effect is to increase an irresponsible power, in the long run the effect is bound to be increased control of corporations by the power of the state. The more it comes to be accepted that corporations ought to be directed in the service of specific 'public interests', the more persuasive becomes the contention that, as government is the appointed guardian of the public interest, government should also have power to tell the corporations what they must do. Their power to do good according to their own judgment is bound to be a merely transitory stage. The price they would soon have to pay for this short-lived freedom will be that they will have to take instructions from the political authority which is supposed to represent the public interest. Unless we believe that the corporations serve the public interest best by devoting their resources to the single aim of securing the largest return in terms of long-run profits, the case for free enterprise breaks down.

I cannot better sum up what I have been trying to say than by quoting a brief statement in which my colleague Professor Milton Friedman expressed the chief contention two years ago: 'If anything is certain to destroy our free society, to undermine its very foundations, it would be a wide-spread acceptance by management of social responsibilities in some sense other than to make as much money as possible. This is a fundamentally subversive doctrine.'[3]

[3] The Social Science Reporter's Eighth Social Science Seminar on 'Three Major Factors in Business Management: Leadership, Decision Making, and Social Responsibility', March 19, 1958. Summary by Walter A. Diehm, Graduate School of Business, Stanford University.

CHAPTER TWENTY-THREE

The Non Sequitur of the 'Dependence Effect'*

For well over a hundred years the critics of the free enterprise system have resorted to the argument that if production were only organized rationally, there would be no economic problem. Rather than face the problem which scarcity creates, socialist reformers have tended to deny that scarcity existed. Ever since the Saint-Simonians their contention has been that the problem of production has been solved and only the problem of distribution remains. However absurd this contention must appear to us with respect to the time when it was first advanced, it still has some persuasive power when repeated with reference to the present.

The latest form of this old contention is expounded in *The Affluent Society* by Professor J. K. Galbraith. He attempts to demonstrate that in our affluent society the important private needs are already satisfied and the urgent need is therefore no longer a further expansion of the output of commodities but an increase of those services which are supplied (and presumably can be supplied only) by government. Though his book has been extensively discussed since its publication in 1958, its central thesis still requires some further examination.

I believe the author would agree that his argument turns upon the 'Dependence Effect' explained in Chapter XI of the book. The argument of this chapter starts from the assertion that a great part of the wants which are still unsatisfied in modern society are not wants which would be experienced spontaneously by the individual if left to himself, but are wants which are created by the process by which they are satisfied. It is then represented as self-evident that for this reason such wants cannot

* Reprinted from *The Southern Economic Journal*, Vol. XXVII, No. 4, April 1961.

be urgent or important. This crucial conclusion appears to be a complete *non sequitur* and it would seem that with it the whole argument of the book collapses.

The first part of the argument is of course perfectly true: we would not desire any of the amenities of civilization—or even of the most primitive culture—if we did not live in a society in which others provide them. The innate wants are probably confined to food, shelter, and sex. All the rest we learn to desire because we see others enjoying various things. To say that a desire is not important because it is not innate is to say that the whole cultural achievement of man is not important.

This cultural origin of practically all the needs of civilized life must of course not be confused with the fact that there are some desires which aim at a satisfaction derived directly not from the use of an object, but only from the status which its consumption is expected to confer. In a passage which Professor Galbraith quotes (p. 118), Lord Keynes seems to treat the latter sort of Veblenesque conspicuous consumption as the only alternative 'to those needs which are absolute in the sense that we feel them whatever the situation of our fellow human beings may be'. If this phrase is interpreted to exclude all the needs for goods which are felt only because these goods are known to be produced, these two Keynesian classes describe of course only extreme types of wants, but disregard the overwhelming majority of goods on which civilized life rests. Very few needs indeed are 'absolute' in the sense that they are independent of social environment or of the example of others and that their satisfaction is an indispensable condition for the preservation of the individual or of the species. Most needs which make us act are needs for things of which only civilization teaches us that they exist at all, and these things are wanted by us because they produce feelings or emotions which we would not know if it were not for our cultural inheritance. Are not in this sense probably all our aesthetic feelings 'acquired tastes'?

How complete a *non sequitur* Professor Galbraith's conclusion represents is seen most clearly if we apply the argument to any product of the arts, be it music, painting, or literature. If the fact that people would not feel the need for something if it were not produced did prove that such products are of small value, all those highest products of human endeavour would be of small value. Professor Galbraith's argument could be easily employed, without any change of the essential terms, to demonstrate the worthlessness of literature or any other form of art. Surely an individual's want for literature is not original with himself in the sense that he would experience it if literature were not produced. Does this then mean that the production of literature cannot be defended as satisfying a want because it is only the production which provokes the demand? In this, as in the case of all cultural needs, it is unquestionably, in Professor Galbraith's words, 'the process of satisfying the wants that creates the wants'. There have never been 'independently determined desires for' literature before literature has been produced and books certainly do not serve 'the simple mode of enjoyment which requires no previous conditioning of the consumer' (p. 217). Clearly my taste for the novels of Jane Austen or Anthony Trollope or C. P. Snow is not 'original with myself'. But is it not rather absurd to conclude from this that it is less important than, say, the need for education? Public education, indeed, seems to regard it as one of its tasks to instil a taste for literature in the young and even employs producers of literature for that purpose. Is this want-creation by the producer reprehensible? Or does the fact that some of the pupils may possess a taste for poetry only because of the efforts of their teachers prove that since 'it does not arise in spontaneous consumer need and the demand would not exist were it not contrived, its utility or urgency, ex contrivance, is zero'?

The appearance that the conclusions follow from the admitted facts is produced by an obscurity of the wording of the argument with respect to which it is difficult to know whether the author is himself the victim of a confusion or whether he skilfully uses ambiguous terms to make his conclusion appear plausible. The obscurity concerns the implied assertion that the wants of the consumers are determined by the producers. Professor Galbraith avoids in this connection any terms as crude and definite as 'determine'. The expressions he employs, such as that wants are 'dependent on' or the 'fruits of' production, or that 'production creates the wants', do, of course, suggest determination but avoid saying so in plain terms. After what has already been said it is of course obvious that the knowledge of what is being produced is one of the many factors on which it depends what people will want. It would scarcely be an exaggeration to say that contemporary man, in all fields where he has not yet formed firm habits, tends to find out what he wants by looking at what his neighbours do and at various displays of goods (physical or in catalogues or advertisements) and then choosing what he likes best.

In this sense the tastes of man, as is also true of his opinions and beliefs and indeed much of his personality, are shaped in great measure by his cultural environment. But though in some contexts it would perhaps be legitimate to express this by a phrase like 'production creates the wants', the circumstances mentioned would clearly not justify the contention that particular producers can deliberately determine the wants of particular consumers. The efforts of all producers will certainly be directed towards that end; but how far any individual producer will succeed will depend not only on what he does but also on what the others do and on a great many other influences operating upon the consumers. The joint but unco-ordinated efforts of the producers merely create one element of the environment by which the wants of the consumers are shaped. It is because each individual producer thinks that the consumers can be persuaded to like his products that he endeavours to influence them. But though this effort is part of the influences which shape consumers' tastes, no producer can in any real sense 'determine' them. This, however, is clearly implied in such statements as that wants are 'both passively and deliberately the fruits of the process by which they are satisfied' (p. 124). If the producer could in fact deliberately determine what the consumers will want, Professor Galbraith's conclusions would have some validity. But though this is skilfully suggested, it is nowhere made credible, and could hardly be made credible because it is not true. Though the range of choice open to the consumers is the joint result of, among other things, the efforts of all producers who vie with each other to make their respective products appear more attractive than those of their competitors, every particular consumer still has the choice between all those different offers.

A fuller examination of this process would, of course, have to consider how, after the efforts of some producers have actually swayed some consumers, it becomes the example of the various consumers thus persuaded which will influence the remaining consumers. This can be mentioned here only to emphasize that even if each consumer were exposed to pressure of only one producer, the harmful effects which are apprehended from this would soon be offset by the much more influential example of his fellows. It is of course fashionable to treat this influence of the example of others (or, what comes to the same thing, the learning from the experience made by others) as if it amounted all to an attempt at keeping up with the Joneses and for that reason was to be regarded as detrimental. It seems to me that not only is the importance of this factor usually greatly exaggerated, but also that it is not really relevant to Professor Galbraith's main thesis. But it might be worthwhile briefly to ask what it would really prove if some expenditure were actually determined solely by the desire to keep up with the Joneses. At least in Europe we used to be familiar with a type of person who often denied himself even enough food in order to maintain an appearance of respectability or gentility in dress and style of life. We may regard this as a misguided effort, but surely it would not prove that the income of such persons was larger than they knew how to use wisely. That the appearance of success, or wealth, may to some people seem more important than many other needs, does in no way prove that the needs they sacrifice to the former are unimportant. In the same way, even though people are often persuaded to spend unwisely, this surely is no evidence that they do not still have important unsatisfied needs.

Professor Galbraith's attempt to give an apparent scientific proof of the contention that the need for the production of more commodities has greatly decreased seems to me to have broken down completely. With it goes the claim to have produced a valid argument which justifies the use of coercion to make people employ their income for those purposes of which he approves. It is not to be denied that there is some originality in this latest version of the old socialist argument. For over a hundred years we have been exhorted to embrace socialism because it would give us more goods. Since it has so lamentably failed to achieve this where it has been tried, we are now urged to adopt it because more goods after all are not important. The aim is still progressively to increase the share of the resources whose use is determined by political authority and the coercion of any dissenting minority. It is not surprising, therefore, that Professor Galbraith's thesis has been most enthusiastically received by the intellectuals of the British Labour Party, among whom his influence bids fair to displace that of the late Lord Keynes. It is more curious that in this country it is not recognized as an outright socialist argument and often seems to appeal to people on the opposite end of the political spectrum. But this is probably only another instance of the familiar fact that on these matters the extremes frequently meet.

CHAPTER TWENTY-FOUR

The Uses of 'Gresham's Law' as an Illustration of 'Historical Theory'*

Mr. A. L. Burns' use of Gresham's Law as an illustration[1] provides a good example for showing how useful it would be for the historian if he examined what Gresham's Law amounts to as a theoretical statement and not merely as an empirical generalization. The empirical generalization that 'bad money drives out good' of course goes back to classical antiquity, when it seems to have been so familiar that Aristophanes (*Frogs*, 891–898) could assume that he would be readily understood when he applied the idea to good and bad politicians. It is pure accident that this empirical rule became attached to the name of Gresham. And as a mere empirical rule it is practically valueless. I remember that in the monetary disturbances of the early 1920's, when people began to use dollars and other solid currencies in the place of the rapidly depreciating mark, a Dutch financier (if I remember rightly, Mr. Vissering) asserted that Gresham's Law was wrong and that it was in fact the other way round and it was the good money that drove out the bad.

If Gresham's Law is properly stated with the conditions in which it applies, it will appear that as a proposition of compositive social theory it can indeed provide a useful tool of historical explanation. The essential condition is that there must be two kinds of money which are of equivalent value for some purposes and of different value for others. The typical instance about which the empirical generalization developed is the simultaneous circulation of a particular coin, say a gold ducat, in a new

---

* Reprinted from *History and Theory*, Vol. I, 1962.
[1] Arthur Lee Burns, 'International Theory and Historical Explanation', *History and Theory*, I, 1 (1960), 62–6.

and a worn state. If such a coin is legal tender in a country, the two different forms are of the same value for the discharge of internal debts. But they may not be for foreign payments, and are clearly not of the same value for the industrial use of the gold contained in them. The two kinds of coin may for a long time circulate side by side and be accepted as equivalent not only internally but even externally if there is a net influx of money into the country concerned. But as soon as its balance of payments turns against it, the position will change. The worn coins will now have only the value which they have as currency of the country using them in its regular internal trade. But in international trade the new and full-weight coins may well have a higher value and the same will apply to the internal industrial uses (by goldsmiths) of the gold contained in them. In certain transactions which take coins out of the internal circulation new full-weight coins will therefore be more useful than worn coins, and the former will tend to go out of circulation.

It would not be a very useful approach to the problem to say 'that at some reasonably brief interval before the specie disappeared from circulation, it had become public knowledge that it was undervalued by a certain amount in terms of the rest of the currency'.[2] No change of this sort need have become newly known. Foreign merchants and goldsmiths may always have been using only new coins. But while as many gold coins (or as much gold to be coined) came into the country as went out, this would not lead to a reduction of the proportion of good coins in circulation. Only when the conditions of a net inflow turned into conditions of a net outflow would a change in the relative composition of the circulation manifest itself.

The historian who knows of Gresham's Law merely as an empirical proposition might well be puzzled when he finds that, after good and bad coins had been circulating concurrently for decades without a noticeable deterioration in the average quality, at one point of time the good coins had suddenly begun to grow very scarce. He would not be able to discover any new information which had become available concerning the 'undervaluation' of one kind of coin. Indeed if he were able to ask those immediately concerned they would tell him that they merely continued to do exactly what they had done before. What theory will tell him is that he must look for some cause which led to a fall of the internal value of both good and bad coins relative to their value in foreign commerce and in industrial uses. He will have to understand that neither wear and tear nor clipping can have caused this relative depreciation. He will have to look for a cause which either increased the relative supply or decreased the relative demand for coins and their substitutes in internal circulation. One need merely read the usual accounts of the events during the 'Kipper and Wipper' period (1621–1623) in Germany, or of those preceding the English re-coinage of 1696, in order to see how easy it is to go wrong without some knowledge of monetary theory. Like most of the theory which is likely to be useful to the historian, it is only very simple and elementary theory which is required; and the usual conception of Gresham's Law is a very good illustration of how theory may and how it will not help the historian.

CHAPTER TWENTY-FIVE

The Economics of Development Charges[*]

I

Few measures of similar importance, at the time they were passed, have probably received so little attention from some of those most affected by them, as was true of the Town and Country Planning Act, 1947. Even now, some nine months after the Act has come into force, few people are aware of its full significance for the economic future of this country. Yet it may well prove to have a decisive and perhaps fatal effect on that increase of industrial efficiency on which our future must depend.

The public can hardly be blamed, however, for not at once appreciating the wider bearing of that measure. One may even doubt whether its drafters and supporters quite understood its implications. The Act applies to a wide field a special theory which has been developed within a narrow circle of town planners with a limited object in view; but the general significance of that theory has never been systematically examined.

This doctrine was first expounded in several reports and documents which were published during the war and which, in consequence, did not receive careful critical examination. The Act itself and its implementation not only went even beyond what was contemplated in those earlier documents; it was also couched in a language so obscure and at the same time so vague that it was scarcely possible to know what some of its most crucial provisions would mean before it was seen how they were administered.

Since on some of the most crucial issues the decisions have not been written into the Act but have been left to the discretion of various

* From *The Financial Times*, April 26, 27, 28, 1949.

government departments, it is only as their policy becomes known that we can form a clearer idea of the probable effects.

On the issue to be considered here, the 'development charges', the operation and the interpretation of the Act has been entrusted to the Central Land Board. This Board has recently explained its intentions in a set of *Practice Notes*[1] which is in more than one respect a remarkable document deserving close study.

There will be opportunity later to comment on the curious light it throws on the political and administrative problems raised by this sort of planning. But the indications it gives of how the Board proposes to assess the development charges raise purely economic problems which require careful examination.

As the document puts it, the Central Land Board has been given 'a monopoly in development rights' in land. 'Development' means now for this purpose not only the turning of hitherto 'undeveloped' agricultural land to industrial or commercial uses; it includes 'redevelopment', that is all material changes in the use of any already developed land, except when the change takes place within certain narrowly defined classes.

All such changes of use require a previous 'planning permission'. Most of them are also subject to a development charge which must be paid before the change can be made. The principle on which these charges are determined will therefore decide what kind of change will still be practicable.

If anybody should still think that these development charges are intended merely to confiscate some special gain due to the beneficial effect of public policy, of a genuine 'betterment' in the old sense of the term, he will soon be undeceived. The development charge has become something altogether different.

It is intended to absorb any increase in value of a particular piece of land due to the permission to change its use. It constitutes in effect a confiscation of the whole advantage derived from any industrial development for which land hitherto used for a different purpose has to be used.

The development charge is in each instance to be equal to 'the difference between the existing use value and the value for the permitted development'; or, in the new terminology introduced, between the 'Refusal Value' and the 'Consent Value' of the piece of land. Until the

[1] Central Land Board, *Practice Notes (First Series)*. Being Notes on the Development Charges under the Town and Country Planning Act, 1947. London: H.M. Stationery Office, 1949.

planning permission is granted, the land is presumed to derive its value exclusively from the existing use.

So far as the owner is concerned this will indeed be true, whatever its potentialities from a social point of view, since all the potentialities for some different and more valuable use have been expropriated and vested in the Central Land Board.

We are not concerned here with the owner's distant prospect in a share of the £300 million set aside for compensation. That he may hope some day to get a sum of uncertain magnitude does not alter the effect of the price which he will have to pay now for the acquisition or re-acquisition of any development right.

The earlier documents in which this scheme was first outlined had proposed development charges amounting to a certain proportion, something like 75 or 80 per cent, of the increase in value. The Act itself left this point characteristically undecided. But the policy announced by the Minister of Town and Country Planning is to fix the charges at 100 per cent of the increase in value.

This means that anyone contemplating a change in the layout of an industrial plant involving a material change in the use of land, before he is allowed to undertake it, will have to hand over the full capitalized value of the expected advantage.

There are, it is true, certain exceptions to this rule. Where the change is confined to an alternation of the use of already existing buildings within certain narrowly defined classes, no charge will arise. But where it involves a change in the use of land between any such categories as office buildings, 'light' industrial buildings, 'general' industrial buildings, or any one of five classes of 'special' industrial buildings, the full charge is due. The exceptions somewhat limit the incidence of the charge. But they do not alter the principle or the general effects of its application.

This principle amounts to nothing less than that the whole of any advantage derived from the reorganization of a manufacturing process which involves a material change in the use of land shall be absorbed by the development charge. What is taken away is thus not merely the special advantage which a particular piece of land may offer compared with others, because of its situation or special qualities.

Since any land, except that already devoted to a certain kind of use, will be available for this use only after the payment of a development charge, the 'advantage' for which the price has to be paid will be the possibility of introducing a new process anywhere.

Since the permission will be granted only with respect to a particular piece of land, that possibility becomes artificially attached to that piece of land and the value of the possibility to introduce the new process becomes similarly tied to the value of that piece of land.

The significance of the new monopoly element thus introduced will be seen more clearly if we consider for a moment how the price of land in a similar situation was determined in the past. Take the problems raised by the expansion of an industrial undertaking surrounded by agricultural land. If the land on all sides was of the same agricultural quality, was owned by different people, and offered the same opportunities to the plant, the pieces needed could have been bought for a price representing its agricultural use value.

This would in most instances have correctly represented the social cost of the change: the loss of the agricultural value would have been the loss to society which would have to be more than offset by the gain from its industrial use if the change was to be beneficial.

Only if some of the land surrounding the plant offered to the undertaking greater advantages than the rest would the owner of that piece of land have been able to hold out for a correspondingly higher price. The undertaking might have had to pay extra, over and above what it would have had to pay for any other land, for any special advantage the particular site offered to it. But this payment would have had to be made for a differential advantage of that piece of land—not for the possibility of expanding at all, but for being able to expand in a particular direction.

Contrast this with the situation where all the land surrounding the plant belonged to one owner; it would then have been the possibility of expanding at all, not merely the possibility of expanding on a particular piece of land, which would depend on the landowner's willingness to sell. He would be in a position to extort a price equal to nearly the whole gain from the expansion. Any piece of land he was prepared to sell would for the undertaking possess the full value of the gain to be expected from expanding on the existing site.

The monopoly of the Land Board will be even more complete than that of such a single owner of all the land surrounding an existing plant. The Board will also control the only two alternatives to expanding on adjoining land: development within the given area—for example, by building higher—or moving the whole plant elsewhere.

All opportunities for expansion will depend on its permission and since only land with a planning permission can be used for the expansion, the 'Consent Value' of any such land will include the whole value of the gain to be expected from the expansion.

It is true that in its *Practice Notes* the Board disclaims the intention of exacting monopoly values. But since at the same time it states that it means to take into account the special value of land to an only possible purchaser, that assurance evidently cannot be taken literally. It is indeed difficult to see how under its instructions the Board can do anything but charge monopoly values. Since what it confers are essentially monopoly values, its concept also has a monopoly value.

The Board has in effect been given 'a monopoly in the development rights' not only *in land*, but, in so far as any development requires some land and since the Board controls all land, it has a monopoly of all industrial development of the kind.

II

Land is a factor which is indispensable in all industrial activity and all change in industrial activity therefore involves a change in the use of land. To make some such changes dependent upon permission and on the payment of a price is to make industrial adjustment to that extent dependent on a permission and the payment of a price. And to fix this price with regard to the advantage depending on the permission amounts in effect to a confiscation of the gain from such industrial change. This is a principle introduced by the Town and Country Planning Act.

The term 'gain', however, in this connection, is rather misleading; it suggests less serious effects of the development charges than they are likely to have. They will not only eliminate a main incentive to socially desirable changes. They will impose an artificial cost on such change to which no genuine social costs correspond. The changes in question may be necessary merely to preserve the usefulness of the land or to maintain the solvency of an enterprise.

It may merely be a question of avoiding loss. Yet where the avoidance of the loss depends on a change made in the use of land, the permission to make it will be worth the whole loss which is thereby avoided, and the development charge will have to be fixed accordingly. Even where the gain expected from the change is a net gain, its value will have to be laid out beforehand and a new risk will be created which the investor will have to incur without any compensating prospect of gain.

Land used for industrial purposes will over long periods retain its value only in so far as its use is adjusted to changing conditions. The value of a particular piece of land for a given purpose constantly changes, and if it were permanently tied to a particular purpose its value would be certain sooner or later to fall. Such losses are usually avoided by switching the land to a different use when its former use becomes less valuable.

Under the new arrangements such a loss must be wholly borne by the owner of the land, since he no longer owns the right to change the use but will have to purchase his right at a price corresponding to the amount he recovers by the change. The land may in the new use be worth less than it has been before the opportunity for its former use disappeared.

Nevertheless, once the value in its former use has fallen, the opportunity of recovering part of the losses by changing the use belongs to the State. In the example given in the *Practice Notes*, 'The slum cottage is to have only its existing use value as a cottage until planning permission is given for redevelopment. Then on payment of the development charge, representing the value due to that permission, the value jumps at one bound to that for the new permitted use.'

In other words, the owner will first have to suffer the loss of obsolescence imposed on him by the prohibition of the change in the use (or because the versatility of his asset has been artificially restricted by law); and he is then deprived of any gain which he might make when the change is permitted.

One wonders indeed whether the inventors of the whole scheme have ever reflected on what it will mean if the development charge makes a change unprofitable, or whether it has ever occurred to them that it will frequently do so.

It should be obvious both that *any* development charge may prevent some desirable change, and that, whenever it has that effect, it will prevent a more productive use of the available resources.

The only exception to this would be where the development charge happened to be equal in value to some indirect damage done by the development to other property, a damage which otherwise would not have been taken into account in calculating the net benefit to be expected. But there is no intention and no practical possibility of relating the development charges to such detrimental effects of the change. We can therefore neglect the possibility of a purely accidental coincidence.

Let us consider a particular case. Suppose an undertaking owns some workers' houses close to its manufacturing plant. If the houses had not already been there, it might long have been advantageous to use the site for some process ancillary to manufacture. But as the houses already exist, the value of their services has to be set against the advantage of having that process on the particular spot.

But sooner or later, as the value of the houses declines, the point will come when that advantage is greater than the value of the services which the houses will give. They will be demolished and the site turned to manufacture precisely when this brings some net saving in the combined costs of producing both the housing services and the industrial product.

This saving of costs may be small, and it will certainly stand in no relation to the difference in value between other similar land in the neighbourhood used for housing and for manufacture respectively. Yet it is on the cumulative effect of many small savings in costs such as this that improvements in industrial efficiency depend.

If in a case like this a development charge is levied, the effect can be only that the change is delayed and perhaps altogether prevented. In future, it will be necessary that the saving in costs should exceed the value of the existing use value, according to established valuation practices, by as much as land available for manufacturing purposes exceeds in value land used for dwelling houses.

The same applies to all similar changes designed to bring about a saving in costs. Such changes will be either prevented or at least the incentive to make them greatly reduced.

This would be bad enough if the gain were only confiscated after it has in fact materialized. Carried out consistently, it would deprive the owners of all interest in cost-saving changes of the kind. We should have to rely on their public spirit for their constantly striving to keep costs as low as possible.

The fact that the development charge has to be paid before the change is made and irrespective of whether the expected benefit actually matures makes the effect, however, even worse. It creates a new private risk which the individual developer has to bear, but to which no social risk corresponds.

The developer must be willing to stake an amount equal to the hoped-for gain, certain that he will lose if his hopes are not fulfilled, but without any prospect of advantage if his expectations prove correct. A grosser form of penalizing risk can hardly be imagined. Wherever there is un-certainty about the outcome it will become much safer to stay put than to sink capital in buying a permission which may prove of little value.

What the whole scheme amounts to is that a penalty is placed upon industrial change. Every adjustment to changed conditions which involves a 'material' change in the use of land is made the occasion for a levy which in effect expropriates the gain that might be expected. The more rapidly and the more often an undertaking tries to meet changes in conditions, the more often part of its capital will be confiscated.

Wherever the gain it can expect from a change is smaller than the

Central Land Board thinks it ought to be, the change will be altogether impossible. And only when a firm can persuade the Board that the gain from the change will be smaller than it in fact expects it to be, will there be any pecuniary advantage in undertaking it.

Let it once more be stressed that in all this 'gain' does not necessarily mean an absolute gain. What is confiscated is the gain relative to the position if the change were prohibited. The change may aim merely at lowering of costs in line with what foreign competitors are doing. Or it may be necessary because a change in demand requires an alteration of the product.

It does not matter. So long as a material change in the use of land is necessary the benefit from the change is taken away. Can there be much doubt that if this principle is carried out as now announced, it cannot but prove to be one of the most serious blows administered to the prospects of increasing the efficiency of British industry?

III

It has been suggested in the first part of this article that the authors of the Town and Country Planning Act did not know what they were planning. After examining the practical significance of the development charges as now interpreted, one must almost hope that this was so.

It is becoming only too clear that the whole scheme has not been adequately thought out beforehand, and that we have been committed to an experiment, of the outcome of which nobody has formed a clear conception. It appears that the unprecedented blanket powers which the Act conferred on the Minister of Town and Country Planning and the Central Land Board were the result of a lack of any clear idea of how these powers were to be used.

The advocates of central planning always assure us that democratic legislation is an adequate safeguard against controls becoming arbitrary. What are we, then, to think of an Act which explicitly leaves undetermined the *general principles* on which the authorities are to use one of the most powerful tools of economic control ever put into their hands?

Yet this is exactly what the Town and Country Planning Act (Sub-section 3 of Section 70) did when it provided that 'regulations made under the Act with the consent of the Treasury may prescribe the general principles to be followed by the Board in determining . . . whether any and if so what development charges are to be paid'.

It was under this provision that it was left to the Minister of Town and Country Planning unexpectedly to issue a Regulation according to which the development charges were normally 'not to be less' than the whole additional value of the land accruing from the planning permission for a particular development.

The general principle stated in that Regulation, however, still provides no more than the most general framework within which the Board must formulate its own policies.

The position in which the Central Land Board has thereby been placed is well illustrated by the Preface which its chairman has contributed to the *Practice Notes* in which it has summed up the principles it proposes to follow. These notes, he explains, 'are meant to describe the principles and working rules in accordance with which any applicant can confidently assume his case will be dealt.' This sounds reassuring until one reads on and finds that the sentence continues: 'unless either he can show good cause for different treatment, or the Board inform him that for special reasons the normal rules do not apply.'

What confidence can there be in any rules if no principles are stated on which it will be decided that the general rules do not apply in a particular case? The Board even explicitly refuses to be tied by a fixed rule: 'A general working rule must always be variable if it does not fit a particular case.'

The Board also refuses to be bound by precedent and announces that 'we have no doubt that from time to time we shall vary our policy' and that such future variations 'can only operate for new cases and cannot reopen old'.

Why this continued vagueness if there is a clear aim? Can it be that the absurdity of the general principle is already half recognized and that it is intended to mitigate the bad effects by concessions in the negotiations with individual applicants? Certain statements made in Parliament and some passages in the Preface to the *PracticeNotes* suggest that this may be the intention.

Is a more dangerous procedure imaginable than first to burden the authorities with the duty of imposing enormous charges on a principle which it is known cannot be consistently applied, and then to leave it to their discretion to modify their claims when it appears that the effects are all too harmful?

The Preface to the *Practice Notes* almost seems to invite precisely this sort of bargaining and to suggest that the Board will always be willing to listen to special considerations if they are pressed hard enough.

The fact is that the task of administering the development charges not only 'fairly' but in such a manner that they do not impede desirable industrial development is an impossible one. In determining the development charge the Board is, in fact, deciding whether a particular development ought to take place or not. It could do so intelligently only if it were in a position to plan the whole industrial development of the country.

In order that it should be in a position to judge the effects of its decisions on industrial efficiency, it would have to have at its disposal, and have to be able to judge, all the data which the individual developer takes into account.

Indeed, if the development charges are to be anything but a harmful obstacle to development, they would have to be used according to a detailed overall plan, which lays down in what form and in which direction each industry, and each plant in each industry, ought to be developed.

This, however, is of course neither the intention nor a practical possibility. Instead, the Land Board is charged with determining one of the essential conditions on which the decision of the private developer must depend, without any possibility (other than the owner's statement) of judging how its action will affect that decision, or what that decision ought to be in the national interest.

Neither the Land Board nor the developer will be able to base his decisions on the objective merits of the situation. Whether the development will take place is made dependent on an artificially created conflict of interests to which no economic facts correspond and which must be detrimental to a wise solution of the genuine economic problems involved.

There exists indeed no *rationale* for the development charges as now conceived. Far from introducing a rational element into the decisions about the use of land, it introduces a completely meaningless factor and falsifies the data on which the developer will have to base his decisions. The costs he will have to take into account will correspond less to the true social costs than ever before.

His opportunity to plan wisely and the likelihood of his serving the best social interest will be greatly decreased. And his energies will have to be bent, not so much to discovering the real facts of the situation, as to finding arguments which will appear plausible to those who have to fix the terms on which he will be allowed to go ahead with his plans.

The direction of industrial progress will more than ever become dependent on the powers of persuasion, the accidents of contacts, and the vicissitudes of official procedure where the most careful calculation ought to decide. The most efficient and conscientious civil service cannot prevent this where no clear direction can be laid down for its actions.

Nobody has yet suggested what these directions ought to be if the development charges are to be beneficial to the increase of industrial efficiency. The only rule which would have that effect would be that there should be no development charges.

APPENDIX: A Review of Charles M. Haar, *Land Planning Law in a Free Society: A Study of the British Town and Country Planning Act*.[2] Cambridge, Mass., Harvard University Press, 1951.

One of the inevitable effects of the progressive extension of government control over economic life is that economic problems are increasingly disposed of by lawyers, technologists and experts in 'administration'. It might be expected that this would lead to an increased understanding of economics in these professions. This expectation has generally been frustrated—it almost seems as if those who ardently believe that they can solve economic problems by central planning in most instances do so precisely because they are unaware of what the economic problems are.

There is no better illustration of this than town planning—a subject which, it must be admitted, has been sadly neglected by economists. And there could be hardly a more telling demonstration of the complete lack of comprehension of the economic problems which the use of land raises for society than the present careful and painstaking study of the new British Town and Country Planning Act of 1947 by an American student of Public Administration. While the book presents a sympathetic interpretation of that experiment, in the sense that Mr. Haar fully shares the outlook which inspires it, it is as devoid of any appreciation of the wider economic issues involved as were the group of architects and administrators who, in the peculiar circumstances of Britain between 1940 and 1947, were almost exclusively responsible for this piece of legislation. The book does not even take notice of the few critical analyses of the Act which appeared when the British economists were at last released from the more important preoccupation of winning the war. In particular the author ignores the masterly analysis of the problem by Sir Arnold Plant[3] and the severe criticism which the measure has received from groups which one might expect to be sympathetic towards it, such as the followers of Henry George.[4]

After reading the book one feels some doubt whether the author, any

[2] Reprinted from the *University of Chicago Law Review*, XIX/3, Spring 1952.
[3] A. Plant, 'Land Planning and the Economic Functions of Ownership', *Journal Chartered Auctioneers and Estate Agents Inst.*, Vol. XXX (1949).
[4] Cf. especially their journal, *Land and Liberty*, London, 1948 and 1949.

more than the legislators or the British public at large, is fully aware of how completely the Act has changed the whole character of the British economic system. While entirely suspending the operation of the price mechanism with regard to land (outside agricultural uses) it has put nothing in its place except arbitrary decision without even a general principle to guide it. What the Act has decreed is nothing less than that all advantage which a private owner could derive from any change in the use made of a piece of land (if it was to be devoted to other than agricultural purposes) shall in future be confiscated by the government, and that, therefore, if the principles of the Act can be consistently applied, no private person or corporation will have any incentive to improve economic efficiency, where this involves a change in the use of land.

To anyone familiar with the history of the Act and the effects which it is producing, the most curious aspect of the present book is that it attempts to emphasize throughout the democratic character of the measure and its compatibility with free institutions, while on the basis of the facts provided by the book itself both are at best pious hopes of highly questionable value. If the author is unaware of the threat to freedom involved, this is probably because he seems equally oblivious to the fact that consistent application of the principles of the Act in the long run implies central direction of all economic activity. Characterization of the measure as particularly democratic squares ill with the admitted facts that when it was discussed in Parliament almost nobody understood the practically unlimited discretionary powers it conferred on administrative agencies. '[T]he Opposition often felt in the position of Joseph who was asked not only to interpret the dream, but to say what the dream was' (p. 177). Furthermore, after the Act had placed in the power of a minister unlimited discretion to lay down even the 'general principle' on which its most important provision was to be administered, the minister in fact issued regulations which 'represent a complete change of mind since the time of the debates of the Act' (p. 111). We shall later have to consider the issue in question. From a lawyer one might also have expected a little more concern about the fact, mentioned like many of the less appealing features of the legislation in the small print of the notes, that 'throughout, the Act seems to avoid any recourse to the courts' (p. 188).

The discussion of the economically most important provisions of the Act is compressed almost entirely into a few pages of Mr. Haar's book (pp. 98–117), and in a brief review we must concentrate on these. As is made abundantly clear throughout the exposition, the basic motive behind all legislation of this kind is 'the ever-present fear of need to pay compensation which constitutes an ever-present threat to bold planning'

(p. 101; cf. pp. 157 and 167). In other words, it is the desire of the town planners to be relieved of the necessity of counting the cost of their activities, and it is freely admitted that many of the things which they regard as desirable would prove impossible if the whole costs, as they are measured in a market economy, had to be paid. The central aim is therefore to enable the planning authorities to acquire control over land below the price it would fetch on a free market. The argument used to justify this aim betrays a complete failure to understand the significance of these costs. We shall not stop to examine at length the arguments used in the present book to show why these costs can in fact not be paid.

The significance of the market value of land as an indicator of the social costs of its use for particular purposes is a more fundamental issue. In town planning literature generally, as in the present book, this question is generally represented as a purely fiscal problem: how these costs are to be met. It is regarded as solved if the burden can be placed on a particular group by a partial expropriation of the landowners. But this is not at all the main social problem involved. The crux of the matter lies in making sure that generally, and in every particular instance, the advantages derived from planning exceed the losses of the developments which the planning restrictions prevent. Paying the owner less than the full value of the land uses which are taken from him does not reduce the costs for society one whit. It merely makes it possible to disregard them and go ahead with planning schemes regardless of whether they repay their total costs. Unless it can be shown that the market prices of land reflect more than the value of the alternative services to the consumers which the land would render if allowed to be put to its more profitable use, the direction of the land to other purposes can be justified only if it can be demonstrated that it will make a contribution to public welfare which is greater than the value lost. This is what the planners can so rarely demonstrate. But, like most planners, the town planners, while pretending to take a more comprehensive view, are usually interested only in a limited range of values and wish to escape the trammels of considerations which they neither understand nor care for, and which probably no central plan could adequately take into account. As the present book characteristically puts it, their hope is that in the future the 'decision on the proper use of a piece of land will not be distorted by either the excessive cost of high development value or of the need of avoiding the payment of compensation, but will be taken strictly on planning merits' (p. 102).

The only serious attempt to justify this approach was made by one of the British commissions of inquiry which preceded the 1947 legislation, the 'Uthwatt Report' on Compensation and Betterment of 1942. This report developed a curious theory of 'floating' and 'shifting' values which, though I doubt whether it is taken seriously by a single reputable economist, appears to have made a considerable impression on town planners and administrators. It is based on the assumption that the total value of all the land in a country is a fixed magnitude, independent of the uses to which the individual pieces of land are put, and that, in consequence, the control of the use of land has only 'the effect of shifting land values: in other words, it increases the value of some land and decreases the value of other land, but it does not destroy land values' (p. 99, quoted from the Uthwatt Report). Now this is not merely, as Mr. Haar suggests, a theory which 'may be open to question on the ground of lack of empirical proof' (*ibid.*). It is sheer nonsense, which empirically could neither be proved nor disproved. There is no useful meaning of the term 'value' of which it could possibly be true. The situation is not much better with regard to the theory of 'floating value': the assertion that as a rule the expectation of impending development will affect the value of more land than will in fact be developed and increase it by more than the value of the actual developments. Yet even though it may occasionally be true that the market value of land on the margin of a town may be based on expectations which cannot all be valid, this surely is a difficulty which could be met by appropriate principles of valuation and which does not justify complete disregard of market values.

All this does not mean that we want to belittle the difficulty caused by the fact that while the cost of planning through reducing the value of some land is not too difficult to recognize and the bearers of the loss are certain to claim compensation, the 'betterment', i.e., the increases in the value of land due to the same planning measures, is much more difficult to ascertain. Nor can there be much question that, so far as specific betterments of this kind are ascertainable, it is desirable that the beneficiaries should be made to contribute to the cost of planning in proportion. There is much to be said for taxing away increments of land value which are demonstrably due to public activity. Indeed, of all kinds of socialism, the nationalization of land would have most to recommend it if it were practicable to distinguish the value of the Ricardian 'indestructible and permanent powers of the soil', to which alone the argument applies, from that value which the efforts of the owner have contributed. The difficulties here are essentially of a practical nature: the impossibility of distinguishing between these two parts of the value of a piece of land, and the problem of so adjusting rent contracts as to give the user of the land the appropriate inducements for investment. However, though 'only' practical, these difficulties have nevertheless proved insuperable.

In effect, this was recognized by the Uthwatt Report which, by a 'bold departure from precedent' on which the authors specially prided themselves, started a new development which in the end perverted that reasonable but impracticable idea of the taxation of betterment values into its opposite: instead of using the taxation of land values as a means of forcing the owners to put their land to the best use, the Town and Country Planning Act of 1947, under the name of the Development Charge, in effect imposed a penalty, on anyone putting land to better use, amounting to the whole gain to be derived from it. This transformation of the initial idea began with the Uthwatt Committee's decision 'to cut the Gordian knot by taking for the community some fixed proportion of the whole of any increase in site values without any attempt at precise analysis of the causes to which they may be due' (p. 98, quoted from the Uthwatt Report). The further steps leading from this to the 1947 Act were that this principle, which the Uthwatt Report intended to apply only to as yet undeveloped land, was extended to include all redevelopment of land already used for non-agricultural purposes; that, instead of making the value at a fixed date the basis for determining the increment, the value of any piece of land in the particular use to which it was devoted at any given time became the measure of the 'gain' due to a change in that use—apparently even if the 'existing use value' had fallen to zero; and finally that, after the measure had been passed by Parliament in the general belief that some 75 or 80 per cent of the difference between the value in the old use and the value in the new use would be taxed away, the minister empowered to fix the percentage decided that it should be 100 per cent. The result is that, as the law now stands, the Central Land Board, entrusted with levying the development charges, is instructed to make it a condition for permitting any development on land that the whole gain derived from it be handed over to the government. It would not seem unfair to sum up this curious evolution by saying that, since what might have made sense theoretically proved practically impossible, and since we must have planning whatever the costs ('even only fairly good planning is to be preferred over the past chaos'—p. 169), even the most nonsensical principle, if it is only administratively feasible, must be adopted.

It will now be clear that what the British government has undertaken is no less than to remove the incentive from practically any change in industrial and commercial activity which involves any substantial change in the use of land (the exceptions are so insignificant that we can disregard them for the present purpose). This is a task which cannot rationally be consummated unless the government takes responsibility for practically all investment decisions. If it were to be consistently carried out, land planning would in the end mean central direction of all commercial and industrial activity. No private person or corporation would have any interest in putting a piece of land to better use or in starting anything new on British soil, because the gain, which can only be obtained by using some British land for new purposes, would have to go to the government. Even worse is the fact that since the prospective value of the development must be paid for in cash before the development can be started, the risk of any uncertain venture will be greatly increased. Sir Arnold Plant, in the address already mentioned, put it mildly when he concluded that the Act, in its present form,

> threatens to ossify our industrial and commercial structure at the very points at which flexibility and speed of redevelopment are the indispensable requirement of successful enterprise in a competitive system.

The illustrations which Sir Arnold offers demonstrate, perhaps better than general discussion, just what the Act means in practice:

> Thus the ground floor of a commercial building cannot be changed over from use as an office to use as a shop, a retail shop cannot undertake new wholesale business, a wholesale warehouse cannot be used for light industry, or *vice versa* [i.e. without previous planning permission and payment of development charges]. You will be pleased to know, if you have not yet caught up with Statutory Instrument No. 195 of 9th February, 1949, that although a shop cannot begin to serve its customers with a meal cooked on the premises, a restaurant may now be turned into a shop. The managements of our great department stores may not yet all be aware that if they increase the proportion of their floor space devoted to the restaurant by more than 10 per cent, without first securing the permission of the local planning authority and paying any development charge demanded by the Central Land Board, they are apparently breaking the law.

Any number of similar illustrations could be given from the actual decisions of the Central Land Board. It is one of the most serious defects of Mr. Haar's book that it gives scarcely any idea of what the application of the new law means in concrete terms. The fact is that it would no longer be worth while to make any changes in the use of land if the law were followed literally and the development charges so fixed as to absorb the whole advantage of the change. But it is scarcely more reassuring for the prospects of preserving a free society that in fact all future 'developments' will depend on the Central Land Board authoritatively so fixing the development charges in each particular instance that those developments it wishes to proceed will still remain profitable while all others become impossible. We cannot attempt to demonstrate here in detail that the two magnitudes whose difference is to determine the development charge, the 'refusal value' (i.e., the value of a piece of land for which permission for *any* development is refused) and the 'consent value' (the value of this land after permission for a particular development has been granted), are not objective magnitudes, ascertainable, as the legislator believed, by 'normal processes of evaluation'. As there can be no longer a market for development values there will also exist no basis for their valuation. The fixing of the development charges of necessity becomes an arbitrary affair, exempt from any objective test, and is bound to degenerate into a process of bargaining. The American observer will have no difficulty in seeing where this is likely to lead when he reads the following remarkable paragraph from the preface to the pamphlet called *Practice Notes*, in which the chairman of the Central Land Board announced the 'principles' which the Board proposed to follow in fixing development charges:

The State now owns the value of all development rights in land. We are the managing agents and have to collect the additional value given to a piece of land by the permission given to develop it for a particular purpose. My colleagues and I are very conscious of the responsibilities of this new task. A study of these Notes will show that 'value' has many meanings and that to adopt one common meaning for all cases must produce absurd results in some. We have been given the discretion to decide which is the fairest to adopt in each case, and have stated some of our present views in these Notes. Each case, however, must depend on its own facts and a general working rule must always be variable if it does not fit a particular case. We have given instructions to our staff and to our advisers to suggest the fairest value possible for the case in question and to consider with care the views of any developer who takes an opposite view. We promise to try to give our own decisions with these points always in mind.[5]

Could the invitation to bargaining be stated in much plainer terms?

There is indeed much that must be explained both to the British and to the American public about this 'daring experiment in social control of the environment' (p. 1) into which the British people appear to have stumbled even more unknowingly than into any of the undesigned institutions which grew up as the result of free development. If Mr. Haar's prediction be true, 'that the 'fifties in the United States will be

[5] *1 Series, Central Land Board, Practice Notes* (1949) at III.

marked by a struggle over land planning in much the same fashion as public housing was the issue in the 'forties', certainly the British experiment should be carefully studied in this country. Mr. Haar has faithfully presented the legislative foundations. Perhaps, as the book appears to be based on a single visit to Britain in 1949, when the Act had only just come into force, we should not expect more than a descriptive account of its provisions and antecedents. We ought to be grateful to Mr. Haar for offering, in readable form, the essence of 'the massive document of 10 Parts, 120 long and involved sections, subdivided into 405 subsections [which] runs to no less than 206 pages in the King's Printers' copy' and which still left 'many of the more important provisions for Regulations, Directions and Orders to be issued by the Minister of Town and Country Planning' which, even at the time of the writing of the book, had become more voluminous and complex than the Act itself (p. 8). Yet, convenient as it is to have available an intelligible account of the British arrangements, the concern with the administrative details tends to obscure rather than point up the wider significance of the measure. Where a definite goal is set the technique of achieving it is a matter of legitimate interest. But where, as appears to be true in the present case, administrative expediency and the narrow considerations of a group of specialists have been allowed to decide one of the most general issues of economic policy, exclusive concern with machinery has little value except as a warning. Few readers will derive from the present book the main lesson the British experience has to teach: the acute danger that a small group of technical specialists may, in suitable circumstances, succeed in leading a democracy into legislation which few of those affected by it would have approved if they had understood what it meant.

Appendix

SCHUMPETER ON THE HISTORY OF ECONOMICS*

Although there is no lack of histories of economics, there are few good ones and most of the latter are no more than sketches. It is, therefore, a real tragedy that it was not given to the late Professor Schumpeter to complete an achievement for which he had almost unique qualifications. Forty years ago, after he had already established a reputation as an original theorist, he had published a brilliant outline of the development of economic theory which many regarded as the best available, but with which he himself was so little satisfied that he would not permit the issue of an English translation of the original German version. Some nine or ten years before his death in 1950 he had started on a revision of this early work which gradually grew into a monumental achievement of scholarship which has no equal in its field and on which he was still engaged at the time of his death. He had then covered almost the entire field he had intended to treat and there are few important gaps in the version now published. But much was still in the form of first drafts and all would probably have undergone very careful revision. The whole is evidently based on a systematic examination of a range of original literature which is truly amazing in its extent; and it shows an encyclopaedic knowledge far beyond the confines of economics which is hardly less impressive. If, as no doubt the author had intended, in the course of the revision the secondary literature had been as fully worked in as the originals had already been, we would have got such a handbook of the history of economics as one would not expect from a single man but only from a committee of specialists. As it was, the author's widow, herself a distinguished economist in her own right, undertook to get the manuscript ready for publication, intent to preserve it as closely as possible as her husband had left it. But Mrs. Schumpeter too died before the task was completed and various friends and pupils of the author appear to have prepared the volume for the press.

There are inevitably many details on which other students will disagree with

* A review of *History of Economic Analysis*, by Joseph A. Schumpeter. Edited from Manuscript by Elizabeth Boody Schumpeter. New York (Oxford University Press); published in abridged form in *The Freeman*, New York, 1954.

the author, but as one reads on all such occasional misgivings pale into insignificance against the impressive nature of the general picture which emerges. In a short review, at any rate, it would not be appropriate to say more about any minor faults one could find and most of which the author himself would have remedied if he had lived. We shall attempt no more than to indicate what he aimed at and has so largely achieved.

The book is designed as a history of the science of economics in the strict sense, not of the wider field of political economy. But as, more than perhaps in the case of any other science, the development of economics is hardly intelligible without the political, sociological and intellectual currents which determined the direction of interests at different times, we are throughout given masterly sketches of this background which make the book much more than a history of merely one branch of knowledge. And although Schumpeter was a man of strong and highly individual and sometimes unpopular views, the manner in which he succeeds on the whole to keep his personal prejudices out is wholly admirable. Indeed, his endeavour to do justice to any genuine effort which in the past had not been given sufficient credit, and to find justification even for the less plausible arguments in the circumstances of the time, goes surprisingly far. To those who know his general theoretical views it will be no surprise to find that Quesnay, Cournot, and Walras ('so far as pure theory is concerned . . . the greatest of all economists') are his heroes, and that he rates Adam Smith, Ricardo and even Marshall decidedly lower than is usual. Most of this is just and all of it can be defended with good argument. A great merit is the proper recognition of the great role played by men like Cantillon, Senior, and Böhm-Bawerk, and compared with this the occasional cavalier treatment of some secondary yet still not unimportant figures like Robert Torrens is a minor matter. Even the great attention given to Karl Marx is probably justified, if not by any important contribution he made to economic theory, yet by the influence he has exercised and by his early efforts to work sociological considerations into economic analysis—which is evidently the aspect of his work which appealed to Schumpeter. Indeed the fact that Schumpeter himself was at times almost as much interested in sociology as in pure economics has contributed a good deal to the character of this last work, some parts of which are fascinating essays in the sociology of science. They are stimulating even where one cannot entirely agree. Readers of this journal will probably be irritated by the unnecessary if not contemptuous manner in which Schumpeter usually refers to nineteenth-century liberalism, individualism, and 'laissez faire'. But they should remember that it comes from an author who knew as well as anybody 'that capitalist evolution tends to peter out because the modern state may crush or paralyse its motive forces', yet who also seems to have had an irrepressible urge to *épater les bourgeois.*

With its over 1,200 closely printed pages this is not likely to be a popular book, though it is so well written that it should give pleasure not only to the specialists. This is not to say that it is an easy book, or suitable for the kindergarten atmosphere in which so much college education proceeds. Nor is it in every respect a 'safe' book: the orthodox of any description must be prepared for constant shocks, and the literal-minded will miss much that is said only between the lines. But for the mature and thoughtful reader, whether he be an economic theorist or merely generally interested in the growth of ideas on human affairs, it should be an invaluable source of instruction. And nobody should profit more from it than the economists of the younger generation: as in other subjects the increasing technicality of the theory carries with it the danger of a narrow specialism which is peculiarly harmful in this field. I know of no better antidote than this book to the belief, which seems to dominate some of the younger men, that nothing that happened before 1936 can be of importance to them, and no work better suited to show what they ought to know if they are to be not merely economists but cultivated persons competent to use their technical knowledge in a complex world. And they will also find in the later part of the book an—alas incomplete—survey of the contemporary state of economics which, at least to one reader, seems much more stimulating and satisfactory than the various collective efforts which have in recent years been directed to the same end.

THE WEBBS AND THEIR WORK*

It would be difficult to overstate the importance of *Our Partnership* for the understanding of British history in the twentieth century. Beyond this, the story of the Webbs provides a unique lesson of what unselfish and single-minded devotion and the methodical hard work of two people can achieve. The strongest impression left by this second part of Beatrice Webb's memoirs is that she and her husband owed the extent of their influence largely to the fact that they cared only for the success of the ideas in which they believed, without any regard to who got the credit for them, that they were willing to operate through any medium, person or party which allowed itself to be used, and above all, that they fully understood, and knew how to make use of, the decisive position which the intellectuals occupy in shaping public opinion.

They had 'little faith in the "average sensual man" ' (p. 120). They set out not 'to organize the unthinking persons into Socialist societies' but 'to make the thinking people socialistic' (p. 132). 'The rank and file of Socialists—especially English Socialists' seemed to them 'unusually silly folk' (p. 134). They knew that if they succeeded in 'converting the country to the philosophy of our scheme . . . the application will follow (whatever persons are in power)' (p. 443). It was because they were known to 'have ideas to give away' (p. 402)

* A review of *Our Partnership*, by Beatrice Webb. Edited by Barbara Drake and Margaret I. Cole. London: Longmans, Green and Co., 1948; published in *Economica*, August 1948.

and because they were always ready to provide articles and memoranda to be used in somebody else's name, that their 'behind the scenes intellectual leadership' (p. 116) was so effective. There can indeed be few important organs of the period, from the *Church Times* and the *Christian World* to the *Daily Mail*, which did not, at one time or another, carry unsigned articles by the Webbs (pp. 70, 257), written, if expediency demanded it, in 'our best style of modest moderation' (p. 455), and some papers like the *Manchester Guardian* and the *Echo* they came to regard as 'practically our organs' (p. 145). They kept the London School of Economics 'honestly non-partisan in its theories' (p. 230) and valued its continued prosperity 'so long as it remains unbiassed and open to collectivist tendencies' (p. 463), not in spite but because of the fact that they saw in it the centre 'from which our views will radiate through personal intercourse' (p. 94). It was part of a scheme which made them 'feel assured that with the School as a teaching body, the Fabian Society as a propagandist organization, the L.C.C. Progressives as an object lesson in electoral success, our books as the only [*sic*] elaborate original work in economic fact and theory, no young man or woman who is anxious to study or to work in public affairs can fail to come under our influence' (p. 145). Towards the end of the period covered by the volume Mrs. Webb was indeed justified in looking forward with confidence to the day when 'hosts of able young men, well trained in Fabian economics and administrative lore, will be crowding into the political arena' (p. 469).

'Behind the scenes' was also the keynote of their direct influence on current politics during the period covered by the volume. (It deals with the years 1892–1911, but the last chapter on 'The Plunge into Propaganda, 1909–1911' is really concerned with what is the beginning of the next phase of their life.) Past masters in the art of wire-pulling, of 'manipulating', and '—to speak plainly—of intrigue' (p. 259), they knew how to get the most out of the personal contacts for which their social standing provided the opportunity. It is a curious irony that the circumstances which gave the two people the power to contribute so much towards the destruction of the capitalist civilization which they hated could exist only within that civilization, and that in the type of society for which they hoped no private persons could wield a similar influence towards its change. It was the 'incomparable luxury of freedom from all care for ourselves' (p. 245), provided by an independent income of £1,000 a year, which not only enabled them to devote themselves wholly to the chosen task, but also to employ all the arts of hospitality and to use all the opportunities of social intercourse with the great in the service of their ideals. Even today it is already difficult to appreciate the opportunities which such an income afforded forty or fifty years ago. In the famous ten-roomed house at 41 Grosvenor Road, which they occupied for forty years and ran with two maids, they were for years able to have twelve persons for dinner most weeks (p. 304, cf. p. 339) and to give from time to time receptions for sixty to eighty people. When a person they wanted to use proved recalcitrant he would be asked to dine with a 'carefully selected party' (p. 334). 'A brilliant little luncheon, typically of the "Webb" set', might consist of Dr. Nansen (now

Norwegian Minister), Gerald and Lady Betty Balfour, the Bernard Shaws, Bertrand Russell, Masterman and Lady Desborough typical in its mixture of opinions, classes, interests' (p. 375). Yet to Mrs. Webb this income seemed 'not much more than a livelihood and working expenses' (p. 339) and only occasionally, as when she smiles at staying 'in the cottage of the millionaire while composing this great collectivist document' (the Minority Report of the Poor Law) (p. 412), or when, before their world tour in 1898, she is 'revelling in buying silks and satins, gloves, underclothing, furs and everything that a sober-minded woman of forty can want to inspire Americans and colonials with a true respect for the refinements of collectivism' (p. 146), some sense of the incongruity of this shows itself.

One may doubt whether any of their contemporaries fully realized the extent of their influence in a world where, as Mrs. Webb noted in her diary, 'every politician one meets wants to be coached—it is really quite comic—it seems to be quite irrelevant whether they are Conservatives, Liberals or Labour Party men' (p. 402). What Mrs. Webb calls with some satisfaction 'perhaps the cleverest caricature—about 1900— . . . a picture of Balfour and Asquith bobbing up and down at the end of wires handled by the "wily Fabian"' (p. 7) at the time probably seemed an exaggeration; it hardly does so to the reader of *Our Partnership*.

The book is, perhaps inevitably, least informative on what was certainly Mrs. Webb's main occupation during the period covered—their research. We do not learn much about their conception of 'the scientific method pure and undefiled' (p. 209) which they feel they are practically the first to apply to 'the establishment of a science of society' (p. 170), or about the nature of 'the sound science of social organization' at which they aimed. But one need perhaps not be surprised that they felt in retrospect that 'every discovery in sociology . . . has strengthened our faith' (p. 16). Certainly, when Mrs. Webb is appointed a member of the Poor Law Commission, strategy and research become curiously intermingled: 'Fortunately, we have already discovered our principles of 1907, and we have already devised our scheme for reform. What we are now manufacturing is the heavy artillery of fact that is to drive both principles and scheme home' (p. 399). On one occasion Mrs. Webb confesses to 'more or less engineering the evidence in my direction' (p. 370) and on another of practising 'tacit deception' on her colleagues on the Commission by carefully selecting those parts of a correspondence which she thought suitable for them to see, 'without, be it added, in any way giving the Commission to understand that I had sent them the whole or the part' (p. 393). When after that one finds Mrs. Webb complaining about the 'packed Commission' (p. 381) one cannot but sympathize a little with the 'rude ejaculations' of one of her colleagues whom she heard saying 'what cheek!' while she questioned a witness (p. 377).

Even with this intimate record of the singularly happy partnership before us, 'The Other One' remains a curiously impersonal and shadowy figure whose only distinct trait seems perfect mental efficiency and balance. Sidney Webb has often been described as the prototype of the Commissar, and the description in the diary as a man who 'has no kind of qualms', who is 'selfless' and 'has a robust conscience', confirms this just a little. But it is the picture of a very urbane kind of Commissar which emerges and certainly not of a fanatic. One does not feel so certain on the last point about Mrs. Webb herself. She describes herself as 'conservative by temperament, and [in her youth] anti-democratic through social environment' (p. 361). 'Authoritarian' would probably have been a better term. With her the belief in the 'wholesale and compulsory management' by the expert (p. 120), in the ' "higher freedom" of corporate life' (p. 222) is a passion, and the dislike of all views, but particularly Gladstonian Liberalism, which 'think in individuals', is a real hatred. It is only expediency which prevents her from attacking 'individualism, or, as we prefer to call it, anarchy, in its stronghold of the home and family' (p. 84), and her craving for a ' "Church", a communion of those who hold the faith' (p. 366-7,) the desire for 'constructing a party with a religion and an applied science' (p. 471), fit as well into this fundamentally totalitarian attitude as her personal asceticism which makes her see sins in 'all my little self-indulgences—the cup of tea or occasional coffee after a meal' (*ibid.*).

HARROD'S LIFE OF KEYNES*

As a biography of a contemporary figure published within five years of his death, this monumental life of Lord Keynes is a remarkable achievement. Written by one of his closest friends and most fervent admirers, it gives a sympathetic yet unsparingly honest picture of one of the most influential and colourful minds of his generation. It is based on a thorough examination of the great mass of private and official documents which are available and gives a vivid picture of the background against which the career of Keynes must be seen.

The profound influence which he exercised on the development of ideas, the role he played in English public life, and the part he took in his last years in Anglo-American relations make the book a major contribution to the history of our time. The almost unbelievable variety of Keynes' activities and interests made such a biography a task of unusual difficulty. But Mr. Harrod was in most respects almost ideally qualified for it. He shared many of Keynes's interests, had followed him both in his theoretical work and in some of his more practical activities, and had personally known most of the circles in which Keynes had moved in his earlier years. He writes an easy and lucid style and succeeds in making intelligible to the layman even some of the intricacies of Keynes' contributions to economic theory. In places one might

* A review of *The Life of John Maynard Keynes*, by R. F. Harrod. New York: Harcourt, Brace and Company, 1951; published in *The Journal of Modern History*, XXIV/2, June 1952.

wish that there were less argument or attempts to defend and justify and more of Keynes' own informal accounts of the working of his mind. But although Mr. Harrod reproduces part of many interesting letters which whet the appetite for more, one gathers that the greater part of Keynes' correspondence will not be suitable for publication during the lifetime of his contemporaries.

Whatever one may think of Keynes as an economist, nobody who knew him will deny that he was one of the outstanding Englishmen of his generation. Indeed the magnitude of his influence as an economist is probably at least as much due to the impressiveness of the man, the universality of his interests, and the power and persuasive charm of his personality, as to the originality or theoretical soundness of his contribution to economics. He owed his success largely to a rare combination of brilliance and quickness of mind with a mastery of the English language in which few contemporaries could rival him and, what is not mentioned in the *Life* but to me seemed always one of his strongest assets, a voice of bewitching persuasiveness. As a scholar he was incisive rather than profound and thorough, guided by a strong intuition which would make him try to prove the same point again and again by different routes. It is not surprising that a man who at one stage was able to divide his time between teaching economics and conducting a ballet, financial speculation and collecting pictures, running an investment trust and directing the finances of a Cambridge College, acting as the director of an insurance company and practically running the Cambridge Arts Theatre and attending there to such details as the food and wine served in its restaurant, should show sometimes surprising lack of knowledge on subjects where his predominantly aesthetic sympathies had not been aroused. While, for instance, his book-collecting activities had given him a rare knowledge of the intellectual history of the seventeenth and eighteenth centuries, his knowledge of nineteenth-century history and even of the economic literature of that period was somewhat meagre. He was able to master the essential outlines of a new subject in a remarkably short time: indeed, he seems to have turned himself into an economist, after a university course in mathematics, in the course of little more than two years filled with many other activities. The result of this, however, was that the scope of his knowledge remained always not only somewhat insular but distinctly 'Cambridge'. He had been unusually fortunate in his background, his early associates, and the group with which he spent his formative years. And he seems to the end of his life to have regarded the views and the outlook of that particular set as the highest flower of civilization.

Although by disposition the young Keynes was a characteristic rationalist radical of his generation, the kind who felt that it was their vocation 'to judge all things anew' (p. 77), a member of a group who were convinced that only they 'knew the rudiments of a true theory of ethics' (p. 114), and who in 1918 described himself as a bolshevik who was not sorry to watch 'the disappearance of the social order as we have known it hitherto' (p. 223), as an economist he was even at the time when he achieved international fame an old-fashioned liberal. In his celebrated articles in the *Manchester Guardian Commercial* in 1921 and 1922 he still defended free trade, the international gold standard, and the need for more saving. There is some reason to doubt whether he ever fully understood the classical theory of international trade on which that position was largely based (even Mr. Harrod has to admit, in another connection, p. 453, that 'he was himself in some confusion about what the classical position really was') and it would probably be possible to trace much of his later developments from certain questionable arguments which he had effectively employed in this field in a good cause in his *Economic Consequences of the Peace* (1919). The great change came before the Great Depression, about the time of Great Britain's return to the Gold Standard in 1925. His own explanation of why he had become convinced of *The End of Laissez Faire* (1927) is, as Mr. Harrod also seems to feel, really appallingly thin and flimsy. But there can be little doubt that with his new beliefs in a managed currency, in controlled investment, and in cartels, he became, together with his great antagonist Lloyd George, the main author of the conversion of the British Liberal Party to the semi-socialist programme expounded in the Liberal Yellow Book (*Britain's Industrial Future*, 1927) (pp. 392–3).

Mr. Harrod takes some pains to defend Keynes against the charge of inconsistency. In this he seems to me not to be very successful. There was, undoubtedly, a continuity of development and a persistence of ultimate aim. But there was also in Keynes a certain puckish delight in shocking his contemporaries, a tendency to overstate his disagreements with current views, and a fondness for stressing his broadminded understanding of the more revolutionary attitudes, which is not very compatible with consistency. Again and again he would surprise his friends by an argument which did not seem to agree with his public pronouncements. I remember particularly one occasion which well illustrates this. He had not long before coined the phrase of the 'euthanasia of the *rentier*', and in a deliberate attempt to draw him out I took the next opportunity in conversation to stress the importance which the man of independent means had had in the English political tradition. Far from contradicting me, this made Keynes launch into a long eulogy of the role played by the propertied class, with many illustrations of their indispensability for the preservation of a decent civilization. Perhaps it was his gift for phrase-making which made him so often overstate his point. Certainly such phrases as the 'humbug of finance', 'the end of laissez faire', and 'in the long run we are all dead' must have often recoiled against their author when he was in a more conservative mood. Even his greatest admirers must have winced a little when in 1933 he chose a German periodical to praise 'National Selfsufficiency' ('Nationale Selbstgenügsamkeit', *Schmollers Jahrbuch*, Vol. 57) and one can only wonder what he can have meant when, three years later in his preface to the German translation of the *General Theory of Employment, Interest, and Money*, he commended the book to its readers on the ground that 'the theory of production as a whole which is the goal of this book can much more easily be adapted to the conditions of a total state' than is true of the competitive theory. Mr. Harrod stresses that towards the end of his life there was some return to free trade views, and some of his occasional utterances seem to suggest this. But as late as October 1943 he had still stressed that the future seemed to him to lie with '(i) State trading for commodities; (ii) International cartels for necessary manufactures; and (iii) Quantitative import restrictions for non-essential manufactures'.

It is perhaps significant that Keynes hated to be addressed as 'Professor' (he never had that title). He was not primarily a scholar. He was a great amateur in many fields of knowledge and the arts; he had all the gifts of a great politician and political pamphleteer; and he knew that 'the ideas of economists and political philosophers, both when they are right and when they are wrong, are more powerful than is generally understood. Indeed the world is ruled by little else' (*General Theory*, etc., p. 338). And as he had a mind capable of recasting, in the intervals of his other occupations, the body of current economic theory, he more than any of his compeers had come to affect current thought. Whether he was right or wrong only the future will show. There are some who fear that if Lenin's statement is correct, of which Keynes himself has reminded us (p. 273), that the best way to destroy the capitalist system is to debauch the currency, it will be largely due to Keynes' influence if this prescription is followed.

Mr. Harrod is very frank about Keynes' temperamental shortcomings, not only 'his minor failings—impetuosity, change of view, speaking beyond his book' (p. 373), but also about his strong propensity to gamble, his ruthlessness and occasional rudeness in discussion ('all seemed fair to him in controversial warfare'—p. 359), his tendency to 'cultivate the appearance of omniscience' (p. 468) and of 'always being ready to guess a figure to illustrate a point' (p. 507). It may be doubted whether 'his flair for "global" estimates' (p. 229) which, owing not least to his influence, has now become the fashion, and his general habit of thinking in terms of aggregates and averages, have been beneficial to the understanding of economic phenomena. Economic activity is not guided by such totals but always by relations between different magnitudes, and the practice of always thinking in 'global' totals can be very misleading. In at least one instance his later arguments against orthodoxy were largely directed against a view which few reputable economists except he himself had ever advocated: against the demand for an all-round cut of wages and salaries to meet unemployment (pp. 361–2). Much of the confusion about the effects of wage reductions has been caused by the fact that Keynes himself was always thinking in terms of a general wage cut, while the argument of his opponents was in favour of allowing some wages to fall.

Perhaps the explanation of much that is puzzling about Keynes' mind lies in the supreme confidence he had acquired in his power to play on public opinion as a supreme master plays on his instrument. He loved to pose in the role of a Cassandra whose warnings were not listened to. But in fact his early success in swinging round public opinion about the peace treaties had given him a probably even exaggerated belief in his powers. I shall never forget one occasion, I believe the last time that I met him, when he startled me by an uncommonly frank expression of this view. It was early in 1946, shortly after he had returned from the strenuous and exhausting negotiations in Washington on the British Loan. Earlier in the evening he had fascinated the company by a detailed account of the American market for Elizabethan books which in any other man would have given the impression that he had devoted most of his time in the United States to that subject. Later a turn in the conversation made me ask him whether he was not concerned about what some of his disciples were making of his theories. After a not very complimentary remark about the persons concerned he proceeded to reassure me: those ideas had been badly needed at the time he had launched them. But I need not be alarmed: if they should ever become dangerous I could rely upon him that he would again quickly swing round public opinion—indicating by a quick movement of his hand how rapidly that would be done. But three months later he was dead.

FREEDOM AND COERCION

Some Comments on a Critique
by Mr. Ronald Hamowy*

In his review of *The Constitution of Liberty*[1] Mr. Hamowy has raised points which are both important and difficult. In the space available I cannot attempt a complete answer but must concentrate on the chief problems. Before I turn to these I must, however, clear up a misunderstanding.

It was not the main thesis of my book that 'freedom may be defined as the absence of coercion'. Rather, as the first sentence of the first chapter explains, its primary concern is 'the condition of men in which coercion of some by others is reduced as much as is possible in society'. I believe I am etymologically correct in describing such a state as one of liberty or freedom. But this is a secondary issue. The reduction of coercion appears to me an objective of the first importance in its own right and it is to this task that the book addresses itself.

I sympathize with Mr. Hamowy's disappointment about my admission that I know of no way of preventing coercion altogether and that all we can hope to achieve is to minimize it or rather its harmful effects. The sad fact is that nobody has yet found a way in which the former can be achieved by deliberate action. Such a happy state of perfect freedom (as I should call it) might conceivably be attained in a society whose members strictly observed a moral code prohibiting all coercion. Until we know how we can produce such a state

---

* Reprinted from *The New Individualist Review*, published by the University of Chicago Chapter of the Intercollegiate Society of Individualists, Vol. 1, No. 2 Summer 1961.

[1] *New Individualist Review*, April 1961, pp. 28–31.

all we can hope for is to create conditions in which people are prevented from coercing each other. But to prevent people from coercing others is to coerce them. This means that coercion can only be reduced or made less harmful but not entirely eliminated. How far we can reduce it depends in part on circumstances which are not in the control of that organ of deliberate action which we call government. It is at least possible (to mention an extreme case which is the cause of one of Mr. Hamowy's chief complaints) that the use of so severe a form of coercion as conscription may be necessary to ward off the danger of worse coercion by an external enemy. I believe that the Swiss owe a long period of unusual freedom precisely to the fact that they recognized this and acted upon it; while some other countries protected by the sea were not under this unfortunate necessity. Where it exists the closest possible approach to perfect freedom may be much further from the ideal and yet the closest which can be achieved.

The two crucial issues which Mr. Hamowy raises concern, however, the definition of coercion and the practical means of limiting it. On the first his objections rest on a misunderstanding for which my exposition is perhaps partly responsible. I certainly did not intend to represent as coercion *every* change in a person's environment brought about by another with the intention of inducing the first to take some action beneficial to the second. Though both the possibility for the coercer to foresee the action of the coerced, and the former's desire to bring about this action, are required, they are not sufficient. To constitute coercion it is also necessary that the action of the coercer should put the coerced in a position which he regards as worse than that in which he would have been without that action. (That was the meaning of the repeated emphasis in my book on the threatened harm.) Surely no change in the environment of a person which merely adds to his previously existing range of opportunities an additional one can without violence to language be called coercion. However certain I may be that somebody will be glad to buy from me a commodity if I offer it to him at a certain price, and however much I may gain from the sale, it would be ridiculous to suggest that I have coerced him by an offer which he regards as a clear advantage.

Normally, therefore, the terms on which somebody is prepared to render me services cannot be regarded as coercion: however important the service in question may be to me, so long as his action adds to the range of my choice something which I desire and which without his action would not be available to me, he places me in a better position than that in which I would be without his action—however high the price he makes me pay.

There seem to me, however, to exist cases which are superficially similar yet have to be judged differently, though the exact distinction may be difficult to draw. The instance I discuss in my book is the situation in which somebody has acquired control of the whole water supply of an oasis and uses this position to exact unusual performances from those whose life depends on access to that water. Other instances of the same kind would be the only doctor available to perform an urgent life-saving operation and similar cases of rescue in an emergency where special unforeseeable circumstances have placed into a single hand the power of rescue from grave danger. They are all instances where I should wish that those in whose hands the life of another is placed should be under a moral and legal obligation to render the help in their power even if they cannot expect any remuneration—though they should of course be entitled to normal remuneration if it is in the power of the rescued. It is because these services are regarded as rights to be counted upon that a refusal to render them except on unusual terms is justly regarded as a harmful alteration of the environment and therefore as coercion. That in such instances the unlimited control of the owner over his property has to give way is good old libertarian doctrine: see David Hume's discussion of the lapse of the *rationale* of property under the conditions of absolute scarcity in a state of siege.

The second chief issue on which Mr. Hamowy dissents is the practical one of the manner in which the power of coercive action by government can be so limited as to be least harmful. Since government needs this power to prevent coercion (and fraud and violence) by individuals, it might at first seem as if the test should be whether it is in the particular instance necessary for that purpose. But to make necessity for the prevention of worse coercion the criterion would inevitably make the decision dependent on somebody's discretion and thereby open the doors to what has long been recognized as one of the most harmful and obnoxious forms of coercion, that dependent on some other man's opinion. While we want to allow coercion by government only in situations where it is necessary to prevent coercion (or violence, etc.) by others, we do not want to allow it in all instances where it could be pretended that it was necessary for that purpose. We need therefore another test to make the use of coercion independent of individual will. It is the distinguishing mark of the Western political tradition that for this purpose coercion has been confined to instances where it is required by general abstract rules, known beforehand and equally applicable to all. It is true that this by itself would not confine coercion to instances where it is necessary to prevent worse coercion; it leaves open possibilities of enforcement of highly oppressive rules on some dissenting group, especially in the field of religious observance, and perhaps also in such restrictions on consumption as Prohibition—though it is very questionable whether the latter kind of restrictions would ever be imposed if they had to take the form of general rules from which no exceptions could be granted. Yet combined with the requirement that such general rules authorizing coercion could be justified only by the general purpose of preventing worse coercion, etc., this principle seems to be as effective a method of minimizing coercion as mankind has yet discovered. It certainly seems to me the best protection yet devised against that administrative despotism which is the greatest danger to individual liberty today.

Index

ABOUT THE AUTHOR

Born and educated in Vienna, Professor F. A. Hayek was for many years a professor of economics at the London School of Economics. He later became Professor of Social and Moral Science at the University of Chicago, and is now Professor of Economics at the University of Freiburg. He is well-known as the author of many important books on various aspects of the social sciences including: *The Road to Serfdom, The Constitution of Liberty, Individualism and Economic Order, The Sensory Order: An Inquiry into the Foundations of Theoretical Psychology,* and (with others) *Capitalism and the Historians.*